JEAN and JOHNNY

19 20

JEAN

and

JOHNNY

By BEVERLY CLEARY

Illustrated by
Joe and Beth Krush

William Morrow & Company, New York, 1959

JEAN and JOHNNY

FOUR ASPECTS OF THE FILM

This is a volume in the
Arno Press collection

ASPECTS OF FILM

Advisory Editor
Garth S. Jowett

See last pages of this volume
for a complete list of titles.

FOUR ASPECTS
OF THE FILM

James L. Limbacher

ARNO PRESS
A New York Times Company
New York • 1978

Editorial Supervision: MARIA CASALE

———◆———

Reprint Edition 1978 by Arno Press Inc.

Reprinted by permission of Land's End Press

ASPECTS OF FILM
ISBN for complete set: 0-405-11125-8
See last pages of this volume for titles.

Manufactured in the United States of America

Publisher's Note: All illustrations have been
reproduced in black and white in this edition.

Page 356A replaces p.357 in this edition.
The text is complete.

———◆———

Library of Congress Cataloging in Publication Data
Limbacher, James L.
    Four aspects of the film.

    (Aspects of film)
    Reprint of the ed. published by Brussel &
Brussel, New York.
    Bibliography: p.
    Includes index.
    1. Wide-screen processes (Cinematography)
2. Color cinematography. I. Title. II. Series.
[TR855.L55 1978]   778.5'3   77-11379
ISBN 0-405-11138-X

FOUR ASPECTS OF THE FILM

James L. Limbacher

1969, BRUSSEL & BRUSSEL INC., 10011

Copyright 1968

James L. Limbacher

DEDICATION

To my Father and Mother —
who let me go to the movies
early and often

TABLE OF CONTENTS

PREFACE

No sooner had motion pictures been developed than attempts were made to improve them artistically. From the first American presentation on a movie screen in 1896, the black-and-white silent movie in an aspect ratio of three times high and four times wide was destined to become the most distinctly American art form so far created.

Within a decade of their introduction, films were appearing in color, with a widescreen effect, with a third dimension and with sound and odors synchronized. However crude these early additions to the art of the film were, they have been perfected through the years to a high degree. They appear, disappear and re-appear at intervals, according to the current public taste.

This book, the result of nearly 20 years of research, covers these exciting aspects of the art of the film. Perhaps the most exciting developments are still to come. Certainly there are new aspects now being developed which will someday become standard. Others will not catch the public's fancy and disappear.

This, then, is the chronicle of color, widescreen, the third dimension, sound and the avant garde aspects of the motion picture. The author can only hope that it will be as thrilling to read about as it was to write.

— James L. Limbacher

PART ONE — COLOR

"I can't bear films in sepia
Except about once ever leap-year.
And about those in Cinecolor
I'm even cynicaller."
— Kenneth Tynan

CHAPTER ONE
THE EARLIEST COLOR FILMS

From the outset of movie making, there have been three types of color motion pictures. They are (a) the hand-painted, tinted or toned film, (b) the additive color film and (c) the subtractive color film.

The theory of color goes back to Sir Isaac Newton, who discovered the components of light and color by means of a prism held up to the sunlight. Other scientists later determined the three basic colors as red, green and indigo (blue-violet). When these three colors were mixed in certain proportions, the result was the sensation of pure white light.

When red and indigo are mixed, the result is magenta; red and green make yellow and green and indigo form blue-green. The act of adding one color to another to produce another color is called an additive color process.

Clerk Maxwell, an English physicist, discovered in 1855 that if a scene were filmed separately on three different black-and-white negatives through filters which transmitted the blue, green and red sections of the spectrum, the scene could be "re-built" in its original colors by superimposing the three positive images onto a screen through the same filters as those which were used in making the negative. This became the basis of the additive color process for motion pictures.

As Raymond Spottiswoode states it, "The additive process is in theory the most perfect form of color reproduction, for it requires no dyed images in the film emulsion, the color residing merely in simple and easily reproducible filters attached to camera and projector."[1]

Conversely, in the subtractive color process, the three negatives are again photographed through red, blue and green filters, but each positive is printed in a color **complementary** to that of the filter through which the corresponding negative was taken. Yellow and blue-green make green; yellow and magenta make red and magenta

and blue-green make indigo. Since these colors are produced by the act of filtering out one or more colors, it is subtractive. These color positives are superimposed to produce the color picture.

Color films are considered to be those to which tints and colors have been added and **natural color** films are those in which the colors are in the film stock itself or added by mechanical or optical means. For this study, however, both these types will be called simply "color films."[2]

TINTING AND TONING

The oldest methods of imparting color to motion picture films are tinting and toning. Still in use today, the tinting of 35mm film is done by applying one or more colors to the film itself. Toning is the bathing of the entire film in a color which imparts the same black-and-white value of that color to each image on the film.[3]

There are three methods of tinting and toning films: (a) applying a liquid tint to the black-and-white film after it has been developed, (b) having the tint already in the film stock before it is exposed in the camera, and (c) applying colors by hand or by stenciling.

The first color motion picture film made for screen projection seems to have been done in 1894.[4] A year later, Robert Paul of England was hand-coloring release prints of short films.

Thomas A. Edison, the pioneer of the motion picture in the United States, tried hand-painting release prints of his films before 1900, but these proved difficult on the eyes. In 1905, a stenciling process was perfected in which sections could be painted on more accurately, but the result was still crude and did not resemble natural color.[5]

Early French films were available in either black-and-white or color versions. The coloring, of course, was not as we know it today, but rather was hand-tinted by a group of fifty "tinters" employed for that purpose. Each person was assigned to one color and these colors were painted on the individual frames of film. Most of these movies were of less than three minutes in running time and were described in glowing terms.

Georges Melies used hand-tinting in many of his early "trick" films such as AN ASTRONOMER'S DREAM (1898) and his first version of A TRIP TO THE MOON (1900).

Of Melies' TRANSFORMATION, it was said, "flowers turn into beautiful women; a baby is taken from the heart of a rose." Of THE FLOWER FAIRY, "the flowers come to life in the spring and the landscape bursts into color."[6]

In an attempt to improve the color quality, Charles Pathe later

invented another improved method of stenciling but, like Edison's, did not gain wide popularity. Some Pathe films were hand-tinted in the United States as well as in Europe and they used various colors to accent the highlights in the story or to indicate a change of mood.

In the 1903 production of THE GREAT TRAIN ROBBERY, the gunshot blast at the end of the film was tinted red. This same device was used 40 years later in Alfred Hitchcock's SPELLBOUND.

Film director D. W. Griffith used tinted sequences in THE BIRTH OF A NATION, THE WHITE ROSE (in which Carol Dempster actually blushed, with the help of some red tint in her cheeks), BROKEN BLOSSOMS, INTOLERANCE and WAY DOWN EAST, among others.

Writer A. R. Fulton describes the original tinted print of INTOLERANCE as "blue for the Judean story, sepia for the French, gray-green for the Babylonian and amber for the modern. Night scenes were blue, sunny exteriors yellow, and night battle scenes red."[7]

BROKEN BLOSSOMS was described by Joe Franklin as having many colors on the release print which were "an integral part of the whole; gentle rose hues, savage reds, rich blues for the night scenes, and other tones matching every mood and nuance. Audiences that see this film in its rare public viewings today almost invariably see a black-and-white print, which is tantamount to seeing but a pale shadow of what the film originally was."[8]

Theodore Huff remembers WAY DOWN EAST as ". . . tinted and toned all through the picture. Many scenes were hand-painted — the dresses at the ball . . . Tone stock was used, then the highlights would be tinted another color by a bath in chemicals. Particularly the scenes by the river: the sunset sky was pink and the rest of the picture blue."[9] In the finale of the film, the ice floe sequence was tinted a dark blue.

In England, the 1913 version of EAST LYNNE and DAVID COPPERFIELD had the night scenes tinted in blue-green.

Erich von Stroheim employed a yellow tint in GREED during the symbolic sequences showing gold and golden objects. A German film, SCHERBEN (SHATTERED) had Werner Krauss as a track walker whose signal lantern radiated a bright red light. Another German film, PEAK OF FATE, used a different color tone on each side of the film. As one film fan remembers it:

"Multiple tinting was perfected to a fine art . . . PEAK OF FATE used a different color tone on each side of the print, resulting in a

beautiful effect as it was projected on the screen."[10] The film is considered by many silent film enthusiasts as one of the most beautiful hand-tinted films ever released to theatres.

Maurice Tourneur's THE BLUEBIRD was a natural for the tinting process, as was the 1925 version of THE LOST WORLD, where the scene of the volcanic eruption was highlighted by red tints.

Russian director Serge Eisenstein used color tints in POTEMKIN (1925) when the flag appeared in red and in THE GENERAL LINE (OLD AND NEW) (1927) in the sequences involving the separator and another involving a bull.

Some of the color in silent films was memorable and effective, but others proved to be distracting, especially when more than one tint was used on the same frame. Monochrome films soon fell into stereotypes. Red represented fire; blue indicated night; green usually accompanied forest scenes and yellow was used when artificial light was represented. But these tints survived the tests of time and are still used occasionally today.

PATHECOLOR

One of the first hand-painted color processes to have a name was Pathecolor. Developed in France around the turn of the century, it was a hand-painted process regarded by viewers as either extremely beautiful or rather gaudy. Despite mixed opinions, the process achieved great success and had a longer life than the other color experiments because it did not need special equipment for projection.

An early Pathecolor print of the 1900 film, THE FLOWER FAIRY, has been reduced and preserved on 16mm color film and proves that the process was amazingly accurate and stands up even by today's standards.

Among the notable Pathecolor films were CINDERELLA (1909) which contained color sequences only; IN ANCIENT GREECE, advertised in 1910 that "the flesh tints (are) so natural that it is hard to believe that the people are only pictures on a screen."[11] Pathecolor graduated to feature-length pictures in 1914 when it was used in THE LIFE OF OUR SAVIOR, filmed by Pathe in Jerusalem.[12]

Pathecolor films were not always in the full range of color, however. In recently examined prints of the process, one finds much mono-color tinting with occasional splashes of color. One scene in a typical print shows the appearance of a demon. Up to this time, the

film has been tinted only blue. As a puff of smoke announces the demon, we see the smoke tinted in orange. The Pathecolor film, despite the fact that it was hand-painted frame by frame, still is exciting to examine since the color has withstood the test of time and some of its pastel tints are lovely.

Other silent feature films which were colored and shown in Pathecolor were A ROSE AMONG THE BRIARS, THE BELOVED VAGABOND, QUEEN MARGARET, THE THREE MASKS and CYRANO DE BERGERAC, which also had the distinction of being a pioneer effort in the all-talking sound film experiments. Of CYRANO, a New York **Sun** critic reported:

"The characters appear in eye-smashing creations, consisting of purple trousers, pink shirts and green capes, or blue gowns, yellow hats and indigo hose. (The result) has all the artistic effectiveness of a succession of penny postal cards!"[13]

The New York Evening **Post** critic agreed that while many of the colors were pleasant and a number of scenes unusually beautiful, the picture "would have been just as satisfying had it been presented in black and white."[14]

The creator of some truly striking color effects, the hand-tinted Pathecolor process continued in films until the advent of sound.

OTHER MULTI-COLOR TINTS

Max Handschiegl, a former St. Louis engraver, worked out an "imbibition" process for tinting films in one or more colors. After a film was completed, the producers would send the finished print to Handschiegl, who would etch, print or hand block a register print containing the sections of the film to be colored. It is from this "color plate" that the release prints were made.[15]

Handschiegl was noted for his tinting of JOAN THE WOMAN for Cecil B. DeMille, as well as Douglas Fairbanks' THE THREE MUSKETEERS and Marion Davies' WHEN KNIGHTHOOD WAS IN FLOWER. Some of the other famous silent films tinted with the process were von Stroheim's GREED and THE MERRY WIDOW, Lon Chaney's THE PHANTOM OF THE OPERA and Coleen Moore's IRENE.

Robert Paul turned out a seven-reel hand-colored version of THE MIRACLE in England, consisting of 112,000 individual frames![16]

By 1920 over 80 per cent of all Hollywood feature films were being tinted in some manner. By the middle 1920's, hand toning and tinting gave way to tinted film stock.

ONE-COLOR TINTS

By the late 1920's, features were being tinted all colors of the rainbow. ACROSS TO SINGAPORE, CIRCUS ROOKIES, THE ENEMY and THE RIVER PIRATE had sequences tinted in blue; THE PLAY GIRL, PLASTERED IN PARIS, STREET ANGEL, A THIEF IN THE DARK, UNDER THE BLACK EAGLE and France's monumental NAPOLEON had lavender scenes; THE FIRST YEAR, MORE PAY — LESS WORK and WHY SAILORS GO WRONG, light amber, and red was the color for HONOR BOUND, THE WEDDING MARCH (in the bordello sequences, appropriately) and in Howard Hughes' HELL'S ANGELS for the flames from the airplane guns.

When the early and crude "talkies" arrived in 1927, tinting of films was temporarily dropped because the tint interfered with the sound track reproduction. But, in 1929, the Society of Motion Picture Engineers (SMPE) announced that it had perfected tints which would not destroy the sound reproduction qualities. They listed seventeen tints which were contained in the film stock itself.[17]

The tinting process continued through the transition into the sound era. A sepia tint then widely used in western films is still found today in several series of outdoor pictures. Among the top sepia films were Fox's THE RAINS CAME, Warner Brothers' THE OKLAHOMA KID and Hal Roach's OF MICE AND MEN (all 1939).

Metro-Goldwyn-Mayer studios widely used the sepia tint in the late 1930's in such films as THE BAD MAN OF BRIMSTONE, BROADWAY SERENADE, CABIN IN THE SKY, THE FIREFLY, THE GIRL OF THE GOLDEN WEST, LET FREEDOM RING, STABLEMATES, STAND UP AND FIGHT and ZIEGFELD GIRL. Fox presented "The March of the Toys" finale in MY LUCKY STAR in sepia.

In 1937, Gustav Brock of New York City announced that he was hand coloring release prints of motion pictures.[18] In 1946, Eastman Kodak announced its series of Sonochrome Tinted Positive films. These were ready-tinted positive films in a variety of colors adjusted so as not to interfere with sound reproduction.

Nearly all the major Hollywood studios used tints at one time or another. Universal tinted the preview trailer of THE BRIDE OF FRANKENSTEIN in green to exploit the eerie atmosphere of the film. Green was also used for the Irish scenes in Fox's LUCK OF THE IRISH (1948) and the storm sequences in Selznick's PORTRAIT OF JENNIE (1948).

Columbia used two tones in ARIZONA in 1940. Daytime exteriors and all interior shots were in amber and nighttime exteriors were in blue. That company's SONG OF INDIA and "Jungle Jim" series employed a sepia tint. RKO Radio used multiple tints in its production of MIGHTY JOE YOUNG with red for the fire sequence at the orphanage and amber for the closing sequences.

Lippert Pictures used a bluish-pink tint for scenes on the planet Mars in ROCKETSHIP X-M and green was used for the lost world sequences of THE LOST CONTINENT. Allied Artists, as well as other companies, employed Sepiatone for outdoor films, including FARGO and TOPEKA. The sepia tint was also used in portions of LEONARDO DA VINCI and THE STEEL LADY in 1953 and in several of the pioneer 3-D films, MAN IN THE DARK and CAT WOMEN OF THE MOON. An amber tone called Wondercolor appeared in a "quickie" film called RHYTHM AND BLUES REVUE in 1955 and a 1961 film, TEENAGE MILLIONAIRE, used "Multicolor," a series of 11 tints to break up the 11 musical numbers in the film. **Variety,** in its review of this film, suggested that "the crude quality (of the color) might suggest to the layman that it consists of nothing more than a colored cellophane lollipop wrapper placed in front of the lens. The colors, each one utilized for a separate break, range from racy chartreuse to kimnovak lavender."[19]

And the tinting process still appears. A Japanese multi-tinted CinemaScope film of 1961 was reported by Commander Herbert B. Wyman in **Motion Picture Herald:**

"The gimmick: use one or at most two tints to convey the director's feeling in an otherwise black-and-white scene . . . Thus a cloud might be pink or blue, a river yellow, a face green, or there might be two clouds of different colors. Also, there were times when a tinted cloud might be purposely out of place, such as in a peasant's hovel. Sometimes the entire scene would be a single hue such as a blue death scene or a red pan of corpses on the battlefield. In one interesting scene, the flame of a candle was red in an otherwise black-and-white film.

"The coloring was crude from the standpoint that it did not always coincide with the obvious physical boundaries which it was supposed to tint. Also, the process as used was reminiscent of the all-red tinting in RKO's MIGHTY JOE YOUNG . . . The only difference here was that the gimmick was used throughout the entire 118-minute film rather than only for a one-sequence 'punch'.

"Without the gimmick, this film would have been a ponderous,

slow-moving, frequently dull cavalcade of rising and then falling
fortunes of a sixteenth century family over a sixty-year span. The
gimmick enhanced the audience interest by creating suspense in
guessing what would happen next colorwise, if not dramatically."[20]

For the record, this garishly tinted movie was called FUEFUKE
RIVER! And since one color is better than none at all, tinting and
toning will probably continue to appear in films of all types in the
future.

[1] Spottiswoode, *Film and Its Techniques*, p. 207.
[2] The proper term is "colored films," but the adjective "color" is almost now universally used.
[3] These films are sometimes known as "monochrome" or one-color films.
[4] George Mitchell, *Films in Review* 6:44, January, 1955.
[5] Leslie Wood, *The Miracle of the Movies*, p. 250.
[6] Quotation from an early Pathe film catalog.
[7] A. R. Fulton, *Motion Pictures: The Development of an Art From Silent Films to the Age of Television*, p. 109.
[8] Joe Franklin, *Classics of the Silent Screen*, pp. 25-26.
[9] Theodore Huff, *Films in Review*, 4:314, June-July, 1953.
[10] Lucien C. Holtzendorff, *Films in Review*, 10:435, August-September, 1959.
[11] Daniel Blum, *A Pictorial History of the Silent Screen*, p. 19.
[12] A. P. Peck, *Educational Screen* 18:13, January, 1939.
[13] Review, *Literary Digest*, 86:29, July 25, 1925.
[14] *Loc. cit.*
[15] William van Doren Kelley, *SMPE Journal*, 10:238, October, 1926.
[16] Mitchell, see footnote 4.
[17] *Science* 69sup:12-14, May 17, 1929.
[18] *Film Daily Production Guide and Director's Annual*, 1937 edition.
[19] *Variety*, 224:6, August 15, 1961.
[20] *Motion Picture Herald*, 224:18, September 27, 1961.

CHAPTER TWO
NATURAL COLOR FILMS

To most moviegoers, natural color film began appearing in the middle thirties. In reality, films in natural color are as old as the film industry itself. When the development of the film took place in the 1890's, color films were immediately thought of as a future possibility.

Natural color photography dates as far back as 1785 but, as William van Doren Kelley, a pioneer in color films, puts it, "Men discovered at that time; later, men forgot; and then men discovered again."[21] Such was the case with color photography. Color processes were discovered and then they disappeared, only to crop up again almost 100 years later.

As early as 1813, A. Vogel discovered the principle of the "dye and bleach" color film and the modern theory of three-color films was recognized as early as 1861.

One of the earliest color still photographs now on record was a three-color carbon print taken by Louis Ducos du Haron in 1877 of the City of Angouleme, France. One of the fathers of color photography, du Haron expounded the complicated theories of color long before there were any means to prove them.[22] Some of his theories were later applied to some of the earliest motion pictures.

EARLY PATENTS

The earliest patent recorded for color films, registered in 1897 by H. Isensee of Berlin, described an invention which would produce motion pictures in natural colors by means of "images being projected rapidly one after another and in regular sequence in . . . red, green and blue."[23]

This invention was the beginning of a series of color films which were additive. Isensee's invention used a rotating disc containing colored glass in red, green and blue which turned before the projector lens.

In 1898, Captain William Norman Lascelles-Davidson of England patented a triple-lens motion picture camera with color filters which could revolve either behind the lens or in front of it.[24]

Following this, Frederick Marshall Lee and Raymond Turner, also of England, were credited with the discovery of the first practical color projector and film. Their work was financed by Charles Urban, a well-known impressario who later was to become a leading figure in the field of the color motion picture. The two men recorded their film in a camera equipped with a single lens which was equipped with rotating filters in red, green and blue. During projection, each picture was shown through each of the three color lenses in turn and three pictures were always projected simultaneously.[25]

By 1900, several color systems were in existence. The McDonough process, an additive system, the Sanger-Shepherd process, which was subtractive, and the Lippman process, which was based on the theory of interference of light waves.[26]

Color pioneer F. E. Ives invented Kromoscope, an additive process, in 1900 and the penny peep shows were showing views in Gaumont Color, a process for still pictures.

None of these systems was successful because of considerable "fringing," that is, the three images would not always be in exact alignment when projected on the screen. The inventors became doubtful that any practical three-color motion picture film could be invented using the additive process.

An early color film was invented by the two French pioneers, the Lumiere Brothers, but it was limited to transparencies for slide projectors and was not used for motion pictures.

E. J. Wall experimented with a dichromated gelatin color film process in 1911 but soon abandoned the project. He felt the only true color film would be one with the color directly on the film as it is exposed in the camera.[27] But it would be a few years before this idea finally came about.

One of the first subtractive color processes was invented by A. Hernandez-Mejia in 1912 called Cinecolorgraph and used color emulsion on both sides of the film.[28]

BIOCOLOR AND CINECHROME

In England, William Friese-Greene was one of the first to introduce color films which gave a stereoscopic effect. Friese-Greene used red, green and blue color filters to obtain his color effects.

These films, however, never progressed beyond the experimental stages. Although Friese-Greene is credited with being one of the pioneers in color motion pictures, film expert Theodore Huff once said:

"I cannot learn that he ever produced anything. I have gone over Friese-Greene's four patents on color photography and have come to the conclusion he was given to hallucinations. While I have not seen his master patent,. I suspect it is no more profound than the four patents I have studied."[29]

Mr. Friese-Greene's Biocolor process was used in four 1914 British productions — THE EARL OF CAMELOT, PRIDE OF THE NATIONS, ROBIN HOOD and SPEAKING PICTURES.

Friese-Greene sold out to Colin Bennett Ltd. in 1911. After three years the company had corrected several of the defects in the earlier process and announced a new and improved color film, Cinechrome. The new color system had two lenses placed behind a prism or "split beam" divider[30] which caused the colors to separate in the camera and register on the film individually. The film had two blank frames between each picture and employed an elaborate triple projector. Cinechrome recorded two adjacent images on one frame of film. A special projection lens superimposed the two images on the screen, thus forming a complete color picture.

Bennett then developed a new and radical type of film. Instead of a single film he used two films double width with three sets of perforations — one set on each side of the film and one set down the middle. On this new type of film, manufactured by the Eastman Kodak Company, the visit of the Prince of Wales to India was recorded. The film was later shown on a special projector at the Stoll Picture Theatre in London in 1921 where it was a great success. The wide film, however, was very cumbersome and it was rejected completely by 1925. That year Cinechrome was abandoned.[31]

English actor Cyril Maude arrived in New York with some color films in 1915 made by superimposing coats of gelatin in red, blue and yellow on the film.

A Roman painter, S. Barricelli, invented the red-yellow-blue visual persistence system which gave the impression of a three-color image, as early as 1909. He photographed each image three times through properly colored screens. A glass disc in three colored sections revolved during the projection of the film, thus giving a three-color illusion. The film, of course, had the disadvantage of being three times as long and was projected three times as fast as an ordinary motion picture.[32]

THE TWO-COLOR PROCESSES

Composed of two separate films, two-color processes are a compromise of the three-color systems. One film is usually sensitive to red, orange and yellow, while the other attracts blue and green. Some other colors are absent from these two-color systems and the remaining colors are not nearly so true as in full color films.

KINEMACOLOR

Charles Urban, one of the pioneers in color film research, perfected an additive system based on the three-color process used for printing art plates. By printing three blocks in exact register, a printer gets a complete color picture. Working on this theory, Urban engaged a chemist, Edward R. Turner, and went to work. He used a single black-and-white negative in the photographic process. During projection, however, the colors sometimes became "out of register," a characteristic of earlier attempts at color films. Also, the projection system was rather complicated. The film required both a special colored light and a rotating color filter on the projector as well as a special fixed-color screen on which to project the image.[33]

They experimented with color in two 1906 films, one covering a state visit of King George and Queen Mary and the other showing the various phases of building the Panama Canal.

A short time later, Turner died. Urban was determined to continue the experiments and engaged a photographer named George Albert Smith to carry on the research on the process he had already named Kinemacolor. Urban and Smith formed the Natural Colour Kinematograph Company in 1908.

Smith discovered it was an easy thing to keep two colors in register, but not three. He then developed a satisfactory system employing black-and-white film and red-orange and blue-green filters. The film was taken at twice the speed of ordinary film so that the film alternated a red-orange image with a blue-green image. An alternating red-orange and blue-green color wheel in front of the projector and persistence of vision in one's eyes brought all the colors together.

Kinemacolor had two main drawbacks: (a) the double speed through the mechanism was hard on the film, and (b) an ordinary projector, of course, could not run the film. If the filters on the projector accidentally got out of register with the corresponding frames of film, strange things happened. One spectator remembered that the blue trousers worn by a column of marching guardsmen

were going across the screen independently and well ahead of their owners' red coats![34]

The first public demonstration of Kinemacolor in 1908 at the Royal Society of Arts in England, however, was hailed as a great success and Smith received the Society's Silver Medal for his work. A film of plant and animal life made in the Kinemacolor process in 1910 called THE BIRTH OF A FLOWER launched this first commercial color film process. The trade name of Kinemacolor became well-known in England.

In 1911, the first public performances of Kinemacolor films opened at the Scala Theatre in England with a series of unrelated views of farmyard and agricultural scenes, topical events, portrait studies, growing flowers and a moving picture play grouped under the title of ROUND THE WORLD IN TWO HOURS. It also produced a Kinemacolor version of THE CORONATION OF GEORGE V.

"The promoters of Kinemacolor," a London critic said, "may be congratulated on having originated an evening of combined instruction and entertainment which is unique of its kind and should prove capable of taking its place among the established attractions of the London theatres."[35]

The British Journal of Photography noted:

"We have had an opportunity of seeing some results achieved by Mr. G. A. Smith of the Urban Trading Company, Rupert St., in cinematography in colors, and while there is yet room for considerable improvement, the progress made is extremely satisfactory. We were able to compare the colors in the pictures projected with some of the actual accessories used, and the rendering of the colors was strikingly accurate, particularly in the case of the reds. Only two taking and projecting filters were used, an orange-red and a blue-green, the usual third or blue-violet filter being dispensed with. Naturally the whites obtained are not pure, but have a slightly yellowish tinge, yet when projected on the screen with brilliant colors this defect is hardly noticeable. The progress achieved is so satisfactory·that we are warranted in saying that the process should be commercially valuable in a very short time."[36]

Urban then began filming movies of major importance. His first big production, and the first well-known color film, was THE DURBAR AT DELHI, India, in 1911. Twenty-three cameramen were on hand to shoot the event. The sun was so hot that Urban, in order to protect the sensitive color film, built a pit of sand under his

bed and slept on the film. THE DURBAR AT DELHI became the rage of London and Paris.

Ralph Flint recalls the film:

". . . when the Indian Durbar in all its colorful pageantry flashed across the screen at Tremont Temple, bringing the wide world miraculously near; and I still recall the moment — we were properly advised by the commentator — when the Kinecolor (sic) camera caught the sudden pink glint in an elephant's eye!"[37]

Because Kinemacolor was an additive process, its defects and weaknesses were soon discovered. The audiences suffered from much eyestrain, and the projection of 32 frames of film per second, instead of the normal 16, necessitated a special projector and reduced the life of the film.

Albuin R. Mariner of the Kinemacolor plant became one of the most noted of the early color cinematographers. In addition to helping film the Durbar, he photographed the Royal Family, the King's shooting box in Scotland[38] and a production of BY ORDER OF NAPOLEON.

Urban's success in America, however, was disappointing. He came to the United States in 1912 and offered the Kinemacolor process to the United States Patents Company. After a successful test showing, they made him a good offer. The offer, however, was intended to suppress his invention and keep him out of the color field. Despite this, Urban established Kinemacolor studios on Long Island and in Los Angeles and produced color film versions of THE SCARLET LETTER, MISSION BELLS, the classic comedy, THE RIVALS, Thomas Dixon's THE CLANSMAN (which was never completed in color, but emerged later as THE BIRTH OF A NATION), a version of LA TOSCA starring Lillian Russell and some medical films for the United States Government.[39] But after a year of activity, the American branch of Kinemacolor was disbanded.

In 1914, a Kinemacolor production of LITTLE LORD FAUNT-LEROY was made in England.[40]

OTHER DEVELOPMENTS

William F. Fox's Natural Color Company patented a color film in 1917 which used color tones of ferric salts for the blue color and uranium for the red. Kinemacolor took over this process when they dropped their additive "color wheel" system.

In Brighton, England, William Friese-Greene exhibited an improved color film similar to Kinemacolor which caused Urban to bring an unsuccessful suit against him. Kinemacolor carried the case

system in New York City on February 14, 1918. Scenes included bathing beauties, Yosemite National Park, a forest fire, Yellowstone National Park and Mount Tamalpais. The **New York Times** commented that "The effect produced is remarkably true to nature, the range of tint being apparently unlimited, depicting all of the delicate shades and hues."[55]

Douglass' two-color process alternated red and green frames and were dyed red and green and projected at double speed. At public showings in New York City, the reaction was less than anticipated and the process was soon abandoned.[56]

KODACHROME

In 1914 the first actual color-on-film subtractive process was perfected by J. G. Capstaff of Kodak Research Laboratories. The process was named Kodachrome. The negatives were taken by a split-beam camera, after which they were dyed red-orange and blue-green to get a positive image.

KESDACOLOR, KELLEYCOLOR and HARRISCOLOR

William van Doren Kelley, who developed the Prizma process, entered into partnership with Carroll H. Dunning in 1918 and introduced a color-on-film system called Kesdacolor. The first film in the process was a short film showing the American flag. The next year, Kelley produced a series of color cartoons and, in 1924, he introduced his own subtractive process, Kelleycolor.

In 1926, Kelley became associated with Max Handschiegl, a film tinter, and formed the Kelleycolor Company which was purchased by Harriscolor in 1928. Kelley's right to the Prizma process, as was noted earlier, went to Consolidated Film Industries. The Kelleycolor process, however, was never as good as the perfected Prizma process.

ZOECHROME

In 1920, T. A. Mills patented an additive color process known as Zoechrome. The system consisted of three lenses in back of a large lens which exposed three pictures on one frame of film through tri-color filters.[57] The resulting black-and-white film was coated with an emulsion for each color. The process suffered from parallax and considerable "fringing" at the edges of the film and was soon abandoned.

POLYCHROMIDE

The Polychromide process was developed in England in 1922 by

Aron Hamburger, an American chemist. It used a beam-splitter camera which utilized two film gates at right angles to each other. A method of dyeing and toning completed the process. Hamburger claimed that the two positive films had a color gradation which gave the effect of a four-color process of red, yellow, green and blue.[58]

COLORCRAFT

Colorcraft, invented by W. H. Peck, was demonstrated in New York City in 1921. Tests were found to be convincing to those who witnessed them. A **New York Times** reporter remarked: "Difficult hues, photographed under trying conditions, were reproduced with no sign of fringe or parallax."[59]

No special projector was used, but rather Peck employed a beam-splitter camera which split the red and green images onto different films. In printing, green images are put on one side of the film and red images on the other.

FRIESE-GREENE

C. H. Friese-Greene, son of the film pioneer, improved a two-color additive process which was begun years before by his father. It used a camera with a red filter alternating with no filter. Every other frame was tinted red after developing and the alternate frames were tinted blue. Although projection was at normal speed, visual fatigue was too noticeable to make the system of much commercial value.[60]

Within a span of twenty-five years, at least twenty-five different color processes — and probably many more unnamed and long since forgotten — had failed. All of them had hoped to conquer the problem of "motion pictures in natural colors" but none of them succeeded in permanently advancing the film beyond its black-and-white existence.

[21] Kelley, SMPE Journal, November, 1919, p. 42.
[22] "An 1877 Color Photograph," Image 3:33, May, 1954.
[23] Cornwell-Clyne, Color Cinematography, pp. 4-5.
[24] Cornwell-Clyne, p. 11
[25] Ibid.
[26] Kelley, SMPE Journal, April, 1919, p. 76.
[27] Cornwell-Clyne, p. 11.
[28] Ibid.
[29] Theodore Huff, Films in Review, n.d.
[30] A beam splitter camera usually entails a prism which deflects the basic colors onto different films, i.e., reds are deflected onto one film and perhaps blues and greens onto another in a two-color process.
[31] New York Times, 64:11, September 10, 1915.
[32] "Stereoscopic Moving Pictures in Natural Colors," Scientific American, 101:256, October 9, 1909.

[33] "Moving Pictures in Natural Colors," *Scientific American*, 100:374, May 15, 1909.

[34] Wood, *op. cit.*, p. 252.

[35] Quoted in *The British Journal of Photography*, April 17, 1911, by Adrian Cornwell-Clyne, p. 8.

[36] *Ibid*, December 6, 1907.

[37] Ralph Flint, "New Look on the Screen," *Christian Science Monitor*, 45:8c, April 8, 1953.

[38] Arthur Edwin Krows, "Motion Pictures — Not for Theatres," *Educational Screen* 18:363, December, 1939.

[39] Wood, *op. cit.*, p. 254.

[40] Roger Manvell, "The Oldest Man in Films," *Films and Filming* 1:8, August, 1955.

[41] *New York Times*, 69:13, Section 2, May 16, 1920.

[42] Quoted by Wood, *op. cit.*, pp. 253-54.

[43] *New York Times*, 69:22, June 12, 1920.

[44] C. E. K. Mees, *SMPE Journal*, 14:137, May, 1922.

[45] *New York Times*, 64:10, February 26, 1917.

[46] *Ibid.*, 68:13, January 20, 1919.

[47] *Ibid.*, 69:2, Section 7, June 20, 1920.

[48] *Ibid.*, 70:16, February 28, 1921.

[49] *New York Times*, 71:18, April 24, 1922.

[50] Kelley, *SMPE Journal*, April, 1919, pp. 77-78.

[51] *New York Times*, 72:31, September 26, 1922.

[52] Mitchell, *ibid.*

[53] Cornwell-Clyne, pp. 17-18.

[54] A film gate is the rectangular opening in the camera and projector through which the light and film are shown on the screen.

[55] *New York Times*, 67:7, February 15, 1918.

[56] Kelley, *SMPE Journal*, November, 1919, p. 42.

[57] Cornwell-Clyne, pp. 17-18.

[58] *Ibid.*, pp. 339-340.

[59] *New York Times*, 70:2, Section VI, May 15, 1921.

[60] Cornwell-Clyne, p. 11.

CHAPTER THREE
THE WORLD OF TECHNICOLOR

Although the Motion Picture Patents Company suppressed Kinemacolor, they could not prevent experimentation in the field of color films. Two experimentalists, who were later to change the entire course of the color motion picture, worked diligently on a new process for making "natural color" films. The inventors, Herbert T. Kalmus and Daniel F. Comstock, worked with color exposed on two films instead of just one. They named their process Technicolor.

Their laboratory was an abandoned railroad car in Boston and they did all the work themselves. In 1917, Kalmus and Comstock took their car to Jacksonville, Florida, where they produced their first Technicolor picture.

The first Technicolor system superimposed the two colored images onto the screen at the same time. The two images together formed the completed color picture. The system, however, required a special projector and was not adaptable to standard projection.[61] The process was still as crude as the other color systems of the day and did not have the qualities of modern Technicolor. In 1917, the process consisted of only two colors — red and green — rather than the now familiar red, green and blue combination.

The Technicolor camera had two apertures — each with its own color filter — separating the image into either red or green. It proved to be the most advanced method of color cinematography which had yet appeared on the market, even though the system was still an additive one.[62]

The first film of its kind to be made with the process was the feature film, THE GULF BETWEEN, a Technicolor production.

Recalling a demonstration of the film in Aeolian Hall in New York in 1917, Dr. Kalmus said:

"I thought the Technicolor inventors and engineers had a practical solution, at least temporarily, so I marched bravely to the

platform of Aeolian Hall. It was a great lesson. We were, of course, introducing the color by projecting through two apertures, each with a color filter, bringing the two components into register on the screen by means of a thin adjusting glass element . . . During my lecture, something happened to the adjusting element and, in spite of frantic efforts of the projectionists, it refused to adjust. And so I displayed fringes wider than anybody had ever seen before. Both the audience and the press were very kind but it didn't help my immediate dilemma or afford an explanation to our financial angels."[63]

The "wide fringes" of which Dr. Kalmus spoke were the separation of the two colors on the two films, sometimes giving a horse two tails or a man two shirts, each of a different color. Dr. Kalmus went back to the laboratory.

In a front-page story in the New York **Times** of September 21, 1922, William Travers Jerome, a former district attorney of New York County, announced the formation of a one-million-dollar syndicate to exploit Daniel F. Comstock's color process which had been in the experimental stages since 1915. Technicolor, however, was not officially chartered until September 12, 1922, with Herbert T. Kalmus as president.[64]

New York **Times** reviewed the September (1922) preview of Technicolor:

"The film was unreeled before an audience consisting mainly of expert picture men, who seemed unanimous in their opinion that the problem of the colored motion picture had been solved."[65]

Dr. Kalmus exhibited 2,000 feet of Technicolor film shot in Florida before the American Institute of Mining Engineers. "I believe the time is here for the big advance, the production of motion pictures in natural color," he urged.[66]

SUBTRACTIVE TECHNICOLOR

By 1921, the Technicolor process had been improved by having the two films welded together after being exposed and dyed in complementary colors. This was known as the Technicolor subtractive method. The first color film made by this method was TOLL OF THE SEA, released by Metro-Goldwyn Pictures in 1921. It was first exhibited in 1922, but, as the Technicolor laboratories were still small, the great demand for the picture over-taxed Technicolor's facilities and it was 1923 before enough prints had been made to make the picture available to the public. The film made over a quarter of a million dollars and Technicolor received over half the profits.[67]

While TOLL OF THE SEA was still in production, much interest in the process was kindled. Rex Ingram, who was directing a production of THE PRISONER OF ZENDA in 1922, asked his company for permission to scrap all the black-and-white scenes already shot and refilm the production in Technicolor.

Two other queries came from D. W. Griffith and Douglas Fairbanks. Griffith, who had filmed several sequences of WAY DOWN EAST in Technicolor in 1920, wanted to film FAUST in the process and Fairbanks inquired about doing a feature. There is no record that THE PRISONER OF ZENDA was re-filmed in Technicolor or that Griffith ever made a version of FAUST, but Fairbanks did make a Technicolor feature, THE BLACK PIRATE, two years later.

In 1923, producer Jesse L. Lasky recalls an early hand-colored attempt:

"Some scenes of THE TEN COMMANDMENTS were in color before an American laboratory color process for motion pictures had been perfected. Every print was painstakingly painted by hand, frame by frame. The tinted objects jumped around on the screen like a cat on a hot tin roof."[68]

Mr. Lasky was ready for a new idea. He would get it soon.

In the meantime, Technicolor shot its first interior scenes early in 1924. Its other ventures had all been shot outdoors under natural lighting. The picture which featured the first indoor lighting scenes was George Fitzmaurice's CYTHEREA for First National Pictures. It was reasonably successful by the day's standards, according to Dr. Kalmus.[69]

The New York **Times** said of CYTHEREA:

"There are some exquisite sequences of color photography, in which one enjoys the sight of the varied hues and tints of Cuban costumes and scenery. There is one delightful bit of color in one interior; one sees an officer in blue and red, women in green and pink, and possibly the most startling effect is in the embroidery on the women's shawls. These are not only beautifully photographed, but they are introduced most realistically . . ."[70]

That same year Paramount (then the Famous Players Corporation under Jesse L. Lasky) took the plunge. As Mr. Lasky recalls:

"Herbert Kalmus came to me shortly after this (THE TEN COMMANDMENTS) and told me that he had a method for photographing natural color. Always a pushover for new ideas, I ordered it used at once in a picture with vistas of scenery to take full advantage of the chromatic effects. Zane Grey's WANDERER OF

THE WASTELAND was the first full-length Technicolor feature sponsored by a major studio, and it gave the new process an enormous boost in its bid for popularity with movie makers and the public. I particularly remember the dramatic use we made of color in one scene where the hero, tracking down the wounded villian who has concealed himself in a gold-mine stamp mill, notices a trickle of muddy water flowing from the mill sluiceway slowly turning red — and is thus lead to the hideout of his quarry."[71]

Print costs for WANDERER OF THE WASTELAND were staggering, since color film scratched more easily than black-and-white film. Another drawback, Dr. Kalmus recalls, was the "cupping" of the cemented films in the projector, causing the films to be out of focus part of the time. A "true imbibition" process was soon worked out, but not soon enough to soothe the headaches of the Technicolor company.

In 1925, a two-reel short, MARIONETTES, was filmed in Technicolor by Henri Diamont-Berger, a Frenchman who entered the film business as the editor-publisher of a trade magazine. The picture was filmed at the Fort Lee Studios in New Jersey.[72]

By 1926 more improvements had been made in the Technicolor process and Douglas Fairbanks made good his promise of two years earlier and produced his 1926 production of THE BLACK PIRATE in Technicolor. Four of the eleven Technicolor cameras in existence were used in the filming. The picture was very successful — and very expensive. But seeing "Doug" in color appealed to movie fans and the picture was another in the string of Fairbanks successes.

COLOR SEQUENCES

Not many producers wanted to risk the expense of producing a film in Technicolor, so "color sequences" became the rage. These sequences were inserted into more than 30 pictures between 1926 and 1932.

In the fall of 1924, according to Dr. Kalmus, four Technicolor cameras were in Rome working on MGM's spectacle, BEN-HUR. The production was black and white, but Technicolor sequences appeared in the original version. When the Wise Men entered the stable, for instance, the entire scene then turned into color.

The fashion show in IRENE (1926) with Colleen Moore was in Technicolor, as was a sequence in RED HAIR (1928) with Clara Bow shown with her bright red hair against a clear blue sky. Other films of the period with Technicolor sequences included THE

UNINVITED GUEST (1924), PRETTY LADIES, THE MER-
RY WIDOW, THE PHANTOM OF THE OPERA and STAGE
STRUCK (1925), THE AMERICAN VENUS (1926), THE
FIRE BRIGADE and KING OF KINGS (1927), and THE
WEDDING MARCH (1928).

Of the several short subjects filmed in Technicolor during the
period, the first was an episode of a story about George Washington
and Betsy Ross. The climax, of course, was the raising of the
American flag in all its colors. Another episode, photographed in
November of 1927, concerned the divorce of Napoleon and
Josephine. MGM produced both these successful short subjects.

Technicolor produced twelve two-reel films including the above-
mentioned subjects. Dr. Kalmus and the company were asked by
MGM to produce a feature film which they would release and
distribute. Dr. Kalmus had always admired the epic quality of
stories about the Norsemen and engaged Jack Cunningham to write
a screenplay called THE VIKING.

"There seemed to be two principal troubles with THE VIKING,"
Dr. Kalmus remembers. "First, it came out among the very last
silent pictures in 1929, and second, whiskers. Leif Erickson, the
Viking hero, true to character, had a long, curling moustache,
whereas American audiences preferred their lovers smooth-shaven.
At times the whole screen seemed filled with Viking whiskers. But
the picture was a good color job and the first to be synchronized
with music and sound effects."[73] Paramount followed THE
VIKING with the first feature-length Technicolor film in sound,
REDSKIN, with Richard Dix.

THE COMING OF SOUND

The emergence of the talking picture ruined many stars whose
voices were not suitable to the sound track. Many producers, caught
unawares, did not believe the sound picture would last. When they
did realize it, they seized upon color as a novelty with a future. Thus
with the arrival of sound, a profusion of "all-talking, all-singing, all-
color pictures" reached the theatre screens. Both MGM and Warner
Brothers were presenting a profusion of Technicolor pictures from
1928 to 1933.

The first all-color sound picture in Technicolor was ON WITH
THE SHOW, produced in 1929 by Warner Brothers.

Other studios, including Pathe, United Artists, Universal,

Paramount and Columbia inserted color sequences into their 1929 talking films, including BROADWAY MELODY, THE DESERT SONG, THE LOTTERY BRIDE, PUTTIN' ON THE RITZ, FOOTLIGHTS AND FOOLS, PARIS, GLORIFYING THE AMERICAN GIRL, BROADWAY, THE HOLLYWOOD RE-VUE, THE SHOW OF SHOWS, MAMMY, THE DANCE OF LIFE, WHOOPEE and KING OF JAZZ.

In Dr. Kalmus' words, "The studios were beginning to be color conscious."[74] Warner Brothers' GOLD DIGGERS OF BROAD-WAY grossed over three million dollars in 1929 — and the Technicolor process was still in hues of only red and green!

Technicolor prints varied during the "rush" years of the coming of sound. Critic Marguerite Orndorff reviewed two 1930 Technicolor pictures thusly: RIO RITA had "lovely color work" but the color sequences were "badly blurred" in NO NO NANETTE.[75] Holly-wood critic Pete Harrison noted that the color in NO NO NANETTE was "tiresome . . . the Technicolor work is the poorest yet seen. The emulsion grain is so noticeable that it makes the picture appear as if the heavens were raining sand. The long shots are one big blur. The color in the medium shots is mostly washed out."[76]

Some of the all-Technicolor features in 1930 were UNDER A TEXAS MOON, HOLD EVERYTHING, SONG OF THE FLAME, THE VAGABOND KING, SONG OF THE WEST, MAMBA, VIENNESE NIGHTS, THE LIFE OF THE PARTY, NO NO NANETTE, RIO RITA, HIT THE DECK, SALLY, IT'S A GREAT LIFE, PARAMOUNT ON PARADE, LORD BYRON OF BROADWAY, ROGUE SONG, BRIDE OF THE REGI-MENT, THE GOLDEN DAWN, SWEET KITTY BELAIRS and FOLLOW THRU.

Many colored shorts appeared in the early 1930's, mostly from the MGM studios, including COLORTONE REVIEWS (1930), COLORTONE NOVELTIES (1931) and COLORTONE MUSI-CALS (1932).

The concerted movement to color was doomed to failure because of audience disinterest and some poor examples of the process, hurriedly developed in the laboratory. By 1932, the production of Technicolor films had dwindled to almost none. The two-color Technicolor system's novelty had worn off. The last two red-and-green Technicolor films were both Warner Brothers horror films —

DOCTOR X (1932) and THE MYSTERY OF THE WAX MUSEUM (1933).

As Dr. Kalmus described the situation:

"During the rush to color, Technicolor had not only its own shortcomings to contend with, but also a surfeit of poor stories that were to be saved by color and monotony of musicals more or less on the same formula. An injustice was no doubt done Technicolor by causing it thus to be identified with musical and period productions. I counseled at the time that producers were no doubt losing an opportunity in not taking advantage of the fact that color can be used to intensify dramatic effect and bring out the best points in personalities, advantages which have been later used with striking effectiveness."[77].

THREE-COLOR TECHNICOLOR

Through much research and development, Technicolor's new three-color component process was completed in 1932, just at the time when the interest in color films had waned. Of the new process, Dr. Kalmus remarked enthusiastically, "The difference between this three-component process was truly extraordinary. Not only was the accuracy of tone and color reproduction greatly improved, (but) the definition was markedly better."[78]

The three-color Technicolor process worked like this:

"Light, reflected from a photographed object, entering from a single lens, strikes a prism. Part of the light passes through the prism and through a green filter to a green-sensitive primary negative. The remainder, deflected at right angles, is absorbed by the two other primary negatives, individually sensitive to blue and red light. These negatives which had recorded the primary color aspects (red, green and blue) of the scene are developed to produce negatives which look like black-and-white negatives, but each is a record of the scene's primary colors. If a red barn were photographed in a green field with a blue sky overhead, the red record negative would have an image of the barn, the green record negative would have the image of the field, and the blue record negative would have the image of the sky. From each of these color separation negatives a special positive relief image is printed and developed. These positives differ from ordinary positives in that the picture graduations are represented by varying thicknesses of hardened gelatin. These positives, which are called 'matrices,' are used as printing plates. They absorb suitably colored dyes and are then used

in a manner similar to the color plates for a lithograph, the dye image from each of the three matrices being transferred one after the other upon the final completed print ready for projection."[79]

To allow time to build new three-color Technicolor cameras and conversion of the processing laboratories, Dr. Kalmus decided to offer the new color system first to the short subject producer — specifically the cartoon producers. No cartoonist, however, would have it.

"We were told," Dr. Kalmus related, "(that) cartoons were good enough in black and white and that of all departments of production, cartoons could least afford the added expense."[80]

Later that year, Walt Disney, who had created Mickey Mouse five years earlier, decided to try Technicolor as an experiment with his cartoon production of FLOWERS AND TREES. It was so successful that Disney contracted for a series. In Christmas of 1932, he released SANTA'S WORK SHOP and, in the Easter of 1933, FUNNY BUNNIES. May of that year brought the immortal THREE LITTLE PIGS which gave a depression-ridden America laughter when they needed it most. When Disney discovered that the **Silly Symphonies** series was making more money than Mickey Mouse films in black-and-white, he adopted Technicolor for both series. The relationship between Disney and Technicolor remains intact 35 years later. All Disney color films have been in Technicolor.

Other cartoon producers followed suit with Celebrity Productions' **Comicolor Cartoons** series in 1934 and Paramount's **Color Classics** and Columbia's **Color Rhapsodies,** both in 1936.

But no studio would produce a feature-length picture in Technicolor, even though the price of Technicolor film was lowered.

PIONEER PICTURES

On May 18, 1933, a momentous day for Technicolor, Merian C. Cooper and John Hay Whitney of Pioneer Pictures (releasing through RKO Radio Pictures) signed a contract for a series of eight productions in Technicolor.

"There were some conditional clauses," Dr. Kalmus remembers, "among others a provision for extensive preliminary tests. Certain doubts remained in the minds of Whitney and his associates as to the performance of our three-component process under certain conditions. Would the process reproduce the various shades of green in a woodland jungle? . . . What about the visibility of extremely

small figures in the distance? . . . Exhaustive sets of tests were made with results satisfactory to Mr. Whitney and Mr. Cooper."[81]

A long search for the right story for the initial production was begun. While the search went on, Pioneer Pictures made still another test, this time by filming a short subject in Technicolor. The film, LA CUCURACHA, made history and caused a tremendous interest in Technicolor. As only three color cameras were in existence, an order was quickly made for four more.

While Pioneer Pictures continued its research, several Technicolor "inserts" were added to pictures in production. The first was for the closing scene of United Artists' THE HOUSE OF ROTHSCHILD; a second for the last sequence of Samuel Goldwyn's KID MILLIONS, a third for Twentieth Century-Fox's THE LITTLE COLONEL and a fourth in THE CAT AND THE FIDDLE at MGM.

The real color revolution came in 1935 when Pioneer Pictures completed plans to film a feature-length Technicolor production of Thackery's historical novel, **Vanity Fair** — re-named BECKY SHARP. Despite the expense, the filming was done on schedule and had its premiere at the Radio City Music Hall in New York City that same year and was hailed as an innovation. After its release, there was no doubt that Technicolor was to be a permanent part of the motion picture industry.

Rouben Mamoulian, who directed BECKY SHARP, stated:
"For more than 20 years cinematographers have varied their key of lighting in photographing black-and-white pictures to make the visual impression enhance the emotional mood of the action. We have become accustomed to a definite language of lighting: low-key effects, with sombre, heavy shadows, express a sombrely dramatic mood; high-key effects, with brilliant lighting and sparkling definition, suggest a lighter mood; harsh contrasts, with velvety shadows and strong lights, strike a melodramatic note . . . (now) we have color — a new medium, basically different in many ways from any dramatic medium previously known, whether the stage or previous black-and-white pictures. And in color we have not only a new dimension of realism but also a tremendously powerful means of expressing dramatic emotion. Is it not logical, therefore, to feel that it is incumbent upon all of us, as film craftsmen, to seek to evolve a photodramatic language of color analogous to the language of light with which we are all so familiar?"[82]

EARLY TECHNICOLOR FEATURES

After the success of BECKY SHARP, five more pictures went before the Hollywood cameras in 1936 including RAMONA at Twentieth Century-Fox; TRAIL OF THE LONESOME PINE at Paramount; DANCING PIRATE at RKO: GOD'S COUNTRY AND THE WOMAN at Warner Brothers and THE GARDEN OF ALLAH at United Artists. The major and minor companies announced a total of twenty full-color features for 1937. Of these, the majority were in Technicolor.

In the field of short subjects, the noted **Fitzpatrick Travelogues** began appearing in Technicolor in 1936. That same year MGM released an all-star short, LA FIESTA DE SANTA BARBARA with Gary Cooper, Robert Taylor, Buster Keaton and Harpo Marx. Warner Brothers' **Color Parade** series appeared in 1937 and Paramount's **Color Cruises** in 1938. Travelogs in color provided much information and entertainment to motion picture audiences.

In 1937 and 1938, many of the "special" pictures were being filmed in Technicolor. They ranged from outdoor dramas such as THE ADVENTURES OF ROBIN HOOD, EBB TIDE and HER JUNGLE LOVE to interiors in NOTHING SACRED, VOGUES OF 1938, A STAR IS BORN, WINGS OF THE MORNING (the first British Technicolor feature), THE ADVENTURES OF TOM SAWYER, THE PRIVATE LIVES OF ELIZABETH AND ESSEX, THE GOLDWYN FOLLIES and the first full-length color cartoon, SNOW WHITE AND THE SEVEN DWARFS.

The most spectacular Technicolor production of the 1930's was GONE WITH THE WIND, produced by David O. Selznick. It has been re-issued several times and has already grossed over 50 million dollars.

COLOR CONSULTANTS

Technicolor had always supplied its own cameramen for every production in their color system because these men were specialists in working with Technicolor film. And Technicolor cameras are only rented, never purchased, by the motion picture companies.

"Color consultants" appear on the staff of every Technicolor production. The consultant works with various departments, helping to coordinate and control the color in relation to the type and mood of the film subject. The color consultants until recently were headed by Dr. Kalmus' wife, Natalie. Sometimes the consultants, together with the color cameraman, went so far as to

"lay out" the entire color plan of a film, or acted in a purely consulting capacity on the staff of the film. Mrs. Kalmus' personal choice as the best Technicolor film of all time is the British production, THE RED SHOES.

Technicolor films were being used to heighten the dramatic qualities of the script, not merely to "dress up" the physical production. Writer Alice Evans Field expressed it this way:

"At first one is inclined to argue that while (color) adds interest to musicals, fantasies and out-of-door pictures where the natural background is of particular beauty, black-and-white photography seems better suited to a certain type of film drama, such as the mystery or melodrama . . . the deep purple shadows, the sepia tones of old wood and the eerie effects of cold-blue and green lighting might add immensely to the mood of a good mystery film."[83]

Dr. Kalmus believes that since 1940, "the improved fidelity of the modern full-range Technicolor process has greatly increased the demands of precision in color control in order that the fine gradations of color now available on the screen may comprise a pleasing harmony."[84]

Technicolor processed 5,526,128 feet of film in 1932; nearly 162,000,000 in 1944 and over one billion feet in 1946. An estimated nine billion dollars had been invested by 1947 in Technicolor films in Hollywood and Great Britain.[85]

TECHNICOLOR MONOPACK

One of the more recent developments in the Technicolor process was the perfection of the monopack (one film) process. With this new system, Technicolor pictures would be filmed in an ordinary studio camera which usually photographs only black-and-white pictures. Monopack was first used for exteriors in LASSIE COME HOME in 1942 and entirely for THUNDERHEAD — SON OF FLICKA for Twentieth Century-Fox and in SON OF LASSIE and EASY TO WED, both for MGM.[86]

In his report for the year ending December 31, 1945, Dr. Kalmus stated that 26 features had been photographed in Technicolor in 1945 — including four in Great Britain. Forty-two features were announced for 1946 and 48 for 1948. In 1949, **Variety** announced that 30 per cent of all new Hollywood films were to be in color and on July 15, 1952, **Film Daily** stated that over 78 per cent of features then in production were to be in color, the majority in Technicolor. In January of 1953, Columbia Pictures Corporation announced the

production of 30 Technicolor features, the greatest number of Technicolor films ever announced by a single Hollywood studio.[87]

With the introduction of the monopack Eastman Color process, Technicolor found its first real color rival. But Technicolor always continued its research and in 1956 announced another "improved" color process with new matrix stock, new blank stock, and improved optical printing procedure.

When the widescreen vogue came into prominence in 1953, Technicolor developed its Technirama process, using Technicolor film combined with an anamorphic lens with half the "squeezing" of the image done in the laboratory and half by the projecting lens, resulting in a clearer and better focused widescreen image. The Technirama process is widely used all over the world for both 70mm "super" productions and regular 35mm anamorphic movies. For nearly 50 years, Technicolor led the field of color films. It still continues as one of the leaders today, although challenged by other systems. The credit line "Color by Technicolor" has always been a potent selling point for avid movie-goers. "Print by Technicolor" now denotes that although the production may have been photographed in Eastman Color, Ferraniacolor, Gevacolor or Ansco Color, the final color control and the release print shown in the theatres is by Technicolor on Technicolor film stock.

Had it not been for Technicolor, the progress of the natural color film might have been a lot slower. But thanks to it, and to the film-makers themselves, the word "Technicolor" has been and still is the word which reminds all filmgoers of movies in color.

[61] Kelley, SMPE Journal, November, 1919, p. 42.
[62] Herbert T. Kalmus, "Technicolor Adventures in Cinemaland," SMPE Journal, 18:565, December, 1938.
[63] Ibid., p. 566.
[64] New York Times, 72:1, September 21, 1922.
[65] Ibid., 72:9, September 22, 1922.
[66] Ibid., 66:9, February 22, 1917.
[67] Kalmus, op. cit., p. 567.
[68] Lasky, Jesse L., I Blow My Own Horn; p. 170.
[69] Kalmus, ibid., p.571.
[70] New York Times, 73:21, May 26, 1924.
[71] Lasky, op. cit., p.170.
[72] Film Daily, 101:1, September 10, 1951.
[73] Kalmus, ibid., p.573.
[74] Kalmus, ibid., p.573.
[75] Educational Screen, 9:18, January, 1930 and 9:84, March, 1930.
[76] Harrison's Reports, 12:6, January 11, 1930.
[77] Kalmus, ibid. p.577.
[78] Kalmus, ibid. p.578.
[79] Margaret Ettinger press release, June 11, 1946.
[80] Kalmus, ibid., p.578.
[81] Kalmus, ibid., p.579.

[62] Quoted by Alice Evans Field in *Hollywood, USA*, p. 188.

[63] Field, *ibid.*, p. 191.

[64] Ettinger, *op. cit.*

[65] *Variety*, February 17, 1947.

[66] Ettinger, *op. cit.*

[67] *Film Daily*, 103:11, January 19, 1953.

CHAPTER FOUR
COLOR AND THE SOUND PICTURE

With the arrival of sound pictures in 1927, color was immediately rediscovered as a novelty to "dress up" the new "talkies."

Since music was easier to record than dialog, many early sound pictures were musicals. This meant large production numbers with spectacular settings. Producers believed that the addition of color would make the early talking pictures seem less crude and keep the audience's mind off the fact that the music was not always in perfect synchronization and the dialog was not always well-recorded. All the color systems were still two-color ones, featuring a base of orange-red and blue-green filters or dyes. These two-color systems were capable of producing some colors on the screen, but not others. Among the colors which **could** be registered were orange-red, orange, pink, salmon, green, blue-green, brown and tan. Those which could not be reproduced included pure red, pure yellow, deep and light blue, violet, purple and the neutral grays.

THREE EARLY SYSTEMS

The records on three early color films invented when sound came to the motion picture are nearly lost in the annals of color film. For example, Omnicolor, an additive system patented in 1928, was a later development of the Kinemacolor and Prizma processes.[88] That same year, two short experimental reels of film in the Tattenham process were copyrighted in America. No record regarding the success or failure of this process seems to have been kept. The Splendicolor process came in at the same time as Omnicolor and Tattenham and is just as obscure today. Although there is no published account of the system, Splendicolor is known to have been a three-color subtractive process with a dyeing system to impart the color.[89]

RAYCOL

In 1928, an English company was formed to exploit another additive process known as Raycol. British International, an English

producing company, was reported interested in the system, but no films were produced. In 1930, Maurice Elvey, the originator of the process, announced that he would make seven features in the Raycol process, including the life of Shakespeare! In 1933, THE SKIPPER OF THE OSPREY was produced by Raycol in London. The projection of the film was so complicated that mechanics had to travel with the film showings in order to be certain that the projection lens was correctly adjusted and the film was in good registration. [90]

The Raycol optical system suffered from serious parallax, but despite the defects, reports said that the color of the film was comparable to anything which had been shown up to that time. The Raycol British Corporation wound up its business in the 1930s and no apparent attempt was made to revive the system.

A BARRAGE OF COLOR SYSTEMS

By 1930, the market was flooded with color systems, both additive and subtractive, all of which seemed to be unsatisfactory in one way or another. They all were obsolete within a few years.

In Utrecht, Holland, the Sirius Kleuren Film Maatschappij was developed. It was a two-color subtractive process using the patents of L. Horst, a German photographer-inventor.   In England, Cinecolor, Ltd.[91] was formed from the patents of Cinechrome. The new additive process differed from the original Cinechrome only in the fact that the pictures on the film were not turned sideways in pairs on the frame. The Cinecolor method had each pair of images right side up on the film frame. In 1937, the patent and interests in Cinecolor were turned over to the Dufay-Chromex Company.

From France came Harmonicolor, invented by Maurice Combes. The process, using Agfa film with two color filters, was premiered at the Curzon Cinema in London.[92] M. L. F. Dassonville of Brussels developed an unusual system of chemical and dye toning for his color film, Dascolor,[93] while a German system, Ufacolor, was processed by UFA studios and in England, under the name of Chemicolor. A Chemicolor feature film, PAGLIACCI, was presented in the new process. William Fox became an active executive in Chemicolor after seeing sequences from this film but American film makers did not seem to be interested.[94] Chemicolor's title was later changed to Spectracolor, but it still remained a relatively unsuccessful attempt.[95]

In 1930, Serge Eisenstein, the Russian director, experimented with color in THE GENERAL LINE (OLD AND NEW). During one

sequence he interpolated splashes of abstract color in an otherwise black-and-white film. The sequence, however, was too **avant garde** in its day and was cut from the versions shown in England and the United States.[96]

FAILURES IN AMERICAN COLOR FILMS

Failure to achieve success with new color films was not limited to the Europeans. Americans saw the advent of several processes which faded in quick succession into oblivion.

Colorfilm, a two-color subtractive film, had images printed on both sides of the film. Colorcraft, invented in 1929, was a new version of an old color film process patented in 1905. The Pathe Exchange in New Jersey announced a short-lived Coloratura process and the Fox Film Corporation developed Fox Color from the early Kodachrome patents.[97] Even Mack Sennett, the famous director of the silent film comedies, announced a two-color subtractive color film. One side of Sennett Color was toned blue and the other side, red-orange.[98]

PHOTOCOLOR

Another now-obsolete film which received favorable comment when first shown was Photocolor. In this system, the camera is equipped with two lenses and the film is run through the camera at two-and-one-half times the normal speed. Two frames of the film are exposed simultaneously, one through a red-yellow filter and the other through a blue-green filter. The half-space between the two frames was eliminated in the processing. The speed of the film, however, made it impractical for sound pictures and for presentation on ordinary projectors.

When the Photocolor film was developed, it was still in black and white. The two colors were dyed on the film, one color on each side. Despite the obvious failings regarding its use in talking pictures, Photocolor impressed the **Scientific American** with the degree of accuracy in reproducing the flesh tints so long a problem in color films. It also observed that blacks and whites were both clearly reproduced.[99]

Another descendant of the Prizma process, Multicolor, was more successful than the other new color films. A two-color bipack process exposing two negatives at once, Multicolor appeared in several early sound pictures including color sequences in HELL'S ANGELS, THE FOX MOVIETONE FOLLIES OF 1929 and THE GREAT

GABBO and a cartoon called GOOFY GOAT in 1931. The Multicolor company built an elaborate and costly plant in Hollywood, but by 1933 the process had been discontinued.[100] The system was later revived under the name of Cinecolor.

CHIMICOLOR

A three-color subtractive process called Chimicolor was developed in France in 1931 by the Syndicate de la Cinematographe des Couleurs. After dyeing, the film received a protective coating of varnish! Chimicolor was used for several foreign cartoons and the camera used was similar to the Technicolor camera.[101]

OTHER ADDITIVE SYSTEMS

Although impractical for commercial use, additive film processes were still being invented and almost as quickly forgotten. The most impractical of all the additive processes ever conceived was that of J. Szczepanik. He used a continuous-motion camera with a chain of eighteen lenses which moved with the film as it sped through the camera with three images being exposed at one time. Even the camera which was used for this process has now been destroyed.[102]

Three British systems were perfected during the 1930's. The Busch process was used chiefly for medical research; the Hillman process drew mild interest from Sir Alexander Korda in London in 1933 until Technicolor came along with its three-color system, and the Herault Trichrome process used black-and-white film tinted in red, green and blue dyes on appropriate frames.

The Societe Chromofilm of France presented the additive Bassani process using a special camera which produced 96 movements of the film gate per second and, according to some reports, achieved some admirable results.[103] The Pinchart system, a three-color invention, was a complicated system using a large number of lenses. America contributed the Morgana process, perfected by the Bell and Howell Company for 16mm film and Gilmore Color, a two-color system which had two images side-by-side in pairs on each frame.

When most of the additive systems disappeared in favor of the subtractive processes, it was assumed that the days of the strange looking cameras and projectors with multiple lenses and special colored screens were over. They were — but only temporarily. After World War II, a sudden resurgence of the additive processes occurred.

GASPARCOLOR

No further advance in the technique of the color film was made until 1934 when Dr. Bela Gaspar introduced a three-color film called Gasparcolor, "capable of yielding extremely beautiful release prints."[104] The process was first perfected in Germany.

That same year, Gasparcolor, Ltd., was formed in England and began making successful advertising films including the delightful abstract color films of Len Lye. The process, however, was not used for feature films due to some undisclosed technical difficulties. During World War II, Dr. Gaspar came to Hollywood and set up a laboratory there. He received little encouragement from the film industry and finally limited himself to research on the problems of still photographs in color. Adrian Cornwell-Clyne, who was one person who believed in the Gasparcolor process, states that a number of excellent release prints were made from Gasparcolor and that "more may yet be heard from this beautiful process."[105]

OPTICOLOR AND FRANCITA

The Opticolor process was the British branch of the Francita color system, owned in England by British Realita Syndicate, Ltd. Although it was an additive process, Opticolor achieved some success in making theatrical films. The system used two small pictures on one frame of film. A feature film was made in France in the Francita process and exhibited in July, 1935, at a Paris theatre. Author Adrian Cornwell-Clyne recalls of the Paris showing that the color was very fine in parts of the film and any defects were due to poor lighting rather than the process. "This film proved," he continued, "that, were it not for the serious commercial problem of special projection apparatus with the likelihood of its getting out of adjustment, the subtractive process would have a serious competitor in additive systems of this type. Considering that the positive . . . images were of substandard dimensions, it is remarkable how good the definition was."[106] THE CORONATION OF KING GEORGE VI was one of the most noted films taken with the Francita process.

HIRLICOLOR

The emergence of Hirlicolor in the middle 1930's gave the smaller film companies a chance to produce color films. Named after film producer George Hirliman, the process was used for a series of

pictures at the Grand National Studios in CAPTAIN CALAMITY, DEVIL ON HORSEBACK and YOU'RE IN THE LEGION NOW and at Republic Studios in THE BOLD CABELLERO in the late 1930's. The Hirlicolor process was also used for low-budget Spanish films. Soon after these films were made, the Hirligraph Laboratories were sold to Consolidated Film Industries, Inc., and Hirlicolor disappeared temporarily only to reappear a few years later under the title of Magnacolor.[107]

DUFAYCOLOR

As early as 1925, the patents of Louis Dufay, a French photographer, were pooled into the Dufay-Chromex, Ltd. In America, the market was handled by the Dufaycolor Company, Inc. During 1934, a color sequence in a film called THE RADIO PARADE was presented by Dufaycolor in England. The original appearance of the color was disappointing, but British Movietone News made some Dufaycolor news pictures of the Jubilee processions, which meant printing large number of copies successfully and rapidly. The prints suffered from a granular effect known as "boiling." More improvements were made and a practical test was run which made a great impression on the public and the film industry alike — the test being a film of the Coronation in 1937. This was followed by several experimental films in Dufaycolor by Norman McLaren of Canada, COLOR COCKTAIL and LOVE ON THE WING.

During 1937 and 1938, a large number of Dufaycolor short subjects were made in England and on the continent. In the United States, an excellent version of a yacht race was filmed in Dufaycolor and released under the title of SAILS AND SAILORS. Other British films in Dufaycolor included TROOPING THE COLOR, ROYAL NAVAL REVIEW, ST. MORITZ, FAREWELL TOP-SAILS, OLD SOLDIERS NEVER DIE and SOUVENIRS. These films proved that Dufaycolor "could equal any process in definition and accuracy of color reproduction."[108]

During World War II, veteran cameraman Arthur Pereira made some experimental films in Dufaycolor. But despite its success in England, Dufaycolor could not compete with Technicolor in the United States. The process differs from the other color systems in that it is a "screen process" — that is, the back of the film is coated with a large number of minute screens in red, blue and green in such proportions that one cannot see any color in the film at all when it is

held at a distance. The screens are arranged to form a regular "grid" or **reseau** and is developed in two stages.[109]

Dufaycolor unfortunately fell into disuse and while the British company continued, the company's American branch failed in 1939.[110]

A SOVIET PROCESS

As early as 1936, the Russians had perfected an unidentified and untitled two-color process and had filmed two pictures, NIGHTIN-GALE and BLUE SEA in the system. In 1938, they filmed SOROCHINSK FAIR and THE LITTLE HUMPBACKED HORSE. Whether the process is a direct descendant of one of the earlier American or European color systems is still a mystery, although the Russian ZKS-1 color camera is believed to have been used to photograph these films.

COSMOCOLOR

First marketed commercially in 1937, Cosmocolor was a two-color subtractive process which used a complex beam-splitter camera with a double-coated positive print. The images were colored by a special method of toning.[111] The only feature picture on record which is known to have been filmed in Cosmocolor was THE ISLE OF DESTINY, produced and released by RKO Radio Pictures in 1940. The process, when projected, looked similar to the Cinecolor and Magnacolor systems.

DUNNINGCOLOR

A process for duplicating 16mm Kodachrome films for the commercial studios, Dunningcolor has been limited mostly to cartoon films and to a South American travelog called TEHUANTEPEC.[112] Carroll H. Dunning and his son, Dodge, perfected the system in 1937. Two colors are obtained photographically and the third, yellow, is applied by a gelatin matrix.[113] It is processed by the Eastman Kodak Company. Mr. Dunning was associated with THE GLORIOUS ADVENTURE, one of the first color films to be produced in the Prizma process.

TELCO-COLOR

An unsuccessful color film of which much seemed to be expected was Telco-Color, a monopack process which used regular film with the color effect secured through the lens. It was announced that a

feature film would be presented in Telco-Color by Universal Pictures in 1936.[114] No record, however, supports the notion that the film, YELLOWSTONE, was filmed in the process.

Telco-Color was used in a Universal short subject, CAVALCADE OF TEXAS, in 1938. It marked the first appearance of President Franklin D. Roosevelt in color. The process later appeared in a feature film, LURE OF THE WASTELAND, released by Monogram Pictures in 1939.

The film critics found the process both poor and distasteful. **Parents Magazine** mentioned that "LURE OF THE WASTE-LAND . . . was marred by unsuccessful color photography."[115] The process seemed to lack any true colors and seemed almost as crude as the early hand-painted films of the early silent days. Like the Arabs, Telco-Color quietly folded up its patents and silently stole away early in the 1940's.

MAGNACOLOR AND TRUCOLOR

Consolidated Film Industries, which bought out several of the earlier two-color processes of the 1930's and combined some of the best and threw out some of the worst, came up with Magnacolor. The system was a descendant of Prizma, Kelleycolor, Hirlicolor and the like. First used in a series of short subjects for Paramount Pictures — UNUSUAL OCCUPATIONS and POPULAR SCIENCE — the system soon began appearing in feature-length outdoor pictures produced by Consolidated's parent company, Republic Pictures. The features included MAN FROM RAINBOW VALLEY, HOME ON THE RANGE, ROUGH RIDERS OF CHEYENNE, LAST FRONTIER UPRISING and SANTA FE SUNSET. Although the process still is used in Hollywood for short subjects and advertising films, the process has been almost completely supplanted by Trucolor, which is a later improvement of the Magnacolor system. Even in its feature films, Magnacolor showed its defects especially in the fringing of the reds and the blue-greens.[116] In one of the outdoor films, the hero's lumberjack shirt had the red and green stripes separating and dancing all over the screen — a very disconcerting item for the observant moviegoer.

Trucolor was a slight improvement over its predecessor. It declared that it incorporates such factors into its process as (1) color is in the film emulsion. No dyes are applied in the developing or the printing. This results in all the prints being exactly alike, with no color deviation from print to print or scene to scene; (2) negative developing and releasing prints are provided with the same quality

standard and speed of black-and-white release prints; (3) it has unprecedented color control and (4) it guarantees uniformity of all release prints.[117]

The Trucolor process has been used for all of Republic's "top budget" western pictures including the Roy Rogers series, as well as for short subjects by Ted Nemeth, including COLOR RHAPSO-DIE, POLKA GRAPH and SPOOK SPORT. Trucolor, only a two-color process, did not always live up to its name. Its tendency toward "orangeness" and "greenness" did not always seem true, but flesh tones and a general softness of color tone were sometimes quite pleasing.

KODACHROME

Although the Eastman Kodak 16mm Kodachrome process is not used in making commercial motion pictures, it is used (after being enlarged to 35mm theatrical film) in many documentaries and travelogs. Features such as JUNGLE MANHUNTERS, SAVAGE SPLENDOR, THE FIGHTING LADY, THE MEMPHIS BELLE and numerous others, bear the credit line "Print by Technicolor." These are Kodachrome films which have been enlarged on Technicolor film by optical printing.

Other 16mm films in this three-color system, made solely for showing in schools and churches, are filmed in Kodachrome. One company, Planet Pictures, produced a series of feature films in the system, including JEEP HERDERS, DETOUR TO DANGER and THE PEOPLE'S CHOICE. The 16mm market being a small one in the 1940's, the films were not shown enough to warrant the cost of filming them and the company soon went bankrupt. The first full-length American experimental film in color, DREAMS THAT MONEY CAN BUY, was filmed by Dr. Hans Richter in Kodachrome. Although it was of 16mm size, it has been shown in commercial theatres.

Kodachrome's greatest business comes from the amateur movie maker, who consumes millions of Kodachrome reels in making film records of his family and friends.

CINECOLOR

Another and more famous descendant of the Prizma process, Cinecolor has been in existence since 1932. The company, on the verge of bankruptcy before World War II, had "fifteen years of mistakes behind it."[118]

With Technicolor almost completely monopolizing the field of color films, William Loss, a director of the Citizens Traction Company in New York City, provided the backing to put Cinecolor back into the business of making color films. True, the process was only a two-color one, but the demand for color films was on the upswing and it was discovered that a poor motion picture in color was making more money than good black-and-white ones.

Cinecolor had several advantages over Technicolor despite the fact that the film could not produce all the colors in the spectrum. It could present "rushes" within 24 hours after they were filmed and it cost only 25 per cent more than black-and-white film. Loss figured that as long as the grass was green and the sky was blue the audience would not notice the lack of pure reds and greens.

"In Cinecolor, makeup was on the light side to avoid a red-orange or sallow appearance. Lip rouge was orange-red since blue-reds photograph much too dark. Dark prints caused skin tones to take on an orange cast rather than the more desirable pink appearance . . . The successful use of two-color bipack required the use of pastel colors in both sets and wardrobe," according to an article in the **Journal of the Society of Motion Picture Engineers.**[119]

The first feature-length picture to appear in Cinecolor was Monogram Pictures' THE GENTLEMAN FROM ARIZONA in 1940. The lesser film companies who had never made a picture in color soon discovered that they could do so with a minimum of extra cost. Another small film company, Producers Releasing Corporation, began using the process for a series of five western features and a full-length fairy tale, THE ENCHANTED FOREST, which proved to be the largest money-making film in that company's history. Production of four "action pictures" by Screen Guild Productions followed until, by 1946, the first major film company signed to do a Cinecolor feature. The picture was GALLANT BESS and the company was MGM. With this picture, Cinecolor entered onto the profit side of the ledger and netted nearly two hundred thousand dollars in 1947. The demand for acceptable pictures in color continued and Cinecolor found itself booked solid through 1947 and 1948. The Hal Roach Studios presented a series of Cinecolor comedies in 1947; Paramount filmed ADVENTURE ISLAND and even Sweden used the process in a film called THE BELLS OF OLD TOWN. Major companies were finding Cinecolor outdoor scenes very natural and interiors, purely by accident, sometimes gave a stereoscopic effect.

By 1949, studios such as Allied Artists, Columbia, Eagle-Lion, Film Classics, MGM, Monogram, Paramount, Twentieth Century-Fox, United Artists and Universal had made films in Cinecolor. In 1951, Azteca, a Mexican producing company, presented its first color film, RANCHO GRANDE, in Cinecolor.

In the short subject field, Cinecolor appeared in many cartoon series, replacing Technicolor temporarily in almost all cases. The process appeared in Paramount's Popeye cartoons, ALL'S FAIR AT THE FAIR and OLIVE FOR PRESIDENT; Noveltoons such as CAT O' NINE AILS; Warner Brothers Merrie Melodies cartoons, including BONE SWEET BONE, DAFFY DILLY, DOUGH RAY ME-OW, ODOR OF THE DAY, RIFF RAFF DAFFY and UPSTANDING SITTER. Twentieth Century-Fox used Cinecolor in some of its **Magic Carpet** travelog series and there were Cinecolor sequences in the 1951 Columbia serial, CAPTAIN VIDEO, marking probably the only use of a color sequence in a movie serial.

For a short time, Cinecolor merged with Film Classics, a producing organization, but soon went back on its own. With the development of its three-color process, Cinecolor Corporation changed its name to Color Corporation of America. Despite this three-color development, Cinecolor never regained the bullish market it developed in the 1940's and the process is seldom seen on theatre screens today.

The last large contract for Cinecolor pictures was from Allied Artists which produced as many as one film per month in the process, including HIAWATHA, THE HIGHWAYMAN, FLAT TOP, ROYAL AFRICAN RIFLES, FIGHTER ATTACK, SON OF BELLE STARR, THE ROSE BOWL STORY and many others, ending in 1955.

VITACOLOR

A process similar to Cinecolor was expanding during the same period. Vitacolor, according to Clyde A. Warne, newly-elected president of the company in 1948, announced a complete reorganization of the company to make Vitacolor film. The photographic method was essentially the same as Cinecolor and other bipack processes, except that Vitacolor claimed an extended color range. Vitacolor employed the three primary colors in making prints.[120] Feature pictures which appeared in Vitacolor were THE LAST OF THE REDMEN at Columbia in 1947 and THE RETURN OF RIN TIN TIN from Eagle-Lion that same year.

After this, the process is believed to have merged with the Cinecolor patents.

SURVIVAL

With the exception of Trucolor and Cinecolor, which both spanned World War II and into the 1950's, the other color processes have all been withdrawn from commercial use. And in the case of the two which remained, they both developed three-color processes which were popular for a time until the rise of the new modern Eastman Color which caused their demise.

[88] Cornwell-Clyne, graph facing p. 32.

[89] Ibid., p. 427.

[90] Cornwell-Clyne, p. 19.

[91] Not to be confused with the later Cinecolor in America.

[92] Cornwell-Clyne, p. 10.

[93] Ibid., p. 332.

[94] New York Times, 86:12, Section X, May 23, 1937

[95] Cornwell-Clyne, pp. 331-332.

[96] Herman G. Weinberg, "Coffee, Brandy and Cigars IV," Films In Review 3:408, October, 1952.

[97] Cornwell-Clyne, pp. 331-332.

[98] Ibid., p. 342.

[99] A. P. Peck, "Movies Take On Color," Scientific American, 142:285, April, 1930.

[100] Cornwell-Clyne, p. 29.

[101] Cornwell-Clyne, pp. 412-413.

[102] Ibid., p. 278.

[103] Ibid., p. 279.

[104] Cornwell-Clyne, pp. 22-23.

[105] Ibid., p. 350.

[106] Quoted by Cornwell-Clyne, p. 280.

[107] A letter from Donald C. Hamilton, The American Institute, May 12, 1952.

[108] Cornwell-Clyne, pp. 21-22.

[109] Spottiswoode, p. 208.

[110] Cornwell-Clyne, pp. 21-22.

[111] Ibid., p. 25.

[112] Letter from Dunningcolor Corporation, July 7, 1952.

[113] Loc. cit.

[114] New York Times 85:5, Section 9, July 12, 1936.

[115] "Family Movie Guide," Parents Magazine, 14:58, October, 1939.

[116] Cornwell-Clyne, p. 141.

[117] Film Daily Yearbook, 1948 edition, p. 113.

[118] William Loss, "Profit Through Loss," Time, 48:88, September 23, 1946.

[119] John W. Boyle and Benjamin Berg, "Studio Production with Two-Color Bipack Motion Picture Film," SMPTE Journal, 48:114, February, 1947.

[120] Film Daily Yearbook, op. cit., p. 113.

CHAPTER FIVE
POST-WAR COLOR DEVELOPMENTS

After World War II, Hollywood used color films increasingly. Newspaper announcements indicated that the movies would soon be flooded with new subtractive color processes of all types, and improvements of already established color systems were being announced. Also, a resurgence of additive color systems began to occur after the war, although none has yet shown any marked degree of success. Technicolor still was the leader in the color field in post-war America and the two-color Cinecolor process seemed to be the main challenger.

POLACOLOR

During the war, the Polaroid Corporation of Cambridge, Massachusetts, developed a three-color film which was used after the war for nearly 25 educational, advertising and theatrical short subjects. Paramount Pictures used the process commercially in a series of **Screen Song** cartoons including CAMPTOWN RACES, GOLDEN STATE, LONE STAR STATE, SING OR SWIM, WINTER DRAWS ON, THE CIRCUS COMES TO CLOWN and BASE BRAWL; in several **Popeye** cartoons, POPEYE MEETS HERCULES, PRE-HYSTERICAL MAN, SNOW PLACE LIKE HOME, WIGWAM WHOOPEE and WOLF IN SHIEK'S CLOTHING and in one **Noveltoon**, FLIP FLOP.

Polacolor's main purpose, however, was to enlarge a great number of color prints of Kodachrome and Ansco Color negatives, both motion picture films and colored slides. The Polacolor process utilized a three-color dye image in a single layer of photographic emulsion.[121] The system, however, was not successful enough to be tried on a feature film and, by 1949, it had passed out of the competition among new and improved color systems.

SYSTEMS FROM FRANCE AND ENGLAND

France presented four new color processes after the war — the Bertrand Process, Kalichrome, Diacolor and Thomson-Color. The first used 16mm film (Kodachrome) for the original record. The 16mm picture was then enlarged to 35mm theatrical film. No record of any film in the system seems to have been kept.

Kalichrome claimed that it could produce either two or three-color prints with double-coated film. The third color, it announced, was obtained through a dyeing and toning process. Another French system, Thomson-Color, was a lenticular one in which three negatives are printed together and then dyed.[122] Diacolor, the most recent of the four, was used for a feature film in 1953 but no technical data seemed to be released about the mechanics of the Diacolor process.[123]

Great Britain announced the perfection of Ilford Color in 1948. The process similar to the Kodachrome 16mm film process, is a product of the Ilford Ltd. Laboratories in Brentwood and is still active today in the field of color film research. Other English systems were Dufaychrome, called a perfection of the British Tricolor process, and a two-color process, Alfacolor, which used Gaevert film.[124]

AMERICOLOR AND FULLCOLOR

Two American systems, both announced almost simultaneously in 1947, had little success. Americolor, a three-color process which was used previously in slide films (filmstrips) was announced as being available soon to film makers. Negotiations were announced with the producers but there were no commercial films made in the process. Filmstrips in Americolor seem thicker than other films, but the color looks fairly natural, if a bit on the bluish side.

Fullcolor fared slightly better than Americolor by actually presenting several commercial pictures, although producing none. The process, different from most other methods, was designed to make prints of older color systems for theatrical release. Known as a "dry lab," Fullcolor successfully made prints of an early Technicolor film, THE GOLDWYN FOLLIES, for reissue in 1947. The process also was used for the United Artists picture, THE ANGRY GOD and Clyde Elliott's short subject, BANNISTER BABY LAND.

ANSCO COLOR AND METROCOLOR

About the same time that Polacolor was being perfected, the

General Aniline and Film Corporation announced the development of a three-color monopack commercial film process called Ansco Color. The process, which could be used in a standard camera, was first tried out on a two-reel short subject, CLIMBING THE MATTERHORN, released by Monogram Pictures in 1948. The film won an Academy Award and assured the acceptance of Ansco Color for future productions. Monogram followed its award-winning short with a feature-length film, SIXTEEN FATHOMS DEEP.

Although the Ansco system is based on the same fundamental patents as the Agfacolor process, it is capable of producing a wider color range.

Lewis Allen presented two features in Ansco Color, THE MAN ON THE EIFFEL TOWER in 1949 and NEW MEXICO in 1951. This was followed in 1952 by an RKO release, TEMBO, and later was used in independent features such as ISLAND OF ALLAH.

Metro-Goldwyn-Mayer, repeating its historical decision in 1946 to launch Cinecolor by using it in a feature film, again took the lead by producing a feature in Ansco color, THE WILD NORTH. With a major company now interested in the system, its future was assured. MGM, who had more than a casual interest in the process, aided in its development.

Of Ansco Color, photographer Margaret Markham exclaimed:

"Quality-wise, the color is excellent. The test prints which we saw on THE WILD NORTH were certainly most pleasing. There is a softer, more natural tone than we are accustomed to seeing. While, perhaps, under some circumstances, the film may not give the lush, saturated colors characteristic of Technicolor, the average production after all does not fall into the super-extravaganza class requiring the rich colors of pomp and pageantry."[125]

The promotion of Ansco Color was further strengthened when Arch Obler announced his first three-dimensional film would be photographed in the process.[126] The film, BWANA DEVIL, was an overnight sensation due to the novelty of the third dimension, but the Ansco Color was not shown to its best advantage.

On its acceptance by the public, Ansco Color launched into full scale production including many MGM pictures as well as those from other studios. The MGM pictures photographed in Ansco Color included RIDE VAQUERO!, TAKE THE HIGH GROUND, KISS ME KATE, ARENA and ESCAPE FROM FORT BRAVO (the last three in 3-D), SEVEN BRIDES FOR

SEVEN BROTHERS, THE STUDENT PRINCE and BRIGA-
DOON (all filmed in CinemaScope).

Other Ansco Color features included United Artists' THE
SCARLET SPEAR, Lansburgh's MYSTERY LAKE (in 3-D),
Lippert's SINS OF JEZEBEL and THE GREAT JESSE JAMES
RAID, and Multifilms' O DESTINO EM APUROS, the first
Brazilian color film.

Good reviews helped Ansco business skyrocket. THE GREAT
JESSE JAMES RAID was reviewed as "The Ansco Color is a great
asset and the scenery is pictorially beautiful . . ."[127] MYSTERY
LAKE was "beautifully lensed."[128] and "expertly filmed in Ansco
Color."[129] In SINS OF JEZEBEL "Ansco Color is an asset."[130]
However, the color in O DESTINO EM APUROS gave "the whole
picture a delicate pastel shade although colors are frequently
blurred."[131]

Once limited to promotional films, such as YOUR KENTUCKY
and theatrical shorts such as RETURN OF GILBERT AND
SULLIVAN, DESIGN FOR SWIMMING and ROYAL WEL-
COME, Ansco Color under the direction of MGM, began rivaling
Technicolor and it soon expanded to handle the processing of many
more feet of film per year.

The Ansco Color film made its next advance in 1955 when it was
reported that the new Ansco film "is a negative-positive process,
which offers more realistic color of the highest fidelity, with far
superior color reproduction in release prints than ever obtainable
before. It is also considerably sharper, permitting better screen and
picture definition."[132] This newer process, re-named Metrocolor, was
first used in LUST FOR LIFE, where it vividly recreated the mood
and coloring of the paintings of Vincent Van Gogh. It also was used
for TEA AND SYMPATHY, TEAHOUSE OF THE AUGUST
MOON, DON'T GO NEAR THE WATER, THE BROTHERS
KARAMAZOV and was soon adopted for most MGM color films
made at the studio.

COLOR CORPORATION OF AMERICA

Natural Color, processed by the Cinecolor Corporation, was
introduced in 1950. A three-color process, Natural Color appeared in
three feature productions — THE LADY IN THE IRON MASK
and ROSE OF CIMARRON, both for Twentieth Century-Fox, and
THREE FOR BEDROOM C for Warner Brothers. Then the
Natural Color label disappeared in favor of SuperCinecolor.

The new SuperCinecolor was announced in January of 1951 and it

soon appeared successfully in seven feature films, THE SWORD OF MONTE CRISTO, produced by Twentieth Century-Fox; HURRI-CANE ISLAND, WHEN THE REDSKINS RODE, THE TEXAS RANGERS, THE MAGIC CARPET, THE BAREFOOT MAILMAN by Columbia Pictures, and DRUMS IN THE DEEP SOUTH by RKO Radio Pictures.

Alan M. Gundelfinger, who helped develop Cinecolor and SuperCinecolor, described the new process as follows:

"The new Cinecolor process is a subtractive process . . . designed for, and depends upon, three-strip separation negatives for its printing medium . . . because of the years of experience which the company has had in the two-color field, the controls which have been developed, and the economics of operation which have been effected, the three-color process was intentionally developed along the lines of the two-color system."[133]

By 1952, the SuperCinecolor process had overcome most of its minor flaws and became a major contender in the rush for supremacy in color films. Other features in the process followed, including ABBOTT AND COSTELLO MEET CAPTAIN KIDD and JACK AND THE BEANSTALK for Warner Brothers and SOUND OFF for Columbia.

In May, 1953, Cinecolor Corporation changed its name to the Color Corporation of America in order to avoid confusing its early two and three-color processing with its present advanced developments. They also believed that a change in name would give a producer a chance to use his own brand name for his Cinecolor and SuperCinecolor productions.[134] Since then, all SuperCinecolor productions have the credit line, "Color by Color Corporation of America."

Other Color Corporation features of 1954 included NEW FACES from Twentieth Century-Fox, TOP BANANA, SABRE JET, RIDERS TO THE STARS and SHARK RIVER, all from United Artists, and THE DIAMOND QUEEN from Warner Brothers.

Of United Artists' SONG OF THE LAND, the **Independent Film Journal** remarked: "The color by Color Corp. of America is rich and revealing."[135]

In May of 1954, Benjamin Smith and Associates took over the control of the Color Corporation and the laboratories in turn were sold to Technicolor in 1955, marking the ending of commercial use of the process.

TRUCOLOR BY CONSOLIDATED

At nearly the same time SuperCinecolor announced its new process, Republic Pictures presented "Trucolor by Consolidated." A development of its two-color process using the new DuPont color stock, Republic immediately earmarked the new Trucolor for a series of its feature films, including John Ford's THIS IS KOREA, HONEYCHILE, OKLAHOMA ANNIE, FAIR WIND TO JAVA, THE LADY WANTS MINK, WOMAN OF THE NORTH COUNTRY, RIDE THE MAN DOWN, THE TOUGHEST MAN IN ARIZONA, JUBILEE TRAIL, JOHNNY GUITAR and SWEETHEARTS ON PARADE.

Of the last-named film, **Variety** remarked: ". . . the Trucolor on the print witnessed wasn't very true, changing colors in midscene upon occasions."[136] Despite this, other scenes rivaled and sometimes outdid Technicolor for sheer color beauty and Republic used the process until its demise as a film-producing studio in 1958. JOHNNY GUITAR was considered "easily the finest example of that process . . ."[137]

With the release of the new Trucolor system, RKO Radio Pictures was put in the awkward position of possessing an old Trucolor film made four years before and as yet not released. When RKO changed management late in 1952, the film, MONTANA BELLE, was reluctantly released. A **Variety** reviewer voiced the sentiments of many when he said of the film, ". . .(the) greenish hues of Trucolor several years ago, compared with current Trucolor prints, evidences the improvement Republic has made in its tint[138] process."[139]

TECHNICHROME

While American producers announced the perfection of many three-color processes which had formerly been only two-color ones, the Technicolor Company of England announced the perfection of a two-color process based upon the three-color Technicolor system. The new color film was named Technichrome.

Since there were few Technicolor cameras in Great Britain, the two-color system was worked out to make possible two-color film prints without altering the standardized three-color Technicolor process and without using any complicated camera equipment. The first example of Technichrome was the filming of THE OLYMPIC GAMES OF 1948. Some twenty cameras were adapted for this two-color photography.

The idea of Technicolor returning to a two-color system seemed to many to be a retrogressive step, according to J. H. Coote, a British

film technician. He remarked, "Whether Technichrome will ever become widely used remains to be seen, but it is at least interesting to note that the combined footage printed by two American two-color processes — Cinecolor and Magnacolor — last year equalled the total three-color footage of Technicolor in America."[140]

Adrian Cornwell-Clyne reviews Technichrome as "an improvement on the original two-color Technicolor, but it inevitably suffers from defective color rendition and the definition leaves much to be desired. Nevertheless, the color is attractive within its limits."[141]

NEW ADDITIVE COLOR SYSTEMS

Earlier additive color films, from the beginning of film history, were doomed to failure because they could not be projected on ordinary film projectors since the film was not always of standard size or perhaps complicated lenses were needed. With few exceptions, additive color films had not been shown in commercial theatres.

With the sudden demand for color films after World War II, the additive films took a new outlook and those who assumed that the days of the strange looking projectors with the multiple lenses and special colored screens were over, suddenly saw no fewer than six additive systems announced within a few years.

Their appearance was logical. Screen audiences were demanding more color films and some persons were not too particular as to what color process was employed. Although these processes did not revolutionize the post-war color film, they are mentioned to make this study more complete and historically valuable.

THOMASCOLOR

The most noted of the additive systems was Thomascolor, patented in 1942 by Richard Thomas. The system involves a prism filter on the camera which separates the light exposing the film into three color components with individual images on each frame for each component. When the film is projected, the film reverses each image through the filter corresponding to that through which it was photographed. The three-color prisms used are red, green and blue-violet.

One of the great differences noted in the Thomascolor system and other additive or subtractive color processes was that the film used to photograph the image is 65mm wide and later is reduced to the regular 35mm theatrical film size.

The process had many virtues: (1) the processing of the film is

simple; (2) a film can be ready for projection two hours after filming; (3) the projection device needed for the system can be manufactured at a nominal cost, thus permitting speedy equipping of theatres, and (4) prints also can be made on regular color film, such as Ansco Color, and projected without projector lens attachments.[142] As the years went by, further experimentation on the process was apparently given up.

ROUXCOLOR

Another French process, Rouxcolor, is similar to Thomascolor and was developed by Lucien and Armand Roux. The process depends upon filtered light and, again, is filmed on regular black-and-white film. Rouxcolor had a highly favorable reception from early showings[143] but the only feature film in the process was THE MILLER'S DAUGHTER in France in 1948.

The Roux Brothers based their process on an earlier system they developed in 1930 called Cineoptichrome, another additive system.

DUGROMACOLOR

Dugromacolor was introduced and demonstrated in France in 1952. Three collaborators — Dumas, Grosset and Marx — combined sections of their names to give the system its title.

The process used a special lens with filters to break the image into three primary color components and put them into 35mm film in three 16mm boxes with the fourth part of each 35mm frame remaining black. The film is developed in the ordinary way. During projection, a special lens attachment goes on the projector so as to superimpose the three images for color rendition.

Dugromacolor conquered the problem of color registration but still had many drawbacks. French producers felt that it would be useless to make a film in Dugromacolor because it would take five years to equip all the theatres with the necessary apparatus. The projector lens cost about five hundred dollars. Also, the 16mm image on the 35mm film lost quality in long-range theatre projection although the fine grain of the film cut down the loss somewhat. The Dugromacolor process was patented in the United States[144] but the process was not further used in either France or America.

LENTICULAR FILM

Another process still in the experimental stage is lenticular film, a process in which the film itself is made up of tiny lenses directly on the face of the film.

With patent settlements in the early 1950's, the lenticular film systems were prepared to offer an abundance of economical color film if it was accepted by the motion picture industry. Whether lenticular film was to be the connecting link between black-and-white and color films was to be determined by the late 1950's, according to color experts.

With fast color film easily available, the lenticular films never progressed beyond the experimental stages. Perhaps it might be the process of the future.

As with other additive systems, lenticular film has special attachments on both the camera and the projector. The film uses minute lenses rolled directly into the film stock. These lenses, semi-cylindrical in shape, separate the three primary colors. When projected through a three-color filter onto a screen, the film emerges in full color.

Again this process had the disadvantage of having special projector attachments, which the film exhibitor was loath to purchase. As a result, experiments with lenticular film have been highly successful in the laboratory, but have not received a good tryout in a movie theatre. Even with large magnification of the image during projection, the width of the stripes of the color filter images is so small that color banding cannot be noticed on the screen.[145]

FOX LENTICULAR FILM

An attempt to popularize the lenticular film process for theatrical releases was announced by Twentieth Century-Fox in January, 1953. They said the first feature picture to be filmed in the process was in the planning stages and would give results comparable to Technicolor but would be much less expensive.[146] The advantage of the film was said to be that it could be projected as a regular black-and-white film without the color lens attachments.[147] The arrival of the CinemaScope era at the Fox studios unfortunately deterred all plans for this lenticular system but perhaps more may yet be heard from it.

KODACOLOR LENTICULAR

First introduced in 1928, Kodacolor Lenticular Film, like others of the lenticular variety, employs a network of minute lenses embossed on the film. The light coming through a three-banded color filter over the camera lens separates the colors into their three basic colors. When the film is projected, the colors re-form into a color

image as they pass through the same lens.[148] This process also was never tested commercially.

KELLER-DORIAN PROCESS

The Keller-Dorian group brought suit against Eastman Kodak and Technicolor in 1952 charging that they were allegedly suppressing the Keller-Dorian Lenticular system in the United States. The suit was settled soon afterwards[149] and it was the widescreen era and not the color companies who caused the untimely death of these lenticular processes.

NEW FOREIGN COLOR FILMS

Overseas, renewed interest in color films was apparent with the announcement of many new or improved color systems. Naturally, most film producers expected one or two color processes to develop in England after the war. But, to their surprise, the majority of the announcements came from other countries — Italy, Japan, Spain, Germany and Russia. All had perfected new color systems which they hoped would challenge United States supremacy in the field of the color motion picture.

AGFACOLOR

The Agfacolor system, which was used before the war in a few foreign films, was perfected by I. G. Farben in Germany in 1939 and put on the "open market" after World War II ended. The German productions of DIE FLEDERMAUS and BARON MUENCH-HAUSEN showed the possibilities of the process. The Russians, who took over the process in 1945, used the monopack process in several of their post-war films. Several motion picture authorities believe that had the Axis powers won the war, they planned to make Agfacolor the supreme color system throughout Europe and eventually the world. Because Russia holds the basic rights, the process is seen in many Communist satellite countries, but very seldom does the free world use the process for theatrical films.

Agfacolor, although now a tripack process, is unique in that the color forming substances remain fast in the emulsions during the stages of development and no color needs to be added in the later developmental stages, thus making it simpler to process than some of the other systems. Ansco Color, perfected from Agfacolor in America, has these same characteristics.[150]

Among the films produced in Agfacolor were LIFE IN BLOOM, LIGHT OVER RUSSIA, MAY DAY — 1952, MAZOWSZE,

NATIONAL LIBERATION DAY, THREE COMRADES, BOR-
IS GODUNOV, MUSSORGSKY, THE STONE FLOWER and
TALE OF SIBERIA in Russia; THE EMPEROR'S NIGHTIN-
GALE in Czechoslovakia, and DON JUAN in Germany. The
filming of THE STONE FLOWER gave the process its best film
record to date.

The most famous Agfacolor feature was BARON MUENCH-
HAUSEN, although it was never shown in the United States. It was
taken over by Sidney Kaufman at a cost of over five hundred
thousand dollars from the UFA studios in Berlin after four years of
clearance arrangements. Always noted as a fabulous production, the
Agfacolor feature included 85 major roles and 65 supporting roles
and included such characters as Catherine the Great, Cagliostro the
magician and Casanova, as well as a sequence showing a trip to the
moon.[151] The film was edited down to two hours in 1955 and dubbed
into English, but it has received almost no showings since that time.

MAGICOLOR

When the Agfacolor patents were thrown open to everyone, the
Russians adopted the name of Magicolor for the process and first
used it for a full-length cartoon, THE MAGIC HORSE, in 1948.
Other short cartoons were produced under the Magicolor name,
including FISH AND THE FISHERMAN, and by 1952, Magicolor
features came in great numbers. These included THE GRAND
CONCERT, SADKO, MAN OF MUSIC, TWELFTH NIGHT,
STARS OF THE UKRAINE, CONCERT OF STARS, USSR
TODAY, LIFE IN THE ARCTIC, 1905, VASILI'S RETURN,
MAXIMA and THE BALLET OF ROMEO AND JULIET.

Technically, the first feature films in Magicolor seemed poor. A
Variety critic pulled no punches in reviewing them. He said of
LIFE IN THE ARCTIC: "Magicolor . . . process leaves plenty to
be desired. Often it is little more than a fine grade sepia, with no
contrasts in tone."[152] Of MAN OF MUSIC, it was said, "Eduoard
Tisse did a fine job with the camera, and hardly can be blamed for
the wishy-washy tinting supplied via the Russo Magicolor process.
This color can be best compared with some of the first experimental
tint work in the US years ago when there was little exact definition
or contrast of color elements."[153] Of CONCERTS OF STARS, the
comment was, "Magicolor . . . tends to bathe the proceedings in
blueish light."[154]

THE GRAND CONCERT, SADKO and VASILI'S RETURN
were given better treatment by reviewers as the system improved.

Of the last mentioned film, **Variety** said, "The Russian film producers have made strides with their Magicolor, used in this, because it is much more lifelike and sharp."[155]

SOVCOLOR

In 1946 a Russian documentary called RUSSIA ON PARADE was shown in the United States in a color process called "Natural Sovcolor." The process was described by the sponsors of the picture as "a secret known only to Soviet film producers and represents years of experimentation."[156] The **Motion Picture Herald,** however, took a different view of the announcement. "What is omitted," said the **Herald,** "is that Russian soldiery occupied the Agfa plant at Wolfen, Germany, in mid-1945, seized the technicians and the Agfacolor process and refused to allow an American commission to visit Wolfen."[157] Sovcolor, then, is just another version of the Agfacolor process, although even 15 years later, Russian color films continued to be presented in the process, including THE ANNA CROSS, STARS OF THE RUSSIAN BALLET, INDONESIA TODAY, OTHELLO, TIGER GIRL, THE GRASSHOPPER, BRIDE WITH A DOWRY, RIMSKY-KORSAKOV, THE INSPECTOR GENERAL and THE FORTY-FIRST, as well as the first Russian Cinerama-type presentation, GREAT IS MY COUNTRY.

CHROME COLOR AND ART CHROME COLOR

Chrome Color and Art Chrome Color, announced as the process for several Russian pictures in the late 1940's, seems to be another name for the Agfacolor process. No other data have been announced, although THE LUCKY BRIDE, PAGEANT OF RUSSIA and TRIUMPH OF YOUTH were three of the films which appeared under these names.

FERRANIACOLOR

Italy, which had never before produced a color film, presented TOTO A COLORI in another newly perfected version of the Agfacolor process, Ferraniacolor. It had previously been tested in several Italian documentary and newsreel films. A **Variety** reviewer described the process in TOTO A COLORI as having "fair to good values under pressure of studio production. Set and color supervision is experimental at best."[158] A short subject of the annual international horse show in Rome, however, showed Ferraniacolor photography to better advantage. The process compares favorably

to Kodachrome in color quality and seemed to fare better in short subjects than spread over a feature-length film. Italy announced 14 color features in 1953, with eight of these in Ferraniacolor.[159] In 1954, 39 color films to be filmed in Ferraniacolor were announced.[160]

Later films in the process fared much better, especially IFE's AIDA which was one of the most popular foreign films of 1955. **Film Daily** lauded the film and added "with high honors going to the Ferraniacolor."[161] **Independent Film Journal** called the color process "excellent."[162]

Other Ferraniacolor films of more recent vintage included THE BOARDER, WOMEN ALONE, WHITE VERTIGO and CHERI-BIBI from Italy, and THE QUEEN OF BABYLON, released by Twentieth Century-Fox.

Ferraniacolor continues in use today for many Italian films and from other countries around the area of Italy.

KONICOLOR, FUJICOLOR, DAIEI COLOR

Japan surprised the motion picture industry by releasing three varied color processes after World War II. Konishi Roku brought out his process, Konicolor, to be used by MGM for 16mm color prints of three preview "trailers," for KIM, THE YEARLING and LITTLE WOMEN. Several MGM cartoons followed, with prints by Konicolor.[163] Soon Konicolor was making 16mm reductions of MGM features, including KING SOLOMON'S MINES and THE YEARLING, plus prints of MGM CinemaScope films.

Fujicolor, another Japanese process, also was pronounced a success with its first full-length film, ADVENTURE OF NATSU-KO. The process bears a strong resemblance to Kodachrome since it is a three-color separation layer film.[164] The film had a lot of exterior shots and Fujicolor came through these tests successfully, according to reports of experts.

Daiei Color is the most recent Japanese process and several pictures were made in the system, although none in the United States.

CINEFOTOCOLOR

A system perfected in Spain, CineFotoColor has been used for two pictures, FLAMENCO and THE TYRANT.[165] The process rivals the early Cinecolor method and tends toward blueishness.

GEVACOLOR

Gaevert in Germany and Belgium perfected a color film similar to

Agfacolor — a monopack process called Gevacolor.[166] It was successfully used for sequences in LEONARDO DA VINCI and in full-color features such as BONGOLO, SHIP OF DAMNED WOMEN, HIS ROYAL HIGHNESS and LAND OF SMILES. The last-mentioned film was reviewed by **Variety** as: "Gevacolor has been used to advantage. It is done here much better than former tries with it."[167] The subtle color of Gevacolor lent excellent values in bringing out the details of the famous paintings used in LEONARDO DA VINCI.

A Gevacolor featurette, CORONATION DAY, however, was considered ". . .patchy and rarely compares in quality with the other processes."[168]

France, which had made only seven previous color features in her entire history, announced 15 new Gevacolor features in 1953. India made a Gevacolor film called PAMPOSH in 1954 of which **Film Daily** declared: "This was the first film to be made in the Belgian process and the colors generally are clear, bright and solid, with red possibly a little too dominant."[169] **Variety** described the 1954 Franco-Italian Gevacolor film, JOAN AT THE STAKE, as in "elegant color."[170]

European countries are still using the Gevacolor process in their feature films.

POLCOLOR

Poland came up with a process called Polcolor (not to be confused with the American Polacolor) which was believed to be another variation on the Agfacolor-Sovcolor system. **Variety,** in reviewing the first Polcolor feature, ADVENTURE IN WARSAW, said, "This is done in Polcolor, the tinting process whipped up in Poland. It shapes as an improvement over Sovcolor and ranks alongside of Eastmancolor in many respects."[171]

BRITISH CHROMART

Announced in 1950, the British Chromart process claims both a two-color and a three-color system based on the patents of Hans von Fraunhofer, a Hungarian living in England. The two-color process is called Chromart Simplex and the three-color process was named Chromart Tricolor. At this time the success of these entries into the color film race cannot be completely evaluated, although nothing more has been heard of either of the Chromart systems in nearly a decade. It and all the other post-war systems, with one or two

exceptions, have been withdrawn for good, leaving only their names for the film history books.

EXOTIC COLOR

Exotic color, perfected in 1952, was a color film presented by Harry Lee and Edward J. Danziger, based on a color process invented in Spain.

They produced two films, BABES IN BAGDAD and THE QUEEN'S MARK (the latter not released theatrically). The process was purported to be the fastest color system in existence anywhere in the world, and yielded full three-color prints. The Danzigers declared that the prints from black-and-white film stock may be had in four to six hours. They estimated that the color film would cost just slightly more than black-and-white film.

BABES IN BAGDAD did not fare so well with the critics. **Variety** said ". . . the color process — Exotic Color — looks as if its only true destiny is the research lab."[172] **Film Daily** added, ". . . (the film) receives added but minor quality from the color process."[173] Nothing more has been done with the Exotic Color system.

COLOR ANNOUNCEMENTS

Many exciting announcements were made during this latest era of color films, but many of them never developed. Hollywood producer Boris Morros was reported interested in a new Czechoslovakian color process in 1952. Test short subjects made in the system had proved successful but no films have as yet appeared in the system, either before or after Mr. Morros' death. The process was said to have used four solutions to impart the color to the film after it is exposed.[174]

DuPont announced a multilayer film for making release prints.[175] One of the advantages of the new DuPont color stock is that it is said to be able to stand elevated temperatures in the processing solution, presumably reducing materially the size and cost of the processing machinery.[176]

EASTMAN COLOR

In 1950 the new Eastman Color, made expressly for theatrical motion pictures, was announced. It had the advantage of needing less light for photographing images as well as being easier to process at a lower cost.[177]

Late in 1952, productions began to appear in Eastman color. The

first recorded use was in ROYAL JOURNEY, a film record of Princess Elizabeth produced by the National Film Board of Canada. In the film, scenes were taken where shooting with other types of color film would have been impossible. But poor lighting and even falling snow did not diminish the quality of the result obtained with the new Eastman Color film.[178]

Eastman Color had the added advantage of having a negative which appeared in complementary colors to the original subject. This negative becomes the "original" from which countless positive color prints could be made. Also, other "duplicate negatives" can be made to handle the running off of other prints so there is no wear and tear on the original negative.[179] Because of its simplicity of handling, the new Eastman Color was used in many of the 3-D films and widescreen films in the middle 1950's.

The process started out slowly but soon became a threat to Ansco Color, Technicolor and the other new systems. Since it was so easy to use, it became more popular than Technicolor because it was less cumbersome and required less light. Twentieth Century-Fox adopted it for its CinemaScope pictures in 1953, which included THE ROBE, HOW TO MARRY A MILLIONAIRE and BENEATH THE TWELVE MILE REEF, although the films carried the credit line, "Color by Technicolor" since Technicolor made their three-color imbibition prints from the Eastman Color negatives.

So in demand was the new film that a near shortage soon developed, but the Eastman company kept up with the supply by rapid conversion in its plants.

Among the 1953 and 1954 releases in Eastman Color were TANGA TIKA, THE HINDU, RING AROUND SATURN, CROSSED SWORDS and THE COWBOY, as well as many short subjects. Even MGM, who was guiding the perfection of the Ansco Color process, was reported considering the switch to Eastman Color because of the better performance it was giving.[180] By 1955, it was a definite observation that the Eastman Color process was becoming the most sought-after new color process and its future in the film industry was assured.

Soon foreign countries began using Eastman Color for their "special" features. From Italy came LA CASTIGLIONE and the CinemaScope feature, THE MILLER'S BEAUTIFUL WIFE. From Spain came CASTLES IN SPAIN, made in cooperation with France, and from France itself, RASPUTIN. Japan used the process in SAMURAI, THE MASK OF DESTINY, GATE OF HELL and

The Covered Wagon was one of many films of the twenties which were expanded to four times their natural size by the use of the Magnascope lens. Usually reserved for the finale, the Magnascope sequence always brought an extra thrill to even the most jaded movie audience. *(Courtesy The Museum of Modern Art Film Library)*

Garbo "talked" for the first time on the screen in *Anna Christie* (1930)
and caused a sensation. *(Courtesy The Museum of Modern Art Film Library)*

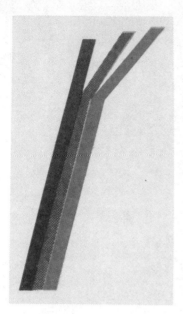

Eastman Color film
with three layers of
colored emulsion

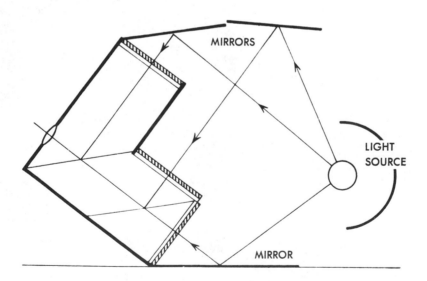

MIRRORS

LIGHT
SOURCE

MIRROR

The principle of the Ives Kromscop

The musical score and sound effects in Fox's *Sunrise* (1927) were among the most creative of the synchronized sound films. *(Courtesy The Museum of Modern Art Film Library)*

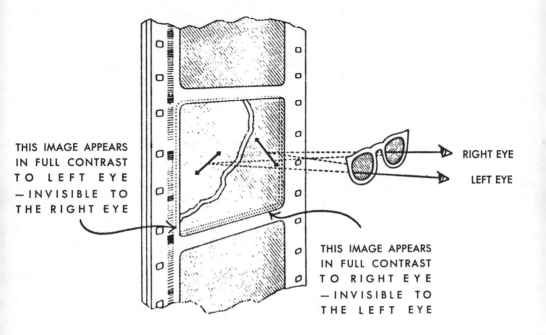

THIS IMAGE APPEARS IN FULL CONTRAST TO LEFT EYE —INVISIBLE TO THE RIGHT EYE

RIGHT EYE

LEFT EYE

THIS IMAGE APPEARS IN FULL CONTRAST TO RIGHT EYE —INVISIBLE TO THE LEFT EYE

The Vectograph 3-D system, which puts both polarized images on two layers of a single film, arrived too late to save the dwindling interest in third dimensional craze in 1953. However, the Vectograph system may still prove to be useful when the next 3-D revival takes place. The great advantages of Vectograph are obvious—two projectors are not needed and neither are any attachments. *(Drawing courtesy* New Screen Techniques, *p. 30)*

The most "far out" of the avant-garde film presentations is the National
Film Board of Canada's *Labyrinth*, which was premiered at Montreal's
"Expo '67." Screens are on the sides and on the floor of the building.

Carol Dempster and Ralph Graves sang a song in D. W. Griffith's *Dream Street* in 1921. *(Courtesy The Museum of Modern Art Film Library)*

Al Jolson both sang and spoke in *The Jazz Singer* (1927) and started a revolution in Hollywood. *(Courtesy The Museum of Modern Art Film Library)*

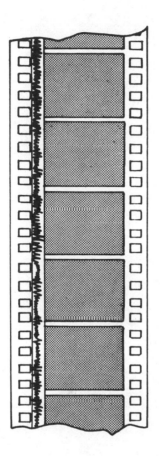 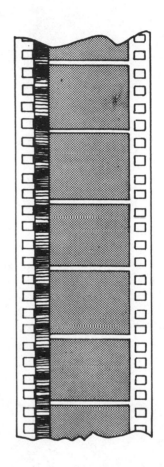

Variable Width
Sound Track

Variable Area
Sound Track

Above is a picture "Squeezed" onto a regular 35mm frame of film by means of an anamorphic lens.

When projected through an anamorphic lens, the subject is spread out to the correct proportion on the movie screen.

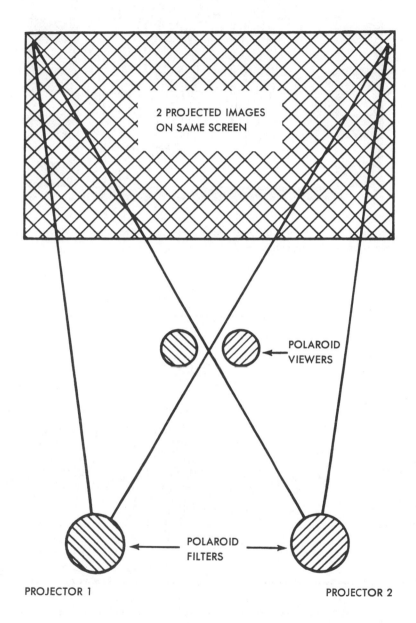

2 PROJECTED IMAGES
ON SAME SCREEN

POLAROID
VIEWERS

POLAROID
FILTERS

PROJECTOR 1

PROJECTOR 2

3-D Projection

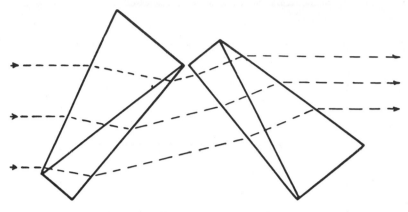

A PAIR OF ACHROMATIZED BREWSTER PRISMS USED
TO EXPAND A PROJECTED IMAGE ANAMORPHICALLY

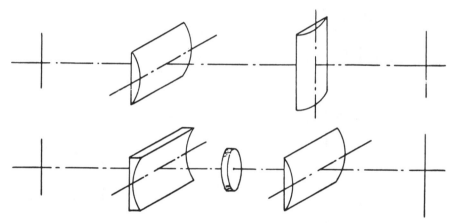

TWO ARRANGEMENTS OF CYLINDRICAL-LENS ANAMORPHOSERS

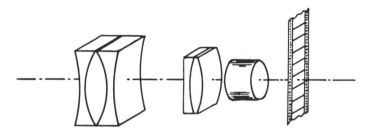

THE "HYPERGONAR" LENS (FROM CHRETIEN'S PATENT)

Types of anamorphic lenses show how the image is "Squeezed" and
"Unsqueezed" by means of optical elements. (*Courtesy* Image, *5:208,
November, 1956, George Eastman House.*)

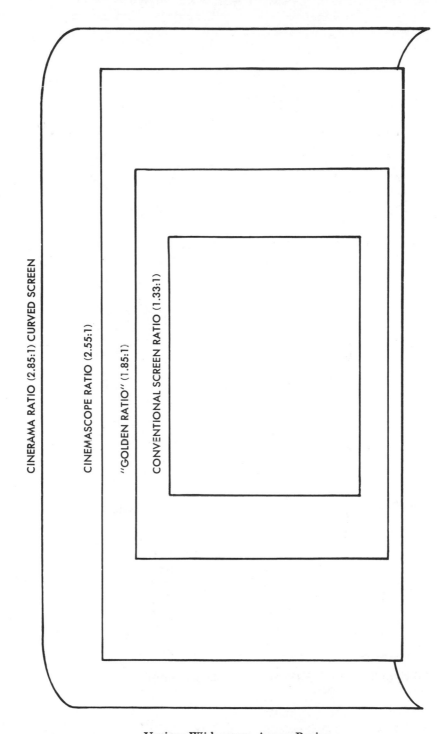

Various Widescreen Aspect Ratios

Of all the thrilling moments put on the screen, the Cinerama "roller coaster" sequences has become one of the best remembered for its sheer size and impact on a film audience. (*From* This is Cinerama; *Roller Coaster Sequence; courtesy Rockaways' Playland Amusement Park, New York*)

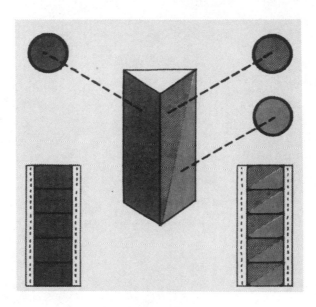

The Technicolor process
using a prism

Early Kinemacolor film

A two-color process, such as Cinecolor, Trucolor or early Technicolor yields a compromise coloring as shown above.

A three-color process, such as technicolor, Eastman Color and Ansco Color gives each color a truer and purer value.

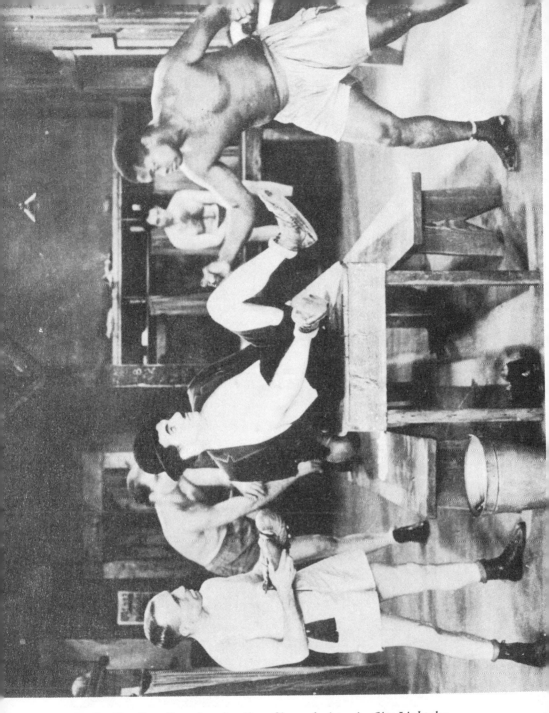

Charlie Chaplin adhered to the silent film technique in *City Lights* by using only synchronized sound effects and a musical score in 1931.

THE GOLDEN DEMON, all of which demonstrated the knack the Japanese had with the Eastman Color system combined with their own artistic sense in the use of color.

A new and faster Eastman Color was used on Paramount's THE RAT RACE in 1959 which is said to photograph more clearly scenes with dim or drab illumination.

TRI-ART, MOVIELAB AND COLOR BY DELUXE

Three "dry-labs" associated with the Eastman process are Tri-Art, Movielab and DeLuxe laboratories. Tri-Art Color Corporation of New York put its name to its own processing of the film including SECRETS OF THE REEF. "Color by Movielab" appeared more recently.

"Color by DeLuxe" became a byword for Eastman Color prints of CinemaScope and standard productions, first at Twentieth Century-Fox and later at several other major studios who had their Eastman release prints made at the DeLuxe Laboratories.

WARNERCOLOR

In 1952, Warner Brothers announced its new color process, "WarnerColor," which was actually the Eastman Color film under another name. The studio installed processing equipment to handle six features a year and soon expanded to twice that amount.

WarnerColor, according to the late Col. Nathan Levinson of the Warners staff, had been "in the experimental stage since 1940." He described the process as "merely the use of Eastman color film stock . . . adapted to our techniques."[181]

During its first year, WarnerColor was used in six productions — THE LION AND THE HORSE, CARSON CITY, SPRINGFIELD RIFLE, STOP YOU'RE KILLING ME!, SHE'S BACK ON BROADWAY and THE MIRACLE OF OUR LADY OF FATIMA.

After the success of its first features, the first WarnerColor 3-D feature was filmed in the Natural Vision process. It proved to be one of the best 3-D films. HOUSE OF WAX grossed over five million dollars its first year. For the first time in its history, Warner Brothers decided to film more features in WarnerColor than in Technicolor.[182]

The 1953-54 WarnerColor productions included HONDO, DIAL M FOR MURDER, THE CHARGE AT FEATHER RIVER and THE PHANTOM OF THE RUE MORGUE (all in 3-D), THE BOUNTY HUNTER, THUNDER OVER THE PLAINS and THE BOY FROM OKLAHOMA.

Warner Brothers soon announced that it was dropping Technicolor completely in favor of their own system. They retracted that statement, however, and said they would still make some films in Technicolor. Warners set up WarnerColor laboratories to serve the East Coast and Great Britain and felt that the future of their version of the Eastman process was secure.

PATHECOLOR

Pathe Laboratories' version of Eastman Color was re-named Pathecolor, adding an ironic touch to the race for color supremacy. Using the name given to the old French hand-painted process used in the early days of the motion picture, Pathe made prints of many Eastman Color pictures for theatrical release, including MISS ROBIN CRUSOE, WAR PAINT, CAPTAIN JOHN SMITH AND POCAHANTAS and LOUISIANA TERRITORY.

Of WAR PAINT, the **Independent Film Journal** remarked: "One bright note is the excellent use of color, which provides some handsome scenes."[183] and **Film Daily** added: ". . . brilliantly photographed."[184]

Pathecolor soon opened laboratories in England to handle the European business, indicating that this version of the Eastman process would also be around for a long time. As in the case of the DeLuxe laboratories, the tag line for Pathecolor was changed to "Eastman Color by Pathe" in order to credit both the film stock and the laboratory.

COLUMBIA COLOR

Columbia Pictures produced its own variation by using "Columbia Color" for many of its 1958 and 1959 productions, including BUCHANAN RIDES ALONE, which was the first entry under the Columbia Color banner. The name was also used on some Columbia travel shorts, but fell into disuse in the early 1960's. In 1965, however, the term began to appear on films again, notably CAT BALLOU.

PANACOLOR

Early in 1961, a new low-cost method of making color release prints was introduced in a process called Panacolor. The system had been in the development stage since 1957.

Its basic difference from other processes is that it uses a black-and-white positive which, when treated in the Panacolor laboratories, comes out as a color-controlled release print. Since the cost of black-

and-white stock is only half the cost of color stock, release print charges can be cut in half.

MGM had taken an interest in the Panacolor process in the early days of its development and in July, 1961, purchased enough stock to gain controlling interest.

It was made clear that Panacolor is not a color film process in itself — that is, the company was not organized to shoot films in color, but merely to make color-controlled release prints for showing in theatres.

Of the over 100 methods of imparting color to motion picture film, the majority have faded into oblivion and few have been hailed as successful.

Within a span of 65 years, from the crude hand-painted films of Edison and Pathe to the latest advances in Technicolor and Eastman Color, the color motion picture has been constantly moving ahead with ever-increasing improvements to bring its public the most beautiful images possible in the theatre.

In the early days of the film, competition was almost non-existent. Today, color films are still highly competitive. With the development of television, there is more need than ever for economical and quick methods of shooting and developing color films. Some processes which faded in recent years might be revived for color television use.

Although there will probably always be black-and-white films, the many excellent color systems now on the market assure a large number of color films as long as there is a market for them.

[121] Polacolor press release, p. 1.
[122] Cornwell-Clyne, pp. 21, 130 and 576.
[123] Variety, 193:12, February 10, 1954.
[124] Cornwell-Clyne, pp. 21, 130 and 576.
[125] Margaret Markham. "Focus on Color," Film News, 12:21, January, 1953.
[126] Independent Film Journal, 16:11, August 23, 1952.
[127] Ibid., 32:28, August 22, 1953.
[128] Variety, 191:6, August 26, 1953.
[129] Independent Film Journal, 32:14, November 28, 1953.
[130] Ibid., 32:17, September 5, 1953.
[131] Variety, 193:18, January 20, 1954.
[132] Film Daily, 109:9, January 6, 1956.
[133] Alan M. Gundelfinger, "Cinecolor Three-Color Process," SMPTE Journal, 54:74, January, 1950.
[134] Film Daily, 103:1, May 19, 1953.
[135] Independent Film Journal, n.d.
[136] Variety, 191:6, June 28, 1953.
[137] Film Daily, 105:7, May 5, 1954.
[138] A Variety term meaning a color process and not a one-tint film as the term might imply.
[139] Variety, 188:6, October 29, 1952.
[140] J. H. Coote, "A Technician's View of the Colour Film," Penguin Film Review 1949, pp. 77-78.
[141] Cornwell-Clyne, p. 325.
[142] New York Times, July 13, 1947.

[143] Cornwell-Clyne, p. 325.
[144] *Variety*, 188:15, August 27, 1952.
[145] Gio Gagliardi, "Lenticulated Film," *Films in Review*, 2:29-33, November, 1951.
[146] *Variety*, 189:5, January 14, 1953.
[147] *Ibid.*, 189:20, January 21, 1953.
[148] Spottiswoode, *op. cit.*, pp. 207-208.
[149] *Film Daily Yearbook*, 1952 edition, p. 63.
[150] see FIAT Report on Agfacolor #976, Office of Military Government for Germany. Also final reports #721. 943 and 977.
[151] *New York Times*, August 29, 1954, Section II, p. 5.
[152] *Variety*, 192:22, September 9, 1953.
[153] *Op. cit.*
[154] *Ibid.*, 189:18, March 4, 1953.
[155] *Ibid.*, 192:22, September 30, 1953.
[156] *10 Eventful Years* (Encyclopaedia Britannica, Volume 3) p. 198.
[157] *Ibid.*
[158] *Variety*, 188:6, May 20, 1952.
[159] *Film Daily*, 103:6, March 3, 1953.
[160] *Ibid.*, 104:4, November 30, 1953.
[161] *Ibid.*, 106:6, October 14, 1954.
[162] *Independent Film Journal*, 34:16, October 16, 1954.
[163] *Film Daily*, 101:1, June 27, 1952.
[164] *Variety*, 189:18, February 25, 1953.
[165] *Ibid.*, 191:8, June 22, 1953.
[166] Cornwell-Clyne, p. 350.
[167] *Variety*, 188:6, November 15, 1952.
[168] *Ibid.*, 191:6, June 10, 1953.
[169] *Film Daily*, 106:6, October 8, 1954.
[170] *Variety*, 196:11, November 3, 1954.
[171] *Variety*, 200:6, November 2, 1955.
[172] *Op. cit.*, 188:7, November 15, 1952.
[173] *Film Daily*, 102:6, December 15, 1952.
[174] *Variety*, 188:7, August 20, 1952.
[175] Cornwell-Clyne, p. 740.
[176] *Variety*, 188:22, November 26, 1952.
[177] Spottiswoode, pp. 214-215.
[178] Markham, *op. cit.*, p. 21.
[179] *Loc. Cit.*
[180] *Variety*, 191:7, August 26, 1953.
[181] Letter from Nathan Levinson, July 1, 1952.
[182] *Variety*, 188:7, October 14, 1952.
[183] *Independent Film Journal*, 21:18, June 11, 1953.
[184] *Film Daily*, 104:6, August 14, 1953.

CHAPTER SIX
THE CREATIVE USE OF COLOR

As with any new innovation, the development of color motion pictures was more of a curse than a blessing to the movie-makers. Problems were found with not only the photographing and the projection of these films, but with their aesthetic use as well.

From all reports from those who remember the early color films, they are recalled as garish, bright and obvious — an attempt to show their audiences that a color film was definitely not a black-and-white one.

The reaction of viewers was a "so what" attitude as well as eyestrain in many cases. The critics usually sided with the audience and if it hadn't been for the development of the three-color system, color films might have disappeared for a longer period than they actually did.

Because of the development of Technicolor, feature films in color were saved from a literal death. There were only two color features in 1932, one in 1933 and none in 1934. But from 1935 on, there has always been a steady stream of color features in many processes.

Once the entire spectrum was re-created on one strip of film, the exhaustive work of decades of experimentation was over. Now it was up to film-makers to make the same creative use of color as they had previously done with cinematography, set designs and sound as they developed from their early awkwardness to art forms in their own right.

The answer was to soften the colors and make them less obvious and more useful to the over-all plan of the film. Color just for color's sake gradually gave way to the use of color for its dramatic and aesthetic values..

Of the many hundreds of color films produced in the many different color systems over the last 70 years, very few stand out because of the creative use of color. And there are many reasons for this.

First, color films are more difficult to photograph, due to the constantly changing light and color values. When the film is edited, the preceding and succeeding scene must "match" not only aesthetically but color-wise. Second, most films (with the exception of many Technicolor films) did not have a "color coordinator" or "color consultant" to work with the writer, designers, director and cinematographer on the production. Third, many productions tended to use color **per se,** as in a musical where everything is so full of color that sometimes the story and the actors are lost in splashes of bold color.

Color, to be used creatively, must seem natural, yet be an essential part of the over-all mood of the production. Carl Th. Dreyer recommends that a color film should have two scripts — the actual script and a "color script" abounding with details — and this second script should be created by preferably a painter who has a knowledge of color.[185]

COLOR EFFECTS

Despite the rapid development in color, the practice of inserting "color sequences" in otherwise black-and-white films continues to be practiced. Some of them have been very short, others running from 10 to 15 minutes in length.

Among the best known color sequences are from JACK THE RIPPER, where red blood spurts from under an elevator where the villain has just been crushed; THE TINGLER, in which a bathtub of red blood appears in contrast to the blacks and whites of the rest of the film; THE PICTURE OF DORIAN GRAY, where the slowly degenerating portrait is shown in all its ghastly horror in color, and in the WAR OF THE COLOSSAL BEAST.

But color sequences were not all used for shock effects in horror films. Many times color would be used for the finale of a film. Some of the finales which suddenly burst into color were SHINE ON HARVEST MOON, TASK FORCE, VICTORIA THE GREAT, THE MOON AND SIXPENCE and SOLID GOLD CADILLAC.

In several films, the "present" was photographed in black and white and the "past" was in lovely color. This device was used successfully in I'LL NEVER FORGET YOU, THE WIZARD OF OZ and BONJOUR TRISTESSE.

The dream world is often represented by color in an otherwise black-and-white movie. Films such as THE SECRET GARDEN, THE SAND CASTLE, THE EIGHTH DAY OF THE WEEK,

ICE FOLLIES OF 1939, the "Alice Blue Gown" sequence from IRENE, and THE RIGHT OF MAN, in which a love scene turned into abstract images and sounds, all had color sequences.

Color sequences in 3-D were added to THE MASK, THIRTEEN GHOSTS and PARADISIO, among others.

Technicolor inserts have been used to create special effects in sound films. In THE NAKED EYE, scenes depicting photographer Edward Weston last works were shown in color, while the rest of the film was in black and white when he photographed only in black and white.

In the PRIVATE AFFAIRS OF BEL AMI, LE NUIT ET LE JOUR from France and THE PASSIONATE STRANGER from England used telling color inserts.

In THE RETURN OF DRACULA, the film turned to color as the stake was driven through the vampire's heart. Pathecolor inserts were used in I WAS A TEENAGE FRANKENSTEIN. In Russia's STORIES ABOUT LENIN, color and black-and-white scenes were alternated. HOW TO MAKE A MONSTER presented the final scene, that of a blazing fire, in color to contrast with the rest of the film. Russia's IVAN THE TERRIBLE, PART II, had the banquet scene as the only color section of the film.

Japan's DAY DREAM shows a short color sequence of a girl bleeding from knife wounds, Italy's BEFORE THE REVOLU-TION has a color sequence in the middle of the film, and France's CLEO FROM 5 TO 7 has the opening fortune-telling sequence in color.

The shortest Technicolor sequence on record was in Alfred Hitchcock's SPELLBOUND when two frames of red Technicolor film were inserted into the black-and-white footage to simulate a gun blast near the end of the film. The effect, to say the least, was considerably heightened by the sharp contrast.

But sequences and short strips of color were many times awkward and obvious, yet they are still in use today for a variety of effects.

THE ARTISTIC USE OF COLOR

Color has been used in films for dramatic effects which make the viewer recall the film because of its color. We recall FUNNY FACE for its "Think Pink" number, and MOULIN ROUGE for its colored filters to simulate the colors in the Toulouse-Lautrec paintings. The dream sequences in THE GIRL MOST LIKELY uses a dominant color for each dream and these colors re-occur at various times in the

story as color leitmotifs, much as Wagner used theme music in his operas. Fellini's JULIET OF THE SPIRITS and Antonioni's RED DESERT sometimes strain for their color effects but they are remembered just the same.

The terrifying contrast of the beautiful sunlit cottage in THE COLLECTOR to the dingy basement where the deranged boy held his victim prisoner made the suspense and irony of that film much more pronounced than it would have been in black-and-white.

A large gamut of lighting effects were used in color films, often for extremely theatrical effects. In THE BROTHERS KARAMAZOV (1958), when the brother's body is discovered hanging in the closet, the viewer is greeted not only by the shocking sight of the body but also an eerie green light which deepens the visual effect through color.

John Huston in MOBY DICK achieved a very subtle color effect by making a black-and-white negative of the completed color print and superimposing it over the color negative. The result was a subdued, yet natural effect. This same technique was used by Rene Clement in France in GERVAISE when he superimposed a black-and-white negative over the Eastmancolor negative. The result was somewhat akin to the old daguerreotypes come to life.

The colors of the spectrum have been given "dramatic values" — that is, red, orange and yellow are warm, passionate colors, whereas green, blue and violet are cool, dispassionate colors. It would be difficult to imagine a daytime desert scene lit in blue or green any more than a nightime scene lit in yellow. Early film producers realized the dramatic value of color when they tinted their daytime scenes in yellow or sepia, night-time scenes in blue and fire scenes in red.

Associations of color have become almost standardized through the centuries. Some of the symbols brought out by the use of various colors include:

Red — blood, fire, anger, danger, stop, blushes, meat, apples and berries, attention, wine, lips.

Orange — the sun, harvest, fruit.

Yellow and gold — hot, dry, desert, cheerfulness, wealth, the holy cross, power, divinity, warmth, charity, illness, cowardice, flowers.

Green — trees, youth, summer, immortality, immaturity, netherworld characters, vegetables, sickness, decay, monsters.

Blue — the sky, coolness, dignity, fidelity, serenity, truth, heaven, melancholy, fair weather.

Violet — royalty, elegance, sunset, sunrise, depression, dignity.

White — purity, virginity, innocence, cleanness, anemia, surrender, goodness, cheerfulness, snow.

Black — night, death, mourning, gloom, fear, horror, wickedness, eternity, profundity, criminality, villainy, storm, dirt.

Gray — sobriety, maturity, fog, dreariness, depression, winter, neutrality.

Each of these colors may vary in brightness, hue and value as well as in its relationship and contrast to the other colors composed in each shot or scene.

These colors can be painted directly onto the set, dyed into the fabrics of the costumes or acquired through the use of various colored gelatins in the lighting apparatus.

PROBLEMS WITH COLOR

The fact that color film stock costs nearly twice as much as black and white is another factor which a budget minded producer must consider before deciding on shooting a film in color. But this is not as large a problem as the actual filming.

Charles Clarke, who filmed THE CAPTAIN FROM CASTILE and SMOKY, feels that color filming is twice as difficult as black and white. As he puts it:

"The first thing to remember is that outdoor color is not always constant, as many people seem to think. Everything is always changing. The green of a tree is entirely different on a cloudy day than it is on a bright one. Even in sunshine the difference between six in the morning and noon is very marked. A red cliff will start the day as maroon and by noon it will be salmon pink. To take care of such variations I do my shooting from ten to four when the colors remain fairly even."[186]

FUTURE OF COLOR

In the 1950's, when television was acquiring a stranglehold on the viewing public, the movies retaliated with color films (as well as widescreen, 3 D and stereophonic sound) to provide their audiences with things they could not see on the small-screen, black-and-white television set.

But by 1965, when all three major TV networks converted almost completely to color, the motion picture had to meet the challenge of making color count and subtlety was the order of the day. Color television was notoriously gaudy and many set owners could not control the colors correctly.

With both motion pictures and television in color, the competition

has ended in a dead heat and each color film, no matter in which medium it is presented, must stand on its own as an artistic entity.

This is the challenge color films face in future years.

[185] Carl Th. Dreyer, "Color and Color Films," *Films in Review*, 6:167, April, 1955.
[186] Quoted from Alice Evans Field, *Hollywood, U.S.A.*, p. 190.

PART TWO — WIDTH

"Movies Are Wider Than Ever!"
— Arthur Knight

CHAPTER ONE
EARLY WIDESCREENS

When critics hailed Cinerama in 1952 as the start of the widescreen revolution, many forgot that widescreen films are as old as movies themselves.

Although directors and cameramen always wanted to "open wide" for dramatic effect, it was usually a problem to get widescreen effects because of the need for special equipment and the extra cost made it prohibitive.

Motion picture films and screens, like any new invention, were not at first standardized. William Friese-Greene's first films were huge strips of celluloid; Pathe used 28mm film; Biograph and Muto-scope used film 2-1/2 inches high and 2-3/4 inches wide;[1] the Lumiere brothers had film with only one sprocket hole per frame and Thomas A. Edison made his movies on 35mm film with four perforations on each side of the film per frame. Because Edison was selling more motion picture equipment than anyone else, his film and screen size — 35mm film and a screen with a 4:3 aspect ratio (four times as wide and 3 times as high) — became the standard of the motion picture industry the world over.

This might not have been the case, according to William E. Waddell. "If early motion pictures had been exhibited in theatres instead of stores," he said, "there would never have been any twenty-foot-wide screens. The natural tendency would have been to make them as wide as the stages."[2]

There are four ways of achieving a widescreen effect on a movie screen: (1) "cropping" the top and bottom of a conventional film, (2) putting two or three films together and project them in a continuous line, (3) use a wide film, or (4) "squeeze" the image onto the film and spread it out on the screen with a special lens.

The earliest widescreen projection device seems to be the Cylindrographe, a panoramic camera invented by P. Moessard and

presented first at the Versailles Photographic Society in July of 1884.[3]

American widescreen presentations first appeared in the travelogs of Lyman H. Howe, who traveled around the country with a group of people who supplied appropriate sound as well as images by making noises backstage to synchronize with the action on the screen. Howe shot his films with short lenses which gave a wide field of vision. This tended to bring the audience right into the scene and made them feel a part of it.[4]

Prof. J. Louis Peck of France demonstrated his curved screen at the Rivoli Theatre in New York in 1920, using scenes from Paramount's EVERYWOMAN. Although the critics were excited about the way the screen brought the image into better focus and eliminated eyestrain, nothing was done to encourage the curved screen until 30 years later.[5]

MAGNASCOPE

Lorenzo Del Riccio introduced the Magnascope in 1924 and the invention proved to have a longevity of nearly 30 years.

A special screen, four times the normal size of the regular theatre screen, is needed for Magnascope projection. Most of the screen is masked by curtains during the regular part of the film. When the Magnascope portion of the film appears, these curtains are raised or pulled aside to reveal the larger screen. This gives the illusion of the picture gradually becoming larger.[6]

Magnascope's main purpose was to "blow up" an especially breathtaking scene (usually the climax of the film) to four times its normal size. To do this, two reels of the same film were run simultaneously through the projector. When it was time for the magnification to take place, the one film was shut off and the other (with the Magnascope lens attached) was enlarged to the new size right before the viewer's eyes.

The Magnascope lens was first used for the finale of Paramount's OLD IRONSIDES and has been effectively used for the battle scenes in THE BIG PARADE, for the stampede in NORTH OF '36, the buffalo roundup in THE THUNDERING HERD, the elephant stampede in CHANG, the ballet in TWINKLETOES, the air sequences in WINGS and the linking of the East and West by railroad in THE IRON HORSE.

Del Riccio's first encounter with Paramount's head of production, Jesse Lasky, is recalled by Lasky himself:

"Del Riccio told me he had invented a supplementary projector lens capable of enlarging a screen image to vast proportions, and would like to demonstrate it to me. I sent him over to the Rivoli and phoned the manager to have our chief projectionist make whatever arrangements were needed and to send for me when they were ready to run a test.

"They reversed a painted backdrop for a screen to fill the whole proscenium arch and threw the picture on the dirty canvas in normal size. Then all of a sudden as OLD IRONSIDES came to the rescue of a merchantman seized by the Tripoli pirates, the picture opened up to more than four times its natural size and the full-rigged ship expanded in all its glory while sailing right into my lap. I've never felt such a dramatic impact from anything in a full lifetime of show business.

"I coined the name 'Magnascope' on the spot, and eagerly authorized the necessary expenditure for a big screen in order to project the sea battle sequences in overwhelming magnitude. We recut the picture to make the most of these scenes. Dr. Hugo Reisenfeld, arranger of the musical score and orchestra leader, stepped up the tempo and volume of the music as the picture suddenly grew gigantic before the startled eyes of the first-night audience. There hadn't been time to advertise the big-screen innovation before the premiere, and everyone was so taken by surprise that all stood up and cheered wildly. The New York **Times** broke precedent the next morning by running its review of the picture on the front page."[7]

Paramount's Adolph Zukor believed that the Magnascope was "the greatest advance in projection during the past twenty years,"[8] but business was so good in the 1920's that theatre managers felt no need of the invention to draw in the customers.

In more recent years, Magnascope has appeared at the Paramount and Rivoli theatres in New York City accompanying the climaxes of such films as PORTRAIT OF JENNY, THE WILD HEART, STAGECOACH, MILLION DOLLAR MERMAID, NIAGARA and TWO FLAGS WEST, but fell into complete disuse with the advent of the widescreen processes.

OTHER DEVELOPMENTS

When the widescreen craze started in 1953, many studios had a large backlog of films made for conventional showing in the 1.33:1 (4:3) screen aspect ratio. In order to give these films the sensation of being filmed and shown as a widescreen film, most studios adopted a

method of "masking" the top or bottom of the screen image to increase its horizontal length and reduce the height. This was accomplished by changing to a different sized film "gate" in the theatre projector. Most of these gates were to change the ratio on the screen from 1.33:1 to 1.66:1, although Universal tried 1.85:1 on some of its conventional films.

Among the films shot in the conventional manner which were shown by these widescreen methods include Paramount's SHANE, which was shown in a ratio of 1.66:1 at the Radio City Music Hall. Stereophonic sound also was dubbed onto that film. Paramount also released THE WAR OF THE WORLDS in the new ratio and later re-issued THE GREATEST SHOW ON EARTH for widescreen exhibition. MGM gave GONE WITH THE WIND a widescreen look during its 1955 reissue, but got complaints from patrons with their widescreen showing of THE BANDWAGON when the feet of Fred Astaire and Cyd Charisse were cut off the screen while they were dancing.

Universal stretched the aspect ratio even further by premiering THUNDER BAY at Loew's State Theatre in New York in a ratio of 1.85:1 with three-channel stereophonic sound. Universal began shooting all its films so they could be shown in ratios up to 2:1.

MGM gave "roadshow" proportions to its JULIUS CAESAR by showing it in a 1.75:1 ratio and adding stereophonic sound to the premiere at the Booth Theatre in New York.

Twentieth Century-Fox, although converted completely to CinemaScope, made ten widescreen films which could be shown in several aspect ratios. Republic geared all its films to be shown from 1.66:1 to 1.85:1. Other studios followed suit. From 1953 on, it was "wider and wider" in Hollywood.

The fact that many actors found their heads chopped off and many dancers found that their feet were not on the screen didn't seem to bother the exhibitor or the theatre patron to any degree. The public was fascinated with the wide screen.

OTHER SYSTEMS

Many other widescreen systems appeared one after the other, most of them being nothing but a film shot with a wide-angle lens, using a masked projection gate in the theatre projector. These systems went under the varied names of Robert Hanover's Photorama; Albert M. Pickus' AMP-O-Vision; MGM's Metrovision and Metroscope; Paramount's Paravision; Republic's Vast-

Vision; RKO's ScenicScope and Twentieth Century-Fox's Widevision.

In other countries, these lenses were Jean Jacques Bessire's Perfect Tone (Switzerland); the Shiga Brothers' Panorama Cinevision (Japan). The Garutso lenses, claiming to give a stereoscopic illusion to motion pictures, were used under the name of Plastorama for a series of German films, ending with Erich Pommer's A LOVE STORY, and a slightly different type of film called Sonoptic, in which a picture is shot on ordinary film and the laboratory prints the image on the film in the exact ratio in which it is to be shown in the theatre. Most of the trial prints in this French process were printed to a 2.55:1, the same ratio as CinemaScope.[9]

A more radical claim for widescreen conversion of conventional films was made by C. V. Whitney, who claimed that his new process would "convert any old film to new aspect ratios and add both color and sound."[10] He announced the first two films to be made under the process would be two old silent features, CHANG and GRASS. So far there has been no more disclosed on this development.

But the real widescreen revolution came with the development of new media for photography and projection. These are all discussed in the following chapters and are classified by the type of process for easier reference and understanding.

[1] E. I. Sponable, "Historical Development of Sound Films," *SMPTE Journal*, 48:414 and *Image*, 8:203, December, 1959.

[2] *New York Times*, 79:6, June 1, 1930.

[3] *Image*, 3:36, May, 1954.

[4] Lewis M. Townsend and William W. Hennessy, *SMPE Journal*, 12:345, April, 1928.

[5] *Literary Digest*, 64:92, January 31, 1920.

[6] H. Rubin, *SMPE Journal*, 12:404, April, 1928.

[7] Lasky, Jesse L., "I Blow My Own Horn," pp. 179-180.

[8] Townsend and Hennessy, *op. cit.*, p. 352.

[9] *Variety*, 191:12, July 29, 1953.

[10] *Film Daily*, 109:1, June 8, 1956.

CHAPTER TWO
MULTIPLE CAMERA PROCESSES

Although one piece of film could give a fairly good widescreen image, many filmmakers and experimenters felt that the only true widescreen image was to put two or three films together, side by side, and project them as one image or as a main image with supplementary images on either side.

The first widescreen motion picture presentation dates back to 1896 when Raoul Grimoin-Sanson presented Cineorama. The system used ten projectors and ten films to throw a panoramic image on a huge circular screen. The Cineorama program consisted of travel films of Europe and Asia.[11] The Cineorama process was shown at the Paris Exposition of 1900 along with another widescreen presentation by the Lumiere Brothers, who projected their movies on a gigantic screen 48 feet high by 63 feet wide.[12]

WIDESCOPE

In 1921 George W. Bingham patented a wide angle projection system called Widescope which he said would "produce a picture showing just twice as much as cameras now in use, making it practical to produce scenes that have until now been considered impossible."[13]

The film used in the Widescope camera was double width. The camera had two lenses — one above the other — each of which put an image on a separate film, thus giving an extended double width image. The double-width film was split into two films and threaded into two interlocked projectors and projected together to give the elongated image.[14]

Bingham envisioned full screen baseball games with the entire diamond in view and each player recognizable. He also claimed that in doubling the image, Widescope eliminated all dangers of eyestrain or cramped eye muscles.

The entire idea, of course, was impractical in its day and Lewis M.

Townsend and William W. Hennessy of the Eastman Theatre in Rochester asked:

"If Widescope or double width pictures are desired, it seems hardly necessary to go to the great trouble and expense involved by using double width film, special projectors, etc., when it would be quite possible to get the same results by using standard film and masking off a portion of the top or bottom or both and then using the proper focus objective lens to project the picture to the size desired."[15]

Thirty-five years later, this theory was finally put in practice (see THRILLARAMA), but it was not considered any more practical than Widescope was in 1921.

THE TRIPLE PANEL

Two Frenchmen, Abel Gance, the noted French director, and Claude Autant-Lara, advanced a different type of widescreen system — the triptych or three-panel screen.

Autant-Lara photographed and projected POUR CONSTRUIRE UN FEU in a process called Hypergonar so that the shape and size of the screen could be varied throughout the picture and subsidiary action could occur on the two smaller panels framing the main screen.

The story concerned the gold hunters of the North and the screen shapes varied in several ways. According to a description in **Films and Filming,** a British magazine, "Screen shapes varied — horizontal for the snows, vertical for the pines — and sometimes the two screens were used simultaneously. (While one man waits patiently in his tent, the other flounders in the white wastes)."[16]

So Hypergonar not only used multiple screens, but also a variable screen. POUR CONSTRUIRE UN FEU was released in 1927 and the negative unfortunately was destroyed in 1932, leaving us with no first-hand record of the Hypergonar system.

Abel Gance, on the other hand, developed the idea of lashing three normal movie screens side by side in a theatre. While the film is shown on the middle screen in the normal fashion, scenes of special importance may be supplemented by images on each side on the second and third screens. The system was first used in his 1927 version of NAPOLEON and was named Polyvision.

Two types of triple images were used — the first was a single panoramic image filling the entire three screens (giving a Cinerama effect) and the second was a series of three separate images complementing and counterpointing each other. For example, in

NAPOLEON, a closeup of Napoleon's head is shown in the center panel, while scenes of the soldiers or a battle are seen on the two flanking panels. It is equivalent to the "flash back" or "dream sequence" without the use of special optical effects.

The original NAPOLEON ran between five and six hours and is considered the longest major film ever to be shown commercially. It opened at the Paris Opera House in April 7, 1927. Thirty-five years later, Abel Gance was still working on his Polyvision process, attempting to perfect his three screens to fit modern screen concepts, which would include quick and smooth changes in the size and shape of today's movie screen.

VITARAMA

There were no more theatrical attempts at popularizing the widescreen or the wide film. But it didn't stop the experiments.

At the World's Fair in New York in 1939, audiences were amazed by the Petroleum Industry exhibit featuring Vitarama, the invention of Fred Waller. He outdid the early Cineorama by using 11 projectors strapped together to project an image on a curved arc with a quarter dome over it telling the history of petroleum.[17] Although Vitarama generated excitement at the World's Fair, it was obviously impractical for theatrical use — or was it? Vitarama, with refinements, emerged in 1952 under the name of Cinerama!

CINERAMA

Fred Waller's Vitarama experienced its birth and death at the World's Fair. It was just too expensive a novelty to have much commercial value. But Waller kept on working on the idea of a huge curved screen although Hollywood had abandoned it as long ago as 1930. Finally, he got the number of projectors down to three and eliminated the quarter dome jutting into the audience. After the end of World War II, Waller decided to try and prove that his new development of the old Vitarama system, re-named Cinerama, would work.

With the help and encouragement of Lowell Thomas, a newscaster, and Merian C. Cooper, a Hollywood veteran, THIS IS CINERAMA was launched at the Broadway Theatre in New York on September 30, 1952, and surprised everyone by creating a sensation. Not only were audiences pleased and thrilled, but also the critics.

The **Associated Press** commented:

"You can now take a roller coaster ride on a roller coaster —

sitting in a movie seat. You'll gasp. Get clammy hands. It's real. It's Cinerama. This is a new movie system of projecting pictures which gives an illusion of third dimension — depth."[18]

Arthur Knight said in the **Saturday Review:**

"The images don't seem to leap off the screen and sit in your lap . . . instead, Cinerama gives a very satisfying **illusion** of space, a space that can extend back to the farthest limits of the eye and up to the very front of the proscenium. It has the further advantage of avoiding the peculiar flatness of image which has characterized all three-dimensional processes to date. These all create space, true, but the figures moving in that space seem flat, as if cut from cardboard. In Cinerama, by contrast, these figures appear to have body, thickness, 'roundness. And finally, the viewer doesn't need tinted or polaroid glasses. He sees the screen as in a normal theatre."[19]

The National Board of Review added:

"It is not only a new kind of movie . . . but a new kind of esthetic, psychological and emotional experience . . . The audience feels that it itself is in the roller coaster, helicopter, airplane . . . The two-hour program of action and scenery now being presented at the Broadway Theatre is an unprecedented, an enthralling, entertainment event. It is also an important event in the history of the evolution of the movies."[20]

Film Daily summed it up this way:

"The motion picture for the first time achieves a startling, even over-powering realism with its amazing screen illusion of both image and sound. The sophisticated first nighters, finding themselves very participants — or so it seemed — in the screen action, which spanned a wide variety of individual subjects, reacted with shrieks, cheers, applause."[21]

Hundreds of inches of copy on the Cinerama premiere appeared in newspapers and magazines and, by the middle of October, tickets for Cinerama were at a premium.

What exactly is Cinerama? How does it differ from the previous attempts at wide-angle and widescreen systems? The basic difference is that it used three cameras and three projectors to record a single image. The three 35mm cameras record three images simultaneously through three 27mm lenses — one of which faces straight ahead, another which looks slightly to the right and a third which looks slightly to the left. Although the film itself is regular 35mm film, each frame is "taller" than the normal film in that it has six sprocket holes per frame in contrast to the four holes on a normal frame.

When projected at 26 frames a second (the normal projection rate is 24), these images are blended together on a screen consisting of 1,110 vertical slats curved to an angle of about 165 degrees. The reels on the projectors hold 7,500 feet of film instead of the normal 2,000 feet. To keep the edges of the films blended together on the screen, a vibrating metal device called a "gigolo" is used and projectors are synchronized by a mechanism operated by a man located independent of the projection booth.

The six projectors are located in three separate booths — one on the left hand side provides the image for the right side of the screen; the right hand one provides the left screen image and the middle projector shoots its image straight ahead. It projects an image of 146 degrees wide and 55 degrees high. This gives the viewer the feeling of actually being involved in the screen image, rather than being just an observer. The screen measurements at the original Broadway Theatre in New York City were 51 feet wide and 25 feet high, but larger screens have been used in later engagements.

It was obvious that Cinerama was not intended for the ordinary theatre with standard projection equipment. Here was an invention which was to start a complete revolution in Hollywood and for film making in general. Cinerama was something "special" and was treated as a "roadshow." It was planned that only the "big" cities would have theatres to show the films and that one Cinerama film would run for years in some cities.

Despite the furor it created, Cinerama still had "bugs" to be worked out and was cruder than most people noticed at the premiere. The lines between the three films were irritatingly obvious; the separate pictures suffered from "jiggling" and people sitting at the sides of the theatre could not see the third screen properly. The Cinerama backers, however, assured the public and the press that all these defects would be ironed out almost immediately. Although some improvements had been made in the process, it remained basically the same after 10 years of exhibition.

It was not only the Cinerama picture that thrilled the spectator. Stereophonic sound had been employed to complete the illusion of reality and dimension. As Arthur Knight put it, ". . . the resulting improvement in sound quality is akin to the difference between an early Edison cylinder and a modern high fidelity recording . . ."[22] The sound was put on six sound tracks and reproduced from speakers located behind the screen as well as on the sides and back walls of the theatre.

CINERAMA OPENINGS

With its initial success, Cinerama quickly made deals to open the new technique in other large theatres throughout the country. The first deal was closed with the Palace Theatre in Chicago, but a projectionists' union struck for a minimum of 17 operators on duty at any one time during a Cinerama showing, but finally settled for 12 operators.[23] Because of this delay, Cinerama opened its second theatre at the Music Hall in Detroit to a huge advance sale and soon surpassed the all-time Detroit box-office record set by GONE WITH THE WIND.

Openings followed in Los Angeles, Chicago, Philadelphia and Pittsburgh, and soon every major city had a "Cinerama Theatre." Most of them toppled previous box office records for films in their respective cities.

Overseas installations of Cinerama equipment, which had now become more portable, made the process available in London, Osaka, Tokyo, Milan, Paris, Rome, Caracas, Marseilles and the Damascus Trade Fair, at which Cinerama almost caused a panic in an effort to obtain tickets.

THIS IS CINERAMA finally broke New York's all-time record for a film by cracking the record of the British film, THE RED SHOES, which ran 108 weeks at the Bijou Theatre several years earlier.

PRODUCTIONS

Now that the Cinerama theatres were settled for long runs, it was obvious that THIS IS CINERAMA could not run forever and that new productions must be made to replace that original film.

Many films were announced, several actually put into work, many costing an outlay of thousands of dollars, but none of them were completed. Among the contemplated productions were Lerner and Loewe's PAINT YOUR WAGON, BLOSSOM TIME, LAWRENCE OF ARABIA (later filmed in Panavision 70 by Columbia), JOSEPH AND HIS BRETHREN, THE CORONATION OF QUEEN ELIZABETH, a projected biography of the life of hunter MARTIN JOHNSON, CAN-CAN (later filmed by Twentieth Century-Fox in Todd-AO) and A FAREWELL TO ARMS (filmed later by Fox in CinemaScope, its own widescreen process).

Finally in October of 1953, over a year after the premiere of Cinerama, Louis de Rochemont, the documentary producer, was hired to produce an original idea for a Cinerama production to be

entitled THE THRILL OF YOUR LIFE, described as "a human drama with an unusual story line."[24] John Halas, the British cartoon producer, was signed to make a cartoon version of THE NIGHT BEFORE CHRISTMAS to be shown with the new feature.[25]

After much difficulty, THE THRILL OF YOUR LIFE became another travel film similar to THIS IS CINERAMA, except for the addition of a young couple selected to be the "stars" of the film and actually take the world-wide tour. The title was changed to CINERAMA HOLIDAY and was the second feature ready for Cinerama presentation. The Christmas cartoon was not completed in Cinerama.

THIS IS CINERAMA, after a record 2,165 showings, gave way on February 8, 1955, to CINERAMA HOLIDAY in New York and in several cases throughout the country, the second feature was more successful than the original. Most reviewers were happy with CINERAMA HOLIDAY, although **Variety** spoke for the entire industry when it said in its review: "Can (they) go on, indefinitely assured of reaping a boxoffice bonanza, without telling a story or going beyond the travel format? The danger of diminishing returns is not immediate, but the third offering, SEVEN WONDERS OF THE WORLD, is apparently lined up as more of the same."[26]

This third production, SEVEN WONDERS OF THE WORLD, originally was begun by John Ford and Merian C. Cooper, but abandoned after its initial planning while Cinerama signed with Warner Brothers to do a film version of the Lewis and Clark Expedition. The story was purchased from RKO for use at Warners. The unique part of the deal was that Warner Brothers would have the rights to release a CinemaScope version of the film after the Cinerama production had played all its theatres. The entire project, however, was never completed, and the third production became the aforementioned SEVEN WONDERS OF THE WORLD, taken over from Ford and Cooper by Lowell Thomas, and opened in New York on April 10, 1955.

By the time the fourth production, SEARCH FOR PARADISE, had opened, the five-year enthusiasm had somewhat abated. Although not the best Cinerama production, SEARCH FOR PARADISE had many thrills and was still packing them in at the box office. Again, **Variety** ended its review with: "The Cinerama medium shouts for that something different which tomorrow will demand. The prediction is not new. But its point jabs home more sharply this time — again because of the trip of David Niven and Cantinflas[27] recently took in another kind of widescreen medium."[28]

After a 31-week run in New York, SEARCH FOR PARADISE was pulled in favor of an eight-week return engagement of the original THIS IS CINERAMA. The management felt that many people had not seen the original — and a new generation was now old enough to see it.

After that return engagement, the fifth Cinerama production, CINERAMA SOUTH SEAS ADVENTURE, produced by Carl Dudley, opened. It was becoming apparent that Cinerama's popularity was on the decline. Cinerama theatres in Buffalo, Atlanta, Oklahoma City and Seattle were closed permanently and Dallas was running on weekends only. Foreign installations, however, were playing to large crowds, especially in Toronto, Vancouver, Havana and the Brussels World's Fair.

In 1960, Cinerama signed a contract with MGM to produce Cinerama films which later could be reduced to CinemaScope prints for showing in regular theatres. The first production, HOW THE WEST WAS WON, was followed by THE WONDERFUL WORLD OF THE BROTHERS GRIMM and both were successful at the box office, even though the conventional prints showed the two dividing lines separating the three films.

In search of product, Cinerama finally refined its process to make it compatible with other 70mm processes, while keeping its special deeply-curved screen. With this decision, the film companies were more eager to have their 70mm films in Cinerama theatres as "Cinerama presentations." Such diverse films as CIRCUS WORLD, THE GREATEST STORY EVER TOLD, and HALLE-LUJAH TRAIL started the trend toward "roadshowing" of regular 70mm films at Cinerama theatres. Although there was some distortion to horizontal lines when shown on the deeply-curved screen, the presentations were otherwise most satisfactory.

Whatever Cinerama's future might be, its past cannot be overlooked. It was Cinerama which started the widescreen revolution and re-interested the public in going to the movies again. It made stereophonic sound something which captured the public's fancy. It caused groups of people to drive as far as 300 miles to see Cinerama. It caused a boom in the tourist business, especially the places where Cinerama had filmed its productions.

President Hazard E. Reeves insists that "It is incorrect to conclude that Cinerama is a freak medium which can only be used to advantage in travel-type productions . . . Our experience in using

this process is still limited. Its potential values in enhancing the telling of a story, we feel, are still almost unlimited."[29]

CINEMIRACLE

When National Theatres president Elmer C. Rhoden announced his organization had developed a "seamless Cinerama" called Cinemiracle in 1955, there wasn't much of a flurry. Despite the fact that Cinemiracle was projected from one booth rather than three as in the case of Cinerama and that the new process virtually eliminated the "joining lines" between the films, there was still not much excitement. As Rhoden described the process:

"Cinemiracle . . . will permit simultaneous photography of three strips of film and their meshing or blending as if it were one continuous film with no joining lines."[30]

He stated that the camera would be be ready to roll within six months and the first film would be called CINEMIRACLE ADVENTURE. In August of 1957, the Cinemiracle camera was unveiled to the press although no footage was shown. In November of that year, the process was demonstrated and many experts felt that Cinemiracle was now equal to, and in several respects superior to, any photographic process that had yet been devised. It so impressed Jack L. Warner that he contracted with National Theatres to use Cinemiracle for the Warner production of THE MIRACLE but, as usual, the deal fell through and THE MIRACLE was filmed instead in Technirama.

The footage shown at the press showing, however, was not to appear in the final picture. At the special screening, there were shots of an auto rushing down the steep streets of San Francisco; a firetruck dashing through Philadelphia; the submerging of a submarine and some scenes filmed aboard a Norwegian naval ship.

Documentary producer Louis de Rochemont, who was earlier affiliated with a Cinerama production, was hired to guide the first Cinemiracle production, but when he saw the miscellaneous footage, he suddenly got the idea of doing the entire film on the Norwegian ship, the "Christian Radich," and soon the production was off and running under the title of WINDJAMMER.

The Roxy Theatre, (which was torn down in 1960), and Grauman's Chinese Theatre in New York and Los Angeles, respectively, were refurbished and redesigned (some seats were covered by curtains at the Roxy so that "periphery" seats would not be sold) for the grand opening of WINDJAMMER.

The world premiere at Grauman's on April 9, 1958, was a smash

hit. It opened soon after at the Roxy with rave reviews. Of the process, **Saturday Review's** Arthur Knight felt:

". . . this one actually succeeds. It is superior in its 'put you in the picture' effect because its wide, curving screen is proportionately higher than Cinerama's. Progress has also been made in circumventing the jiggling join lines, bane of the Cinerama people. The sound is seven-channel stereophonic, as in Cinerama, but mercifully achieving a maximum of hi-fi without splitting the eardrum."[31]

Variety agreed:

"This is a big, rounding, beautifully photographed picture, fresh and gay with the accent on youth and overwhelming in its pictorial impact on the huge screen. Here is one of those special attractions which will gain not only via the introduction of Cinemiracle, which certainly is impressive enough, but also because it has the kind of imagination and charm that will appeal to a very wide audience . . . Since it also looks like a million dollars and manages to come across as the biggest ever, it should clean up at the box-office everywhere."[32]

Since the Cinemiracle process was compatible in every way with Cinerama, the Cinerama theatres were soon showing WINDJAMMER and a merger took place, resulting in no more productions as of this date of Cinemiracle pictures.

THRILLARAMA AND WONDERAMA

Thrillarama, using two cameras and two projectors, had all the impact and all the faults of Cinerama, which outdid this latter-day process by one projector and one camera. The idea was developed by Albert H. Reynolds and the process is described thusly:

"Two regular conventional motion picture projectors are locked together and two films are projected simultaneously (with crossed beams) each covering one-half of the screen's surface. A special patented device dovetails the two scenes where they meet in the center of the screen. Another patented device is attached to the base of the projector for horizontal adjustments on the screen. Large film reels are used and there is a short intermission period in the middle of the program for the changeover. No alterations are needed in the regular (projection) booth. All needed booth attachments are supplied on a loan basis, by Thrillarama, Inc."[33]

Thrillarama, with its two 35mm films side by side, was about equal to Todd-AO's 70mm film.

After several delays, the first film, THRILLARAMA ADVEN-

TURE, opened in Houston, Texas on August 9, 1956, with many interested film persons attending. But despite some enthusiastic reviews, Thrillarama found itself faced with the same problems Cinerama had been trying to solve. Its "wrap-around" screen was fine, but the "seam" between the two pictures was readily apparent and the two Technicolor prints were not evenly matched as to color and intensity.

Louis Alexander, who reported the Thrillarama premiere for **Film Daily,** said that the process "lies somewhere between Todd-AO and Cinerama" and that "most of the first-night audience accepted it enthusiastically." Some of the visitors from the film industry were interested in the advantages of its low cost and mobility.

Variety felt the subjects in the film were "well chosen" but also was disconcerted about the "seam."[34]

After a week in Houston, Thrillarama closed because of mechanical troubles.[35]

In its Philadelphia bow, Thrillarama drew a neutral reception, according to **Film Daily.** "The two-projector process failed to prove as impressive as Cinerama," it said, "providing little sense of audience participation. The seam running down the center of the adjustable screen . . . proved to be a big distraction. There was a noticeable color difference in the two halves of the picture on the screen."[36] The sound and the musical score, however, were given praise.

Improvements in the process were announced and a second Thrillarama production was planned, but never undertaken.

Almost the same fate lay ahead for the Walter Reade-Sterling process, Wonderama. It was a process which was originally shot in 70mm, then split in half and the two halves of the picture put on different parts of a conventional frame of film. A complicated lens arrangement "re-constituted" the film into a widescreen image. After one or two successful engagements and a few unsuccessful ones, plus some less-than-promising reviews, the first Wonderama film, MEDITERRANEAN HOLIDAY, was released and shown as a Cinerama film in 1965.

KINOPANORAMA

Russia's version of the three-strip widescreen film presentation came to light in March of 1958 when its first film, GREAT IS MY COUNTRY (also called HOW BROAD IS MY COUNTRY and WIDE IS MY COUNTRY) was premiered in Moscow's Mir Theatre on a screen 107.7 feet wide by 37.7 feet high. There were 120

loudspeakers spotted all around the circular theatre, which was built especially for the presentation.

Included in the film were an airplane trip through the Caucasus Mountains, motorboat and electric train rides, and a dangerous trip down the rapids on a log raft. The last part of the film was devoted to the Sixth World Youth Festival in Moscow.

Although the film lacked the "thrill" gimmicks of Cinerama, it was not without its creative aspects, according to Irving R. Levine, NBC's Moscow correspondent:

"In showing the Winter Palace in Leningrad, now a state museum, the three segments of the screen suddenly switch from a single color picture to three panels of black and white. The center panel shows V. I. Lenin addressing a crowd. The side panels depict the Communist-inspired workers, peasants, and soldiers storming the gates of the Winter Palace in 1916 . . . Whatever the inadequacies of the Panoramic film — including such deficiencies as general over-exposure, resulting in washed-out colors, uneven exposure among the three panels of the curved screen and frequent visibility of the margins between the panels — it does provide the best trip on film to date through the USSR. It may well be that in the exchange of films that is to follow the recently concluded cultural agreement between the US and Russia, an exchange of a Cinerama film and this Panoramic film might provide an excellent beginning."[37]

Together with another film, THE ENCHANTED MIRROR, Kinopanorama was shown at the Mayfair Theatre (now the DeMille) in New York during the Russian Exhibit in the summer of 1959. Of THE ENCHANTED MIRROR, **Film Daily** said:

"Described as a 'fantasy-documentary,' the film utilizes animation and takes the theme of familiar fairy tales . . . In general it is a mixture of exciting and dull moments . . . Audiences with a yen to get a glimpse of Soviet life, even a one-sided one, may want to see it."[38]

Variety's quite frank review of GREAT IS MY COUNTRY found the production lacking in most respects, when compared to Cinerama.

"They may have been ahead with the sputniks. They're certainly behind when it comes to widescreen . . . Photographically (the film) contains some very exciting sequences . . . But the overall impact suffers from the inadequacy of the process . . . three panels are divided by very prominent matchlines and the images don't always match. There is a great deal of distortion on both sides, the side panels have a tendency to jiggle and blur, and objects on the screen

literally change directions as they reach one of the matchlines. Also, the color in the three panels (representing three separate strips of film) rarely matches so that a river will be blue on the left, almost black in the middle and a dirty gray on the right.

"The much-vaunted nine-channel stereophonic sound (Cinerama uses seven channels) adds little to this show. In fact, the male commentator is difficult to understand, which isn't much of a loss since the narration borders on the inane.

"Although the Kinopanorama process won the Grand Prize at the Brussels Fair, it remains a puzzle why the Soviets would present such a technically inferior product to Americans whom they are trying to impress with the very opposite. GREAT IS MY COUNTRY is hard on the eyes (particularly when the camera pans along a subject and tends to be static . . . It's a curiosity item because it was made in the Soviet Union."[39]

Another comparatively inexpensive "Cinerama type" projection system was announced early in 1956 by Leon Bronesky, head of Hi-Lux Tape Corporation. Whereas Cinerama, Cinemiracle and Panoramic use three cameras and projectors and Thrillarama uses two, the new and as yet unnamed process uses only one camera and one projector but two images on each film frame. Bronesky's technique is described as follows:

"The process employs a split-frame film projected through the two lenses onto the screen as two separate duplicate images which are joined on the screen without showing any break line . . . The film used is standard 35mm, separated on the same stock into two images each 17½mm wide."[40]

No films have ever been made in the process, but another new and radical process actually had demonstrations. Italy's Aviorama, invented by A. Moretti, "requires that one screen slightly tilted toward the viewer be placed in a hole in the floor. Another screen occupies a normal vertical position and a third screen, this one also tilted toward the viewer is fastened to the ceiling. Three projectors are needed to fill the three screens. When a spectator at the Aviorama theatre looks up, straight ahead or down, he sees part of a composite image that makes up an aerial view of Italian landmarks."[41] Aviorama, to put it plainly, was a vertical version of Cinerama.

QUADRAVISION

The Ford Motor Company developed a process called Quadravision which consisted of four projectors operating simultaneously

onto four embossed fabric screens, each screen equipped with its own speaker. Action may take place on all four screens at once or on individual screens, or move from one screen to another. Even dialog occurs on two screens at once without jumble. The first Quadravision production was a 12-minute color film, DESIGN FOR SUBURBAN LIVING, which was presented in a tent at shopping centers in the fall of 1959.

CIRCARAMA

Walt Disney's Circarama exhibit at the Brussels World Fair in 1958, under the sponsorship of Eastman Kodak, used 11 projectors. The spectator could watch any or all of the eleven moving panels, while the 19-minute film (in three languages) unfolded before him. There were no seats, but the audience rather strolled through the theatre at the back of the United States Pavilion.

The Circarama system is also on display at Disneyland where it attracts hundreds of thousands yearly. Although obviously not practical for conventional movie theatres, it is a delightful display gimmick and will probably be in use for many years to come.

Among the complex items used in the Circarama system were eleven 16mm cameras mounted in a special circular mount, four magnetic soundtracks on a single but separate 35mm magnetic film run in interlock with the projectors, eleven banks of loudspeakers (one beneath each projector), and eleven 8 x 11 ft. screens with six-inch frames between each screen.

The Soviet version of Circarama is exactly double the American version. The Russian process utilizes 22 projectors and 22 screens in two rows — one circle of screens above the other — with the top row of screens slightly smaller than the bottom row. The projectors in the Russian system were mounted "piggy back" to cover both top and bottom screens.

Film Daily reported that the United States Circarama had beautiful color and its 22-minute live-action trip through America was shown 26 times a day to a maximum of 550 persons per showing. On the other hand, the Soviet version showed only five times daily to audiences of 200.

The Soviet process ran only 13 minutes and opened with a cartoon, followed by a train trip through various sections of Russia, an air trip over Moscow and Leningrad featuring glimpses of Red Square on May Day and closed with another cartoon depicting rockets going off, fireworks, sputniks, etc.

While the competition went on between the American and Soviet

versions of Circarama, the thoughts of film scholars were turned back to 1896 and Cineorama. The multiple camera processes have seemingly come full circle.

At the 1964-65 World's Fair in New York, the unanimous "hit" of the many film presentations was Francis Thompson's TO BE ALIVE!, a three-film process on three screens which were separated by a foot or two of space, rather than lashed together as one unit. With this division, Thompson could juggle his images so that three identical items could be shown or three contrasting ones or even one idea flowing either left or right from one screen to the next. Accompanied by excellent stereophonic sound, a great deal more may be heard from this process.

[11] Gavin Lambert, "Report on New Dimensions," *Sight and Sound,* 22:157, April-June, 1953.

[12] "Are 3-D Movies Really New?," *Science Digest,* 33:26-28, May, 1953.

[13] *New York Times,* 70:2, Section 6, February 20, 1921.

[14] John D. Elms, *SMPE Journal,* 6:124-126, October, 1922.

[15] *Ibid.,* 12:353, April, 1928.

[16] *Films and Filming,* 7:11, October, 1960.

[17] Ralph Walker, "The Birth of an Idea," *"New Screen Techniques,* p. 116.

[18] *Associated Press,* October 1, 1952.

[19] Arthur Knight, *Saturday Review,* 35:40, October 4, 1952.

[20] National Board of Review of Motion Pictures, *Weekly Guide to Motion Pictures,* October 4, 1952.

[21] *Film Daily,* 102:1, December 31, 1952.

[22] Knight, *op. cit.*

[23] *Film Daily,* 103:6, Febrruary 11, 1953.

[24] *Film Daily,* 104:1, October 30, 1953.

[25] *Ibid.,* December 1, 1953.

[26] *Variety,* 197:10, February 9, 1955.

[27] Stars of the first Todd-AO film, *Around the World in 80 Days,* which took several Academy Awards in 1957.

[28] *Variety,* 208:6, September 24, 1957.

[29] *Film Daily,* 109:11, April 13, 1956.

[30] *Ibid.,* 107:1, June 24, 1955.

[31] Arthur Knight, *Saturday Review,* 41:29, April 19, 1958.

[32] *Variety,* 210:6, April 9, 1958.

[33] *Film Daily,* 110:1, August 13, 1956.

[34] *Variety,* 203:6, August 15, 1956.

[35] *Film Daily,* 110:2, August 15, 1956.

[36] *Ibid.,* 111:1, February 25, 1957.

[37] *Variety,* 201:1, March 12, 1958.

[38] *Film Daily,* 116:7, June 23, 1959.

[39] *Variety,* 215:7, July 1, 1959.

[40] *Film Daily,* 101:9, February 3, 1956.

[41] H. Sidney Newcomer, *New Screen Techniques,* pp. 195-196.

CHAPTER THREE
ANAMORPHIC LENSES

"Anamorphosis" is a process by which an image coming through the lens onto ordinary movie film **compresses** and distorts the image. In projection with the same type of anamorphic lens, the image is "spread out" to give the image more width than the ordinary motion picture image ratio of 1.33:1.

Sir David Brewster is credited with the discovery of the anamorphosis theory and the idea was patented in Britain as early as 1862. Prof. Ernst Abbe of the Zeiss Company in Germany filed an anamorphoser patent in 1898.

Ernst Zollinger of Italy used an anamorphic lens in 1910 to compress a motion picture vertically to half its size in order to permit the use of a two-color additive motion picture process. The two films were then expanded by another lens and super-imposed.[42]

In 1929 Dr. H. Sidney Newcomer announced an invention called "Anamorphosa" which would take as well as project a widescreen image with ordinary film. He exhibited the invention in New York in 1930, but the film industry was not interested, since it had decided against any widescreen projection while the studios were converting to sound films.

The late Prof. Henri Chretien, who had presented a paper on the ideas of anamorphosis as early as 1927, developed his "squeeze" lens in 1931 and in 1935, Paramount Pictures took an option on the system, shot 10 reels of tests, then decided against further development. In 1937, Prof. Chretien exhibited his widescreen system at the Paris Exhibition, but there still were no takers from the film industry.[43]

Jacques Flaud, director general of the Center National de la Cinematographie in France, told French producers in 1951 that they should start making films in the Chretien process, but his idea went unheeded. In 1954, he was quoted as saying that French producers again had "missed the boat."[44]

CINEMASCOPE

After the success of Cinerama, all the studios were alerted to the fact that there might be a future in widescreen films after all. On December 18, 1952, after seeing a demonstration of the Chretien system, Twentieth Century-Fox took an option on it and renamed it CinemaScope. The system, as stated above, had already been dropped by the French film industry, as well as J. Arthur Rank in England.

Some test footage was shot and the results were laudable enough to make Fox president Spyros Skouras announce that from then on all Twentieth Century-Fox films would be made in CinemaScope, beginning with THE ROBE.

The CinemaScope image was two and one-half times as wide as it was high (2.66:1) but with the addition of four-track magnetic stereophonic sound, that ratio was reduced to 2.55:1 to accommodate the sound tracks on the film. Theatres which did not have screens and stages wide enough to carry the full CinemaScope image sometimes carried as much of it as they could, which resulted in a character speaking "off camera" when in reality he should have been seen on the screen.

On September 16, 1953, THE ROBE opened at the Roxy Theatre in New York to enthusiastic acclaim by the public, if not the critics. Although the picture itself left much to be desired, the CinemaScope process was highly praised.

The National Board of Review noted: "What is shown on CinemaScope's widescreen is more lifelike, richer in detail and incident, than what has hitherto been shown on conventional screens in an aspect ratio of 1.33:1."[45]

Fox's "all out" attitude toward CinemaScope caused theatres to become wired for stereophonic sound and to have CinemaScope lenses installed. The second CinemaScope release, HOW TO MARRY A MILLIONAIRE, opened simultaneously in two Broadway theatres and was a hit in both. Soon the widescreen films came at a faster rate from Fox — BENEATH THE 12-MILE REEF, KING OF THE KHYBER RIFLES, HELL AND HIGH WATER, NEW FACES, NIGHT PEOPLE, PRINCE VALIANT, RIVER OF NO RETURN, THREE COINS IN THE FOUNTAIN, GARDEN OF EVIL and DEMETRIUS AND THE GLADIATORS, a sequel to THE ROBE.

Soon Metro-Goldwyn-Mayer, Allied Artists, Universal-International, Columbia, Walt Disney and United Artists announced

CinemaScope productions. The main holdouts were Warner Brothers, Paramount, RKO and Republic.

WARNERSCOPE

While Fox's CinemaScope was premiering in New York, Warner Brothers announced it had developed its own anamorphic system which was compatible with CinemaScope, called WarnerSuperScope, using lenses manufactured by Zeiss-Opton in Germany.[46]

In an industry which was trying desperately to standardize, the Warner Brothers announcement came as a shock.

WarnerSuperScope, in reality, was Vistarama, another anamorphic lens system, just as WarnerColor was Eastman Color and WarnerPhonic Sound was RCA stereophonic sound. Warners soon shortened the name to WarnerScope and announced that it was filming REAR GUARD in the new process, in addition to six other films. Since the Zeiss lenses did not arrive on time, Warners used the lenses of the Vistarama system. But the pressure from the industry finally forced the Warner Brothers studio to make the official announcement that it was abandoning WarnerScope and "going CinemaScope." Its already-completed REAR GUARD was changed to THE COMMAND and, with Fox's permission, released as a CinemaScope production. The public never knew the difference since the lenses were basically the same.

The second Warners CinemaScope film, LUCKY ME, followed soon after. Unlike Fox, Warners did not demand that stereophonic sound be used, which gave many theatres who could not afford installation of stereophonic sound a chance to show CinemaScope productions, which soon included A STAR IS BORN, THE HIGH AND THE MIGHTY, RING OF FEAR, BATTLE CRY, MR. ROBERTS and HELEN OF TROY.

THE RISE OF CINEMASCOPE

Twentieth Century Fox's multi-million dollar gamble with CinemaScope had paid off by the middle of 1954 when 75 films were announced as being filmed or recently completed in the CinemaScope process. All the companies with the exception of RKO, Paramount and Republic were making CinemaScope films. CinemaScope theatre installations with four-channel stereophonic sound was shooting toward the 5,000 mark. Fox's insistence on the special sound, however, was relaxed in May of 1954 and even more theatres converted to the system.

January of 1954 saw the top seven films in the monthly **Variety**

poll of top-grossing films as "new dimension films." Four were in CinemaScope, one in Cinerama and two in 3-D. By April the top five included Cinerama and four CinemaScope films.

Some of the pioneer CinemaScope pictures from the studios other than Twentieth Century-Fox and Warner Brothers included: KNIGHTS OF THE ROUND TABLE, ROSE-MARIE, BRIGA-DOON, SEVEN BRIDES FOR SEVEN BROTHERS and THE STUDENT PRINCE from Metro-Goldwyn-Mayer; THE BLACK SHIELD OF FALWORTH and SIGN OF THE PAGAN from Universal-International; THREE FOR THE SHOW and THE LONG GRAY LINE from Columbia; 20,000 LEAGUES UNDER THE SEA and LADY AND THE TRAMP from Walt Disney; SITTING BULL from United Artists; THE WARRIORS and THE BLACK PRINCE from Allied Artists and DER KOMMAN-DANT in Germany. The late Errol Flynn began THE STORY OF WILLIAM TELL in CinemaScope, but it was never completed.

To get more theatres to play the pictures, several companies began issuing standard versions of their CinemaScope films, usually shot at the same time as the widescreen version. These began appearing in June of 1954 with Warner's THE COMMAND and Fox's THE ROBE. Universal and United Artists also began releasing standard versions of their widescreen films.

By the middle of 1955, there were 20,682 theatres over the globe which could show CinemaScope films. Nearly every key theatre in the United States and Canada was equipped with the special lens, which was constantly being improved. Beginning with Fox's production of BROKEN LANCE and THE EGYPTIAN, the lenses were giving a much better defined screen image and these two films were lauded for their increased clarity and definition.

The standard CinemaScope ratio, which began in 1953 as 2.66:1, was shaved to 2.55:1 when magnetic sound was added and had settled at 2.35:1, which was considered about the maximum width most conventional theatres could project. Many theatres with small proscenium arches never have been able to project the anamor-phic image as wide as it was meant to be shown.

Another CinemaScope rule set down by Fox was that all films made with CinemaScope lenses must be filmed in color. To do anything else would be a retrogressive step, they announced. But in 1956, Fox relented by producing TEENAGE REBEL in black-and-white CinemaScope when they discovered that many serious dramatic films are much more effective without color. Fox also inaugurated a series of low-budget pictures in the same anamorphic

process, released under the trade name of "RegalScope." Soon other companies were making black-and-white CinemaScope films, among the most effective being A HATFUL OF RAIN and THE POWER AND THE PRIZE.

The third Fox standard, that of presenting all CinemaScope films from their company with four-track magnetic sound, soon became a compromise of "magoptical" print which could be shown on either a standard sound projector or one adapted for magnetic sound tracks.

The final indication that CinemaScope had "arrived" and had become the standard anamorphic system was the conversion of theatrical films into 16mm CinemaScope prints for showing in churches, schools and organizations. Many schools and libraries immediately adapted their projectors with an anamorphic lens and by 1957 were showing THE ROBE, THE HIGH AND THE MIGHTY, among others, during school recesses and at library film showings.

CINEMASCOPE 55

In order to get an even sharper image, Fox experimented with a larger negative, much as the Todd-AO group was doing. Fox came up with a 55mm negative in 1955 which would give each frame four times the negative area as the conventional 35mm film. Their idea was to film "super specials" in the 55mm process and show them on a special projector adapted to show the new width film. After much discussion, however, it was decided to reduce the large area negative onto standard 35mm film so no more conversion of theatre projectors would be required.

The first two very successful productions in CinemaScope 55 were the Rodgers and Hammerstein musicals, CAROUSEL and THE KING AND I, both of which were marked by extremely good color rendition and very sharp focus and depth. In 1961, Fox re-released THE KING AND I in large negative form for showing at the Rivoli Theatre in New York — the only time that CinemaScope 55 was shown in its original form.

Fox announced that CinemaScope 55 would be reserved for spectacular pictures, but when Todd-AO's production of SOUTH PACIFIC was released by Fox, the company decided that all future large-negative productions at their studio would be in Todd-AO, a non-anamorphic process.

With standardization in nearly every theatre in America, the regular 35mm CinemaScope was definitely the top widescreen process in the Hollywood era of new screen dimensions.

VISTARAMA

Another anamorphic system compatible with CinemaScope is Vistarama, promoted by Carl Dudley and developed by the Simpson Optical Company of Chicago. The first Vistarama demonstration in New York presented a short on Hawaii, ALOHA NUI, which was quite successful. **Variety** commented: "Reproduction on the widescreen had good definition, plenty of light and came through impressively even though in many scenes straight lines appeared slightly curved."[47] The last comment, of course, was brought about by the sudden showing of wide films on curved screens.

The first pictures announced in Vistarama were TOBOR and FESTIVAL IN SALZBURG (the first to combine anamorphosis with 3-D) and AROUND THE WORLD WITH JINX FALKEN-BERG.

Promoter Dudley is much franker about anamorphosis than Warners or Fox. He remarked that "CinemaScope, WarnerScope and Vistarama are all one in the same, each being merely a trade name for a squeeze-type motion picture employing anamorphic lenses . . . Any theatre equipped with any anamorphic lens can project any picture made under any of these trade names."[48]

TECHNISCOPE

Technicolor developed a razor-sharp anamorphic system which was comparable to the other widescreen processes and has been used successfully since 1964 in many feature films in the United States, as well as in England and on the continent.

SUPERSCOPE AND PANAVISION

Two different types of anamorphic lenses appeared in April of 1954 with resounding effect on the widescreen race. The two lenses — of the variable prismatic type — were SuperScope and Panavision.

SuperScope was invented by the Tushinsky Brothers of RKO Radio Pictures and premiered in New York with enthusiastic acclaim. The lens was capable of showing regular CinemaScope pictures as well as other films from an aspect ratio of 1.33:1 to 3:1 if necessary. Anamorphic prints were issued in two ranges — 1.875:1 (which can be shown from 1.75:1 to 2:1) and 2.15:1 (which can be shown from 2:1 to 2.25:1). The turn of a knob on the lens is all that is needed to change the aspect ratio.

The Panavision lens, invented by Robert E. Gottschalk, is similar to the SuperScope lens and is capable of the same variable aspect ratios. In both systems, however, the correct type of prints must be used or excessive distortion will result.

Some of the films shot or adapted for SuperScope projection at RKO were UNDERWATER!, SON OF SINBAD, SLIGHTLY SCARLET and TENNESSEE'S PARTNER, all of which could be shown with a CinemaScope lens at an aspect ratio of 2:1. Other SuperScope features included Allied Artists' THE RETURN OF JACK SLADE; United Artists' DESERT SANDS and VERA CRUZ; Mexico's EL SIETE LEGUAS and THE CHARGE OF THE RURALES, and adapted versions of two conventional films for re-issue, FANTASIA and HENRY V. In England, SuperScope was called RKO-Scope and was first used for Sol Lesser's TARZAN AND THE LOST SAFARI.

"SuperScope 235," with an aspect ratio of 2.35:1, standardized nearly all anamorphic systems at this ratio.

Panavision, however, became the more successful of the two systems and is still in use today, both as an anamorphic and a wide film process. Even Paramount, which had declined to make any films in an anamorphic process , finally adopted Panavision for its widescreen films in 1961 after a seven-year holdout.

SuperScope, along with many other early widescreen anamorphic systems, gradually disappeared in favor of CinemaScope. In the case of SuperScope, the demise of RKO studio helped the process to a quick end.

NATURAMA

Not to be confused with the 3-D system of the same title, Naturama was adopted by Republic Pictures for its big-budget (and later for small-budget) productions. The lens is a French anamorphic type called Cinepanoramic. The aspect ratio and end result were much the same as CinemaScope, except that Republic did not have to rent CinemaScope lenses from Fox.

The first production in Naturama was THE MAVERICK QUEEN and was technically very successful. **Variety** remarked that "As for Naturama, it is excellent and the 2.35:1 aspect ratio makes it adaptable to present squeeze lens projection installations in any theatre."[49] **Film Daily** found Naturama ". . . quite capable of transmitting to the screen a picture of fine resolution" and concluded that ". . . Hollywood's technical advancements in the new media progressed further with Naturama."[50]

Other Naturama productions from Republic, all filmed in Trucolor, include LISBON, SPOILERS OF THE FOREST, and a series of black-and-white low-budget films. Republic left the field of theatrical production in 1957.

PANOSCOPE

The only anamorphic lens system which was not compatible with CinemaScope and its family of lenses was Panoscope, developed by Goerz Optical Company. The system used a 2:1 aspect ratio, rather than the 2.55:1 used by the other processes, since it was felt that a 2:1 ratio would fit better onto most of the world's theatre screens.[51]

Paramount, which had been the most important holdout to CinemaScope, was reported interested in the Panoscope system, even though if adopted it would mean another couple of thousand dollars to the already financially-drained theatre owner. But Panoscope was soon forgotten when Paramount developed its VistaVision process in 1954.

OTHER AMERICAN SYSTEMS

Other compatible systems worthy of mention were Superama, used at the American-International studios for small-budget films such as MACHINE GUN KELLY and THE BONNIE PARKER STORY, and for amateur 16mm movie making; the Atlas anamorphic lens, and Walter Futter's Vidoscope lens.

FOREIGN COMPATIBLE SYSTEMS

As with any new and exciting invention, there were many other anamorphic lens systems such as the afore-mentioned Vistarama, which were nearly identical with CinemaScope and could be used interchangeably with it. By 1957, nearly every country had a variant on the anamorphic lens.

A Netherlands system, Vistascope, and Delrama, a Dutch system, were both compatible, the latter using a pair of anamorphic mirrors in the form of a periscope rather than actual lenses. It was developed by Albert Bouwers, who developed the X-Ray tube.

FRANCE

The French introduced Cinepanoramic in 1953. An invention of Prof. Ernst Abbe, a pioneer in anamorphic lens photography, the process was used for many French feature films, but was not as successful as its American counterpart (Naturama). Cinepanoramic was renamed Franscope and was first used in a 1956 film called

DIMANCHE, which won the all-nations prize at the Cannes Film Festival that year.

Another French anamorphic process, Dyaliscope, was first used for CE SOIR LES JUPONS VOLENT in 1956. **Variety,** in reviewing the Agfacolor film, said it was neither completely clear in definition nor too perfect in color rendition. But all these systems improved remarkably within a period of two years.

ITALY

Italy's anamorphic contribution was UltraScope and was used in THE LAST PARADISE (a sequel to THE LOST CONTINENT) and in two American shorts, ARABESQUES and FIESTA IN SEVILLE. A second Italian process, with the unwieldy name of Superfilmscope, was used in 1956 for a film called LE DICIOT-TENNI, produced by Carlo Ponti. Colorscope and Supercinescope were other trade names used for Italian motion pictures filmed in anamorphic processes.

SCANDINAVIA

Norway presented NorwayScope, which was an all-dimension projector which could project all film from 8mm to CinemaScope size by means of adjustable prisms. Sweden, via Aga Laboratories in Stockholm, came out with the AgaScope process which premiered in LOVE ALONG A RIVER which one critic compared in photographic clarity and color smoothness to CinemaScope 55! Arne Sucksdorff, the famed Swedish cinematographer (THE GREAT ADVENTURE) who had always filmed in black and white, made his first color film in Technicolor and AgaScope in 1958, EN DJUNGLESAGA, called THE FLUTE AND THE ARROW in English-speaking countries.

OTHER COUNTRIES

Two un-named anamorphic processes came from Switzerland and Russia. The Swiss presented THE TENTH OF MAY in their system, while the Russians did a large-scale production of DON QUIXOTE in Sovcolor and widescreen. American visitors to Russia said that the Russian process compared very favorably to the CinemaScope process. At its North American premiere at the 1958 Stratford (Ontario) Film Festival, DON QUIXOTE was well-received. It is believed that the process used was what is now called Sovscope.

Japan's systems, patterned directly after CinemaScope, were

called "Sharpscope," Tohoscope, DaieiScope and Nikkatuscope, the strange names coming from the studios which used them.

Mexico brought out its Mexiscope in 1957 with HER LAST MELODY (EL ULTIMO COUPLET). Germany's Sinoscope process was introduced in 1957 and Argentina's Alexscope appeared in the 1958 film, ROSURA A LAS DIEZ. East Germany calls its systems TotalScope and TotalVision.

The British used France's Cinepanoramic lenses under the title of CameraScope first in a 1955 film called YOU LUCKY PEOPLE. Another British group, Archway Film Distributors, developed a process known as CosmoScope and used it for the first time in FIVE GUINEAS A WEEK.[52] SpectaScope was a third trade name use for such releases as KONGA.

Under whatever name, the anamorphic lens had widened the screen's horizons in less than a decade in nearly every movie theatre in the world. Since the anamorphic films can be shown on conventional projectors, it has been an important factor in bringing inexpensive widescreen films to movie viewers everywhere.

[42] *Science Digest*, 33:27, May, 1953.
[43] *Time*, 61:71, June 8, 1953.
[44] *Film Daily*, 105:1, April 5, 1954.
[45] National Board of Review of Motion Pictures, *Weekly Guide to Motion Pictures*, October 3, 1953.
[46] *Variety*, 191·7, September 2, 1953.
[47] *Variety*, 192:7, September 9, 1953.
[48] *Independent Film Journal*, 32:19, September 5, 1953.
[49] *Variety*, 202:6, May 2, 1956.
[50] *Film Daily*, 109:1, April 20, 1956
[51] *Variety*, 192:4, September 16, 1953.
[52] *Film Daily*, 110:2, July 27, 1956.

CHAPTER FOUR
WIDE FILMS

Film stock other than the standard 35mm gauge has always been considered "experimental" until recent years when wide films finally won favor with film technicians and audiences alike. Since 1897 when the film Fitzsimmons-Corbett prize fight was shot on the wide Veriscope film, experiments have continued in the field of the wide film.

TRI-ERGON

In the middle of the 1920's the Germans introduced a 42mm film which gave a widescreen image and named it Tri-Ergon. They previewed the system in America at the Cameo Theatre in New York City and featured an outdoor feature film.[53] The Tri-Ergon film, however, aroused no more enthusiasm than Widescope or the curved screen had previously aroused and it, too, soon disappeared.

NATURAL VISION

The Essanay Studios, which had closed in 1916 to work on a new widescreen technique, finally announced the results of its seven-year research by presenting "Natural Vision."[54] The invention used a film 70mm wide (as opposed to the standard of 35mm) and was shown on a screen 70 feet wide by 34 feet high.

It was the work of George K. Spoor and P. John Berggren and was said to also give a stereoscopic effect, due to mechanical and optical "shutters" which "blinded" the film as it came through the projector. The screen was not only wider, but it also consisted of two screens — one transparent and one opaque — which made the image free from distortion no matter where it was viewed in the theatre.

The camera for Natural Vision was more than four times the size of the conventional camera in use in most studios at the time. The lenses were three inches apart and super-imposed two images on the one strip of film.[55]

During the three years of experimentation, the Spoor-Berggren Natural Vision system was developed to a point where RKO agreed to produce a film in the process. The production was DANGER LIGHTS with Jean Arthur and Robert Armstrong.

Mr. Spoor described the results himself in 1953:

"The Natural Vision picture DANGER LIGHTS opened November 1, 1930, at the State-Lake Theatre in Chicago to capacity business at $1.00 admission, filling the theatre five times daily for the entire month of November. It was then moved into the Mayfair Theatre in New York where it remained, also to capacity business, for seven weeks, starting December 1, also at $1.00 top . . ."

"The Motion Picture Producers Association, of which RKO had become a member during the filming of DANGER LIGHTS, called the management of RKO in and (said) that if they, RKO, expected to receive any pictures for its chain of theatres (some 450 houses) which Natural Vision could not supply at the time, that they, RKO, must disassociate themselves from all connection with Spoor and Natural Vision Pictures. They had no alternative. And consequently Natural Vision was without theatres to show in and likewise through. Laboratory equipment and projection machines for twelve theatres went into storage where it is now and where it will remain. If there ever was a commercial murder, this was it. And I was the victim at the hands of men, most of whom I put into the picture business."[56]

GRANDEUR

Somewhat the same fate befell the first re-appearance of 70mm film at Gramercy Studio of the Radio Corporation of America. The experiment was presented on a glass screen 30 feet high by 52 feet wide. As a witness described it:

"An ordinary sized motion picture was first projected . . . Then . . . this film was blacked out and the entire screen was suddenly filled with another picture, Gargantuan in size, with the life-like figures of a dozen chorus girls singing their songs, accompanied by an invisible orchestra. There was a spontaneous burst of applause from the audience.

"In the Niagara Falls picture, the stupendous sweep of Horseshoe Falls was shown. The great cascades seemed to splash out upon the studio floor . . . Objects appearing from the foreground to the back seemed to have a dimensional perspective."[57]

With this successful presentation, Fox purchased the rights to Natural Vision and improved the system, re-named it Grandeur and

premiered the new process at the Gaiety Theatre in New York City on September 17, 1929.

Included on the program was the Grandeur Newsreel including the original footage from Niagara Falls previously shown; a tennis match with Bill Tilden; a baseball game and glimpses of the Twentieth Century Limited, West Point cadet drill, the Tiller Dancers, Manhattan and a Long Island duck farm. After an intermission, a special Grandeur version of the FOX MOVIETONE FOLLIES OF 1929 was shown. This feature, however, did not fare so well as the newsreel since it was shot simultaneously with the standard version and not as a widescreen feature.

New York audiences were impressed with Grandeur but theatre owners, already in debt with having their theatres wired for sound, were not too receptive to the new wide film and wide screen. But Fox optimistically felt that within a year no important director would consider making a picture unless it was on wide film.[58] Their ads heralded that "Grandeur does for vision what Movietone does for sound."[59]

Fox began installing Grandeur equipment in their flagship house, the Roxy in New York City, in anticipation of complete acceptance by both the public and the theatres. The builders installed the 42 by 20 feet screen at night. The new type screen was made of finely woven cotton cloth knit together by a layer of adhesive. A thin layer of ground glass was spread on top.[60] The Grandeur sound track was three times as wide as on regular 35mm film and resulted in better modulation and more natural sound.

The second Grandeur feature, HAPPY DAYS, opened at the Roxy late in 1929, followed by THE BIG TRAIL in 1930.

But the Grandeur system failed to revolutionize the film industry, even though the General Theatres Equipment, Inc., announced that they had developed a projector which could project films of any width from 35mm to 70mm.[61] The fact that Grandeur required new projectors, new screens, new cameras, new printing machines, larger sets and increased lighting sealed its doom by 1931.

MAGNIFILM

Lorenzo del Riccio, whose Magnascope was a popular way of giving films a new size and dimension, introduced his 56mm Magnifilm under the sponsorship of Paramount Pictures. As Jesse Lasky remembers it:

"(del Riccio) was building a camera to use 56mm film. This would make it possible to project on a much wider screen in the theatre

without any loss of clarity. The picture quality would be better than with the Magnascope, which merely enlarged. With a slight alteration, existing projection equipment would accommodate film 56mm wide, but no wider. Del Riccio determined that his new frame should have a height-to-width ratio of 1 to 1.85 after going to the Metropolitan Museum of Art and making a statistical survey of what the old masters had found to be the most pleasing proportions for pictorial representation."[62]

The first film in the process, WE'RE IN THE NAVY NOW, was premiered at the Rivoli Theatre in New York City on July 18, 1929, on a screen 40 by 20 feet but was subsequently released only in 35mm to theatres. The basic advantage of the Magnifilm process was that 56mm film could be used in a regular 35mm projector. But despite this advantage, Magnifilm disappeared from Broadway quickly and prepared itself for a long rest on the shelf of the Paramount laboratory.

REALIFE

Metro-Goldwyn-Mayer's wide film bid was Realife, first used on King Vidor's BILLY THE KID in 1930. Differing from the other widescreen systems, Realife used standard sized 35mm film with a special lens enlarging the image on the screen. A special-sized film was used in taking the picture and this film was reduced optically on regular theatrical film. Only 10 theatres showed Realife film and it was soon withdrawn.

Despite the poor reception of Realife, director King Vidor was still enthusiastic:

"In one sequence in BILLY THE KID, we have a holdup scene in the foreground of the picture. By means of the depth illusion produced by the new wide screen, a rescue party is seen starting in the background, several miles away. The oncoming party does not know what is happening in front, but the audience observes every movement of both with more suspense than would be possible by any system of cut backs."[63]

After a second Realife film, GREAT MEADOW, in 1931, MGM abandoned the wide film system.

OTHER WIDE FILM SYSTEMS

Warner Brothers, like other major studios, made a widescreen bid with its 65mm wide film, used in KISMET in 1930 and THE LASH in 1931. Joseph Schenk photographed his 1930 production of THE

BAT WHISPERS in 65mm, but both systems failed to make a difference at the boxoffice.

Russia's Sergei Eisenstein, in his 1930 visit to Hollywood, suggested to the Academy of Motion Picture Arts and Sciences that the idea of an enlarged screen with extended action be seriously considered as a standard. But with the failure of four widescreen systems within a span of just over two years, Hollywood was not interested.

George Hill, a British film engineer, and Professor Alberini, an Italian inventor, worked on a widescreen system in 1928 composed of double 35mm frames of film running horizontally through the camera and projected in like fashion. The combination of lack of finances and the "wrong" time in film history discouraged perfection of the process. However, Hill did some scenes filmed in Picadilly Circus in the process. The same idea was resurrected in 1954 by Paramount as VistaVision.[64]

An English widescreen film was premiered in 1930 at the Regal Theatre in London under the name of "Giant Expanding Pictures." The inventor of the system was the projectionist at the Regal Theatre. But London, as well as the United States, feared the widescreen since it might upset the already confused theatremen — now confronted with sound films as well as a national depression.

So, by almost mutual consent, the widescreens and wide films were abandoned for the present until such time as they might be needed for added screen impact. It was Adolph Zukor of Paramount who, speaking for the Producers Association of America, assured England and America that they had "decided it would be folly to bring out the wide film and place additional burdens on the exhibitors. I can assure you that the producers of America have decided to delay the advent of the wide film until such time as it is necessary again to provide an attraction to the public."[65]

TODD-AO

For over two decades, wide film was completely dead. But the advent and quick popularity of Cinerama brought it to life again. Michael Todd, one of the original members of the Cinerama company, sold his stock and severed his connection with the company in March, 1953, and announced that he and the American Optical Company had joined forces to produce films by a new panoramic system using 65mm film, which was perfected by Dr. Brian O'Brien of the company. The process was named Todd-AO. The 65mm cameras used were the same ones which Lorenzo del

Riccio had developed at Paramount in the 1920's, but abandoned when Paramount and Warner Brothers were talking about a merger.

At a time when many widescreen systems were announced, this new method would not have ordinarily caused much excitement, were it not for the fact that Todd-AO had a million dollar commitment to film the Rodgers and Hammerstein hit, OKLAHO-MA, in the process. Rodgers and Hammerstein had previously turned down all offers to produce OKLAHOMA but were so impressed with the Todd-AO system that they finally gave their permission.

In addition to Todd, Rodgers and Hammerstein, the new producing company unit also included Joseph Schenk (who had used 65mm film in 1930), George P. Skouras, Arthur Hornblow, Jr., Lee Shubert, Edward Small and later Fred Zinnemann.

Like Cinerama, Todd-AO film would be shown only in especially-equipped theatres since the 65mm film required special projectors. The screen is composed of a plastic fabric with aluminum squares which were supposed to reflect more light than screens used in other widescreen systems.[66] Todd himself predicted that the new 65mm film would eventually replace the regular 35mm films which had been standard since the early days of motion pictures.[67]

The Magna Theatre Corporation came into partnership with Todd by view of the extra financing it offered. OKLAHOMA finally went into production in July, 1954, at MGM studios with a budget of four million dollars. The nation saw its release in 1955.

OKLAHOMA was a smash hit. The sound was exciting to hear, the opening scene of the "corn as high as an elephant's eye" giving way to a clear blue sky in an almost faultless print was breathtaking to behold. Todd considered it a "show" and not just a "movie." He even refused to let popcorn be sold at any Todd-AO presentation of the film.

The gamble had apparently paid off. Even the special projectors required for the process could also be used for other types of film presentations with just slight conversions. This amazing projector could show CinemaScope, Todd-AO and any other 70mm film at either 24 or 30 frames per second with up to seven sound tracks, either magnetic or optical. The only type of film it could not project was, of course, Cinerama.

OKLAHOMA was shown on a "road show" basis with usually eight or ten showings a week at raised admission prices. After the success of the first openings in the large American cities, a short subject called THE MIRACLE OF TODD-AO was added to the

program. It included a roller coaster ride similar to the one in Cinerama, a plane flight, skiing at Sun Valley, a fast motorcycle ride through the San Francisco hills and Pope John XXIII's coronation.

After a year of showings, OKLAHOMA was "printed down" into CinemaScope form and shown at smaller theatres as a regular film at regular admission prices.

But OKLAHOMA was to be topped by the biggest show of them all, Todd's own production of the Jules Verne novel, AROUND THE WORLD IN 80 DAYS, which replaced OKLAHOMA as the second production at Todd-AO theatres late in 1956. It proved to be a stunning, star-studded satire, beautifully photographed and blessed with a theme song by Victor Young which swept the nation. Fifty stars played cameo roles in the film. At Academy Award time, it garnered its share of Oscars, including the award for the "best picture of the year."

With the success of his first two films, Todd went back to work on a version of WAR AND PEACE, but Paramount already had the edge and owing to some trouble with the use of Yugoslavian troops in the projected film version, Todd abandoned the project and turned to his next production, DON QUIXOTE, while Twentieth Century-Fox began filming their second Rodgers and Hammerstein vehicle in Todd-AO, SOUTH PACIFIC. Just as SOUTH PACIFIC was replacing AROUND THE WORLD IN 80 DAYS in Todd-AO theatres, Mike Todd was killed in an airplane crash in New Mexico. DON QUIXOTE was dropped and SOUTH PACIFIC opened to a mixed press reaction.

The process which bears his name, however, continues. Some in the film industry predict it will eventually become a standard film process. For clarity and beauty, it is difficult to surpass. Universal-International's THIS EARTH IS MINE was scheduled for the Todd-AO treatment in 1958, but the plan was abandoned and CinemaScope was used instead. However, Sam Goldwyn's PORGY AND BESS, Fox's CAN-CAN and United Artists' THE ALAMO all were completed in the Todd-AO process.

When Twentieth Century-Fox purchased the major stock in the Magna Theatre Corporation which controlled the Todd-AO process, it began shooting its "blockbusters" in the system. Of the scheduled films announced for Todd-AO shooting, only CLEOPATRA and THE SOUND OF MUSIC finally utilized the process, but other films followed, including THOSE MAGNIFICENT MEN IN THEIR FLYING MACHINES, THE AGONY AND THE ECSTASY, and THE SAND PEBBLES.

Michael Todd, Jr., developed Todd 70, a refinement of Todd-AO film for his SCENT OF MYSTERY (see AVANT GARDE). Todd 70 is actually the same as Todd-AO and was used under that credit line only in the one film.

GLAMORAMA AND SUPERAMA

Douglas Leigh, previously known as the creator of spectacular Broadway advertising displays, entered the widescreen race in 1953 with Glamorama and Superama.

Glamorama could be projected from the orchestra pit of the theatre, Leigh claimed. The system would be of the "road show" variety like Cinerama. The images were taken vertically in the camera, but each image took up about two and one-half normal frames. A special lens "turned" the vertical image into a horizontal one and projected it on the wide screen.[68] After making several major changes, such as running the film horizontally and discarding the special lens, Paramount perfected the system and brought it to the public as VistaVision.

Superama, on the other hand, could be used in any aspect ratio from 1.66:1 to 2.66:1. Superama lenses were used on the Paramount lot for test shots, but Superama was soon dropped in favor of the revamped VistaVision. The company, however, is said to hold the rights to both systems. Superama, as an anamorphic system, re-appeared in 1958 in low-budget films for American International.

VISTAVISION

The Glamorama concept of motion picture film being exposed **horizontally** rather than vertically came to full fruition as VistaVision. With Paramount as the major holdout against CinemaScope, VistaVision was their answer. They decided that the CinemaScope aspect ratio of 2.66:1 was too long and narrow and looked as though the film was being projected through a mail slot. Paramount preferred the "golden ratio" (also approved by Arch Obler, Lorenzo del Riccio and others) of 1.85:1, which provided "head room" and still gave the picture a new scope and dimension.

The VistaVision system is described as follows:

"VistaVision is a process of photography in the studio by which a wider image is photographed **on the film negative.** This is accomplished by running the negative film through the camera horizontally and producing a photographic image the width of 8 sprocket holes, or about double the width possible if the film were run through the camera vertically, as has been done on every picture

made up to the advent of VistaVision. In producing positive prints
. . . the image that has been photographed twice as wide as normal,
is processed so that it is reduced in size and appears on the positive
print in the usual position.

". . . Its wide negative image can also be used more easily than
conventionally photographed subjects, to produce positive films in
anamorphic or 'squeezed' form."[69]

As the first serious competitor to CinemaScope, it premiered at
the Radio City Music Hall April 27, 1954, with WHITE
CHRISTMAS. After its early morning premiere, the reaction was
nothing short of enthusiastic. The film was shown on a screen 30 by
55 feet.

"This VistaVision process must be good," one exhibitor remarked.
"I like it, even on an empty stomach. And that's a pretty severe
test."[70] Within a month, several pictures were shooting with the
system, including THREE RING CIRCUS, STRATEGIC AIR
COMMAND, THE GIRL RUSH, THE ROSE TATOO, Cecil B.
DeMille's THE TEN COMMANDMENTS, TO CATCH A
THIEF, WE'RE NO ANGELS and RUN FOR COVER.

Loren L. Ryder, head of engineering and recording at Paramount,
laid down four reasons why VistaVision would be good for any
theatre, large or small:

1. VistaVision can be shown in any aspect ratio from 1.33:1 to
   2:1.
2. VistaVision does not require the purchase of any additional
equipment.
3. VistaVision will not reduce the seating capacity of any
theatre.
4. VistaVision will permit the patrons to see more and gain more
enjoyment.[71]

VistaVision pictures are shot in a "loose" aspect ratio of 1.66:1 so
they can be shown at 1.75:1, 1.85:1 (the recommended aperture) and
as wide as 2:1. At one time, Paramount planned to present "non-
compatible" anamorphic prints to be shown at the 1.85:1 ratio.

In some theatres, such as the New York Paramount, early
VistaVision films were shown "horizontally" to give a truly bright
and clear picture. But most presentations have always been in a
"printed down" 35mm version. Barney Balaban of Paramount
called the horizontal projection method "the Tiffany of projection
methods."

The critics liked the system. **Variety** said it "has an impressive

vastness with color clarity and sharp definition that adds greatly to the visual quality of the production."[72] The **Independent Film Journal** said the system "possesses a clarity of color and definition that is extremely impressive."[73]

When the second VistaVision film, STRATEGIC AIR COMMAND, premiered at the refurbished New York Paramount (selected as the VistaVision "flagship") the success of the process was assured. Again shown "horizontally," STRATEGIC AIR COMMAND had aerial scenes which were breathtaking and the sharpness of the image was much clearer than in CinemaScope or a conventional 35mm film.

Even when VistaVision got to the smaller theatres and was shown in the conventional manner, there was still a marked gain in clarity of the image and the process was heralded as "motion picture high fidelity." By the time the monumental Paramount productions, WAR AND PEACE and THE TEN COMMANDMENTS were released, VistaVision had gone beyond the walls of Paramount Studios and was being used at Warner Brothers for THE SEARCHERS (called by some critics "the best VistaVision production to date"); at MGM for HIGH SOCIETY; at United Artists for Stanley Kramer's THE PRIDE AND THE PASSION, and at Universal-International in AWAY ALL BOATS, in addition to the adoption of the process by J. Arthur Rank in England.

VistaVision won an Oscar for its developers and also the "best color cinematography" award for TO CATCH A THIEF in 1956.

Unlike the other widescreen processes, VistaVision shied away from magnetic sound. It uses only PerspectaSound employing a single optical track on the side of the film. This sound process also was adopted by MGM.

With its simplicity of operation and clarity of image, VistaVision ranked as one of the finer developments in the wide film era. However, with the perfection of the Panavision process, Paramount withdrew the VistaVision system in 1961 with ONE EYED JACKS being the last major production in the process.

PANAVISION

Robert E. Gottschalk's Panavision lenses and 65mm film were decided upon for MGM's new widescreen system early in 1955. Under tests made by Douglas Shearer, the 65mm negative was printed onto a 35mm positive print and revealed a print free of distortion and with a much better definition. It was made clear that

MGM was not going to clutter the field with another film size, but merely to make better 35mm prints for theatrical distribution, whether standard or CinemaScope films. The 65mm film was first used by MGM in 1930 for BILLY THE KID.

As its first 65mm production, MGM chose RAINTREE COUNTY in 1958, followed by a remake of a 1926 silent film, BEN-HUR. Independent Panavision productions (called Panavision 70 when shown with the original negative) included THE BIG FISHERMAN and THE UNFORGIVEN.

Today, Panavision lenses are used at several of the major studios for many of their anamorphic films, as well as special 70mm productions, including EXODUS, MUTINY ON THE BOUNTY, HAWAII and many Cinerama productions.

TECHNIRAMA

An anamorphic process of a different sort which uses wide film is Technirama, developed by the Technicolor Company from a Dutch process. The film was first used for the 1957 Universal-International releases, ESCAPADE IN JAPAN (filmed by RKO) and NIGHT PASSAGE. William E. Snyder, director of photography for ESCAPADE IN JAPAN, described the process as:

"Basic to the system is a mirror-prism anamorphic lens which squeezes the image 50 per cent in shooting, as against CinemaScope's 100 per cent. An additional squeeze of 50 per cent is accomplished in printing. The positive prints can be projected in any of the various ratios."[74]

Technirama is photographed on a double-width negative and the process is noted for its very sharp image and depth of focus and is especially good in outdoor films. Other pioneer Technirama films include SAYONARA, THE MONTE CARLO STORY, LEGEND OF THE LOST, THE TRIALS OF OSCAR WILDE (later retitled THE GREEN CARNATION), THE SAVAGE INNOCENTS, and THIS ANGRY AGE, among others.

The versatility of the process and its large negative photography is that it can present standard, anamorphic or "road show" widescreen prints all from one original negative. This gives Technirama the same stature as VistaVision, Todd-AO and Panavision.

But it is as a 70mm original negative process which gave Technirama its largest share of fame. With the advent of the wide films, "Technirama 70" was perfected for such special productions as SPARTACUS, SLEEPING BEAUTY, SOLOMON AND

SHEBA, EL CID, KING OF KINGS, BLACK TIGHTS, BARABBAS, LAWRENCE OF ARABIA and SODOM AND GOMORRAH.

Film Daily describes the process in a review of SLEEPING BEAUTY as:

"a process which travels (the) negative through the camera horizontally, exposing two frames at a time, instead of one, thus catching twice as much detail and depth as the standard camera . . . A pan-micro Pantar anamorphic printer lens was used in connection with preparing the print."[75]

The results of Technirama are easily noticeable when a regular CinemaScope or conventional print is shown on the same program. The depth of focus and clarity of the image is superb in the large Technirama 70 negative. It is difficult to beat when it comes to overpowering screen special effects.

Perhaps **Variety's** reviewer, "Holl," sums it up best in his comments on Technirama's THE BIG COUNTRY:

"This is one of the best photography jobs of the year and compares with anything that has been accomplished with Cinerama, Todd-AO or Cinemiracle."[76]

OTHER WIDE FILM SYSTEMS

An un-named process using 42mm film has been demonstrated in New York City which is said to give a "Cinerama effect" on a screen 44 feet wide and about 20 feet high. The process uses a wide film with a split image and is projected through prisms in an aspect ratio up to 3:1.[77]

Carl Dudley announced in 1955 a "Super Vistarama" process which would be similar to CinemaScope 55 in that a wide negative would be used (in this case 65mm film) and modified Vistarama lenses.[78]

Frank Caldwell's version of "Super VistaVision" called Cyclotrona, was first shown in 1955 and emerged again in 1958 as "Cinema 160," named after the degree of image shown on the screen. Utilizing a horizontal negative such as that used by VistaVision and Technirama, Cinema 160 exposed three frames at one time, as compared to two frames for VistaVision and Technirama. The result is said to have an optical range of 160 degrees, which is 14 degrees wider than Cinerama.[79]

Abel Gance's Magirama is a new concept by the developer of the triptych screen and is projected on a screen 90 feet in length.[80] No feature films have as yet appeared in this system.

A widescreen process which claims to give the effect of Cinerama without the dividing lines by merely attaching a lens-prism device to the projection has been premiered in England with encouraging results. Using film shot in Technirama 70 and color — BLACK TIGHTS — the process, called ARC-120, is yet to be seen commercially.

THE WIDESCREEN IMAGE

Since 1960, film sizes have become standardized at 8mm for home movies, 16mm for educational films, 35mm for theatrical releases and 70mm for "roadshow" presentations. Yet this standardization did not come easily or quickly. Over the years, there have been nearly 25 different widths, most of them now obsolete. Only the four sizes named above still exist in any abundance.

Some of these film sizes are reviewed below:

8mm — A substandard size consisting of a 16mm film split down the center and used by amateur movie makers for their home movies. A new Super 8mm film, introduced in 1965, now features 50 per cent more information per frame by reducing the size of the sprocket holes at the side of the film.

9.5mm — A substandard size used for Pathex amateur movies in Europe. The film had a single sprocket hole at the top and bottom of each frame, rather than on the sides of the film.

15mm — Used by Chrono de Poche Gaumont camera, this film had a single row of perforations down the center of the film.

16mm — The standard size used by professional cinematographers for non-theatrical films and by advanced amateurs for home movies. Regular theatrical films made in 35mm are optically reduced for 16mm showings in churches, schools and other institutions. In some art theatres, the 16mm projector shares space with the regular 35mm projectors for showing special films not readily available in 35mm.

17.5mm — Pathe-Rural substandard size formerly used in Europe. Also called "split 35mm." Still in use in some film laboratories, although now obsolete in most countries.

19mm — At one time the proposed standard in France on which the picture image would be 16mm size and the sound track would be enlarged to the width of the sound track on a 35mm film.

20mm — Once proposed as the American standard with the same specifications as the 19mm film.

21mm — Size of the Mirographe film which had notches along the sides of the film rather than perforations.

22mm — Edison's "Home Kinetoscope" movie camera used this size. The film consisted of three rows of pictures, each slightly less than 8mm wide. The middle row was upside down, allowing the film to be projected as three strips of film, one after the other.

26mm — The size of the Pathescope film developed by Pathe Freres in 1912.

28mm — The size in Canada and Europe until around 1937.

32mm — Also known as "Double 16," this film has twice as many sprocket holes along the side of the film as 35mm. When the film is split down the middle, two regular strips of 16mm sound film are formed. Used mostly for a more economical 16mm processing.

35mm — The standard film gauge used all over the world for theatrical exhibition. The 35mm film has been standard since about 1900.

38mm — Another theatrical film size used in the pre-1900 days before standardization in Europe.

42mm — An early film size called Tri-Ergon used in Germany for experimental sound and widescreen productions.

48mm — Another size of film used in pre-1900 Europe before standardization took effect.

55mm — A size experimented with by Twentieth Century-Fox before the adoption of CinemaScope. Also used for "roadshow" versions of two of Fox's early "CinemaScope 55" presentations.

56mm — A size once used for a process called Magnifilm developed for the Famous Players-Lasky (later Paramount).

60mm — A film size used in the Demeny Chronophotographe motion picture camera, developed in 1893, but rendered obsolete when 35mm film became the standard.

63mm — A size used by "Natural Vision," a process developed by the Essanay Corporation.

65mm — First used by Paramount and later by Warner Brothers, it was adopted in 1942 for the Thomascolor process and resurrected again in 1957 for MGM's "Camera 65."

70mm — The largest film size used commercially was first developed for the early Mutograph camera, then again in 1929 as Fox's Grandeur Film and much later as the base for Todd-AO, Super Technirama, Panavision 70 and other "roadshow" presentations.

It is not difficult to see that it was only because Thomas A. Edison was producing more movies than anyone else that 35mm was adopted as the standard. It might have been otherwise had the

Lumiere Brothers or someone in another country been producing the largest number of films.

The same applies to the aspect ratios used for projecting movies on the screen. The 35mm image sets the screen size at 1.33:1, or three times high to four times wide. This was kept as standard until the widescreen revolution of 1953, when every conceivable manner of making films look wider was attempted. Some of these included the Bolex Stereo System (Triorama) which had its image ratio as 1:1.33, or higher than it was wide, but this was limited to only one theatrical showing and was otherwise used only for home movies.

Other aspect ratios have been—

1.37:1 — The smallest ratio set for MGM's Variscope system which could expand to 2.66:1.

1.66:1 — The ratio recommended by Paramount and Republic, consisting of "cropping" the images 10 per cent on the top and bottom of the film frame. Also used as the ratio for many films not prepared for widescreen presentation to give them a widescreen effect (and chopping off some heads in the process).

1.75:1 — Presumably the widest possible ratio for showing conventional films without changes in the mode of shooting. Used by MGM for many of its 1953 and 1954 films, including a re-issue of GONE WITH THE WIND.

1.85:1 — The "Golden Ratio" recommended by Paramount for its VistaVision system and also used by Universal's THUNDER BAY, as well as by the Superama, Columbia and Vistascope processes.

2:1 — Achieved by shooting a film through guide lines while otherwise photographing the scene conventionally. Now used to shoot almost all conventional films so they can be shown at either 1:33 or at any succeeding widescreen aspect ratio up to 2:1. It is also the ratio used for the 70mm Todd-AO process.

2.17:1 — Ratio used by the Naturescope process.

2.25:1 — Ratio used by Glamorama, which later developed into VistaVision.

2.3:1 — The ratio for CinemaScope pictures which used a regular optical film sound track.

2.44:1 — The ratio of a system named Stereocolor.

2.5:1 — The ratio used for Cinepanoramic and Sonoptic processes as well as 16mm CinemaScope.

2.55:1 — The standard ratio for CinemaScope and Vistarama.

2.66:1 — The original ratio for anamorphic widescreen films

before the addition of four magnetic sound tracks on the film. Also used for Superama in its largest ratio.

2.85:1 — The ratio of Cinerama and other 70mm productions in Super Panavision, Super Technirama, etc.

3:1 — This ratio is said to be coming soon as the new standard for several processes still being developed in the laboratories.

And the future? Anything is possible.

[53] *New York Times,* 78:34, September 18, 1929.

[54] Not to be confused with the Natural Vision third-dimensional process of M. L. Gunzburg.

[55] *New York Times,* 72:4, Section 7, September 9, 1923.

[56] *Image,* 5:184, October, 1956.

[57] *New York Times,* 78:16, May 25, 1929.

[58] *Ibid.,* 79:7, Section 9, September 22, 1929.

[59] *Ibid.,* 78:34, September 18, 1929.

[60] *Ibid.,* 79:5, Section 9, February 16, 1930.

[61] *Ibid.,* 80:26, May 16, 1931.

[62] Lasky, op. cit., p. 183.

[63] *New York Times,* 80:5, Section 9, October 19, 1930.

[64] Christopher Brunel, "Widescreens, Etc., in Britain," *Films in Review,* 5:418, October, 1954.

[65] *New York Times,* 79:5, Section 9, June 8, 1930.

[66] *Variety,* 190:1, March 25, 1953.

[67] *Ibid.,* 190:29, April 1, 1953.

[68] *Variety,* 191:18, June 10, 1953.

[69] *Film Daily,* 105:6, April 9, 1954.

[70] *Variety,* 194:3, April 28, 1954.

[71] *Independent Film Journal,* 33:25, March 20, 1954.

[72] *Variety,* 195:6, September 1, 1954.

[73] *Independent Film Journal,* 34:10, September 4, 1954.

[74] *Independent Film Journal,* 35:12, April 30, 1955.

[75] *Film Daily,* 106:5, November 26, 115:6, January 16, 1959.

[76] *Variety,* 211:6, August 13, 1958.

[77] *Film Daily,* 106:5, November 26, 1954.

[78] *Independent Film Journal,* 35:12, April 30, 1955.

[79] *Film Daily,* 113:2, April 21, 1958.

[80] *Film and Filming,* 3:17, February, 1957.

PART THREE — DEPTH

"I've been spat at and thrown at
And I've ducked evil passes;
But they wouldn't dare hit me
While I'm wearing glasses."
— Leonard Spinrad

CHAPTER ONE
THE THIRD DIMENSION

Acclaimed as a "new" dimension in 1952, stereoscopic motion pictures, like color and sound, have been with the film in some form almost since its inception.

Of course, third dimension can be traced back to about 550 B. C. where Egyptian and Greek works of art show the use of "interposition" to get the effect of depth and perspective.[1] Euclid presented a definition of stereoscopy as early as 280 B. C.

The Fantascope, invented by Robertson in 1799, was a projector on wheels which, when moved toward or away from the screen with continuous refocusing, gave the impression of an approaching or receding figure.[2]

In the 19th century, two Viennese pioneers had animated a three-dimensional image of an athlete performing a high jump. In 1877, M. Raynaud presented his Theatre Optique[3], which featured three-dimensional figures.

Before the movies were invented, grandmother's stereoptican, which showed two pictures side-by-side as one picture in third dimension when viewed through a viewer with two lenses, was proof that this invention was not new. Some of these various stereoscopic inventions were the products of Sir Charles Wheatstone, Sir David Brewster and Oliver Wendell Holmes!

In England in 1858, J. Ch. D'Almeida developed three-dimensional lantern slides which were given to the French Academy of Science after his death.

DIMENSIONS IN THE MOVIES

There are four ways of taking true stereoscopic films: (a) using two cameras; (b) using one camera with two lenses; (c) using optical devices such as mirrors and prisms on the camera lens, and (d) using a camera which takes alternate pictures in which the medial lines are not on the same planes.

William Friese-Greene, the British motion picture pioneer, patented a third-dimensional movie process before 1900. He used two films projected side-by-side on the screen. The viewer had to use an actual stereoptican to see the depth, which made it impractical at that time for theatrical use.

Frederic Eugene Ives invented a 35mm two-film stereo movie camera in 1900. The fixed center lenses were one and three-fourths inches apart and were coupled together.[4] In 1903, stereoscopic movies were shown at the Paris Exposition under the guidance of French movie pioneers, Auguste and Louis Lumiere.

A. Manuelli, an Italian, obtained a French patent in 1908 for a sound camera whose pictures produced a stereoscopic effect. The machine used three separate films.[5] Jean Zafiropulo developed a 3-D film using the lenticular principle around the same period.

In England around 1909, Friese-Greene introduced a color film which gave a third-dimensional effect. These pictures, however, never got past the experimental stage.[6]

In the 1920's, extra film supplements were used to get novel dimension effects. For FIREMAN SAVE MY CHILD at the Eastman Theatre in Rochester, a special film showing flames was shown on the white velvet curtain before the feature began. During the titles, a special cartoon of Wallace Beery and Raymond Hatton was shown as they seemingly fell downward from floor to floor of a tall, flame-filled building. This type of dimension was prevalent at some "class" movie theatres in the 1920's.

THE ANAGLYPH SYSTEMS

Although an Irishman named P. A. Powers reported a "new technique" in 1918 in which a film had a stereoscopic effect requiring only a small lens in the projector and no red-and-green glasses, most of the systems of the twenties were of the "red-and-green" variety.

In 1921, both Vienna and America were showing successful third-dimensional films. Jacob Leventhal, the pioneer stereographer, introduced Plastigrams to the movie world, with the aid of G. W. (Billy) Bitzer, D. W. Griffith's cameraman. These Plastigrams were shown for nearly three years thereafter before their popularity diminished. The premiere was held at the Cameo Theatre in New York and the consensus of opinion was that the public would never consent to look through viewers in order to see depth in a movie.[7] The Plastigram system used the "anaglyph" method in which the two images are photographed and projected through different color

filters — usually one in red and the other in green. Both images were on one strip of film. When the eye looks through the corresponding colors in the viewer, the images separate and the one eye sees only red images and the other eye, green ones.

According to Leventhal:

"The introduction of pictures of this type was beset with many difficulties, one of which was the handling of the spectacles in conjunction with the film. The physical handling and selling of motion pictures is a rock-ribbed affair and hard to dent. Here was a type of film that meant a departure from routine in every department, from the home office of the national distributor down to the porters that clean the theatre. It was obvious at the beginning that if the exhibitors were to accept this kind of picture, it would be necessary to emphasize the spectacular side and make scenes that would startle the audience, rather than views of streets and scenery . . . Some improvements being made in this system will eliminate most of the trouble, and then we may hope to see stereoscopic pictures shown very often, but they will probably never be shown without viewing apparatus of some kind. Therefore, they can never occupy more than a few minutes on a program."[8]

Another of the anaglyph red-and-green systems was Plasticon, which was perfected by William van Doren Kelley. The camera was a converted color camera and used prisms to get the two images on the same film. Plasticon was premiered at the Rivoli Theatre in New York in December of 1922, the same time as Plastigrams. The Plasticon film was a short subject featuring scenes of New York City and a gimmick film in which dual images were put on a single print. By looking through the red glass, the viewer saw a different scene from the one he saw when looking through the green side. The viewer himself could decide whether he wanted a happy or an unhappy ending to the film by closing either his left or his right eye.[9] Later, the Rivoli featured a Plasticon travelog on Washington, D.C.[10]

FAIRALL

The first picture shown in the Fairall Process, invented by Harry K. Fairall, a former cinematographer, and Robert F. Elder, was THE POWER OF LOVE, presented at the Ambassador Hotel Theatre in Los Angeles in 1922. Again the anaglyph system was used, with each image printed on a double-coated positive film. One was printed in red and the other in green. Patent rights to the

process were held by William J. Worthington of Haworth Pictures Corporation.

The Fairall camera is a forerunner of the modern Natural Vision camera in that the two lenses were side by side and the same distance apart as the human eyes. The two projectors superimposed the red and green images on the screen and the viewers gave the pictures depth.[11]

Although the Fairall system was not as popular as some of the other anaglyph systems, there were enthusiastic comments. **The New York Times** noted:

"In viewing through a special appliance pictures taken with the binocular stereoscopic camera, the screen seems to disappear. There is no consciousness of a motion picture having two dimensions, exposed on a flat surface. Instead, by the use of 'viewing screens' (red and green glasses) in complementary colors, the objects viewed appear to have a roundness, their contours are visible and as figures approach the spectator they seem to step right out of the scene."[12]

After these systems had been premiered, interest in the anaglyph systems waned and they disappeared for over ten years, after which they made a fairly successful come-back in the middle 1930's.

TELEVIEW

The Teleview Company presented a more radical system during the Christmas season of 1922. Invented by Cornell graduates Lawrence Hammond and William F. Cassidy, the system worked like this:

"Two negatives are used and films are taken through lenses 2-5/8 inches apart. The two prints are projected on the screen together, each frame of one following the corresponding frame of the other and seen through a circular aluminum casing containing a motor, an opaque revolving shutter and a piece of plate glass."[13]

Much enthusiasm was generated for the Teleview method when it was premiered at the Selwyn Theatre in New York, although it was conceded that in its present form, it was not practical for movie theatres as the mechanical viewers were too costly.

Among the comments on Teleview were:

"The impression of objects in relief that one gets . . . is startling, so real that it seems inappropriate to speak of it as an illusion . . . Every object has thickness, as well as length and breadth, and stands appreciably in front of or behind every other object."[14]

"The Teleview Corporation has made and exhibited genuinely

stereoscopic motion pictures . . . which may mark an epoch in the development of cinematography."[15]

The Teleview program featured perspective drawings, still and motion travel pictures and a feature film.

The drawings included a jug marked "Rye" which extended from the screen out into the audience. Then a dragon came out over the orchestra pit. This was followed by stereo shots of the Canadian Rockies and some movies of the Hopi and Navajo Indians. All of these views were quite successful.

The feature picture, however, was not as popular. As **The New York Times** noted:

"The program ended with "M. A. R. S.," a stereoscopic photoplay which, unfortunately, did not prove very impressive as a dramatic composition . . . It illustrated the use of the third dimension, however, and the part of its action laid on the planet Mars . . . permitted a number of bizarre effects . . .

"The faces of people sometimes seem more clear in them (Teleview) than on the usual screen, but at other times it is harder to distinguish expression, either because the Teleview cuts down the illumination or because there was insufficient illumination when the scenes were photographed."[16]

Despite its shortcomings, Teleview had a distinct advantage that the other dimension systems did not advertise. Either of the two Teleview prints could be shown in a regular theatre as a "flat" feature.

But the enthusiasm for Teleview, like the other systems, was short-lived and scientists went back to the laboratory.

OTHER SYSTEMS OF THE 1920'S

George K. Spoor, the founder of Essanay Studios in Chicago, and P. John Berggren announced their 3-D camera in January, 1921. It consisted of one camera with two lenses side by side and a projector consisting of similar lenses.[17] They announced an improved system in 1923 but no enthusiasm was aroused.

William E. Waddell and John D. Elms experimented with third-dimensional films in the 1920's, but turned with greater enthusiasm to widescreen films and were responsible for the Grandeur process in 1929.[18]

Lorenzo del Riccio discovered his Magnascope lens by accident while working on 3-D motion pictures.[19]

Spectra, a single-strip 3-D illusion system by Charles V. Henkel of

New York, was demonstrated in 1921. In addition to being more simplified than the Berggren-Spoor camera, he claimed that his films also had "color values." Since all motion picture prints have this value, even though it is not visible to the naked eye, Henkel insisted that his Spectra process makes these colors visible and gives the impression of depth to the picture.[20]

Another single-strip illusion process was shown by Walter Parkes of Oakland, California, in 1923 at the American Releasing Corporation screening room. Scenes of Grand Canyon were shown and viewers saw a decided depth in some shots and not much in others. It was felt that the Parkes process was not as good as far as depth was concerned as were the anaglyph and Teleview systems but, as **The New York Times** expressed it, ". . . there is hardly any distortion, and none in objects near to, it has a distinct advantage over the other attempts."[21]

In 1925, a series of four stereoscopic shorts were released by Pathe with the intriguing titles of LUNA-CY, OUCH, A RUNAWAY TAXI and ZOWIE!

L. E. Randall, a Texas inventor, demonstrated his system on July 10, 1929 in New York. It used a special screen, two projectors (one projecting images with violet rays and the other, light which is deficient in actinic rays). The two images build on the crossed lines in the screen into images, giving the impression of depth to the audience.

"Extensive work has to be done before the machines can be used in theatres," Randall said humbly.[22]

In 1926 one of the first pictures advertised as having a stereoscopic illusion was filmed in the third dimension, THE SHIP OF SOULS. Filmed by the Stereoscopic Film Company, Inc., of Los Angeles in the Max O. Miller process, the film, like so many others of the 1920's, was only "pseudoscopic" and did not give a true two-eyed depth.[23]

Some other attempts of the period included a system which used vertical "grids" in both the projector and the viewer; another which used two images side by side on the screen and supplied the audience with opera glasses which had prisms placed in front to help turn each eye toward only one image, and a third which used a special two-colored "fan" which worked much like the red and green viewers of the anaglyph systems.[24] All of these were obviously not practical for commercial use.

[1] *Film Daily,* 103:3, May 15, 1953.

[2] Anthony R. Michaelis, "Science, Research and Film," *Sight and Sound,* 17:184. Winter, 1948-49.

[3] See the 16mm sound film, "Animated Cartoons — the Toy That Grew Up."

[4] John A. Norling, "Basic Principles of 3-D Photography and Projection," *New Screen Techniques,* p. 48.

[5] E. I. Sponable, "Historical Development of Sound Films,"*SMPE Journal,* 48:280, April, 1947.

[6] "Stereoscopic Moving Pictures in Natural Colors," *Scientific American,* 101:256, October 9, 1909.

[7] Sidney Skolsky, "That's Hollywood For You," *Photoplay,* 44:21, September, 1953.

[8] Jacob Leventhal, *SMPE Journal,* May, 1926, pp. 25-26.

[9] *Film Daily,* 119:3, October 30, 1961.

[10] William van Doren Kelley, *SMPE Journal,* October, 1923, p. 51.

[11] *Film Daily,* September 30, 1922, quoted by Kelley, *op. cit.,* p. 150.

[12] *New York Times,* 76:5, Section 7, February 20, 1927.

[13] *Ibid.,* 72:2, Section 8, October 22, 1922.

[14] *Loc. cit.*

[15] *New York Times,* 72:20, December 28, 1922.

[16] *Loc. cit.*

[17] *New York Times,* 70:2, Section 6, January 23, 1921.

[18] *Ibid.,* 79:6, June 1, 1930.

[19] *Ibid.,* 77:29, April 24, 1928.

[20] *Ibid.,* 70:2, Section 6, January 30, 1921.

[21] *Ibid.,* 72:22, May 15, 1923.

[22] *New York Times,* 78:15, July 11, 1929.

[23] *Film Daily,* 103:12, March 12, 1953.

[24] *SMPE Journal,* October, 1919, p. 37.

CHAPTER TWO
THE THIRTIES

The late George K. Spoor, who had been announcing his stereoscope system for many years, finally presented a picture at the Chicago State Lake Theatre in 1930 but the film failed to catch on.[25] This was to be Spoor's last contribution to the film industry after previously making third-dimensional films of Niagara Falls and a roller coaster ride in 1926, which paralleled the same locales later used in Cinerama.[26] A 3-D short, CAMPUS SWEETHEARTS, appeared in the Spoor system in 1930.

That same year, Dr. Herbert E. Ives of the Bell Telephone Company, one of the pioneer stereographers, introduced a new concept of third dimension, the "parallax panoramagram." He first demonstrated the system to the American Optical Society on October 30, 1930. He photographed the images as seen in a curved mirror and then projected the image on the rear of the screen using multiple projectors.[27]

This theory was later used by the Russians for their third-dimensional "parallax stereogram" system.

Dr. R. T. A. Innes, a South African astronomer, devised a stereoscopic system in which "the special optical appliance was placed near the screen."[28] The system was never worked commercially.

The system invented by Douglas F. Winnek of New York University in 1931 made possible "a perspective of three dimensions without the necessity for any special viewing devices."[29]

The screen used had a beaded cellophane surface with each tiny bead acting as a lens. The projector combined the images on the screen after the camera had taken alternate right and left eye images.

Another stereoscopic illusion system which was cited by cinematographer Gregg Toland as something which would start another Hollywood revolution was the invention of William Adler of

Pasadena, California, a former cinematographer. An attachment on the camera, consisting of a three-angled mirror, was the only equipment change. As the mirror revolves on the camera, it reflects the image onto the film. Each three frames, therefore, will have a forward view and the other two will have views of different sides of the subject. When projected at Grauman's Chinese Theatre by Adler and Samuel Goldwyn, they found the images in any section of the house to be "startlingly clear."[30] The main drawback to the system was that each subject had to be lighted on all sides to get the third dimension.

THE RETURN OF THE ANAGLYPH

The anaglyph returned to the screen for a short stay via MGM's AUDIOSCOPIKS in 1936, THE NEW AUDIOSCOPIKS in 1938 and THIRD DIMENSION MURDER in 1941. The last of these was promoted under the title of Metroscopics after some improvements had been made by the process by MGM. These films, all short subjects, were developed by Jacob Leventhal and John Norling, the latter of whom is still active in the 3-D film industry today.

Of AUDIOSCOPIKS, the **New York Times** remarked:

"A pitcher winds up and throws a ball into the audience and a magician conjures up a white mouse onto the tip of his wand and pokes it into the audience."[31]

With the addition of sound, the old anaglyph movies again tickled the fancy of the public and they enjoyed having a torch thrown into their face by a fire eater, as well as seltzer water, a woman on a swing, a witch with a spider on her broomstick, and a skeleton.

Leventhal and Norling dyed one negative blue and the other red and had Technicolor make composite prints. MGM had three million eyeglasses made of red and green cellophane to be used with AUDIOSCOPIKS. The cost: less than four dollars a thousand.

With over 200 patents for 3-D movies filed during the era of the silent film, the addition of sound to the motion picture soon separated the crackpots from the earnest inventors who had practical commercial systems. Good 3-D short films began appearing with more rapidity after 1935.

Auguste Lumiere perfected his 3-D system in that year and his films were shown in Paris, Lyon, Marseilles and Nice.[32]

Italy produced BEGGAR'S WEDDING (NOZZE VAGABONE) in the third dimension in 1936. In 1937, Germany made probably the first 3-D sound film in genuine color, YOU CAN NEARLY

TOUCH IT (ZUM GREIFEN NAH) in the Boehner system using lenses made by Zeiss-Icon. This was followed by SIX GIRLS DRIVE INTO THE WEEKEND (SECHS MADEL ROLLEN INS WOCHENEND) in 1939. These films were seen through polarized viewers made by the Zeiss Company.[33] This type of viewer was slowly replacing the red-green anaglyph viewers and marked another significant step ahead in practical third dimensional motion pictures.

WORLD'S FAIR FILMS

John A. Norling's third-dimensional films delighted over 1,500,000 persons at the New York World's Fair in 1939. Two projectors and polaroid glasses were used. Of the Chrysler film, which premiered on May 4, 1939, photography expert Adrian Cornwell-Clyne noted:

"The remarkable Technicolor stereoscopic film presented by Chrysler at the New York World's Fair in 1939 is the largest scale public exhibition of three-dimensional motion pictures so far given. The film had a projection length of some 15 minutes and consisted of a stop motion sequence in which the parts of a Plymouth automobile march, dance or sail into their correct position in the chassis in time with musical accompaniment. The scenario was written by J. A. Norling of the Loucks and Norling Studios in New York. Norling also did the whole of the technical control. Part of the film — the part using live models — was made with a pair of Technicolor beam-splitter cameras, but the mechanical animation was photographed with a pair of cameras using single film and successive sets of red, green and blue frames."[34]

Narrator of the film was Major Edward Bowes of the popular Amateur Hour on radio. He appeared in a "live action" sequence which was believed to be the first "live action — live dialog" sequence ever made in a third dimensional film.[35]

Stereoscopic films by Loucks and Norling also were made for the Pennsylvania Railroad display at the Golden Gate Exposition in San Francisco in 1940.

THE PARALLAX STEREOGRAM

In Russia, Semyon Ivanov was working on a different principle of third dimension, the parallax stereogram. His system, premiered at the Stereokino in 1941, was composed of double-width film with images side-by-side, projected onto a screen consisting of tiny projections which reflected light.[36]

The "grid" system of the screen contained 36,000 copper wires

radiating in three directions. The first film in the process was FILM CONCERT in 1940.

The disadvantages of the system were many — despite the fact that no glasses were needed. The Soyuzdetfilm Studios in Moscow were turned over completely to stereo film production in 1947 and over 4,500,000 patrons had already seen these productions by 1948.[37]

Credited to Ivanov, the Russian system is actually based on the work of many inventors, including the late Frederic Ives in America. Reports from observers say that the screen was originally made of wire netting, but that this type of screen let through too much light and was replaced by slats and later by pin point prisms and special transparent lenses. But the system has always been referred to as the wire "grid"system.

In 1947, the Stereokino premiered its first feature film, ROBINSON CRUSOE. After a long run, NIGHT IN MAY was shown. Two more features, LALIM, based on a Chekhov story, and ALEKO, based on a Pushkin poem and a Rachmaninoff opera, have also been shown in the theatre and played to "standing room only" in the five theatres equipped to play the grid system.[38]

A Russian embassy officer, on seeing an early demonstration of the system, described the Ivanov method differently from the previous reports in the trade papers:

"The development consists of two principal parts. The first part is a new type projection screen made of glass, about three-quarters of an inch thick. The present model is three feet by five feet, though there is no reason why there should be any limitation of size. The back of the screen is engraved with closely spaced lines, perpendicular, but tending to fan out right and left from the center line as they move from top to bottom. The lines in the original model were black, but the color has been omitted from the screen now used.

"The second change has been made in the camera and the projector. The camera, instead of facing the subject, is at right angles to it, and the image is reflected into the lens by a mirror which is at a 45-degree angle to both lens and subject. The mirror is actually two mirrors separated by a vertical gap.

"The lens is bisected vertically by a narrow bar which coincides with the break between the mirrors. Hence the film bears two parallel images of each photograph, which are identical except for the slight change of perspective caused by the two mirrors. Similarly the projector has the same bar-and-mirror arrangement as the camera, and the image is reflected from the mirrors to the screen.

The reflection of the back of the screen produces the three-dimensional effect.

"The illusion produced is complete and the focus perfect in any one of some six different positions while sitting in any given chair. In between these positions the image becomes blurred and the third-dimensional effect disappears."[39]

The Russians believed that as soon as it was perfected that the system would become standard for all motion pictures, even though it required rear projection. After reading the complicated explanations, America admitted that the Russian system had about as much chance of becoming the industry standard as would some of the early 3-D methods.

George H. Elsin, general secretary of the Association of Cinematograph and Allied Technicians in London was disappointed in what he saw at a later demonstration at the Stereokino and maintained that the British technicians seemed much farther ahead of the Russians "both in obtaining greater depth of focus and in avoiding strain on the eyes."[40]

Russian film director Gregori Roshall was less kind to the system. He insisted that "like every new technical discovery, it is, as yet, far from perfect. In fact, not every shot is fully stereoscopic, not all scenes are photographed in an interesting manner, and the technique of screening, it seems to me, should be considerably improved. (Yet) the stereo-cinema will become the main form of cinematography in the future."[41]

Joseph MacLeod, another witness at the Stereokino, described his reaction to the later improved version of the parallax stereogram:

"The Moscow stereo cinema is a former concert hall seating about 220 . . . The screen, which is made, I was told, of millions of chips of glass, looks like any ordinary screen, though it was pitched high. Occasionally something like a sound track was visible on the left side. We used no special lenses or apparatus of any kind. At first the unusual nature of the projection is not noticed, for credit titles are superimposed on a background of mountainous seas, and it may be that the double focus so created destroyed the vividness of the background. By the time the credits are gone your eyes are used to the seas. The story was ROBINSON CRUSOE, a second, improved version. It was only when Crusoe in his shipwreck throws a rope to a drowning sailor that you get the first shock. The rope comes hurtling and curling right over your head. At you! You duck. We all did. After that we were ready for anything . . . You soon accept the new screen convention of Crusoe's personal **roundness** and take it for

granted. Other chances must be taken to keep the new medium alive. They come from the animals which Crusoe encounters. Each is startlingly real; and when a civet cat crawls out on a branch over the auditorium our delight is unbounded. Another useful introduction is Crusoe's dog, rescued from the wreck, a kind of lightly-built St. Bernard with a curled tail. He keeps space alive and personal around Crusoe, even when there is no photographic frame in the foreground. But in the main, advantage is continually taken of shooting through fore-frames of ropes or branches or the archway of a tree . . . Out in the auditorium, about three rows in front of you, leaves and lianas materialize in the air, dangle and dance, and float away into Crusoe's face. Parakeets and small birds sit on them; or fly at you from the screen and vanish over your head . . . Their musical chattering is also in the air all around you and there is no need here as in ordinary cinema to adjust this depth of sound to the flat conventions on the screen several yards away.

"Personally, I am allergic to spiders. I was nauseated by an immense brute as real as life and half as large as the screen within what appeared to be a hand's grasp of my nose!

"Darker scenes are apt to be blurred. But the lighter scenes are brilliant, though lighting seems to be as tricky for color films. There are no dissolves. A scene is ended with a fade or, for passage of time, with a wipe . . ."[42]

Another observer behind the Iron Curtain gave his impressions of the system — "A screen composed of thousands of parallel strips, placed in front of the main screen, allows the left eye to see only one of two projected images through its slits. The complementary picture intended for the right eye is hid by the opaque strips . . . As each eye sees only the image it should see, a 3-D effect results. Close-up, the result looks like a film projected on a zebra. From where the audience sits, however, the striped images merge like the dots of a half-tone illustration."[43]

With such a variance of descriptions of the same system, we will never be sure exactly how the process works until it is shown in the United States. The New Cameo theatre in New York City, which shows Russian films almost exclusively, announced that provision was being made for the Ivanov 3-D process if it was possible to install it in the new theatre.[44] But this was in 1955, and America as yet has not seen this dimension process.

In 1954, announcements from behind the iron curtain reported that the Ivanov system had been "modified completely," indicating that a single-film system is now in use, implying that the frames are

arranged alternately on standard film. The frames are probably projected simultaneously in pairs while the film moves two frames at a time. It has been named "The Modified Ivanov System," according to these reports.

Sergei Eisenstein, the Russian director, has theoretically divided stereoscopic films into three classifications: (1) those resembling a flat alto-relievo, balanced somewhere in the plane of the mirror screen, (2) those which pierce through the depth of the screen, taking the spectator into previously unseen distance, and (3) those in which the image "pours" out of the screen into the auditorium. At time of his death, Eisenstein was working on a study of the third-dimensional film. Whether he would have been pleased with recent advances in 3-D films remains an unanswered question.

VERI-VISION AND BIOPTICAN

A Dutch process, Frank A. Weber's VeriVision camera shot a 3-D image on a single film. The special camera pulled down six sprockets instead of the normal four. The system, however, had a very short life, although it boasted the production of the first 3-D newsreel.[45] It also produced and exhibited two short subjects, QUEEN JULIANA and STAR OF THE SCREEN.

The British "Bioptican" system was announced early in 1948 and it was to give a "terrific boost to British Films" by producing the world's first natural full-length stereoscopic motion picture. The Bioptican process used a standard camera, film, projector and screen. No glasses were needed. The process relied solely on an oscillating mechanism, which moved in such a way that alternate shots were taken from different angles. The eye fuses these two images together on the screen into one 3-D image. Ted Maxwell-Harvey was responsible for the introduction of the Bioptican process and, according to him, was the "result of 20 years' experiments."[46] No film, however, has appeared in the system.

THE FESTIVAL OF BRITAIN

In 1951, in honor of the Festival of Britain, the first theatre built especially for third-dimensional films (excluding Russia's Stereoki-no) — the Telecinema — was erected in London. Films for the presentation were made by Stereo-Techniques under the direction of Raymond Spottiswoode and included five short subjects: A SOLID EXPLANATION, ROYAL RIVER, THE BLACK SWAN, and two Norman McLaren films, NOW IS THE TIME (TO PUT ON YOUR GLASSES) and ROUND IS AROUND. The Stereo-

Techniques organization also was reported as having completed two feature films in 3-D, THE LIFE OF JESUS and THE FIRE-BIRD[47] but this apparently was just a publicity announcement.

The Stereo-Techniques system, based on the English Dudley Camera, was optioned for showing and production in the United States by veteran Sol Lesser, who re-named the system Tri-Optican and later, Stereo-Cine. The program of short subjects from the Festival was also shown in Berlin, Brussels, Cologne, Frankfort, Hamburg, Lucerne and Paris as well as London, New York and Chicago.

In America, the Stereo-Cine shorts opened to critical acclaim, especially the two Norman McLaren subjects which featured abstract figures dancing merrily out over the heads of the startled audience, who were wearing permanent polaroid viewers. Broadway and Chicago audiences reached capacity and were delighted with the Sadlers Wells group doing THE BLACK SWAN, the lovely Technicolor and depth of ROYAL RIVER and the seals in a zoo splashing water into the very front row of the audience.

An un-named 3-D process was developed in Hungary at the same time Stereo-Techniques was being shown in Britain. In Budapest, many thousands saw A WALK IN THE ZOO, ARTISTS EXAMINATION and MAY DAY, 1952. The system was later used for a feature version of WINTER TALE featuring members of a Hungarian ice skating revue. But compared to 1953, all the many years of stereo films which preceded it seemed minute and unimportant when "3-Dementia" came to Hollywood.

[25] Variety, 192:83, December 2, 1953.
[26] Film Daily, 104:1, November 25, 1953.
[27] New York Times, 80:19, October 31, 1930 and 82:25, April 28, 1933.
[28] Ibid., 80:8, September 20, 1931.
[29] New York Times, 81:27, November 24, 1931.
[30] Ibid., 84:5, Section 10, January 20, 1935.
[31] New York Times, 85:6, Section 10, December 8, 1935.
[32] Auguste Lumiere, quoted in Sight and Sound, 17:70, Summer, 1948.
[33] Frank A. Weber, "3-D in Europe," New Screen Techniques, p. 71.
[34] Cornwell-Clyne, op. cit., pp. 614-617.
[35] John A. Norling, "The Stereoscopic Art," SMPTE Journal, March, 1953, pp. 287 and 289.
[36] Variety, 192:5, October 28, 1953.
[37] Winchester Screen Encyclopedia, 1948, p. 236.
[38] Variety, 192:5, October 28, 1953.
[39] Hollywood Quarterly, 1:237-238, January, 1946.
[40] Christopher-Brunel, "3-D in England," Films in Review, 6:228-229, May, 1953.
[41] Grigori Roshall, "The Soviet Film," Experiment in the Film, pp. 162-164.
[42] Joseph MacLeod, "Stereoscopic Film," Sight and Sound, 16:118, Autumn, 1947.
[43] Variety, 199:2, June 29, 1955.
[44] Film Daily, 107:6, May 16, 1955.
[45] Frank A. Weber, New Screen Techniques, p. 70.
[46] Frank G. Barnes, "The Third Dimension," Monthly Film Review, 6:17, February, 1948.
[47] Film Daily, 103:1, March 16, 1953.

CHAPTER THREE
COMES THE REVOLUTION

The first era of the third dimensional film was summed up by Gio Gagliardi when he mentioned the five basic types of stereoscopic films shown in commercial theatres up to 1950:

1. SCREEN DIVIDER AND VIEWER — images shown side by side and viewed through the stereoptican.

2. MECHANICAL ECLIPSE — two images projected alternately on the screen with a shutter device.

3. COLOR ANAGLYPH — red and green images and glasses used to get the stereo effect.

4. FREE VISION — Vertical grid blocks off left and right eye pictures from audience one at a time.

5. POLARIZED FILTER — polarized filter on projector and polaroid glasses for the audience.[48]

Although all these five types of 3-D systems had been demonstrated with some degree of success, only the last-named remained to enter the second era of the third dimension motion picture.

In 1952, American movie audiences, previously at 80 million, had dropped to 46 million. The situation was attributed mostly to the inroads made by television in the American home. People were staying home to watch movies — despite the fact that TV movies were then limited to vintage releases of mediocre pictures.

Late in that year, Cinerama was introduced to wide-eyed filmgoers in New York. At the same time, Arch Obler, a radio writer turned movie producer, was completing shooting on a full-length stereoscopic film in Ansco Color. The film, BWANA DEVIL, was released late in 1952 and, coupled with Cinerama, started the greatest Hollywood revolution since sound.

Obler decided that now was the time for a revolution. "I think that the industry will turn to three dimension," he commented. "They will have to, out of the sheer facts of life. Motion picture

audiences will not accept less after seeing third dimension. This is the medium that is going to resurrect the motion picture business."[49]

The process used in the film was Natural Vision, invented by Milton L. Gunzburg, his brother Julian, an eye specialist, and Friend Baker, a Hollywood camera engineer. The process is based on the old "convergence" principle used in the anaglyph and other polaroid methods. As Obler explained it:

"Images are photographed from two different points of view. Each lens, focusing and converging on an object almost precisely as do the human eyes, provides a separate and complete two dimensional picture . . . In the theatre the normal two projectors in a booth project the two separate pictures onto the screen in superimposition, much as in nature they are projected into the 'brain eye.' The right and left images pass through polaroid filters placed in the portholes of the projection booth. The two images are superimposed almost as one on a reflective type screen.[50] The images are reflected back to the viewer who is equipped with polaroid glasses, which serve to accept the correct image intended for that eye."[51]

Gunzburg had previously given an option on the Natural Vision system to MGM, but they soon dropped it. Columbia, Fox and Paramount were not interested at the time.

Before BWANA DEVIL filled the screen, a prolog was presented featuring Lloyd Nolan, who explained the third dimensional technique and introduced TV puppets, "Beanie and Cecil," who added their comments in 3-D.

Of BWANA DEVIL, **Film Daily** remarked:

"BWANA DEVIL is the most conspicuous and outstanding movie of the moment, not because of story or performance, but because of its importance as an innovation in technical production . . . a novelty all of which adds up to cash at the box office, and a promise of renewed interest in movie going . . . The audiences applauded the stereoscopic effect, obtained by the new photographic technique, especially in the brilliant shots of mountains and groups of natives working in the scenes."[52]

Home Movies magazine, however, was a little more frank about the process:

". . . The film has very few perfectly exposed shots, and in the main, the color balance is horrible (not the fault of the film) and is reminiscent of the poorest color films. In many cases, one half of a scene was well exposed while the other half was completely over-exposed. Focus was off, more often than not. In one particular scene containing two people against a background of palm leaves, we

found that when we looked directly at the actors they were in focus and the leaves were not. Glancing at the leaves, they were sharp and the actors were not. Overall sharpness was not present in anything but the longest of long shots. The cameraman got a little too cute (for our liking) when he persisted in using large masses in the foreground in order to heighten the stereo effect. To sum up, very few shots were good, many were terrible, and the whole thing felt (to this viewer) as if we were seeing the film through a wet glass sheet. The picture was a flop in our books and we think that Obler had better pull up his socks. There is no excuse for sloppy technique. If the process was not perfected at the time of shooting, then it should not have been foisted on the public in this brazen way."[53]

Despite the fact that the film was probably one of the dullest and most inept ever produced, it broke box office records in many theatres. It had nothing to offer except **depth** — but the public was both fascinated and annoyed by the polaroid glasses they wore and thrilled at some good and bad stereoscopic shots. After several months in independent release, BWANA DEVIL was sold outright to United Artists who continued its distribution into the waiting arms of the public. Obler got a half-million-dollar advance from the distribution deal and the film racked up unbelievable profits.

The Natural Vision system had its draw-backs. The camera was heavy since it employed two regular sized cameras. Also, projection was awkward, requiring the use of both projectors in the theatre at once as well as an automatic interlocking device to keep the two films in synchronization as they went through the projector. The projectionist and theatre owner longed for the old Audioscopiks days when the 3-D image was on just one film. Since the audience wore glasses, these cut down the amount of light to reach the eye. Therefore, more light was required at the source of the projection to keep the film from appearing too dark by the time it had penetrated the viewers.

Despite all these disadvantages, BWANA DEVIL was bringing Hollywood temporarily back to life.

VIEWING GLASSES

Polaroid was discovered by Edwin H. Land in 1932 after many failures. It is in reality a sheet of plastic dipped into an iodine solution. The iodine-plastic molecules are aligned uniformly but in different directions — at 55 degree right angles to each other. By putting the same type of filters on the projector lens, the depth illusion results.[54]

Until 1953, Polaroid glasses were used for looking at stereoscopic snapshots and the company turned out only a few thousand pairs a year. After BWANA DEVIL, the Polaroid Company turned out glasses at the rate of six million pairs a week.

Gunzburg was exclusive distributor for the glasses until July 15, 1953. He bought the cardboard-framed glasses at six cents a pair and sold them to theatres for ten cents a pair. Exhibitors added ten cents to their admission price to cover the cost.

Improvements came quickly. Soon the polaroid glasses were notched so they could fit over the glasses already worn by the moviegoer. Clip-ons followed and soon plastic-rimmed viewers appeared.

There were naturally complaints about wearing the glasses and most critics predicted that 3-D movies would become obsolete within a year or so, but they apparently regarded the glasses as a greater nuisance than did the moviegoing public. Certified Reports, Inc., took a poll of filmgoers over 15 years of age and the ones who complained the most were between 20 and 35. Complaints included eyestrain, headaches, slippage, pressure and the small size of the lens. Nearly half, however, had no complaints at all.[55] When asked if the wearing of glasses would deter them from seeing subsequent 3-D films, most of them answered a decided "no."[56]

Optometrists came to the movies' defense with statements that if viewers got headaches from 3-D glasses, it is the fault of the person's eyes and not the film or the glasses. Another claimed that the 3-D glasses were an eye saver in that they gave the wearer valuable exercise.[57] Still another said that 3-D could save 10 per cent of the world's population from blindness and even death by pointing out flaws in their vision.[58]

Perhaps the most amusing incident and the most favorable one in the eyes of the Polaroid producers was the case of a Copenhagen woman, aged 74, who had been seeing double for the last eight years. She went to see BWANA DEVIL and, after donning the polaroids, saw correctly. She now wears a permanent pair of polaroids.[59]

But glasses or no glasses, Hollywood had finally opened its eyes to the fact that here was the box-office hypo it needed to bring the ailing patient back to life. By the beginning of 1953, nearly all the major studios had announced at least one 3-D production and 3-D glasses were soon standardized.

WARNER BROTHERS PIONEER AGAIN

Warner Brothers, who had pioneered with the first practical sound

films, also pioneered with "the first 3-D film in color from a major company." They chose to remake one of their early sound hits, THE MYSTERY OF THE WAX MUSEUM, retitled HOUSE OF WAX. Following the lead of Cinerama, they added stereophonic sound to the film. With this combination, Warner Brothers thought, they could not miss. And they were right. HOUSE OF WAX made BWANA DEVIL look sick by comparison and it is still one of the slickest and best 3-D films ever made. It broke more box office records and soared toward a record gross of five million dollars, making it the highest-grossing 3-D film ever made.

Despite its rousing success with the public, HOUSE OF WAX, like BWANA DEVIL, found mixed critical reception. **Film Daily,** coining the motto, "Don't Throw Those Glasses Away!" said:

"Here is the shape of things to come . . . The old show business axiom — scare the hell out of an audience and they'll love it — has been perfectly applied here with a skilled hand and a know how that will without doubt result in vast purchase of tickets and the full-to-capacity house."[60]

The **Christian Science Monitor,** however, was at the other extreme:

"HOUSE OF WAX is a three-dimensional movie with a one-dimensional purpose: to scare the daylights out of the spectator. That it succeeds is no credit to anyone in particular. The initial Warner Brothers entry in the current 3-D race represents a new low in sensationalism and violence for their own sake. The inane screenplay . . . comes off the Warner horror shelf where it has reposed since the first version, 20 years ago . . . Watching HOUSE OF WAX is rather like spending an hour and a half on the rack. One comes away feeling physically assaulted and numbed."[61]

The film's most terrifying moment occurred when smoke from a fire seemed to pour from the screen out into the audience and the most sensuous was a barker batting a paddle ball out into the audience until it seemed to touch the end of the nose.

Following HOUSE OF WAX, films came at a faster rate from several studios, some filmed in the Natural Vision process and others with similar cameras which had been gathering dust in studio basements. From Warner Brothers came three more 3-D films — THE CHARGE AT FEATHER RIVER, THE MOONLIGHTER and HONDO. The first was a gimmicked-up successor to HOUSE OF WAX with rocks, sabres, tomahawks, spears, fists and even a venomous snake ending up in the viewer's lap. The film even went so far as to spit in the patron's face!

THE MOONLIGHTER, in black-and-white, was a disappointment, both as a film and as 3-D. Despite Barbara Stanwyck and Fred MacMurray in the leading roles, 3-D added nothing to the film and the moving titles at the beginning were nerve wracking to watch.

HONDO, an off-beat western, was shown in both 3-D and widescreen and the depth photography was good. The National Board of Review remarked:

"HONDO's 3-D photography is the best to date. There are **many** moments in HONDO in which the illusion is complete of there being no screen, and of images moving as objects and people do in reality. HONDO should give proponents of CinemaScope pause, and should be seen by all who wish to keep abreast of the technological changes now transforming the motion picture."[62]

Despite their success with 3-D films, Warner Brothers — who seemed to have the most faith in them — dropped 3-D production after releasing THE PHANTOM OF RUE MORGUE and DIAL M FOR MURDER.

STEREO-CINE

Sol Lesser was joined by producer Walter Wanger in planning a wide production program for Stereo-Cine, which had already proved as a potential "draw" with its five short subjects already shown in America. They now planned two features, THE RUNAWAY TRAIN and THREE-D FOLLIES, plus a feature cartoon, six two-reel shorts and a film of the coronation of Queen Elizabeth. Of all these productions, only THREE-D FOLLIES was even partially completed.[63]

Stereo-Cine, however, did release theatrical films. Its first, THE ROCKY MARCIANO-JOE WALCOTT FIGHT of May 15, 1953, was filmed and released to the theatres, although the production had to be "padded" to 17 minutes when the knockout came in the first round. An advertising film used with the London premiere of BWANA DEVIL also used the process and the first 3-D cartoon, THE OWL AND THE PUSSYCAT appeared that same year in England. Several Stereo-Cine featurettes filmed in Great Britain, were released by Robert L. Lippert in America including A DAY IN THE COUNTRY, CAMPUS CAPERS and BANDIT ISLAND.

The first feature-length American Stereo-Cine film was HANNAH LEE, filmed in Pathecolor. Critics, however, found it not on par with other 3-D systems on the market and it did not enjoy much success.

Britain announced its first feature, THE DIAMOND WIZARD, in the Stereo-Cine system using the new Space Master camera designed by the company. By this time, however, the interest in 3-D had declined and the film was released only in the standard version.[64]

COLUMBIA PICTURES

Columbia was another enthusiastic backer of third dimension films and produced even more depth films than Warner Brothers. Like the Warners, they made their first depth film a remake of a former production, THE MAN WHO LIVED TWICE, re-named MAN IN THE DARK. It grossed over a million dollars in its first five weeks in release and beat HOUSE OF WAX to Broadway by two days. Columbia also produced FORT TI, THE STRANGER WORE A GUN, THE NEBRASKAN, MISS SADIE THOMPSON, GUN FURY, DRUMS OF TAHITI, JESSE JAMES VS. THE DALTONS and THE MAD MAGICIAN in 3-D.

MAN IN THE DARK, tinted in sepia, was considered by critics to be strictly second-rate melodrama but enhanced by the dimension effects. The picture shot off a gun in the face of the audience, dropped a flower pot into their laps, poked surgical instruments into their faces, let a crazed bat fly into the auditorium and climaxed the film with the inevitable roller coaster sequence which Cinerama had made so popular.

FORT TI used the gimmick game even further. The Indians hurled spears, arrows, torches and other Indians into the audience. One San Francisco moviegoer socked the theatre manager in the jaw for playing THE NEBRASKAN. He didn't like boiling oil and arrows coming out at him.[65]

UNIVERSAL

Universal took the non-gimmick approach to its dimensional films and produced two "thrillers" — IT CAME FROM OUTER SPACE and THE CREATURE FROM THE BLACK LAGOON, both featuring good dimensional photography. The former had stereophonic sound and both were shown on wide screens.

The company also produced four other 3-D films — WINGS OF THE HAWK, THE GLASS WEB, TAZA, SON OF COCHISE and REVENGE OF THE CREATURE — the last-named being made in 1955 as a last attempt to revive interest in depth films. All of these films were only mildly successful.

PARAMOUNT

Paramount produced five depth films in 1953, all of which achieved some success but most of them fared better when shown in regular flat versions. SANGAREE, based on a historical novel, was on the dullish side, but kept the gimmicks to a minimum. THOSE REDHEADS FROM SEATTLE was billed as "the first 3-D musical." FLIGHT TO TANGIER and CEASE FIRE had good depth photography while MONEY FROM HOME, a Martin and Lewis comedy, gained very little depth in 3-D. After these productions, Paramount dropped depth films in order to concentrate on its new widescreen process, VistaVision.

METRO-GOLDWYN-MAYER

MGM filmed two 3-D productions, ARENA and KISS ME KATE. The latter was the first film actually designed for the third dimension and contained some exciting perspective scenery plus the fact that it was an outstanding musical film in any dimension. Its box-office reception, however, was disappointing. Of KISS ME KATE, **Variety** remarked:

"Why 3-D? KATE has all the dimension it needs in 2-D. The pictorial effects achieved with 3-D lensing mean little in added entertainment. The necessity of wearing viewing glasses, to us, proved a pain in the eyebrows."[66]

Its other film, ARENA, relied on men, furniture, bottles, Brahma steers and spirited broncos flying into the audience's lap.

With the disappointment of its first two attempts, MGM converted to CinemaScope and regular widescreen production and avoided further dimensional films.

RKO RADIO

RKO (now Desilu), like Warner Brothers and Columbia, went into 3-D "all the way" and was reasonably successful. They presented SECOND CHANCE, SON OF SINBAD, DEVIL'S CANYON, LOUISIANA TERRITORY, DANGEROUS MISSION and THE FRENCH LINE as depth features. The last-named, a Jane Russell musical, used 3-D to little advantage and was more notable for its censorship and record-breaking runs than for its depth. The cable car sequence in SECOND CHANCE, however, remains one of the most exciting 3-D scenes ever filmed as the cable car hurtles down a canyon after a suspense-filled ride.

TWENTIETH CENTURY-FOX

Fox, which went all out for the CinemaScope system, produced only two 3-D films. The first, INFERNO, was one of the best — both in story, photography and performances. Besides achieving good depth and perspective, its Technicolor hues added dramatic value to the story and the suspenseful editing was exceptionally effective. Scenes contrasting Robert Ryan stranded on the hot yellow desert and Rhonda Fleming and William Lundigan dining in an air-conditioned restaurant was one of the exciting contrasts which showed that 3-D could be an interesting medium of expression. Fox's second 3-D film, GORILLA AT LARGE, was a thriller filmed by Leonard Goldstein's Panoramic Productions and released through Fox while it was converting to CinemaScope production.

UNITED ARTISTS

United Artists released several films in three dimensions — all produced by members of its family of independent companies. In addition to BWANA DEVIL, it released HANNAH LEE, THE DIAMOND, I THE JURY, GOG and SOUTHWEST PASSAGE and announced that there would be more upcoming 3-D films on its release schedules.

THE DIAMOND and GOG, both released during the decline of 3-D, were released "flat" although **Variety** felt that "probably the chase at the tag end and the gunplay would have come out better in 3-D"[67] in THE DIAMOND and considered that 3-D and color might help GOG, but "the depth treatment should have had more gimmicks to go with it."[68]

ALLIED ARTISTS

Allied Artists (formerly Monogram) released THE MAZE, notable mostly for its last sequence when a hideous, frog-like creature jumps toward the startled audience. As a good old-fashioned melodrama and as one of the first 3-D's, THE MAZE created quite a furor at the box office. The second Allied Artists feature, DRAGONFLY SQUADRON, although filmed in 3-D was released "flat" after the 3-D appeal at the box office dwindled.

3-D SHORT SUBJECTS

Short subjects posed a problem for the major studios. None of them wanted to be stuck with shorts which would be shown only in a

few theatres as the short subject business was dropping to a new low as it was. Everyone proceeded with caution with Universal finally breaking the ice with a short two-reel musical featuring Nat "King" Cole and shown with IT CAME FROM OUTER SPACE. At the same studio, Walter Lantz made the first 3-D cartoon, THE HYPNOTIC HICK featuring Woody Woodpecker.

Columbia presented two Three Stooges comedies, SPOOKS and PARDON MY BACKFIRE as well as a UPA cartoon, THE TELL-TALE HEART. In SPOOKS, 3-D hit a new low in gimmicks with everything which was not nailed down thrown at the audience.

Warner Brothers released a Bugs Bunny cartoon, LUMBER JACK RABBIT and Paramount, BOO MOON with Casper the Friendly Ghost and POPEYE, ACE OF SPACE. RKO presented Walt Disney's MELODY and a musical short, MOTOR RHYTHM.

In Europe, the AUDIOSCOPIKS from the 1930's were successfully re-released.

The Rialto Theatre in New York showed four shorts made with the Bolex 16mm stereo system, BOLEX STEREO, SUNDAY IN STEREO, INDIAN SUMMER and AMERICAN LIFE to cash in on the 3-D craze, even though the images were higher than they were wide. There were no other theatrical showings of this "home movie" stereo.

THE YEAR OF DECISION

The year of 1954, however successful 3-D was in 1953, proved to be the decisive year. By the end of 1953, 3-D films were slowly dying at the box office, mainly because of the expense and trouble of projecting them and the fact that many presentations were sub-standard. Some of the early films were cheaply and hurriedly made in order to get on the "3-D bandwagon." When the bandwagon lost a wheel, the market fell apart.

By the time the "big" 3-D films arrived with good stories and top stars, the popularity had waned. Even KISS ME KATE and MISS SADIE THOMPSON, top quality productions in any dimension, soon were forced to show regular flat versions only. No one wanted the depth versions.

Producers also realized that it was the "type" of picture that counted in 3-D. Not all films lent themselves to depth treatment. Horror and science fiction stories did — as IT CAME FROM

OUTER SPACE, HOUSE OF WAX and PHANTOM OF THE RUE MORGUE testified. Comedies didn't. MONEY FROM HOME and THE FRENCH LINE seemed to have little or no depth.

The theatre owner boiled it down to this: "Either we get 3-D films of good quality which are as easy to project as regular 2-D films, or we don't want them."

There was a solution but no one would take the initiative. With over 5,000 theatres equipped to show 3-D films, the answer was to put both images on one film, thus eliminating out-of-sync projection, patron's complaints and frayed nerves in the projection booth.

Single-strip systems were available. Why weren't they adopted?

In 1954, two companies pulled 3-D back from the grave by adopting two of the several single-strip systems on the market.

COLUMBIA AND THE NORD PROCESS

The Nord single-strip process was first demonstrated in June, 1953, and it was announced that the secret of the system would be passed onto the movie industry without charge.[69] The process was invented by Nathan Supak, Harry Ratner and Roy Clapp.

It used a corrective prism-type lens and put the two images on the frame of the film vertically. The first film to be tested was one reel of the United Artists film, I THE JURY. Although the demonstration was successful, only one company — Columbia — took the system to use for its films.

Prints of GUN FURY, THE NEBRASKAN, MISS SADIE THOMPSON, DRUMS OF TAHITI, JESSE JAMES VS. THE DALTONS and THE MAD MAGICIAN were made available in the Nord system. The only charge to the theatre owner was the purchase of Magic-Vuers polaroid glasses which were an improvement over the old cardboard frame polaroid glasses.

MOROPTICAN AND POLA-LITE

The most important development in the single-strip field was Moroptican, named after producer Boris Morros, who acquired the rights to the system in Vienna. He claimed that the system would allow more light to get to the screen and projection would be very simple.

In the first demonstrations in September, 1953, results were successful. Scenes from TAZA, SON OF COCHISE were shown and they were reported as sharp, clear and bright.[70]

Soon after these demonstrations, the Pola-Lite Company, which formerly had manufactured just 3-D viewers, took over the system and offered it under their name to any theatre in the United States for just one hundred dollars. This again included a commitment to buy Pola-Lite viewers to use with the system.

The idea appealed to the theatre owners and was the biggest boon to 3-D since BWANA DEVIL. Universal announced that TAZA, SON OF COCHISE AND CREATURE FROM THE BLACK LAGOON would be available on Pola-Lite, while United Artists released GOG and SOUTHWEST PASSAGE and Fox, GORILLA AT LARGE. With just an attachment to put on the front of the projector the simple Pola-Lite system seemed the logical answer to the 3-D projection problem, yet hardly any theatres bothered with the single-strip systems.

OTHER SINGLE-STRIP SYSTEMS

Although other single-strip systems were announced, most of them were never put to commercial use.

The Norling system used alternate frames — a right eye picture alternating with a left eye picture on one strip of film. When the film was projected, the two images fused on the screen.[71]

Vectograph, invented by Polaroid, dated back to 1938 and was used by the Navy during World War II. The process superimposed right and left eye images on the front and back sides of polarized film.[72] By the time Polaroid and Technicolor had begun a joint development of this system, the 3-D craze had subsided.

Naturama, presented by Col. Robert V. Bernier of Dayton, Ohio, was announced as "ready for use" in April, 1954. The Naturama system incorporated both right and left eye images on a single strip much like the other systems. The only equipment needed for projection was the "Naturama attachment," which consisted of a two-plane "window" between the projector and the projection room port hole.[73]

The first theatre to install Naturama was the Ames Theatre in Dayton.

Arch Obler, producer of BWANA DEVIL, announced in July, 1954, that he would use the Naturama system for his next production. However, when Naturama actually turned up on the movie screens, it was a widescreen system under the ageis of Republic Studios and the 3-D Naturama was not heard from again.

The Motion Picture Research Council developed a new single-projector technique which was considered "too bulky" for general

use, although it was reported as imparting much more light on the screen than some of the other systems had provided.[74]

The Astor 3-D Single Camera Optican Unit was a single strip of film running through the camera at double the normal speed, exposing the left and right eye images alternately. The negative could be separated for double-strip 3-D showing if desired. The camera weighed only 11 pounds.[75]

BACK FROM THE GRAVE

The single-strip system saved the 3-D film from death for a short while and the industry felt that dimensional films were here to stay.

Typical of the renewed interest in 3-D was keynoted by a column in **Film Daily** magazine, a trade paper which summed up the situation:

"Meaning no disrespect or lack of interest in Cinerama, CinemaScope, VistaVision, SuperScope and all the other major processes intriguing the industry, Phil M. this Monday morn would like to say a few kind words in behalf of simonpure 3-D . . . To Phil M. frankly, 'twould be a pity and a folly to give 3-D the old heave-ho . . . Actually, 3-D has been more sinned against than sinning . . . Which is to say that the trouble with 3-D has been not in the process, but the use made of it, particularly in the early stages . . . The temptation proved too strong: A process in short order became just a production gimmick . . . You can attract a quick customer buck that way, to be sure . . . But it's no way to bring 'em back alive to the box office time and time again.

"There were other unfortunate circumstances, too . . . There was the requirement for dual projection . . . And there also was the fact that some of the early viewers or glasses were hardly designed to make 3-D attendance attractive . . . Well, you no longer require dual projection, the drawbacks to which hardly need spelling out here . . . And if you've used the new type viewers available from several sources, you know that this problem, too, has been solved . . . Meanwhile, of course, research in 3-D is being carried forward. And one of these days, it's conceivable that there will be a 3-D system which does not require viewers . . . And it may be possible to 'marry' 3-D to one of the other widescreen processes, too.

"Should we forego 3-D until this transpires? . . . Phil M. doesn't think so . . . He believes the industry, if it is really smart, will see to it that some 3-D production continues . . . Making certain, of course, that the story property is suited to it and for it . . . After all, 3-D can do more than — for example — toss a spear into the

audience . . . Why not give it a chance to do so? . . . Actually, Hollywood has done comparatively little experimentation with 3-D . . . One of these days, it well may regret it . . . A process which rolled up those tremendous grosses really could be a handy thing to have around."[76]

Despite "Phil M. Daly's" kind words about the third dimension, it came too late to save it. Public apathy, industry misuse and many other causes gave rise to its demise. But that didn't mean that research and experimentation didn't continue. It did.

[48]Gio Gagliardi, *Films in Review*, 2:24, February, 1951.

[49] *Independent Film Journal*, 16:31, December 13, 1952.

[50] Ordinary screens depolarize the light from the image and the screens must be coated with a non-polarizing material in order to show the pictures correctly.

[51] *Independent Film Journal, ibid.*

[52] *Film Daily*, 102:6, December 2, 1952.

[53] *Home Movies*, January, 1953, p. 6.

[54] *New Yorker*, 29:26, May 16, 1953.

[55] *Variety*, 191:16, August 3, 1953.

[56] *Film Daily*, 32:12, August 8, 1953.

[57] *Film Daily*, 32:12, August 8, 1953.

[58] *Variety*, 191:15, June 17, 1953.

[59] *Film Daily*, 103:1, April 28, 1953.

[60] *Film Daily*, 103:8, April 13, 1953.

[61] *Christian Science Monitor*, April 14, 1953, p. 4C.

[62] "Weekly Guide to Motion Pictures," *National Board of Review*, December 26, 1953.

[63] *Variety*, 190:8, May 6, 1953.

[64] *Film Daily*, 104:1, September 3, 1953.

[65] *Variety*, 193:7, February 24, 1954.

[66] *Variety*, 192:6, October 28, 1953.

[67] *Variety*, 195:6, July 14, 1954.

[68] *Ibid.*, 195:6, June 5, 1954.

[69] *Variety*, 191:15, June 17, 1953.

[70] *Film Daily*, 104:1, September 10, 1953.

[71] *Variety*, 191:8, June 24, 1953.

[72] *Loc. cit.*

[73] *Film Daily*, 105:1, April 19, 1954.

[74] *Ibid.*, 104:1, December 8, 1953.

[75] *Loc. cit.*

[76] *Film Daily*, 105:3, April 19, 1954.

CHAPTER FOUR
OTHER THIRD-DIMENSIONAL SYSTEMS

Although foreign countries discovered and perfected many 3-D processes, America still led the way, announcing many competing systems during 1953 and 1954, each guaranteed to work better than those systems already in existence. All required viewing glasses to get the 3-D effect.

THE DUNNING PROCESS

The Dunning process fared better than some of the systems introduced during the 3-D renaissance in that it was used for several interesting films. Developed by Carroll and Dodge Dunning of the Dunningcolor Company, the system used only a single lightweight camera and no mirrors. The camera weighed 68 pounds and the surrounding "blimp" about 40 pounds.[77]

The first important film in the Dunning process was the filming of the Las Vegas Atom Blast on March 17, 1953. It was filmed in both black-and-white and color and was released by 3-D Productions, which had an arrangement to use the Dunning camera on all future 3-D productions.[78]

The system was put to the real test when it appeared in the feature film, I THE JURY, which proved to be one of the best stereo features to date. In long shots, depth was sharp and in close-ups, the roundness was astonishingly realistic. The film avoided gimmicks and concentrated on depth. When shown on a wide, curved screen, as it was at the Criterion Theatre in New York, the depth was even more realistic.

THE CHRISTIANI CAMERA

Luigi Christiani, an engineer from Florence, Italy, developed a four-lens combination which could be slipped over an ordinary camera lens and again on the projector to give 3-D images.

The process was considered as a "thunderbolt" by Sir Alexander Korda and some film industry spokesmen admitted that it was

much less costly and more effective than some of the Hollywood systems. The Richardson Camera Company lost no time in getting the American rights and Paramount grabbed the contract to release films made in the process.[79]

The Christiani system, advertised in America as "The Richardson Camera," first filmed TAILOR MADE BEAUTIES in Italy and then THE ODYSSEY starring Kirk Douglas and Sylvana Mangano. The 3-D version was planned in Gevacolor and the "flat" version was in Eastman Color. When 3-D declined, THE ODYSSEY was released in its 2-D version only.

Also scrapped were plans to release a 3-D comedy, THE FUNNIEST SHOW ON EARTH, with Italian comedian, Toto, and made in the Christiani system.

BOLEX TRIORAMA SYSTEM

The Bolex single-strip stereo system for 16mm films was a radical departure from the other inventions. Its images were vertical, i.e., the image was taller than it was wide, giving the effect of a tall picture frame. The system, called Triorama for its short Broadway run, was premiered at the Rialto Theatre in New York City on February 12, 1953, mostly to cash in on the current 3-D rage. The program consisted of four short subjects. Reviewers made it clear that this was strictly an amateur process and left much to be desired as a theatrical release. There was not much depth noticeable and the image, being twice as high as it was wide, was considered irritating and uncomfortable.[80]

Despite its faults for theatrical use, the Bolex system was used for some 16mm industrial films and it was the first process to be used to film a major baseball game in 3-D. The game was between the Milwaukee Braves and the Chicago Cubs and was released by Academy Film Productions.[81] Since the Bolex process uses the same "taking" and "projecting" lens, it was simple enough even for an amateur to use. If 3-D films come back in fashion, we may hear more from the Bolex system.

STEREOCOLOR

Dr. R. E. Schensted of Marshalltown, Iowa, entered the 3-D sweepstakes with Stereocolor, which produced color images on black-and-white film. His partner, Col. B. J. Palmer, demonstrated the process at several film conventions and at each one, mechanical difficulties plagued the showings. Flicker was apparent during the showings but Palmer insisted that he was demonstrating on a

workshop model and this flicker would be eliminated on the proper projector.[82]

The camera used one strip of black-and-white film with the color being secured through the use of a red-green-blue color wheel and through the color filters on the camera lens. How the stereo effect was obtained seemed to be a dark secret. MGM was about the only one interested in the process, but even its interest soon waned. The Stereocolor system showed that it was more and more impractical due to the color wheel technique, which was shoved aside by the movie industry as early as 1911 and by the television industry as early as 1946.[83] Later Stereocolor demonstrations added stereophonic sound for added effect and was projected at an aspect ratio of 2.44:1, but by the end of 1954, experimentation was discontinued.[84]

THE NORLING CAMERA

John A. Norling, who was responsible for AUDIOSCOPIKS in 1936, used his camera for all RKO 3-D films produced at that studio. The Norling Camera, handled as a regular camera, had a double film magazine and a binocular viewfinder which helped the scenes to be composed three-dimensionally. The camera was used most successfully in SECOND CHANCE.

OTHER SYSTEMS WITH GLASSES

Universal's process was put to practical use in their 3-D films beginning with IT CAME FROM OUTER SPACE and proved quite successful. Other systems meeting with some degree of success were RCA's 16mm 3-D system for use with dimension films overseas and the Tru-Stereo system, exploited by Al Zimbalist and used for ROBOT MONSTER in 1953. Reviewers considered it especially easy on the eyes and clear at all times.[85]

Other systems did not fare so well. Dr. Edgar I. Fuller's Naturescope was reported to be fuzzy and out of focus in its first demonstrations.[86] Friend Baker, who helped develop Natural Vision, announced his own variation of the system and demonstrated it to the American Society of Cinematographers.[87] Depth-O-Vision, developed by Howard Anderson and son, announced a feature film in the process, BARCELONA, which, if made at all, was not released domestically.[88]

3-D CARTOONS

For cartoon films, three systems adapted for 3-D were being used. Famous Studios, releasing through Paramount, brought out

Stereotoon, a system which was used for POPEYE, ACE OF SPACE and BOO MOON.

Walter Lantz developed a process which shot cartoon drawings for the left eye and then moved slightly and shot a second film for the right eye. The invention was first used successfully in THE HYPNOTIC HICK, a Woody Woodpecker cartoon.[89]

The third system, unnamed, was developed by John R. Bray and Max Fleischer, both veteran cartoon producers.

OPERATIONS IN 3-D

The American College of Surgeons got their first look at the Floyd Ramsdell system in a 3-D color picture of a stomach operation in March, 1953. Ramsdell claimed that it would revolutionize surgery teaching methods with the addition of depth a very potent factor in showing operation details. Patented in 1949, the system used a movable mirror for the dimension effect. The Ramsdell system was described as devoid of eyestrain and lens distortion.[90] The first "mobile 3-D theatre" seating eight persons was sent on the road in 1954, using a film called A WAY OF THINKING made in the Ramsdell 3-D system.

FOREIGN DIMENSION PROCESSES

Among the foreign 3-D systems using polaroid glasses were a one-camera system using a rubberized screen and projection from mid-theatre, announced by George Palmer of Australia.[91]

With great rapidity came many other versions. Hong Kong came up with an amateurish film called THE FORTUNE HUNTERS which was shown at the Sun Sing Theatre in New York in an unnamed 3-D system. Only the children were impressed, a reviewer stated, with the various articles which came out of the screen at them. In addition, dialog in the film was in Cantonese, which is slowly dying out in New York as a spoken language.[92]

Germany's Boehner system used a single strip of film with Zeiss-Icon lenses and was resurrected after being idle since 1939. Renewed interest was shown in the system by Warner Brothers, but it was the King Brothers releasing through RKO, who filmed THE CARNIVAL STORY successfully in the process, using Agfacolor film.[93] In most cases, however, it was released as a regular flat film.

Japan announced two systems almost simultaneously. Tovision, used at Toho Studios, filmed two short subjects, JUMPING OUT SUNDAY and I AM MARKED in the process.[94] The other system, Shockitu Vision, produced a feature picture in the system, which

required only one camera and one projector. Special lenses were used on both the camera and projector.[95]

Adolpho Acosto Briceno of Mexico announced a system with both images on one film.[96] The first Mexican 3-D film to play in the United States was EL CORAZON Y LA ESPADA, starring Cesar Romero and Katy Jurado. Since the images were on one film, it was inexpensive for Spanish language theatres to show it. The Mexican 3-D films were shown mostly in American cities where there were Spanish theatres and in Texas and New Mexico. The market since the advent of television has decreased to a few scattered theatres today. What became of this one-projector system is a mystery.

3-D FOR STANDARD FILMS

From the Union of South Africa came the startling news in April, 1954, that three Cape Town residents — C. R. Brougham-Cook, Bert Fisher and Eddie Pentz, had developed a method of projecting any standard film in 3-D on a single strip of film by means of a simple attachment on the projector lens and the use of polaroid glasses by the audience. They called the invention Tru Dimension.

After the fantastic claims for "crackpot" processes which had appeared in the previous two years, experts were sure that this was another invention that would never get out of the experimental stage. But S. M. Kirsch, a **Film Daily** staff correspondent, actually witnessed a private demonstration of the system in both 16mm and 35mm and among his enthusiastic comments were:

". . . (The) demonstration included ordinary 2-D prints of a 16mm color version of a standard feature. 16mm black-and-white short subjects, and a 35mm U.S. feature. The effect in each case was remarkable. The 35mm feature's depth of vision was extraordinarily enhanced by the fact that some of the sequences were of horses, paddocks and corrals, with the fencing disappearing into the distance from the front of the screen.

"It was notable, too, that no eye straining was experienced, while there was no diminishing in size of the screen image as in conventional 3-D. This correspondent tested the depth of vision effect from all angles and from various distances from the screen, to find that the depth effect was fully obtained from all stations."[97]

Another system of this type was invented by Merf Evans of Denver and demonstrated for the press in 1954. The patented device worked on a system of mirrors and lenses. Glasses were required to see the final pictures and it was said to be adaptable for television as well as movies.[98]

STEREOSCOPIC ILLUSION FILMS

Stereoscopic films without the use of viewing glasses are also as old as the film medium itself. As early as 1910, a Hale's Tour travelog, UP MOUNT TAMALPAIS, attained some astounding accidental depth in some of its scenes. Stereo illusion films were seen in the 1920's and Walt Disney's Multiplane Camera gave a sense of depth to some of his short films and feature cartoons in the late 1930's and 1940's.

The Garutso Balanced Lenses were used for several feature films in the late 1940's including a series of Lippert Films — APACHE CHIEF, DEPUTY MARSHAL, and TOUGH ASSIGNMENT, as well as Stanley Kramer's production of CYRANO DE BERGE-RAC. None of these systems, however, gave a depth effect enough to excite a contented movie industry to adopt them as standards.

But with BWANA DEVIL and the advent of polaroid glasses, everyone began to scramble for a stereoscopic system which would give depth without wearing special glasses. Several announcements were made which claimed to solve the problem, but most of them never got past the announcement stage, although some were put into use for a short time.

THE BETTI SYSTEM

Perhaps the most impractical film of the viewerless type was the Betti process, invented in Italy by Alberto and Adriano Betti. They took their film on two strips in two cameras. When it was projected onto a screen, a giant wheel with hundreds of spokes alternating mirrored and black bands is placed in front of the projector. In front of and below this wheel was another mirror and the dimensional effect was achieved without glasses by having the image from one projector hit the black band while the other images hit the mirrored band. Then this was reversed. When the wheel was speeded up, the illusion was formed.[99]

Simple? Yes, but there was one drawback. In order to view the film, the spectator had to sit in a seat similar to a barber's chair with a headrest on it. If one moved his head out of the headrest, the 3-D effect was lost!

CYCLOSTEREOSCOPE

In Paris, Francois Savoye announced that his Cyclostereoscope 3-D system, which was premiered in May at the Clichy-Palace Theatre, needed no viewers. This was in 1954, at the height of the 3-D craze. M. Savoye stated that any 3-D film could be shown on the

special screen, which had a rotating conic grill which surrounded the screen. This grill was synchronized with the projectors.[100]

The system, it was announced, would eliminate the need for polaroid viewers and pictures would not suffer from light losses. However, the grill, one-half again as large as the diameter of the screen, meant a loss of seating capacity in the theatre and installation would be costly.

Another Parisian, Pierre Boyer, announced another "glassless" 3-D system which he told the press would be ready soon. It never was.[101]

THE MORROS SYSTEM

Producer Boris Morros, who later became famed as a U.S. counterspy, announced in 1954 that he had purchased the rights to an Austrian dimensional system which required no glasses or special projecting equipment. Instead, a special screen was used containing seven reflecting surfaces, each behind the other. In addition to giving a stereoscopic illusion to regular "flat" films, this special screen was supposed to give complete depth to regular 3-D films without the use of viewers.[102] Morros' enthusiasm about the fact that the process would cost no more than a regular screen and give added values to conventional films, did not seem to impress the Hollywood powers-that-be. No picture was attempted with the system.

TRI-DIM

A method which had a slightly longer longevity than most of the other 3-D systems (or at least it seemed so) was Tri-Dim, invented by Stuart Sheldon and Dr. Henry Goldman of Trotwood, Ohio. Sheldon began experimentation nearly 20 years before. The original system, announced in June of 1954, was:

"Tri-Dim is a system that projects film at the rate of 120 frames per minute as against the conventional 90, and while the original taking camera uses two films, one to record the right eye and the other the left eye, the single print reaching the theatre will have the images for each eye alternating. It is the eyes' power to retain one image while the other is being superimposed that gives the three-dimensional effect."[103]

Several major movie companies had reported their interest after seeing the demonstration in Sheldon's basement theatre. The 3-D effect, it was said, was good and there was no eyestrain.

Sheldon used a system of prisms in the taking cameras and the

film was pulled through the projector two frames at a time. Any type of widescreen system (VistaVision, CinemaScope, SuperScope, etc.) could be adapted to Tri-Dim.

Sheldon made his 400-ft. demonstration film with a hand-made camera, flat flood lighting and no exposure meter. Yet, there was roundness and depth on the screen.

"The success of Tri-Dim," as Sheldon himself put it, "is in its ability to project two separate images, yet the eyes only see a composite of the two in one image on the screen."[104]

By the middle of 1956, all tests had been completed and Tri-Dim was ready to go into the theatres on a "roadshow" basis, but by then interest in 3-D films was at its nadir.

OTHER ILLUSION SYSTEMS

Another system which was said to have given depth to ordinary films was AMP-O-Vision, invented by Albert M. Pickus, a theatre owner in Stratford, Conn. He worked on the process in his basement and it was a completely "home-made" affair. It featured a large curved screen giving a widescreen image as well as a depth illusion.[105]

Sol Lesser, who had brought Tri-Optican to America, obtained the U. S. rights to a system which gave films depth and panoramic size by means of a lenticular screen consisting of little "lenses" and a set of wings jutting out from each side. The picture was allowed to "bleed" over on these wings, giving a depth illusion.[106]

David Gordon's system got the 3-D effect by filming two successive images, one of which was predominant and the second, subordinate. The latter contained the image, which, when viewed in rapid succession to the former, provided a halo image with respect to the foreground objects in the picture.[107]

Keisuke Yamazaki of Japan used a slow motion camera attachment and a special lens which permitted the subject to be photographed in the same way as the human eye sees him. To compensate for the slow motion photography, the speed of the projector was accelerated for showing.[108]

A Belgium system used a large viewing glass in front of the screen to separate the two images, replacing the glasses.[109]

The Russians attempted to cash in on the 3-D rage by exhibiting ADMIRAL USHAKOV, the dimensional effect of which was apparently in the minds of the press agents who presented the film. As **Films in Review** summed it up:

"As for Sovscope, it is an invention of the ad writers. No '3-D

effect' whatever is visible in the print of ADMIRAL USHAKOV being shown here."[110]

Other inventions included Max Fleischer's "glassless 3-D camera;"[111] Ralph Huber's "Huber System" which projected each image on a screen so constructed that each view is reflected into the proper eye of each member of the audience regardless of his location in the theatre;[112] William (Hopalong Cassidy) Boyd's "secret process" which never has been disclosed;[113] Dr. Edgar Fuller's Matriscope and the aforementioned Garutso Balanced Lenses which were tried again.

Alexandre Filippi, a French engineer, announced a "glassless" 3-D process in February 1952, which used a grid and raster arrangement.

Another process which was said to have given a 3-D illusion to any regular theatrical motion picture was announced in Brussels by A. Garikian and P. de Wit. In their method, the image is first projected on a normally situated screen. This screen is powerfully reflective and possesses a calculated curve, so that it throws the image onto another screen placed opposite. The image from the second screen is again reflected back to the first, which is placed higher than the second. Although persons who witnessed demonstrations of the system say that it is not quite as three-dimensional as some of the other systems, but is closer to actual vision.[114]

The Garutso Realife Process, which featured a multiple source lens which produced a 3-D effect on a single film, was another variant on the Garutso Balanced Lenses.[115] Unlike most of the illusion processes, the Garutso Realife system was used on a feature film, Erich Pommer's A LOVE STORY filmed in Germany, in widescreen.

But the 3-D "illusion" systems were shattered like the 3-D illusion itself. After two years of excitement, the third dimensional film became as obsolete as button shoes and it looked as if it would never be revived again.

[77] *Variety*, 190:7, March 4, 1953.
[78] *Film Daily*, 103:6, March 17, 1953.
[79] Marcia McEwan, "Italian Invents 3-D Device," *Christian Science Monitor*, April 14, 1953, p. 4C.
[80] *Variety*, 189:6, February 18, 1953.
[81] *Film Daily*, 104:8, August 25, 1953.
[82] *Film Daily*, 103:1, June 2, 1953.
[83] Charles Urban's Kinemacolor system used a color wheel in 1911 and the CBS color television system used the same technique in the 1940's. Both were found impractical and abandoned.
[84] *Film Daily*, 104:10, November 2, 1953.
[85] *Variety*, 191:16, June 17, 1953.
[86] *Film Daily*, 103:1, May 15, 1953.
[87] *Ibid.*. 103:7, April 27, 1953.

[88] *Variety*, 190:27, March 25, 1953.
[89] *Variety*, 190:5, May 20, 1953.
[90] *Ibid.*, 190:7, April 1, 1953.
[91] *Film Daily*, 104:1, July 31, 1953.
[92] *Variety*, 192:15, September 30, 1953.
[93] *Ibid.*, 190:5, April 8, 1953.
[94] *Ibid.*, 190:18, April 1, 1953.
[95] *Ibid.*, 190:12, April 22, 1953.
[96] *Film Daily*, 104:1, August 12, 1953.
[97] S. M. Kirsch, *Film Daily*, 105:1, April 2, 1954.
[98] *Independent Film Journal*, 33:10, May 29, 1954.
[99] *Film Daily*, 103:11, March 4, 1953.
[100] *Variety*, 193:7, March 5, 1954.
[101] *Variety*, 193:7, March 5, 1954.
[102] *Loc. cit.*
[103] *Film Daily*, 106:9, July 30, 1954.
[104] *Ibid.*, 107:10, April 29, 1955.
[105] *Film Daily*, 103:1, March 2, 1953.
[106] *Ibid.*, 103:1, February 10, 1953.
[107] *Ibid.*, 103:5, April 13, 1953.
[108] *Loc. cit.*
[109] *Variety*, 189:16, March 4, 1953.
[110] *Films in Review*, 5:146, March, 1954.
[111] *Variety*, 189:7, February 25, 1953.
[112] *Film Daily*, 103:1, February 9, 1953.
[113] *Ibid.*, 104:7, June 14, 1953.
[114] *Independent Film Journal*, 33:8, April 17, 1954.
[115] *Film Daily*, 105:1, April 23, 1954.

CHAPTER FIVE
THE THIRD-DIMENSION IN THE
TELEVISION ERA

Two 3-D television systems, both using polaroid glasses, were announced in 1953, although neither one is as yet in commercial use.

Bolex Stereo system, which had exhibited its Triorama in New York, used a special stereoptican lens placed in front of the television camera lens to get the 3-D effect.[116]

The Genoscope process, perfected in Bloomington, Illinois, tested its process in actual TV broadcasts. The two lenses on the camera are mounted in shadow boxes. The left image is deterred by a special lens so it is seen a fraction of a second later than the right eye image.[117]

In 1954, a TV series called ANGEL'S AUDITIONS was announced as going into 3-D production under the direction of L.P. Dudley, a British stereoscopic expert.[118] The program was said to have been viewable by the aid of polaroid glasses in 3-D and without glasses in 2-D. Nothing seemed to happen to this project, however, as it never appeared on the networks.

By 1956, a compatible dimensional system was announced for television presentation by "Compatible 3-D-TV Corp." The system could be seen in 3-D or in flat versions and the films were to be made in the Langberg system. Glasses again would be needed to see the 3-D versions.[119]

Tri-Visional TV Commercials, Inc., announced it would produce short subjects with a depth effect attained by means of composite plate photography.[120]

Stuart Sheldon, who invented the Tri-Dim process for the movies, said his system would be adapted for both "live" and filmed television productions. Sets not adapted to the new system would be able to pick up the picture in its flat version.[121]

So far, none of these 3-D television systems has been put to any practical use. And while television occupied more people in their living rooms, the 3-D movies died out in the big cities while 3-D held

on in the smaller towns as late as October of 1954. As **Variety** put it, "3-D Lingers in Sticks."[122] But soon even the "sticks" gave up altogether.

Yet while 3-D films were as dead as could be in the United States, other countries were still excited about the new movie concept. RKO and Warner Brothers ordered more than a million pairs of viewers for Formosa, Puerto Rico, Columbia, Argentina, Montevideo and Italy.

Despite the excitement in these places, polaroid earnings for the first six months of 1954 slipped from over 13 million dollars to less than 10 million.

A SHORT REVIVAL

In 1955, Universal tried a revival of the 3-D film with glasses in its REVENGE OF THE CREATURE which was to be a "test case" as to whether the dimensional motion picture could make a comeback in the theatres. The film, according to Universal, was photographed with a view to avoiding past mistakes at the technical and photographic end. Since theatres were still equipped to show the double-film 3-D systems, they could lose nothing.

After a big Detroit premiere in which the film chalked up nearly record business, even Universal was at a loss as to why it was such a hit. Even though exhibitors had a choice of both 3-D and 2-D prints, most of them chose the former. Polaroid rallied its support and it looked as if 3-D might come back in a limited number of productions each year.

As for the picture itself, it got fair reviews, although most reviewers felt that 3-D didn't add too much to the film.

So despite this slight upsurge, REVENGE OF THE CREATURE did not cause a 3-D comeback. Yet just as the CREATURE keeps reappearing in films, 3-D constantly re-occurs in one form or another. Warner's HOUSE OF WAX and PHANTOM OF THE RUE MORGUE were revived in 1958 and several critics felt that a re-issue of old 3-D films once in a while was a good lift to the box office and offered a chance to a new generation to see these films.

Alvin Marks of Marks Polarized Corporation announced a new 3-D technique, Cinetrox in June, 1956. He described it as compatible with present widescreen systems and the theatre could be converted for less than ten thousand dollars.[123] But with TV cutting into theatre business that year, the theatres were not interested.

The answer to successful 3-D seemed to be in a perfected system which could show the depth without glasses. That was still to come.

TAKE OFF THOSE GLASSES!

Research on dimensional films still continued in the 1960's and the claims of "3-D without glasses" still echoed throughout Filmland.

A French process called Heraclorama, developed by M. Bourdiaux, claimed to bring depth to ordinary films without the use of glasses. It consisted of a slatted screen and a special lens. According to those who have witnessed a demonstration of Heraclorama, the method actually works.

A **Variety** reporter at a Brussels demonstration said: "There was plenty of cheering when extracts of several films suddenly came to life within three dimensions. These included extracts from Lamorisse's (THE RED BALLOON) and WEST SIDE STORY . . . which currently is showing at the same cinema . . . He has brought to the cinema a feeling of depth, without the use of glasses, or so it seemed to viewers here."[124]

It is said that the slats of the screen are curved to follow the shape of the retina of the eye. As of this writing, the Heraclorama method has not been demonstrated in the United States.

Other "depth effect" screens include the "Maika" screen from Japan and the double, semi-transparent screen of Alvin and Mortimer Marks of Long Island.

A three-lens unit is the key to Giantscope, another development of the Technicolor technicians; Stereorama is an undisclosed "glassless" process developed in New Castle, Indiana; CineDepth, a development financed by Paramount, was announced in 1959, but was later dropped by the studio, and a system touted by Texas millionaire Glenn H. McCarthy which has yet to be named.

3-D and CINEMASCOPE

A rather aborted attempt to combine 3-D and CinemaScope showed up in 1960 in SEPTEMBER STORM, released by Fox. Rather than adopting the double image on the same film, the Fox release used the old two-projector system — the system which killed 3-D in theatres a few years earlier.

Advertised as "perfected," it proved to be only more of the same.

The combination of poor story and poor projection killed SEPTEMBER STORM very early and it was shown in most of its few engagements as a regular "flat" film. The public couldn't have cared less. The process, for the record, was called "Stereovision."

At its premiere at the Fox Theatre in Detroit, the two projectors got so far out of synchronization at one showing (witnessed by this

writer) that hero Mark Stevens had four arms and the fringing got so bad that the second projector was turned off and the rest of the film was shown flat. The management, however, failed to notify the audience of this fact and the entire audience (which was small) sat through the entire second half of the film with their glasses on — with no depth to see.

THE ANAGLYPH RETURNS — AGAIN!

After the grave of the polaroid glasses had been dug, the film industry occasionally reverted back to the old anaglyph 3-D method to put a little spark into some of its "exploitation" films.

In 1960, William Castle, a producer who was never averse to using a new gimmick to spice up his horror films, revived the orange and blue glasses (a variant on the red and green ones) in which a look through the orange viewer would make ghosts appear on the screen and a look through the blue side of the viewer would make them disappear.

Outside of this gimmick, the film 13 GHOSTS had nothing else to recommend it. And even the 3-D effect was anything but astounding and the picture was relegated to the Saturday matinees for the kids.

The following year Warner Brothers contracted to release a Canadian film about the supernatural, THE MASK, which used the red and green glasses for "dream sequences" during this film about a mask which drives people mad. Each time the hero dons the mask, the audience dons its 3-D viewers. As with 13 GHOSTS, what was seen through the glasses was never as horrible as one's own imagination might conjure up. The camera used was said to have been developed by the British government at great expense. Judging from the box office returns, the great expense wasn't worth it.

With the rise in popularity of the "nudie" films in the 1960's, it was only a matter of time until 3-D was utilized as a gimmick in one of these films. The time came in 1962 with PARADISIO, the story of a man who found a pair of glasses which, when put on, made everyone appear nude. You can guess the rest. Like the other reversions to the anaglyph system, PARADISIO was quickly forgotten.

THE FUTURE OF THE THIRD DIMENSION

Where is 3-D heading in the next few years? Is there a big future for it in television as well as motion pictures? Can true "glassless" 3-D ever come about?

As of now, the old true stereoscopic effect is through two images

projected on one screen with some method (usually viewing glasses) to separate the left and right images in the eye.

But science says it is possible that someday we will have true depth films without viewing glasses. And science is working on it.

The first break-through in true glassless 3-D came in magazine photography in 1964. Look Magazine tried it first, followed by other advertisers. Using the "parallax panoramagram" process (similar to the Russian's "Parallax Stereogram" system), it has already been proved that it can produce depth without mechanical aids. This is apparently the process worked on "under wraps" by MGM and which the New York University College of Engineering had been working on.[125]

While some insist that it is only a matter of months until the solution to "glassless" 3-D is found, Col. Robert V. Bernier, one of the pioneers in stereoscopic vision without glasses, insists that it might be 50 years before 3-D without glasses would be commercially available, although some experimental exhibits might be held. He continued:

"The overall efforts both physically and economically which would be needed to make such movies possible, even when limited to this country alone, would be almost analogous to our atomic energy program.

"The principle of how such movies can be made and exhibited is well known. It is also well known that an efficient and genuine 3-D motion picture (that) can be seen without glasses requires not just two slightly different stereo images, but a multiplicity of images. It would be impractical to utilize a film a foot or more wide, a size it might well have to be to accommodate all those images.

"Further, the best vision that the brain could form from the resultant inferior synthetic images would be far short of a re-creation of the original physical scene. The three-dimensional vision that can be had today by the expedient of wearing a comfortable pair of viewers is far superior in its ability to duplicate the original physical scene."[126]

Other 3-D pioneers envision even more radical changes in future dimensional systems, even if glasses are still used. John Norling conservatively stated that the "stereo window" isn't necessary and that 3-D images would fare much better in "space" where the margins of the screen are vignetted, gradually shaded off from outer darkness to the full illumination of the picture itself."[127]

Arch Obler, who started the 3-D craze, envisions an entire elimination of the theatre screen and have the picture electronically received in space.[128] He predicts that this may be only a dozen years away.

Fred Schwartz, president of Century Theatres, envisions a "fish tank" type of screen which would be filled with activated glasses similar to a neon sign which would receive the 3-D images.[129]

Melville Terwilliger's "Inspacian Depthdimension" claims to be the only method of suspending images in space, but Mr. Terwilliger's invention doesn't seem to be taking Hollywood by storm — if indeed, it exists at all.[130]

Seemingly the best invention of all is one of man's latent talents, according to Wilton Melhorn, instructor at the University of Michigan. When he found that 3-D glasses hurt his eyes, he took them off, squinted, blinked and wham — things came into focus all by themselves — and in perfect 3-D. He insists that anyone can do it.[131]

But content is still the most important item to a creative artist and to the many movie fans throughout the world. As director George Stevens once stated, "Unless we come to our senses, we'll end up with a magnificently huge screen, no picture and no audience."[132]

So whether the 3-D systems are with or without glasses, there is definitely a future for a good dimension system sometime in the future. Hollywood lost the ball in the 1950's. It will try not to make the same mistake again. There are still many people who have faith in 3-D films and who see artistic possibilities for them.

Among them is Jonas Mekas, who expressed this hope:

"It seems to me that we have recently missed a promising opportunity to create a unique form of expression: I have in mind stereoscopic cinema. However primitive the first 3-D films were — BWANA DEVIL or IT CAME FROM OUTER SPACE — there was a certain excitement in watching them, even when suffering under the uncomfortable glasses. Even the crudest plot, like that of HOUSE OF WAX, gained new dimensions from the process. However, the experiment was abandoned in its infancy, unjustly and tragically, in the face of competition from easier-to-achieve gimmicks — the large screens. There is little hope that anybody will take it up again soon. The impression has been created that 3-D had proved unsuccessful financially and artistically. But those who saw McLaren's AROUND IS AROUND can clearly recall the experience of viewing this stereoscopic film (making use of the

mobile patterns generated by a cathode-ray oscillograph) on an immense screen — his dots and lines and ellipses and parabolas swinging and moving in a fascinating game. It takes an artist to reveal the artistic possibilities of a new technical process."[133] And so it does.

Despite the on again-off again status of motion pictures in depth, the future is bound to see the perfection of 3-D systems which can be seen with the naked eye and which will revolutionize film projection as we know it today. As with color and sound, the basic rudiments have always been inherent in our universe. It remains only for someone to develop 3-D to the point where it can be used easily and inexpensively.

The answer to natural third dimensional motion pictures may be in the recent development of the "hologram," which utilizes the amazing new Laser beam. It provides a genuine 3-D picture in which the view is in correct perspective to each individual person in the audience. The system has already been used for advertising displays and it is only a matter of time until it is adapted for the motion picture screen. Its perfection could revolutionize motion picture production as we now know it. Only future experimentation in this new science will provide the answer.

All of us, if we have two fairly normal eyes, "see" in depth and there is no doubt that motion pictures in 3-D will add a naturalness to films, and also a sense of drama and involvement which has never been possible with conventional "flat" films. The dramatic possibilities of 3-D have yet to be genuinely explored by film artists, who have been limited to throwing things out into the audience, making them more irritated than involved. When depth can be used to involve rather than to assault the viewer, it will be a most welcome addition to the art of the film.

When the viewer can see a situation unfolding in another room with a complete naturalness of spatial dimension, it will become difficult for him to disassociate himself from the scene and there will be little doubt that he will derive more pleasure from the scene on the screen.

Aesthetically, the third dimension has no bounds — except that of the "frame" of the movie screen itself. When the problem of these boundaries has been solved (either by the image seeming to "float in space" or having no "edges" on the wall or screen) then the viewer

will see the most natural and most exciting images ever offered to the moviegoers of the world.

The possibilities of 3-D are endless and they **will** become a permanent part of all films sometime in the future. Of this there is no doubt. All that is needed is the man to solve the depth equation.

[116] *Film Daily,* 104:1, February 6, 1953.
[117] *Ibid.,* 104:1, December 3, 1953.
[118] *Variety,* 196:45, September 8, 1954.
[119] *Film Daily,* 110:6, August 13, 1956.
[120] *Ibid.,* 107:7, February 8, 1955.
[121] *Film Daily,* 108:10, October 14, 1955.
[122] *Variety,* 196:4, October 13, 1954.
[123] *Variety,* 203:17, June 13, 1956.
[124] *Variety,* 232:14, October 16, 1963.
[125] *Variety,* 105:1, April 9, 1954.
[126] *Ibid.,* 105:7, February 11, 1954.
[127] *Variety,* 190:13, June 3, 1953.
[128] *Film Daily,* 103:1, February 4, 1953.
[129] *Ibid.,* 103:1, February 18, 1953.
[130] *Variety,* 191:2, August 12, 1953.
[131] *Loc. cit.*
[132] *Theatre Arts,* 37:72, September, 1953.
[133] Jonas Mekas, *Experiment in the Film,* p. 150.

PART FOUR — SOUND

"Wait a minute. Wait a minute.
You ain't heard nothin' yet!"
— Al Jolson in **The Jazz Singer**

CHAPTER ONE
EARLY ATTEMPTS AT SOUND FILMS

Ever since Thomas A. Edison invented the phonograph in 1877 and premiered the first modern motion picture in America in 1896, inventors were looking toward the day when these two great discoveries could be wedded into a "talking picture."

Despite comments to the contrary, there have been sound films shown in movie theatres not only from the earliest days of the film, but also before it. But before discussing these early talking movies, let's examine the easiest way of making sound films — using people instead of electronics.

HUMAN SOUND FILMS

Most early producers understood the excitement of films with sound and made many brave attempts to give their audiences this extra dimension. Many "man-made talkies" appeared in the early days of the movies.

The Italian comedian, Leopold Fregoli, helped pioneer the "do-it-yourself" sound film as early as 1898. He made a series of short comedies and projected them at the end of his stage performances. Fregoli would stand behind the screen and speak or sing in synchronization with the image.

Another version of this method was used by Lyman H. Howe, whose companies would travel around the country showing travel films while, behind the screen, a group of men would make the appropriate sound effects. The Howe company did the sound for two 1911 films, Reliance's THE GRAY OF THE DAWN and Rex's FATE.

In 1910 a cast of actors were stationed back of the screen during the Vitagraph presentation of UNCLE TOM'S CABIN and did a complete "talkie" version of that famous play when they mouthed the words.

D. W. Griffith used this same method on some of the "road show"

tours of his film version of THE BIRTH OF A NATION. As one of the sound men recalls one of these performances:

"I was just a high school student at the time and I was given the privilege of helping make the sound effects . . . I was given instructions to slap two boards together when a certain red light flashed on. We could see the film through the back of the screen to be sure we got our synchronization correctly. But I was glued to that red light. When it came on, I slammed the two boards together. When I looked at the screen, I discovered that I had just shot Abraham Lincoln!"[1]

The famous Hale's Tours, which began in 1903, used films shot with a wide angle lens and projected in a train car, giving the effect of taking a train trip. The lens gave the films a widescreen effect and, although the train was standing still, Hale added train noises to further the realism for the audience.

Some early pianists provided sound effects by the use of noisemakers — sandpaper, castanets, whistles, etc. — to underscore the images on the screen. Also used were "noise machines" which recreated the sounds of automobile motors, horns, hoofbeats of horses, train sounds and other standard sound effects.

EARLY SOUND FILMS

The first "sound film" using mechanical means seems to be that of Demeny's Chronophotophone which combined a phonograph and magic lantern slides. This was followed by Edison's Kinetophone, a combination of the cylinder phonograph and the Kinetoscope machine. By inserting what looked like a stethoscope into the ears, an individual viewer could see and hear a short sound movie. It was merely a novelty and interest soon waned on the part of the peep show habitues and only 50 Kinetophones were manufactured and sold.

In 1889, Thomas A. Edison's assistant, Laurie Dickson, became the first talking picture star when he demonstrated the Kinetophone to Mr. Edison, who had just returned from Europe. On a small four-foot screen, Dickson entered the frame on film, raised his hat and said "Good morning, Mr. Edison, glad to see you back. Hope you will like the Kinetophone. To show the synchronization I will lift my hand and count up to ten."[2] He then raised and lowered his hands and counted to ten. There was no hitch and the picture was fairly steady.

The Kinetophone used a complicated belt which was attached to a phonograph on the stage with the projector in the booth. It had a

successful run at the Keith Theatre in New York and played engagements in other key American theatres and in England. Due mostly to the fact that a fire gutted the Edison Laboratory in 1914, the production of Kinetophone films was never resumed after the disaster.

SOUND IN ENGLAND

The turn of the century brought many sound film experiments. In England, a film called LITTLE TICH AND HIS BIG BOOTS used an orchestral recording to accompany the film.

The French Chronophone appeared at the London Hippodrome in 1904 and by 1906 it was a popular item in many English theatres. It was again a system using Edison records more or less synchronized with a film.

The most popular sound system of the period was the Animatophone, an outgrowth of the earlier Simplex system which presented the inevitable vaudeville "turns" so popular there. An English company also presented a sound film version of THE MIKADO, produced about 1911, but the problem of good synchronization and adequate sound reproduction defeated its future use. The 1911 Kinemacolor film of the CORONATION OF KING GEORGE V also contained recorded sound.[3]

Early systems which competed in England were devices under such diversified names as Chronomegaphone, Appollogramaphone, Filmophone, Replicaphone, Vivaphone and the Warwick Cinephone. All actually were used in theatres and although they earned some popularity, none of them survived past 1912.[4]

In succeeding years, England produced such film-and-record combinations as THE MIDNIGHT SUN, KITTY MALONE, THE LAMBETH CAKEWALK and a 46-minute sound film version of FAUST.

The Gaumont system was not only one of the earliest sound film systems, but it also showed the films in color. The sound was furnished by a recording amplified with compressed air. As the system was described:

"Synchronization was attempted through a system of rotating brushes and collector rings. By means of an electrically-operated clutch, either one of two turntables could be rotated. A control panel was provided to be placed at the screen to synchronize sound and picture manually should the collector ring system fail to operate."[5]

In 1913, the British Gaumont Color films were premiered at the 39th Street Theatre in New York City and advertised as "talking

pictures in natural colors." That same year, Erich Pommer prepared an original musical score on records which were synchronized with the German film LES HEURES (DIE STUNDEN).

Even later, the Blatnerphone Corporation in London developed soundtracks on magnetized wire, but this system lost out in favor of the optical soundtrack in the 1920's.

FRANCE AND ITALY

Leon Gaumont in France was presenting a sound film each week at his chain of theatres in 1900 with his Chronophone system. Another French system, Phono-Scenes was popular with moviegoers.

By 1902, the stage stars of the day, including the incredible Yvette Guilbert, appeared in short talking films with recordings synchronized more or less to the films of their specialty acts. A talking film, THE DRESS, was presented with sound that same year.

The Paris Exposition presented the duel scene from CYRANO DE BERGERAC, a scene from LES PRECIEUSES RIDICULES and Sarah Bernhardt speaking in a play scene. The CYRANO scene has been re-recorded and can now be seen as a sequence in the documentary film, THE MOVIES LEARN TO TALK.

In 1916, two Italian films, L'AMICA and RAPSODIA SATANICA, had especially-composed music by Pietro Mascagni played behind the screen on synchronized phonograph records.

THE UNITED STATES

Sigmund Lubin, one of the pioneer film distributors, marketed the Cinephone, which was a movie film combined with a Victor Talking Machine phonograph.

In 1905, a variant on Edison's Kinetophone named Cameraphone, was put on the market and featured filmed vaudeville acts including Eva Tanguay singing her classic "I Don't Care" number, Blanche Ring and Anna Held. But like the other early attempts at sound films, the time was not right — either artistically or technically — and Cameraphone disappeared after 1908 for lack of interest and customers.

An article in **Moving Picture World** of 1909, however, speaks very highly of the Cameraphone films and had favorable comments on three of the 1908 sound film productions — THE CORSICAN BROTHERS, COON SONG and SCENE IN A TURKISH BATH — and predicted that the "speaking films" would become as common as the silent films.[6]

Carl Laemmle of Universal Pictures, commercialized the Synchronophone in 1907 using records and films. It attained some success that year.

The Edison Studios added sound-on-disc accompaniment to two 1912 films — THE INDIAN GIRL'S REVENGE and THE CHARGE OF THE LIGHT BRIGADE.

In 1913, the Vi-T-Phone system (not related to the later Vitaphone system of the Warner Brothers) announced it had over 100 American-made singing and talking subjects ready and was releasing six new subjects every week, including a three-reel sound film version of PAGLIACCI!

Sir Harry Lauder did a series of phonograph films for Selig Polyscope in 1914 and a year later, the Commercial Biophone presented some rather expert sound films featuring scenes from FAUST, THE BARBER OF SEVILLE and LA BOHEME, among others.

GRIFFITH AND SOUND

D. W. Griffith, who had used man-made sound effects in THE BIRTH OF A NATION, tried a genuine sound film in 1921 called DREAM STREET in the Phonokinema Process. The sound came from synchronized phonograph records which contained a special sound score. The stars, Ralph Graves and Carol Dempster sang as well as spoke during a few minutes of the film while music accompanied the remainder of the picture. The film was pronounced a hit at the Town Hall Theatre in New York City and everyone had thought the "talkies" had arrived, but lack of financial backing and Griffith's philosophy that sound films would only confine the movies to only English-speaking people caused the entire idea to be abandoned.

Griffith was quoted as saying the following about sound films:

"Speaking movies are impossible. When a century has passed, all thought of our so-called speaking movies will have been abandoned. It will never be possible to synchronize the voice with the picture."[7]

Just how wrong his prediction was to be was shown within the next five years as experimentation reached a fever pitch during this period.

SOUND-ON-FILM PROCESSES

In 1900, J. Poliakoff patented a sound reproducing system using

the photo-electric cell, which is the basis of modern talking pictures. This patent, plus the patents of A. G. Bell, C. A. Bell and S. Tainter of a variable-area and variable-density method of sound recording were the key factors in the development of sound pictures as we know them today.

Other sound recording apparatus was patented between 1901 and 1907, including Ernest Ruhmer's Photogramaphon, similar to today's sound camera; Valdemar Poulsen for wire and tape recording and Eugene A. Lauste for variable area recording.

Mr. Lauste, of the Edison Laboratory, took out his patent in 1906 and by 1910 had made the first picture with the sound track printed directly on the film. He used a mechanical shutter that opened and closed to let varied amounts of light record on the film, according to the type of sound being made.

E. E. Ries patented a sound-on-film device which he later sold to Lee deForest, a pioneer in television and sound pictures.

T. H. Nakken patented another device similar to the sound-on-film device of Dr. Lee deForest, which he sold to Warner Brothers. In 1920, H. C. Bullis patented a sound system using a double film with the image on one film and the sound track on the other.

That same year, the General Electric Company demonstrated a sound-on-film system.

The first sound-on-film motion pictures in Europe were shown in Berlin in 1922 in the Tri-Ergon system which was recorded on film approximately 42mm wide with the sound placed outside the sprocket holes. Fox Films expressed an interest in the process and bought the American patent rights. Tri-Ergon later developed into the process known today as Movietone.

Dr. Lee deForest, who had purchased the Ries sound-on-film process, had been working on sound films with only indifferent success since 1919 but finally perfected a sound system in 1923 which was considered workable. He gave a demonstration of the process before the New York Electrical Society on April 4, 1923.

As Mr. deForest explained the system:

"I have simply photographed the voice onto an ordinary film. It is on the same film with the picture, a narrow strip down one side, so narrow that the picture is not spoiled."[8]

He tried to interest Carl Laemmle of Universal and Adolph Zukor of Paramount in the new system, but they were not interested at the time.

The process, having passed the first test, was named Phonofilm and was first presented publicly at the Rivoli Theatre in New York

City in April of 1923. The public was not too excited over the demonstration and deForest continued to improve it. During 1924, he presented nearly 24 "road show" performances. In July of 1924, sound films of President Coolidge and Sen. LaFollette were made in Washington. These are considered the first talking newsreels.

PHONOFILM'S RISE

By the middle of 1924, interest in Phonofilm had developed at such a rate that over 30 theatres were wired to show Phonofilms and 50 more were being wired at the rate of two a week. The company produced a two-reel sound film called LOVE'S OLD SWEET SONG, an episode in the life of Abraham Lincoln, starring Una Merkel and Mrs. deForest. These films were shown mostly in vaudeville theatres as a novelty. Miles Mander, who was later to become a film actor, directed some of these early films, which were made at the Norma Talmadge Studios in New York City.

The first exciting Phonofilm full-length production was a sound track of the orchestration for THE COVERED WAGON.

The early Phonofilm productions were made in a room ten feet square with the walls covered with hair felt. The camera was placed outside the studio and its lens focused through a hole in one of the studio walls. The subjects, because of the hot lights, could not remain in the studio for more than a few minutes at a time without coming out for air.

The Phonofilm camera underwent more improvements and, by 1926, the process was felt ready for complete commercialization. But in order to successfully prove that Phonofilm was practical, a feature film had to be made. Demonstrations of Phonofilm were presented for William Fox of Fox Films. Several sound film sequences were made at the Fox Studios, including RETRIBU-TION, and Fox was convinced that talking pictures could be successful with the American public.

But deForest, like Edison and Griffith, never seemed to have complete confidence in the power of the sound film. When asked if talking pictures would ever replace the silent film, he replied:

"In my opinion, the answer is 'no,' for the two forms of entertainment are essentially different. The Phonofilm will never attempt to tell the same form of story adapted for pantomime nor will it draw its talent from the regular motion picture field."[9]

He also predicted that Phonofilm versions of famous stage musicals and plays would replace road shows of these productions.

Fox Films bought the German Tri-Ergon patents in 1927 and

merged them with their Phonofilm patents. The process was named Fox-Case, then changed to Movietone in April of 1927 when the Fox Movietone Newsreel was inaugurated. Such personalities as Mussolini, Shaw and Coolidge appeared in short speaking films. "The talkies" were beginning to arrive. Even in France, their 1925 version of CYRANO DE BERGERAC was in both color and sound.

But Edison, like the others, went on record as seeing no future in sound films.

[1] Dr. Averill J. Hammer, professor of chemistry at Bowling Green State University in a 1950 speech.

[2] *Variety*, 205:38, January 7, 1957.

[3] *Moving Picture World* 9:548, August 26, 1911.

[4] Rachel Low, *The History of the British Film*, 1906-1914, pp. 265-266.

[6] *Moving Picture World*, 4:71, January 16, 1909.

[7] *Educational Screen*, September, 1924.

[8] Georgette Carneal, *Conqueror of Space*, p. 282.

[9] Dr. Lee deForest, *SMPE Journal*, October, 1924, p. 17.

CHAPTER TWO
THE TURNING POINT

On April 20, 1926, Western Electric Company and Warner Brothers formed the Vitaphone Company in New York City to develop a sound-on-disc system for motion pictures. The late Sam Warner was the guiding light in Vitaphone. He told his brother Harry to "go to the Western Electric Company and see what I consider the greatest thing in the world."

Harry went.

"I had heard and seen talking pictures so much that I would not have walked across the street to look at one. But when I heard a twelve-piece orchestra on the screen at the Bell Telephone Laboratories, I could not believe my own ears. I walked in back of the screen to see if they did not have an orchestra there synchronizing with the picture. They all laughed at me. The whole affair was in a ten by twelve room. There were a lot of bulbs working and things I know nothing about, but there was not any concealed orchestra."[10]

By August, the company had perfected the system enough to present a group of short subjects and a feature film with a synchronized musical score at the Warner Theatre. The feature was DON JUAN starring John Barrymore and the shorts included a talk by Will Hays and music by the New York Philharmonic Orchestra, Marion Talley, Efrem Zimbalist and Harold Bauer, Roy Smeck, Anna Case, Mischa Elman and Giovanni Martinelli. The score for the feature film, played by the New York Philharmonic, was on discs.

The Warner Theatre used four projectors for the premiere with each set of projectors using identical films and records. In case one of the films got "out of sync" with the record, the other projector and record were turned up and the out-of-sync one faded out. Three operators were assigned to each machine.

Despite all these precautions, things did go wrong at subsequent

performances. One night an operator put on the wrong record for Will Hays' speech and as he spoke, a banjo played.

The Vitaphone system used 16-inch one-sided phonograph records which played at 33-1/3 revolutions per minute. Each record lasted for one reel.

On Christmas Day in 1926, the premiere of Warner Brothers' THE BETTER 'OLE featured a synchronized musical score, plus all-talking short subjects with Al Jolson, George Jessel, Elsie Janis and Willie and Eugene Howard. The showing was held at the Colony Theatre in New York City.

The Vitaphone equipment was moved to Hollywood in the spring of 1927 and soon after, Warner Brothers, who were on the verge of bankruptcy, acquired 100 per cent interest in the Vitaphone system and took a big chance.

HISTORY IS MADE

For the premiere sound film in the new process, Warner Brothers chose THE JAZZ SINGER and persuaded singer Al Jolson to star in it. The film was not an all-talking picture, but did contain several song sequences and two short sections of dialog with the remainder of the film silent with musical background. As awkward as it seems today, especially with the possibilities of the disc getting out of synchronization, THE JAZZ SINGER made history. Soon Warner Brothers was on its feet financially and they plunged into the business of making sound films even though only 100 theatres were wired for sound when THE JAZZ SINGER was released.

Warners first added musical accompaniment to WHEN A MAN LOVES followed by dialog sequences in GLORIOUS BETSY, MIDNIGHT TAXI, MY MAN, STATE STREET SADIE and WOMEN THEY TALK ABOUT.

By the end of 1928, Warners had made six all-talking films, LIGHTS OF NEW YORK, THE LION AND THE MOUSE, ON TRIAL, THE TERROR, THE SINGING FOOL and THE HOMETOWNERS.

But the sound-on-disc films had many drawbacks. It was difficult to keep the film and sound together and, once the record had begun to pick up the sound, it could not be stopped for fear of never getting the synchronization back again.

DISSATISFACTION GROWS

Lee deForest, however, was not satisfied with the Vitaphone system and neither were the other film companies. They were

convinced that "talking pictures" were just a fad and would die as soon as the novelty wore off.

deForest was looking ahead.

"I find myself," he said, "more than ever firmly convinced that the right way to solve the problem of the talking motion picture, and the musically accompanied feature picture, is that of photographing the sound waves on the film rather than by means of the synchronized phonograph. In any event I am glad to note that the film industry, for the first time since the inception of the art, is ready to welcome the so-called 'talking pictures' and am convinced that in a very short time they will prove a most important part of every program."[11]

MOVIETONE

Movietone became the first popular system to employ a sound track directly on the film, and it proved to be the turning point for talking pictures and set the standard for sound films still used today.

Under the direction of Theodore W. Case, William Fox and Earl I. Sponable, and with the cooperation of General Electric, Movietone began making test films. The first was by Sir Harry Lauder, who had previously appeared in some sound-on-disc shorts. He sang his famous "Roamin' in the Gloamin' " and to be sure that the film would not be shown commercially, Sir Harry stopped in the middle of the song and inserted the phrase, "This is a test." And a successful test it was.

HOW IT WORKS

Movietone operated on the principle of the photo-electric cell. When sound is photographed on a film, each sound makes an image. When projected, the projector scans the sound track, with its variations of white, gray and black, and the light-sensitive photo-electric cell flickers as the film passes it. This flicker is transferred back into electrical impulses which are in turn converted back into sound.

Fox went ahead with plans to film some one-reel sound films to "test" in regular motion picture theatres. Early in 1927, Fox presented several sound shorts with its feature release, WHAT PRICE GLORY? Audience reaction was good but, as Mr. Sponable put it, "there was no stampede."[12]

Author Walter Pitkin has perhaps the easiest way of explaining how a sound film is made:

". . . a player on the movie set speaks the line, 'I love you.' As the words leave his lips, sound waves travel from his mouth to the microphone. As the microphone vibrates to these air waves, sound waves travel from the microphone to an electric light shining through a slit on a moving film in the camera. As the microphone currents strike the electric light, it flickers, changing its brightness in sensitive response to the microphone current. Or perhaps instead, a light shines upon the film and changes its size automatically. The different quantities or the different intensities of light set up minute ether waves which travel rapidly to the sensitized film. When these strike the film, they cause the chemicals on the film to change or develop in various degrees of light and shade. These chemical changes on the film are then fixed and furnish permanent records: corresponding precisely to the original sound waves caused by the words 'I love you,' which the actor spoke. 'I love you' then becomes, in photographic form, a series of black and white lines on the edge of a strip of celluloid."[13]

Because of the problems inherent in keeping the sound discs and the film image in synchronization, the Fox Movietone system with the sound actually on the film itself soon gained the upper hand and the cumbersome sound-on-disc system was assigned to the scrap heap within two years.

OUT OF THE STUDIO

The greatest difficulty of the early sound films was the question of where to put the loudspeakers from which the sound came. This was solved by Mr. Sponable's perfection of a new type of movie screen filled with little holes which reflected a good picture image while, at the same time, letting the sound pass through the screen from speakers placed behind it. The entire industry accepted this new type of screen, which is still very much the standard in most theatres today.

With successful recording in a soundproof studio, Movietone went outdoors to record a West Point review. Another unit went to Italy to film the Pope and Mussolini.

The West Point film opened at the Roxy Theatre in New York City in May of 1927, as a short subject with a regular silent feature. That same month, another series of Movietone shorts opened at the Harris Theatre with Fox's film, SEVENTH HEAVEN. The feature picture had a musical score synchronized on the sound track.

In June of that year, Fox recorded Lindbergh's welcome in

Washington and, coupled with a speech by Mussolini, created a sensation with the two films and launched them in September at the Times Square Theatre with Fox's SUNRISE with both music and sound on the film. There was still no dialog in the feature films.

The still popular Fox Movietone Newsreel was first presented on October 28, 1927, at the Roxy Theatre in New York City and contained the following: Niagara Falls, Romance of the Iron Horse, Army-Yale Football Game, New York Rodeo, King George V, Lloyd George, Marshal Foch and the Crowned Prince of Sweden.

Development and refinement continued. "Noise" was reduced on the sound track and other technical developments were made. Movietone newsreels were coming out nearly twice a month. More silent Fox pictures were synchronized with sound, including BLINDFOLDED, FAZIL, FOUR SONS, ME GANGSTER, MOTHER MACHREE, PLASTERED IN PARIS, PREP AND PEP, RED DANCE, RILEY THE COP and RIVER PIRATE. Synchronized sound effects also were added to a cartoon film and a test was made combining sound with two-color Technicolor film.

With all these tests successful, Fox went to work on a two-reel comedy with dialog, THE FAMILY PICNIC. This comedy opened at the Globe Theatre in New York City with THE AIR CIRCUS, another part-talking picture. Other "part-talking" films of 1928 were MOTHER KNOWS BEST and THE RIVER.

Soon other companies began realizing the values of sound films and Fox accelerated its sound film program and ordered equipment for 24 recording units. In September, 1928, Fox Movietone City was dedicated, which is now the site of Twentieth Century-Fox Studios.

Three months later, the first out-of-door sound feature, IN OLD ARIZONA, was premiered at the Criterion Theatre in Los Angeles. This Cisco Kid adventure, starring Warner Baxter, won an Academy Award for him. It was said of the film:

"This film was photographed and recorded against a sweeping background of natural beauty, and in it sound recording achieved its highest artistic success up to that time. Filmed and recorded right in the vast open spaces, the scenes and human voice and all the accompanying sounds were reproduced with a clearness and naturalness that attracted wide attention. The Movietone process caught and reproduced with fidelity not only the voices of the actors, but actually the natural sounds of the outdoors: the whispering of the wind, the song of the birds. The picture was thus notable in combining the perfected technique of the silent film with the faithful recording of music, dialog and sound."[14]

With the release of IN OLD ARIZONA, sound-on-film came into its own. Movietone newsreels were increased to three issues per month and by June, 1929, a weekly sound newsreel was issued.

Other all-talking pictures in the Movietone system quickly followed, including THRU DIFFERENT EYES, HEARTS IN DIXIE, BEHIND THAT CURTAIN, COCKEYED WORLD, FROZEN JUSTICE, GHOST TALKS, GIRL FROM HAVANA, ROMANCE OF THE RIO GRANDE, SEVEN FACES, SIDE STREET, SONG OF KENTUCKY and THE VALIANT.

ACROSS THE SEAS

British Movietone Newsreel, the first foreign newsreel in sound, began in 1929 in London with an issue of two reels a week.

But this was not the beginning of sound films in England, however. The first British theatre was wired for sound in 1925. British Acoustic company produced a sound film called A WET NIGHT in February of 1926. Gaumont filmed CHANGING THE GUARD AT BUCKINGHAM PALACE with great success. Dame Sibyl Thorndike did a five-minute scene from SAINT JOAN on sound film and some of the early dialog pictures were AS WE LIE, THE SENTENCE OF DEATH and ANTIDOTE, which some insist was released before THE JAZZ SINGER!

Burlington Pictures had almost completed a silent film called KITTY when they decided to make the last reels with dialog and release it as a sound film. The first reels were synchronized for sound and music only. Since there were no sound studios in Britain, the cast was shipped to New York City and the film was completed there.

This film was followed by the first full-length British talkie, BLACKMAIL, directed by Alfred Hitchcock. Anny Ondra, star of German films, had the lead in the film, but Joan Barry's voice was dubbed on the sound track since Miss Ondra spoke no English.

Gaumont followed with HIGH TREASON in 1929 and soon Britain was as "talk crazy" as Hollywood.

The early French sound films, including L'EAU NIL, LA NUIT EST A NOUS, LA ROUTE EST BELLE and LES TROIS MASQUES, were made in London studios, since the French studios were not yet equipped for the new sound medium. These early French sound films have been described as crude in sound quality and there seemed to be little grasp of the sound medium by the

French film-makers in the transition period between the death of the silent film and the creative use of sound on film.

The Russian films also suffered setbacks when the sound films caught on. Although Soviet inventors Tager and Shorin had developed a sound-on-film recording system as early as 1926,[15] the first Russian film with synchronized music and sound effects, ALONE, did not appear until 1931. Its first full-length talking picture, THE ROAD TO LIFE, appeared later that year. Despite the fact that it was a maiden effort, THE ROAD TO LIFE managed to make some creative use of sound effects to underscore the screen images.

THE KEY YEAR

Once it was established that the moviegoing public was hungry for sound films, nearly every feature film in the vaults of the studios was re-evaluated and brought "up to date" by adding some sort of sound. Many had only a synchronized musical "track," others had inserted dialog sequences and a few were touted as "all-talking" in 1928.

For 1928 was the key year in the transition from silent films to sound. Warner Brothers happily bragged about its Vitaphone system, Fox was high on Movietone and Paramount, MGM, United Artists, First National, Columbia, Universal, Hal Roach and Christie closed agreements with Fox and Western Electric to use the system. The other studios, RKO-Pathe, Sennett and Tiffany-Stahl allied themselves with the Photophone system.

Installations of these systems, depending upon the seating capacity of the individual theatre, ran from $8,500 to $20,000. A lack of trained engineers to keep the equipment in top shape caused many a tragic incident in the early days of sound films. Other problems, such as the wrong discs being shipped with the film, caused many headaches.

In an attempt to cash in on the new talkie fad, film companies did what they could with already-completed feature films and many resorted to slapdash methods which did the studios no credit.

Of the early days of sound, Jesse L. Lasky of Paramount recalls:

"Our special-effect man, Roy Pomeroy, had recorded some sound effects that would pass for the chatter of machine guns and various other noises. They were amplified on a set of three turntables during the dogfight sequences of WINGS. It enhanced the realism of those scenes so much that each of the dozen road-show units of the picture carried turntables and a prop man to watch the picture from the

wings of the theatre and turn on the records at appropriate times.

". . . Walter Wanger proposed that we retroactively add sound effects to Richard Dix's just-completed silent picture, WARMING UP, a baseball story. He rushed a print of it to Camden, New Jersey, where Victor Talking Machine engineers embellished it with the crack of the bat against the ball, and the roar of the cheering crowd when the hero hit a home run. These two noises qualified it for scarehead advertising as 'Part Sound' and enormously increased the financial returns. This 'goat-gland' operation, as it was called, rejuvenated many a silent picture which otherwise would have died with few mourners at the box office . . . Uncompleted portions of silent pictures already in work were finished in sound, so that the screen was apt to snap, crackle and pop at any point, and then go quiet a reel later."[16]

Many times sound was quickly dubbed into a scene by voices other than the actors appearing in the film. There were also cases of the actors lips stopping and the dialog they were supposedly speaking continuing to pour forth from the speakers.

But the public was thrilled, even if the critics and the industry were not. Since the Photophone, Movietone and Vitaphone systems became compatible once all talking films had the sound on the film itself, the three types of films could be inter-changed on the various projectors, although sound quality varied.

PIONEERS IN SOUND

Among the synchronized sound pictures with music and sound effects released in 1928 and not previously mentioned include ACROSS THE ATLANTIC, BEWARE OF MARRIED MEN, CRIMSON CITY, DOMESTIC TROUBLE, FIVE AND TEN CENT ANNIE, LITTLE SNOB, PAY AS YOU ENTER, POWDER MY BACK, RACE FOR LIFE and RINTY OF THE DESERT from Warner Brothers; ADORATION, GOODBYE KISS, THE HAUNTED HOUSE, LILAC TIME, NIGHT WATCH, OUTCAST and SCARLET SEAS from First National, which was merged with the Warner Brothers; AWAKENING, BATTLE OF THE SEXES, GIVE AND TAKE, REVENGE and THE WOMAN DISPUTED from United Artists; BABY CY-CLONE, MASKS OF THE DEVIL and SHOW PEOPLE from MGM; THE CAVALIER and THE TOILERS from Tiffany-Stahl; MAN, WOMAN AND WIFE from Universal and HIS PRIVATE LIFE, MANHATTAN COCKTAIL, THE PATRIOT and SAW-DUST PARADISE from Paramount.

"Part-Talking" pictures of 1928, which included some dialog sequences of varying lengths (from a few minutes to about 30 minutes) as well as music and sound effects, were ALIAS JIMMY VALENTINE from MGM; THE BARKER from First National; CAUGHT IN THE FOG from Warner Brothers; BEGGARS OF LIFE and VARSITY from Paramount; GERALDINE, SHOW FOLKS and SHADY LADY from RKO-Pathe and SHOWBOAT from Universal.

The "All-Talking" films of 1928 included COLLEGE SWING and INTERFERENCE from Paramount; GREASED LIGHT-NING and MELODY OF LOVE from Universal, and LADIES' NIGHT IN A TURKISH BATH from First National.

Despite the rash of sound films, there were still dissenters. One of them, David Barrist in **The Exhibitor** of Philadelphia insisted that:

"The complete flop of the Vocafilm in New York, the rapid downslide that Vitaphone is taking and the utter lack of interest in Movietone and the other 'talkies' simply proves what shrewd observers have long contended — that the talking movie is merely a novelty to be used sparingly and that any attempt to offer it as regular fare is doomed to failure.

"It is absurd to talk of supplanting in public favor the magnificent orchestras and really fine organs in the average first-class theatre with the cold, rasping Noisytone inventions. It's a mighty poor theatre today which cannot afford an organ of a popular make. And these organs have proved over a long period of years their ability to satisfy musical tastes of the moviegoers . . . Edison was right and Harry Warner (was) wrong. The public does not want talking movies in preference to its present entertainment."[17]

[10] Quoted by Stanlie McConnell in *Bulletin of the National Film Music Council*, p. 1.
[11] DeForest, *SMPE Journal*, October, 1926, pp. 69-70.
[12] Earl Sponable, *SMPE Journal*, May, 1947, p. 412.
[13] Walter Pitkin, *The Art of Sound Pictures*, p. 224.
[14] Sponable, *SMPE Journal, op. cit.*
[15] Catherine de la Roche and Thorold Dickenson, *Soviet Cinema*, p. 37.
[16] Lasky, *op. cit.* p. 213-215.
[17] Quoted in *Harrison's Reports*, 9:1, September 24, 1927.

CHAPTER THREE
THE TRANSITION YEARS

The year 1929 is generally recognized as the most important year in the movies' technical history. All phases of movie making were rapidly developed, altered and adapted to meet the demands of talking pictures and the creative possibilities of sound were gradually discovered.

Producers had to adapt many new techniques which were virtually unknown before sound. Many of them did not know how to use the new "toy" which had been given them to play with. The public wanted to hear people talk and the film makers, in conforming to this demand, forgot to include action. As a result, some early sound films literally talked themselves to death.

MICROPHONICS

The large black specter which now loomed over every Hollywood set was the microphone and the subject of "microphonics" baffled many a Hollywood director as well as most actors. On the early sets, when an actor entered a room, he would speak his first line into an overhead microphone and then walk to a chalk line for his second speech into another microphone. This rigidity caused the early sound film to lose its fluidity developed during the silent era. The vacuum-tube microphones were sensitive but only for one direction and some of the sounds it picked up were unbearable.

It now became important to use ingenuity in placing the microphone where it would do the most good. In the first all-talking film, LIGHTS OF NEW YORK, we see "The Boss" and two of his henchmen sitting at a desk. Near them, in a prominent position, is an upright telephone. Inside it is the hidden microphone to pick up the dialog for that scene.

In IN OLD ARIZONA we see Warner Baxter speaking his lines near a clump of sagebrush. The sagebrush contained the microphone, of course.

The situation did improve, as one Hollywoodite recalled many years later:

"If it was fraught with danger to move the amplifier with its supersensitive vacuum tube, someone said, why not move the consenser microphone attached to the amplifier? The actor would thereby at least be able to turn around, instead of remaining glued to the floor, at the spot marked X. Any action was better than none.

"Thus the actor was able to walk about slightly. The increased radius of action was only 3 to 5 feet — the length of the flexible gooseneck which ran from the amplifier to the microphone. In this way, the periodically paralyzed actor began to amble once more, and the director heaved a (small) sigh of relief."[18]

Some microphones were concealed in flower vases, clocks, under ashtrays and in other undesirable locations. In MGM's satirical film of 25 years later, SINGIN' IN THE RAIN, the problems of microphonics was covered in an amusing yet authentic way.

Finally, the 'mike boom' was perfected which could follow above the heads of the actors, out of camera range, and catch their every sound. This invention is sometimes credited to Lionel Barrymore, an actor who also directed several early sound films. Finally the actors could return to their flexible actions which characterized the silent film.

RCA PHOTOPHONE

The Radio Corporation of America brought about the merger of several different sound systems in 1927, mainly the Pallophoto-phone and Kinegraphophone inventions of General Electric, and announced they would compete with Movietone and Vitaphone in the sound film scramble.

Their first attempt was late in 1927 with a sound score for Paramount's epic film, WINGS, starring Clara Bow and Buddy Rogers. Different theatres used the sound in different ways. At the New York Criterion Theatre, the airplane sounds were amplified from disc recordings on a multiple turntable. Other theatres used a sound-on-film score.

Despite this confusion of non-standardization, WINGS was highly successful. But a single standard would have to be adopted. RCA soon combined the General Electric and Westinghouse systems into a variable area system[19] and re-named it Photophone. In order to insure that the sound system would be used to its best advantage, RCA acquired the FBO producing company and began producing its own sound films. The first sound film under the FBO banner was

THE PERFECT CRIME, which featured a synchronized musical score and some dialog. Other sound films presented by FBO were BLOCKADE, GANG WAR, CIRCUS KID and STEPPING HIGH.

FBO and Pathe merged in February of 1929 and later became RKO Radio Pictures, which is now Desilu Studios. The Pathe company adopted the Photophone system and added musical synchronization to CAPTAIN SWAGGER, ANNAPOLIS, MARKED MONKEY and NED McCOBB'S DAUGHTER.

This was followed by the Pathe sound newsreel recorded by the Photophone process. By the end of 1929, RCA had equipped nearly 1,200 theatres for Photophone in the United States and about 600 theatres abroad.

OTHER SYSTEMS

Within a span of two years, the motion picture industry was plagued with many other sound film systems. The Remaphone in 1926 consisted of two phonograph turntables connected to the two projection machines. The Synchrophone system also used synchronized phonograph records.

In 1927, Vocafilm was premiered at the Longacre Theatre in New York. Orchestraphone was unveiled at the Tivoli Theatre and Bristolphone was demonstrated at the Franklin Institute.

By the end of 1929, most of these systems had faded or been pooled with other existing systems. Confused theatre owners had a total of 234 different types of sound systems installed in their theatres. Most of them were of the sound-on-disc variety, including such names as Firnatone, Cinetone, Phonoactinion, Tonfilm, Photion, Thermophone, Moviephone and Titaniaphone. It was obvious that standardization would have to come soon. By 1930, sound-on-film processes had become the standard and the discs were discarded.

THE LAST OF THE SILENTS

One of the most famous silent pictures made in 1929 was A WOMAN OF AFFAIRS starring Greta Garbo, who insisted upon making a silent picture because of her Swedish accent. Other notable silent films during the period of the sound revolution were King Vidor's THE WIND, Erich von Stroheim's THE WEDDING MARCH, Charlie Chaplin's THE CIRCUS and SADIE THOMPSON. As late as 1931, Chaplin made CITY LIGHTS with synchronized sound and music, but no dialog.

Most of the famous directors, such as Cecil B. DeMille, Joseph von Sternberg, King Vidor and Clarence Brown took the leap from silent to sound pictures gracefully. So, it seemed, did D. W. Griffith, whose first talkie, ABRAHAM LINCOLN, was one of the finest productions of 1930. But his next, THE STRUGGLE, in 1931, brought about his abrupt retirement. Of the film, the **New York Times** said:

". . . neither Miss Loos, Mr. Emerson[20] or Mr. Griffith have accomplished anything particularly novel by this screen work, for, with strong drink as its menace, it seldom rises above that old-time contribution, **The Face on the Barroom Floor.**"[21]

That sound films made enemies as well as friends was made clear by Mordaunt Hall regarding Emil Jannings' last silent picture which was released with synchronized sound by Paramount:

". . . It was decided that Emil Jannings' great picture, THE PATRIOT, must be presented with sound effects, but it happened that in the enthusiasm for sound the people who added these effects decided to make Jannings heard in a couple of sequences and have a dog bark, which, to my mind, was a mistake, for this production was quite satisfying in its silence, or at least without any vocal additions to characters who were mute in most of the proceedings. This made enemies for sound."[22]

Directors soon discovered that the image and the microphone could work independently of each other. Alfred Hitchcock used this effectively in BLACKMAIL. BROADWAY MELODY and HALLELUJAH! used natural sounds while the image was showing a contrasting idea.

In the case of musical numbers, a new technique was developing. A singing scene would be shot without sound and later the music would be recorded several times, combining the best moments from each recording into the finished film. Since musical recording was easier to process than that of dialog, a rash of "all-talking, all-singing" pictures appeared, including BROADWAY MELODY, which received the Academy Award for the best picture of that year; PARAMOUNT ON PARADE, FOX MOVIETONE FOL-LIES OF 1929, SUNNY SIDE UP and WORDS AND MUSIC.

SOUND REFINEMENT

By 1930, sound was becoming refined and technique was improving. It was beginning to play a useful as well as a creative part in film making.

In Fox's THE BIG TRAIL in 1930, it was said:

"Unlike the former pictures of pioneer life, the silence of the broad open spaces is now filled with the sound of the moving caravan, the Indians' war whoops, the raging elements and the thud of the buffalo herds."[23]

Sound recording was becoming quieter, too. The premiere of THE RIGHT TO LOVE was lauded for its sound in the **New York Times:**

"The first picture to be presented by the recently discovered process whereby all noises, such as grating, popping and other surface sounds are eliminated is THE RIGHT TO LOVE . . . the excluding of bothersome noises is highly successful for, because of the background of silence, the player's voice is more life-like than ever. The quiet may seem at times too noticeable, but this is only because one has become accustomed to hearing the intrusive mechanical undertones."[24]

And despite the Depression, moviegoers had jumped from 57 million to 97 million in America.

SOUND AND THE INTERNATIONAL MARKET

Sound films killed the "international market" that films had enjoyed for several decades. Now audiences hissed or booed when the dialog was in French or German. The only solution was to make several versions of each film, each in a different language. This proved too costly, however, and was soon dropped in favor of dubbing dialog from various foreign actors onto the sound track and shipping these "dubbed" versions to the countries which spoke that language. Soon each country was dubbing its own translations from other films. Dubbing is still used today, along with superimposed subtitles, for foreign language films.

By 1932, it was taken for granted that every film should be in sound. Only Chaplin remained silent until 1940 when he spoke in THE GREAT DICTATOR. The only other "silent" film made since then has been THE THIEF, filmed with only natural sound and music by United Artists in 1953.

With sound no longer a novelty, movie attendance soon dropped off and exhibitors resorted to "Bank Night," "Screeno," free dishes and, worst of all, double features.

The motion picture industry in 1938 took the situation in hand and worked out the most spectacular drive in film history, the

"Movie Quiz." It was this drive which brought out the slogan, "Motion Pictures Are Your Best Entertainment."

World War II brought the greatest era of prosperity Hollywood had ever known. Many average pictures were grossing over four million dollars. By 1949, however, another "menace" loomed on the horizon — television.

[18] Mueller and Rettinger, *SMPE Journal*, July, 1945, p. 50.

[19] Variable area soundtracks look much like a wiggly line down the side of the film. A variable density track looks like a long gray line of variations in shades of gray.

[20] Authors of the screenplay.

[21] *New York Times*, 80:35, December 11, 1931.

[22] Mordaunt Hall, *SMPE Journal*, 12:605, September, 1928.

[23] *National Board of Review Magazine*, 5:14, December, 1930.

[24] *New York Times*, 80:25, January 2, 1931.

CHAPTER FOUR
DIRECTIONAL SOUND

But the films, in their darkest hour, again survived by presenting something the competition could not show — large-screen, color spectacles like Cinerama, VistaVision and CinemaScope and a new presentation in sound films — stereophonic sound!

As writer Raymond Spottiswoode put it, "Stereophonic sound removed the . . . great disability of present-day electrical reproduction — its one-eared character."[25]

Stereophonic sound was first demonstrated in 1881 in Paris by Clement Ader, a French scientist. Telephonic arrangements were made in four rooms at the electrical exhibition at the Palais de l'Industrie. The audience could hear clearly an opera with four separate sets of sounds — the singers, the orchestra, the murmur of the audience and the applause. Ader installed twelve microphones in the footlights at the opera house. When the listener put on earphones, he heard the things emitting from the left side of the stage in his left ear and things on the right side in his right ear. This is the same basic concept that is employed in the modern stereophonic sound systems.

As far as the motion picture is concerned, it had to wait until sound came along in 1927 before experiments in movie sound could be conducted. Warner Brothers, the pioneers in sound movies, pioneered again with stereophonic sound in 1940 in two of their films, SANTA FE TRAIL and FOUR WIVES. The innovation, called Vitasound, was not a momentous one, as hardly any theatre wanted to be bothered with wiring their theatres for the special sound. So the Vistasound system went back to gather dust in the laboratory.

Two years later, Walt Disney produced FANTASIA with a new system called Fantasound. But only six theatres used the stereophonic sound version.

The turning point for stereophonic sound came with the premiere of THIS IS CINERAMA in September, 1952. With speakers

planted all around the Broadway Theatre in New York City and six sound tracks going at once, one could hardly tell whether or not it was the audience or the people in the movie who were screaming during the roller coaster sequence. Nearly everyone cast a glance into the orchestra pit of the theatre after the performance to convince themselves that there was really no orchestra there. This is how "alive" the sound was.

With Cinerama's success, Warner Brothers decided to add stereophonic sound to its first third-dimensional feature film, HOUSE OF WAX, and running true to form, took the RCA stereo sound system and affixed its own name to it. WarnerPhonic sound was the extra dimension needed to complete the illusion of 3-D films. At the premiere at New York's Paramount Theatre, 25 speakers were installed throughout the auditorium. A separate film containing the extra four magnetic sound tracks was run along with the film.

The success of the film was not shared by all the critics however. **Independent Film Journal** thought that ". . . WarnerPhonic sound in HOUSE OF WAX scored some startling effects to capture the fancy of, if not distract from, the viewer's attention."[26] When the girl screamed at the approaching madman in the film, the entire house was filled with blood-curdling reverberations. A **Christian Science Monitor** reviewer termed the film as ". . . a cacophony of sound hurtling relentlessly at one from all directions."[27]

Despite these remarks, the audiences did not seem to mind the stereo effects and studios began dubbing stereo sound onto separate sound tracks to be played along with already completed films. Some of these dubbed films include THE 5,000 FINGERS OF DR. T, GILBERT AND SULLIVAN, SCARED STIFF, MELBA, SHANE, THE CADDY, CRUISIN' DOWN THE RIVER, LET'S DO IT AGAIN, JULIUS CAESAR, FROM HERE TO ETERNITY, THE JOLSON STORY, YOUNG BESS, WAR OF THE WORLDS, MOGAMBO, THUNDER BAY, and GONE WITH THE WIND, among many others. Columbia Pictures announced that they would add stereo sound to all their upcoming pictures, but no studio ever got around to using the dimensional sound for all productions.

Many of these dubbings were less than successful. If the magnetic sound strip and the regular sound track on the film were not synchronized, the result was bedlam and panicked projectionists were faced with the same problems they previously faced in 1927 when Vitaphone synchronized discs were causing the headaches.

Many films were much enriched by the new sound. Of JULIUS CAESAR **Film Daily** remarked:

"It could be that Metro's JULIUS CAESAR may bring back, at least in some degree, the orchestral overture which in times gone by was virtually a 'must' for deluxe theatres . . . At the Booth Theatre, where JULIUS CAESAR opened auspiciously last night, Metro precedes the Shakespearean feature with a stereophonic recording of Tchaikovsky's 'Capriccio Italien,' magnificently played by the augmented MGM studio orchestra . . . the stereophonic sound's employment (is) impressive . . . orchestral overtures given the benefit of stereo sound could make their own contribution . . . Music frequently can establish a mood more effectively, more speedily than any other medium . . . And you have only to experience 'Capriccio Italien' in association with JULIUS CAESAR to appreciate that fact."[28]

In 1954, THE JOLSON STORY was re-issued with a new stereophonic four-channel sound track and became the first dubbed stereo sound to achieve widespread popularity. At the premiere in Brooklyn, audience reaction was unprecedented. The **Film Daily** remarked:

"The scene was Brooklyn . . . (The theatre) has special sound equipment for directional projection and the print that went on display was supplied with a newly recorded, auxiliary track . . . Never once showing its age, THE JOLSON STORY is still a magnetic and highly rewarding entertainment that holds the audience enrapt and with this new sound process to emphasize and amplify the proceedings there is rich diversion pouring forth from the screen for better than two hours . . . The singing was in high volume and realized the rich qualities of the recorded Jolson voice."[29]

Many 3-D films also added stereophonic sound, but with so many different sound systems on the market and lack of standardization, exhibitors refused to invest their money in new sound equipment. The ones that did in the early months of 1953 found their equipment obsolete within a few months as new developments came along.

Soon the market was flooded with "perfected" stereo systems, just as the early days of sound films saw a deluge of "perfected" sound systems waiting to be grabbed up by exhibitors. Some of the systems of the middle-1950's included RCA, Altec, Ampex, Westrex, Simplex, Reeves, Motiograph, Multi-Directional, Kinevox, Natural Sound, Magnaphonic, WarnerPhonic, Ballantyne "Four-Runner," Cinematic, Panaphonic, Dorsett, and a myriad of others.

With the advent of CinemaScope films in the fall of 1953, magnetic sound tracks were developed which would go directly on the film, instead of being run separately, thus eliminating the danger of the extra sound being out of synchronization with the regular sound track.

The stereo sound used with CinemaScope was impressive. HOW TO MARRY A MILLIONAIRE was better than THE ROBE in this respect. Merlin Lewis reported the sound in HOW TO MARRY A MILLIONAIRE as the high point of the film:

"Stereophonic sound heard at the New York City premiere of HOW TO MARRY A MILLIONAIRE seems to this observer to have accomplished the ultimate in transmitting to the audience a sense of participation in the picture's unfolding.

"There was no gimmicked use of the audience speakers to call attention of the audience to the fact that the theatre had installed stereophonic sound but there was a naturalness of sound and movement from place to place on the gigantic screen as the actors moved from place to place or as sound in the background drew nearer and nearer.

"This naturalness — this kind of high fidelity, good quality sound is the end result of true stereophonic sound installation — one that adds to, rather than distracts from the audience's enjoyment of a motion picture . . . Good stereophonic sound systems now achieve what they are intended to achieve — an enhancement of entertainment."[30]

CREATIVE USE OF SOUND

The fact that so many early sound films talked themselves to death has caused later film-makers to attempt to use the sound medium as creatively as possible. And they have many times succeeded.

The many fine sound men working in film studios all over the world have produced some excellent creative sound tracks. There is no denying the artistry of an apt sound track, even though the average viewer probably would not be aware of this artistry.

They were aware of sound, however, when it was used in the 1951 film, THE THIEF — a film in which not a word was spoken. The entire film depended upon the image and the sound track to tell the story about a spy in New York City. Although the lack of dialog was publicized so highly that it became nothing but a gimmick, THE THIEF did show that sound was an important factor in every film.

Film-makers also discovered that sound need not always be

natural. For instance, when Gregory Peck is recovering from a hangover in DESIGNING WOMEN, a door slam is heard at twice its volume and the audience laughed out of both recognition and sympathy. When Catherine Deneuve, her mind slowly decaying, turns on a light switch in REPULSION and the wall cracks with a thunderous roar, we as an audience discover that we are hearing first-hand the distortion of what a mentally deranged woman would hear. And the marvelous sounds which come from the laboratory of Alec Guinness in THE MAN IN THE WHITE SUIT are still amusing to hear.

Citing more examples of the creative use of sound would only take up space, for every individual could probably cite many cases he himself remembers. Yet the general run of films see to it that the sound is so natural and right that it is **not** noticeable. This, of course, is a compliment to the brilliant sound engineers working today to use sound in the most exciting way.

It is in the short film where the creative use of sound has reached its zenith. The rise of the art theatre has provided an outlet for experimental films with sound and visuals which have caught the viewers' fancy. Who can ever forget the rhythmic "swoosh" of the windmills in PRAISE THE SEA or the delicious combination of sound and music in GLASS?

Sound can be used as a counterpoint to an image as well as an accompaniment to it, much as a narrator is speaking of one subject while something else is being shown on the screen. There are endless variations for the use of sound — distortion, amplification, etc., which can be most effective.

With stereophonic sound as the ultimate achievement in sound films, what lies ahead for sound? Perhaps only the surface has been scratched. We know we have had sound films in some form ever since motion pictures were invented. There is reason to think that undreamed-of improvements and ideas will enhance the sound film even further in coming years. Any art which is dynamic enough to progress from a phonograph record leashed to a movie projector to four highly directional magnetic sound tracks on a CinemaScope film in less than 60 years certainly will find something even more exciting to capture the public's fancy.

[25] Spottiswoode, *op. cit.*, p. 307.
[26] *Independent Film Journal*, 21:13, April 18, 1953.
[27] *Christian Science Monitor*, April 13, 1953, p. 4C.
[28] *Film Daily*, 103:3, June 5, 1953.
[29] *Film Daily*, 105:4, March 29, 1954.
[30] *Film Daily*, 104:7, November 20, 1953.

PART FIVE — THE AVANTE-GARDE

"They've just announced that
the admission for a Smell-O-Vision
picture will be two dollars...
People with colds, a dollar
fifty."
　　— Milton Berle

CHAPTER ONE
VARIABLE SCREEN DEVELOPMENTS

There seems to be no end to the imaginations and experimentations of the movie inventors. Hence, for the record, this final chapter will cover such developments as variable screens, multiple screens, domes, "live" and film combinations, subliminal films and films with "smells" attached.

Many systems were presented which could vary the size of the screen according to whether the scene being shown was an intimate one or one of vast scope. The Magnascope, in essence, used this theory in the days of the silent film. But more recently, there have been four systems which used black masks to change the aspect ratio of the screen. Variascope was designed by Ben Schlanger, Variscope was sponsored by MGM, Mobilia by Robert W. Dowling, and Synthetic Vision was first installed at the Ames Theatre, Dayton, as an experiment.

Mobilia's name was later changed to Vari-Form. The process controlled the variability of the screen by using a standard 35mm film electronically. This film controlled the intensity of light, changed focus and enlarged or reduced the size of the screen mask — horizontally, vertically, or both.[1]

Two Lopert films were used as experiments for Vari-Form in New York City — GILBERT AND SULLIVAN at the Bijou and SUMMERTIME at the Astor. Herbert Wilcox also announced that his latest film, THE GLORIOUS DAYS, would use Vari-Form, but the film was not released in this manner.[2]

"Synthetic Vision" is capable of changing the aspect ratio of the screen to one of four sizes by a touch of the button, thus allowing the newsreel to be shown at 1.33:1, the shorts at 1.85:1 and the feature in CinemaScope. Exhibitors hailed the invention as highly successful, and many large theatres have installed equipment of a similar nature.

VARIABLE ASPECT RATIOS ON FILM

A different type of variable aspect ratio was used by Walt Disney in his re-issue of FANTASIA. An interlocking mechanism controlling screen width and the anamorphic aspect ratio allowed live action scenes to be shown in standard ratio and the cartoons in SuperScope (2:1) or CinemaScope (2.55:1). Again, the film was electronically cued so the changes were made automatically. The film itself changed size without variation or switches in lenses.[3]

Dynamic Frame, developed by the British Film Institute, is another variable screen process invented by an American, Glenn Alvey, Jr., which involves a series of mattes which control the size and shape of the film area and the screen image.

Arthur Knight, in **The Liveliest Art,** describes the first demonstration Dynamic Frame production, THE DOOR IN THE WALL:

"For his drawing-room and conversational scenes . . . (the artist) generally chose a medium-sized rectangular frame, blacking out the remainder with his mattes. In the fantasy sequences, however, the shape of the frame is varied to emphasize every change in mood and action. When the boy first discovers the little green door, the screen is small and square — just large enough to encompass the child, the door and a portion of the wall. Then as he passes into the enchanted garden beyond, the camera follows after him and the screen slowly widens out to full size before his wondering gaze. But when he sits down to rest at the base of a tree, the main part of the screen is blacked out again and the image is contained in a small rectangle at the lower left-hand corner of the frame. He is scarcely seated, however, when he realizes that the tree trunk is actually the leg of a tremendous beast! As he leaps up in alarm, the frame parallels his movement by shooting upward to reveal the monster."[4]

There is no denying the artistic possibilities of this new method of telling a story by variations in screen aspect ratios. If not misused or overdone, it could become a popular means of film expression. It requires no extra equipment in the booth or on the screen. Still admittedly in its early stages, there seems to be no limit to what this process could do (it is in some ways akin to the early days of the silent film when D. W. Griffith used mattes to cover various areas of the screen image to accent a dramatic situation or picture). As Jonas Mekas said of the process:

". . . although jarring and otherwise imperfect, (Dynamic Frame) demonstrates some examples of the functional use of different screen

shapes and sizes, thereby pointing in the right (and little explored) direction."[5]

[1] *Film Daily*, 107:11, January 21, 1955.
[2] *Variety*, 195:24, September 1, 1954.
[3] *Film Daily*, 109:1, February 7, 1956.
[4] Arthur Knight, *The Liveliest Art*, pp. 337-338.
[5] Jonas Mekas, "Experiment in the Fifties," *Film: Book I*, p. 149.

CHAPTER TWO
DOMES AND PEOPLE

Have we reached the ultimate in new screen dimensions? Not if the exhibits at the various world's fairs and trade fairs in the past decade are any indication.

In only five years, we have seen anamorphic systems as CinemaScope; the "horizontal" VistaVision process; the three-strip systems such as Cinerama and CineMiracle, and literally hundreds of other similar attempts to give a sweep and scope to the theatrical film. But the future seems even more exciting to contemplate, with the showing of many new systems at the Brussels World's Fair, plus the re-emergence of an old one.

The old one is Circarama in which a complete battery of projectors surrounds the audience and brings us right back to where we started 60 years ago in the evolution of the widescreen motion picture. The new ones will be discussed below.

SEPTORAMA

Seven 35mm films in a geodesic dome are the main components of Septorama which premiered at the United States Information Service section of the American Exhibit in Moscow in August of 1959. The dome accommodated over 500 persons at each showing and was always full of wide-eyed viewers of the presentation, which was developed by industrial designer Charles Eames. Over 2,000 individual photographs, divided into 300 sets of seven each, were projected onto the seven screens during the 13-minute show.

The pictures were photographed on 35mm film and run through a regular projector which gives the still pictures a feeling of motion and of flowing from screen to screen. The screens were not in a circle, but rather in two rows — four screens on the top row and three screens on the bottom.

The Technicolor presentation, entitled GLIMPSES OF THE USA, consisted mainly of "Americana" with one exception. Once

during the presentation did all seven screens have the same thing on it — Marilyn Monroe!

VISTA-DOME

"Putting you in the picture" seems to be the cry of all the film experimenters. When the Navy developed a hemispherical lens after World War II, others also worked on specialized lens systems.

The Jam Handy Organization of Detroit presented its Vista-Dome process (also called the Cine-Sphere) to help in driver training. Consisting of a lens which photographs a horizontal view of 180 degrees and a vertical view of 90 degrees, Vista-Dome was first shown at the Chevrolet Exhibit of the Detroit Auto Show in 1958 and later at the Chicago Auto Show and the New York World's Fair in 1964.

The camera was mounted on a Chevrolet and driven on the Detroit expressways at a fast rate of speed. Those watching the film attempt to steer and apply brakes to avoid possible "accidents" which seem imminent as the film progresses.

The single 35mm film is shown on a screen shaped like one quarter of a sphere, giving the effect of looking through an automobile windshield.

The process requires, due to the short focal-length lens, that the projector be almost at the edge of the domed screen and it cannot be shown at distances. Also, the audience is limited to about 20 or 30 people, seated on both sides of the projector. Like CinemaScope, the Vista-Dome lens is interchangeable on the camera and the projector.

CINEDOME

The United States Government developed a process in which the screen curves around and over the spectators, which was first shown at the United States Exhibit at the World Agriculture Fair in New Delhi, India, in 1959. The picture was a color documentary, THE ATOM ON THE FARM, and opened with a sequence which was said to give the spectator the feeling of being "inside" the atom with electrons hurling all around the dome-like screen.

CINETARIUM

Germany came out with the ultimate in "surround" projection — a 360 degree projection system called "The Cinetarium" in which the viewer can sit on a swivel chair and view an unbroken picture all around the ball-shaped theatre.

Using only one camera and one projector, Cinetarium was

invented by Adalbert Baltes, a West-German documentary producer who adapted the principle of aerial photography to the motion picture.

He hangs a silver ball above the scene to be photographed and the ball reflects the surrounding scene. The camera photographs from beneath the ball, catching the reflected scene. The film is shown through a projector sunk in the center of the floor onto a screen consisting of a silver-coated half-sphere. As the viewer watches the film, he is always in the center of the action. As inventor Baltes expressed it:

"Patrons sit in swivel chairs, swiveling to follow the action . . . at an auto race, cars will skid around him. At a ballet, the dancers surround him. In a shooting scene, he will be right in the middle."[6]

Cinetarium also provides stereophonic sound to give the effect of "spatial realism" at eight different points around the dome. The technique, naturally, is quite specialized and Baltes has conceded there would be difficulties in making Cinetarium commercially feasible. First, dome-shaped movie theatres would have to be constructed and second, film production techniques would have to be revamped radically. "But," Baltes concludes, "the principles of CinemaScope and Cinerama were worked out in the 1920's." Baltes also envisioned that the process would give the viewer the actual impression of being, say, in Hawaii. "You will see Hawaii's mountains in front of you, a blue sky above and the beach in the rear. I can even turn on the heat to give you more reality."[7]

MULTIPLE SCREENS

In the United States Pavilion at the New York World's Fair in 1964, Cinerama presented a new system utilizing 130 different screens in what looks like a long winding tunnel. As the viewers (2,500 of them an hour) are whisked through the tunnel on contour seats with stereo earphones and headrests, they see a variety of subjects on many different-sized screens ranging from the bottom of the ocean floor to outer space. The narration can be dialed in five languages and the entire performance lasts just under 15 minutes.

POLYCRAN

Combining people and film images has been an aim of theatre people for several generations, and the first attempt seems to be a **feerie** which combined live action, ballet and color film at the Chatalet (England) in 1896. England's "Crazy Gang" ran off the stage and onto the screen of a film in a late 1930 musical revue.

Like most other inventions connected with the film, the combining of live actors and film is not new. George Beban, a silent film star, appeared in SIGN OF THE ROSE in 1922, consisting of himself on a screen, then appearing "live" in front of the screen as the image continues. He then carries on a dialog with himself.

A new process, a tremendously fascinating idea, is Czechoslovakia's Polycran (Also called "Poly-Ecran") invented by Joseph Sloboda and Alfred and Emil Rakok. It works like this:

"(Polycran) uses eight screens and uses them in an unusual way. These screens are of different shapes and sizes and are scattered over a large black background. Average size of the screens is about six feet by four feet. The result is projection of related but separated motion picture images to obtain an overall effect somewhat like that sought after in abstract art.

"Following is an example of how the different screens are used in the Czech process: While symphony musicians are shown playing on two of the screens, their audience is shown on another. Scenes showing flowers, clouds and statuary are shown on the other screens to create atmosphere. — Instead of editing a movie so that it runs from one scene to another, the Czechs make the action move from one screen to another. In a ballet sequence, a dancer enters the scene on one screen, leaps to another and then to a third. The other screens carried images of the feet of many dancers."[8]

MAGIC LANTERN

Czechoslovakia's LANTERNE MAGIQUE was a hit at the Brussels World's Fair with its combination of music, jazz, songs, dances and travelogs on film. Invented by Alfred Rakok, who was also involved in Polycran, the process and the first production is best described in **Sight and Sound,** the British film magazine:

"MAGIC LANTERN is an appropriate name for what is, when all is said and done, a delightful toy with about the same artistic range as the Victorian Parlor delight. The novelty is to combine moving stages and live performers — singers, dancers and musicians — with film projected on to a number of screens of varying shapes and sizes which materialize and vanish at different points about the stage. It was first seen at the Brussels Fair in 1958, opened in Prague a little later, and in Moscow a week or so before it arrived in London. The program we are seeing here appears to be a selection of

the best of the Brussels and Prague programs, adapted to British tastes in association with Wendy Toye.

"One immediate, more sophisticated reaction against mere technical trickery are here rather disarmed by the ingenuity and precision involved, and by the intelligent exploitation of the restricted aesthetic possibilities. The principal fascination for its devisers (the chief of whom is Alfred Radok, who made OLD MAN MOTOR CAR) is evidently the dynamism that can for some reason or another be generated by counter-pointing different kinds of movement in the theatre. Quite undistinguished choreography and fairly undistinguished moving picture images can be juxtaposed with explosive effect. "The Spartakiade," for instance, with a sport ballet going on in front of the films of parading athletes, is irresistible.

"The high spot of the evening . . . is an academically facetious history of the cinema (which is worth taking note of; it does justice to neglected European figures like the inventor Purkyne). It culminates in the simultaneous projection of an old slapstick farce, THE LOVER IN THE WARDROBE, and a film of Verdi's OTELLO. The two screens become rather confused, and (shuttling from one to the other in the farcical wardrobe) the Moor and Desdemona get mixed up with the crazy trio from 1905. It ends with the three gentlemen on one screen pelting the two ladies on the other with assorted bric-a-brac. Not all the program, it is only fair to say, comes up to this; but the strain of stretching one technical novelty to fill a whole variety bill is not too evident."[9]

LIVING SCREEN

Scenic designer Ralph Alswang demonstrated his Living Screen process to the press in September, 1960, using films shown by rear projection on a three-wall stage, supplemented by real actors in front. Critics felt that the process had possibilities and more would be heard of it in the future.

By 1964, Mr. Alswang presented an original two-act musical comedy in London, IS THERE INTELLIGENT LIFE ON EARTH? In the out-of-town review in Brighton, **Variety** commented:

"Living Screen is a substantial advance on the Czech process demonstrated some six years ago at the Brussels World Fair . . . (Alswang) has made a bold effort to combine both film and live action into a unified whole . . . . its potentialities are enormous and

. . . it opens up possibilities on the widest scale, demonstrating that these two visual arts can be jointly harnessed to provide a new dimension in mass entertainment."[10]

The Living Screen presentation depicted a Martian landing on earth in a flying saucer, via an animated film by John Halas. From then on, it is a combination of live actors and music and filmed sequences. The future of the Living Screen process remains to be seen as it is presented before more audiences in the coming years.

Another live-and-film process, developed by John S. Rush, has been named Living Spectocade or 4-D. It is being developed mostly for night-club acts where a star first appears on film, then comes on live. In all these processes, perfect synchronization is the largest stumbling block in the successful future for these avant-garde presentations.

[6] *Detroit News* 87:5, January 4, 1959.
[7] *New Yorker*, 34:154, September 27, 1958.
[8] *Knight, op. cit.*, p. 338.
[9] *Sight and Sound*, 30:91, Spring, 1961.
[10] *Variety*, 234:80, April 8, 1964.

CHAPTER THREE
SUBLIMINAL AND SMELLS

Various attempts at introducing subliminal images into motion pictures have been less than successful, partly due to the physical limitations of the idea itself and partly because of the dangers such productions could have on the minds of the viewing audience. Subliminal films go on the theory that the mind can receive images which it later cannot recall having directly received. In most cases, words or images are put on the screen for a fraction of a second only. The audience is supposed to subconsciously retain the word or image. The images are either communicated to the viewer on one frame of the regular movie film (which would flash on the screen for 1/24 of a second) or by an independent "flasher."

Two subliminal feature films have been made in the Precon Process, dubbed "Psychorama" for commercial purposes, and were of the "horror" variety. In MY WORLD DIES SCREAMING (later changed to TERROR IN THE HAUNTED HOUSE), "subconscious" images are superimposed in several scenes, such as two fluttering hearts (love), a crawling snake (hate), a skull (terror) and as the topper, the word BLOOD spelled out. A second film, A DATE WITH DEATH, used the same technique.

A different type of subliminal suggestion was offered in Allied Artists' THE HYPNOTIC EYE. A hypnotist manages to lure beautiful women into mutilating themselves. The film was accompanied by an eight-minute "lecture" daring the audience to unclasp their hands or lift the balloons which were passed out to them as they came in. As a frank gimmick to capitalize on the "subliminal" craze, the picture did poorly at the box office and was not tried in the same form again.

In 1961, Warner Brothers released a Canadian film called THE MASK in which the "red and green" anaglyph third-dimensional film system was resurrected to aid the audience to participate in the weird dreams of the leading character. When the man donned the

supposedly cursed mask, the audience put on their red and green glasses (in the form of a mask), shared the experience, and then returned to the regular black-and-white movie. This film also was not too successful at the box office, but there will be other attempts at this type of film in succeeding years.

THE SENSE OF SMELL

It was only natural that Edison's idea to combine films and sound would lead to someone deciding to combine films and odors. There had been many such experiences in the history of the theatre. The legitimate theatre, being older than the movies by at least 5,000 years, can lay claim to having "smells" first. **Variety** lists "smellies" as early as 1868 in the London production of THE FAIRY ACORN TREE at the Alhambra Theatre. The scents were dispensed by vaporizers.[11] Composer Alexander Scriabin experimented with odors in his operas and playwright Oscar Wilde's original stage directions for SALOME indicated "braziers of perfume should take the place of an orchestra — a new perfume for each emotion."[12]

THE MUSIC BOX REVUE OF 1923 used a special chemical compound squirted from the orchestra pit into the audience as John Steel and Grace Moore sang "An Orange Grove in California."[13] EARL CARROLL'S VANITIES OF 1931 had a perfumed curtain reeking of Odor de la Noche by Raquel, Inc. The most disastrous attempt at combining smell with drama was in the Broadway play, THE FRENCH TOUCH, in 1945. With Arlene Francis and Brian Aherne as stars, the play was to go down in history — but not as a great drama. The press agent had the playbills and usherettes sprayed with French perfume on opening night, and decided also to blow some of the scent through the ventilating system. The overall effect was staggering. The audience either fell asleep or left and the actors grew nauseous. The perfume gimmick was not tried again in the legitimate theatre for a long time.

DOLLARS AND SCENTS

As early as 1906, S. L. "Roxy" Rothafel had tried adding the dimension of "smell" to the motion picture. At his silent film theatre in Forest City, Pennsylvania, Rothafel dipped cotton in a rose essence and put it in front of an electric fan, allowing the smell of roses to drift out into the audience during the newsreel showing the Pasadena Rose Bowl Game.[14]

In Boston at the Fenway Theatre, Albert E. Fowler (the manager) wrote to **Variety** describing his early "smell" experiment with the Colleen Moore film, LILAC TIME, in 1929:

"After careful trial-and-error timing, a pint of lilac perfume (not imported) was carefully spilled in the plenium chamber of the theatre's ventilating system. The large intake fan gradually forced the lilac-scented air up through the ducts, finally releasing it through the 'mushrooms' under the orchestra seats. Now, the success of the experiment lay in the timing, so that the audience would begin to sniff (suspecting at first their next-seat neighbor) just as the picture's title, LILAC TIME, appeared on the screen. And, believe me, the audience applauded at every single performance!"[15]

That same year the finale of MGM's HOLLYWOOD REVUE was scented. While Charles King sang "Orange Blossom Time," an orange aroma drifted into at least one theatre in America where the manager was scent-oriented.

During the 1950's Charles Eames invented a multiple-screen projection system for slides which contained a device that coordinated visual images with smells. This invention developed into the Septorama process which was exhibited at the American Exhibition at Moscow in 1959.[16]

In May of 1958, British inventor William Rose developed a device for releasing aromas from a television receiver by means of an electric impulse from the transmitter. But it was left to the motion picture industry to come up with genuine smell movies (although some critics insisted that movies had been smelling for almost 60 years anyway.) They came up with not one, but two systems almost simultaneously.

AROMARAMA

The first of the two processes to reach Broadway was AromaRama, which added scents to an already completed film, BEHIND THE GREAT WALL, filmed in Totalscope, printed in DeLuxe Color and featuring stereophonic sound. The odors included various foods, incenses and other "indoor" scents as well as many outdoor smells.

AromaRama was conceived and developed by Charles Weiss, with the help of Rhodia, Inc., which developed the 72 odors capable of being transmitted by the triggering and timing mechanism in the theatre. The odors are fed to the audience through the regular air circulating system.

BEHIND THE GREAT WALL opened at the DeMille Theatre on December 2, 1959, and the critics got their best puns out of the mothballs. The Detroit **Free Press** article called AromaRama "A Real Stinker."[17]

United Press International stated:

"The first motion picture that really smells had its world premiere . . . No one in the audience wanted popcorn. They got hungry for Chinese food. During a Hong Kong night club scene, the smell of Oriental spices, incense and smoke prickled the noses of the spectators . . . When a procession of torchbearers crossed the screen, the stench of burning pitch wafted through the theatre. A shot of a barnyard full of geese smelled like a barnyard full of geese . . . Each smell came and went in perfect timing . . ."[18]

Film Daily's reviewer added:

". . . There are some who may not go for many of the strong, pungent, heavy Oriental odors . . . such as the incense of the mystic scenes duplicating odors inhaled during Buddhist temple rites, or the spicy character of the smells rising from the streets of Hongkong (sic), of the burning resin odors of the tiger hunt. However, the mouthpuckering odor of a luscious ripe orange that comes . . . over the auditorium in a prologue to the introduction of Aro-ma-Rama — well, that may be something else of a cinematic breathing experience. It was delicious."[19]

Since BEHIND THE GREAT WALL had already won two awards at the Brussels Film Exposition **sans** smell, the film itself was not overlooked in the reviews and most critics found it an excellent documentary, with or without AromaRama. The odor gimmick, however, did have its dissenters. **Variety,** with its usual frankness, insisted that:

"The prologue makes a comparison of this scent-yielding process with such cinematic milestones as sound, color and widescreen, and this simply is unrealistic; there's no new screen dimension added, such as provided by Cinerama. But the immodesty can be forgiven, for the presentation in good part does live up to its you-must-breathe-it-to-believe-it promises. Effective smells permeate the theatre . . . with remarkable precision. Net result is a travelog with a good commercial one-shot gimmick."[20]

And a "one-shot" gimmick is what AromaRama was destined to be. Although the company announced that THE SCENT OF NEW MOWN HAY would go into production soon and that there were the inevitable "negotiations with major studios," AromaRama and

BEHIND THE GREAT WALL parted company after a plan failed to play the process in small towns when they discovered that it didn't seem to be a "big city picture" for sophisticated movie audiences.[21]

Even the announcement that Japan's Daiei Studios would pipe the scent of roses into the theatre for its film, ROSE FLOWER BLOOMS (BARANOKINI BARANOHANSSAKU), did not revive the jaded interest of the public in "odor" films. But BEHIND THE GREAT WALL was re-released to theatres quite successfully on its own merits and remains a fine widescreen documentary.

SMELL-O-VISION

In what was called "the film battle of the century," Michael Todd, Jr., paired off against AromaRama to make his own "smell" feature, SCENT OF MYSTERY. Although announced before BEHIND THE GREAT WALL, it was not premiered until January 12, 1960, at the Cinestage in Chicago. The Todd film was shot in 70mm film, Technicolor and stereophonic sound.

Smell-O-Vision differs from AromaRama in that the "smells" are sent to each individual seat by means of tubing aimed at the person sitting in back of the seat. The smells are pumped to each individual seat in the theatre by means of an invention by Hans Laube in which each scent is contained in a vial on a rotating drum, then projected to each member of the audience when a signal is triggered from the "smell track" of the film. Todd claimed that even people with allergies to certain odors need not worry, since all odors were checked out with toxicologists.

Among the Smell-O-Vision odors are roses, peaches, wood shavings, bread, bananas, boot polish, pipe tobacco, perfume, salty ocean breeze, oil paint, wine, sugar cane, garlic, gun smoke, clover, coffee, brandy, peppermint, lavender, carnation, incense, friction and lemon.

As a tongue-in-cheek murder mystery, SCENT OF MYSTERY fared fairly well with the critics. But with the odors added, the reactions varied.

The New York **Herald-Tribune** commented:

". . . some odors elicited sneezes from the spectators. There is also the matter of synchronizing one's breathing with the piping of the smells, for if the breath is let out at the wrong time, one is liable to miss a meaningful odor."[22]

The New York **Times** added:

". . . whatever novel stimulation it might afford with the projection of smells appears to be dubious and dependent upon the

noses of the individual viewers and the smell-projector's whims
. . ."[23]

Time agreed:

"The 'olfactions' themselves are on the whole no more accurate or
creditable than those employed by AromaRama, but at least they
don't stink so loud . . . most customers will probably agree that the
smell they liked best was the one that they got during intermission:
fresh air."[24]

Variety added:

". . . the new dimension will be nothing more than a passing whiff.
Except for providing a novelty value, the accompanying odors
neither add nor detract from the basic enjoyment of a motion
picture."[25]

Film Daily was the most enthusiastic:

"A large assortment of scents are used, with some of them,
perfume and tobacco playing a vital part in advancing the plot and
serving as a clue to solving the mystery of the story . . . The scents
that are emitted add further entertainment value . . . It is a picture
which by every indication should strike a solid response with the
ticket-buying public."[26]

Saturday Review concluded:

"I predict remarkably little controversy over the respective merits
of the two competing smell systems, AromaRama and Glorious
Smell-O-Vision! since neither is particularly successful or desirable.
Differ though they may in technology, the smells are equally
synthetic and equally erratic. That is, the people in the balcony may
be smelling attar of roses while the orchestra is getting the odor of
freshly brewed coffee. Or it may have been poltergeists playing hob
with the processes while I was in attendance. Some odors came
early, some late, and some not at all, and the whole business made
me confused, especially when I was trying to equate the evidence of
my eyes with the evidence of my nose . . . I hope when the Feelies
come, that the promotors will boldly tell us that we can stop living
and simply **be** movies."[27]

With the advent of "smell," the Broadway and Hollywood wags
had a field day. Even the author of the first "smellie," Bill Roos,
was quoted in the **Saturday Review** as saying, "We're scared to
death that on opening night the competition will come to the theatre
armed with Air-Wick."[28]

So Smell-O-Vision disappeared almost as soon as its debut.
SCENT OF MYSTERY was re-titled HOLIDAY IN SPAIN and

shown at Cinerama theatres without odors, where it made little or no sense to unsophisticated audiences unaware of its original purpose for being made. Like other ideas to give the motion picture new dimensions, however, the sense of smell may again be attempted in future years.

[11] *Variety*, 217:6, January 13, 1960.
[12] *Ibid.*, 225:15, January 10, 1962.
[13] *Ibid*, 216:1, November 4, 1959.
[14] *Film Daily*, 114:1, September 10, 1958.
[15] *Variety*, 217:6, January 13, 1960.
[16] *Film and A-V World*, 15:436, October, 1959.
[17] *Detroit Free Press*, May, 1959, n.d.
[18] *Detroit Free Press*, 129:1, December 9, 1959.
[19] *Film Daily*, 116:1, December 10, 1959.
[20] *Variety*, 217:6, December 16, 1959.
[21] *Ibid.*, 218:3, March 30, 1960.
[22] *New York Herald-Tribune*, February 19, 1960, n.d.
[23] *New York Times*, 109:23, February 19, 1960.
[24] *Time*, 75:98, February 29, 1960.
[25] *Variety*, 217:6, January 13, 1960.
[26] *Film Daily*, 117:6, January 8, 1960.
[27] *Saturday Review*, 43:27, January 30, 1960.
[28] *Ibid*, 42:6, January 24, 1959.

BIBLIOGRAPHY

BIBLIOGRAPHY
Books and Periodicals

BOOKS

Bardeche, Maurice, and Robert Brassillach; tr. Iris Barry, *The History of Motion Pictures* (Norton and the Museum of Modern Art, 1938)

Blum, Daniel, *A Pictorial History of the Silent Screen* (Putnam, 1953) and *A Pictorial History of the Talkies* (Putnam, 1958)

Carneal, Georgette, *Conquerer of Space* (Liveright, 1930)

Cornwell-Clyne, Adrian, *Color Cinematography,* Third Edition (Chapman and Hall, 1951)

Dewhurst, H., *Introduction to 3-D* (Chapman and Hall, 1954)

Dickinson, Thorold, and Catherine de la Roche, *Soviet Cinema* (Falcon, 1948)

Eisenstein, Sergei; ed. Jay Leyda, *Film Form* (Harcourt, Brace, 1949)

Evans, Ralph, *Eye, Film and Camera in Color Photography* (Wiley, 1959)

Field, Alice Evans, *Hollywood USA* (Vantage, 1952)

Film Daily Yearbook, annual edition (Film Daily)

Franklin, Joe, *Classics of the Silent Screen* (Citadel, 1959)

Friedman, Joseph S., *The History of Color Photography* (American Photography, 1944)

Fulton, A. R., *Motion Pictures: The Development of an Art from Silent Films to the Age of Television* (University of Oklahoma, 1960)

Griffith, Richard, and Arthur Mayer, *The Movies* (Simon and Schuster, 1957)

Hardy, Forsyth, *Scandinavian Film* (Falcon, 1952)

Hughes, Robert, ed., *Film: Book I* (Evergreen, 1959)

Huntley, John, *British Technicolor Films* (Focal, c1949)

International Motion Picture Almanac, annual edition (Quigley)

Jacobs, Lewis, *The Rise of the American Film* (Harcourt, Brace, 1939)

Jarratt, Vernon, *The Italian Cinema* (Falcon, 1952)

Knight, Arthur, *The Liveliest Art* (Macmillan, 1957)

Lasky, Jesse L. *I Blow My Own Horn* (Doubleday, 1957)

Leyda, Jay, *Kino: A History of the Russian and Soviet Film* (Macmillan, 1960)

Lindgren, Ernest, *A Picture History of the Cinema* (Vista, 1960)

Low, Rachel, *The History of the British Film: 1896-1906* (Allen and Unwin, 1948), *1906-1914* (Allen and Unwin, 1949) and *1914-1918* (Allen and Unwin, 1950)

Macgowan, Kenneth, *Behind the Screen* (Delacorte, 1965)

Manvell, Roger, *Experiment in the Film* (Grey Walls, 1949) and *The Film and the Public* (Penguin, 1955)

Motion Pictures, 1894-1912 (United States Copyright Office, 1953)

Motion Pictures, 1912-1939 (United States Copyright Office, 1951)

Motion Pictures, 1940-1949 (United States Copyright Office, 1953)

Motion Pictures, 1950-1959 (United States Copyright Office, 1961)

Norling, John A., *The Stereoscopic Art* (Society of Motion Picture and Television Engineers, 1953)

Pitkin, Walter, *The Art of Sound Pictures* (Appleton, 1930)

Production Encyclopaedia, 1947 and 1952 editions (Hollywood Reporter)

Quigley, Martin, ed., *New Screen Techniques* (Quigley, 1953)

Ramsaye, Terry, *A Million and One Nights* (Simon and Schuster, 1964)

Rosten, Leo C., *Hollywood* (Harcourt, Brace, 1941)

Rotha, Paul, and Richard Griffith, *The Film Till Now* (Funk and Wagnalls, 1949)

Sadoul, Georges, *French Film* (Falcon, 1953)

Seldes, Gilbert, *An Hour with the Movies and the Talkies* (Lippincott, 1929) and *The 7 Lively Arts* (Sagamore, 1957)

Spottiswoode, Raymond, *Film and Its Techniques* (University of California, 1953)

Spottiswoode, Raymond and Nigel, *The Theory of Stereoscopic Transmission* (Faber, 1954)

Taylor, Deems, *A Pictorial History of the Movies* (Simon and Schuster, 1950)

Weinberg, Herman G., ed., *Fifty Years of Italian Cinema*, American Edition (Bestetti, 1954)

Widescreen Motion Picture Systems (Society of Motion Picture and Television Engineers, 1965)

Wood, Leslie, *The Miracle of the Movies* (Burke, 1948)

PERIODICALS

THE AMERICAN CINEMATOGRAPHER, 1782 N. Orange Dr., Hollywood, California 90028.

BOXOFFICE, 825 Van Brunt Blvd., Kansas City, Missouri 64124.

CHRISTIAN SCIENCE MONITOR, 1 Norway St., Boston, Massachusetts 02115.

DAILY VARIETY, 6404 Sunset Blvd., Hollywood, California 90028.

EDUCATIONAL SCREEN AND A-V GUIDE, 415 N. Dearborn St., Chicago, Illinois 60610.

FILM COMMENT, 838 West End Ave., New York, New York, 10025

FILM DAILY, 1600 Broadway, New York, New York 10019

FILM NEWS, 250 W. 57th St., New York, New York 10019.

FILM QUARTERLY, University of California Press, Berkeley, California 94720.

FILMS AND FILMING, 16 Buckingham Palace Rd., London, S.W. 1, England.

FILMS IN REVIEW, 31 Union Square West, New York, New York 10003.

THE GREEN SHEETS, Motion Picture Association of America, 522 Fifth Ave., New York, New York 10036.

HOLLYWOOD QUARTERLY (see FILM QUARTERLY)

THE HOLLYWOOD REPORTER, 6715 Sunset Blvd., Hollywood, California 90028.

IMAGE, George Eastman House, 900 East Ave., Rochester, New York 14607.

INDEPENDENT FILM JOURNAL, 165 W. 46th St., New York, New York 10036.

INTERNATIONAL PHOTOGRAPHER, 7715 Sunset Blvd., Hollywood, California 90046.

INTERNATIONAL PROJECTIONIST, 1645 Hennepin Ave., Minneapolis, Minnesota 55403.

JOURNAL OF THE SOCIETY OF MOTION PICTURE AND TELEVISION ENGINEERS (see SMPE and SMPTE JOURNAL)

MOTION PICTURE DAILY, 1270 Avenue of the Americas, New York, New York 10020.

MOTION PICTURE EXHIBITOR, 317 N. Broad St., Philadelphia, Pennsylvania 19107.

MOTION PICTURE HERALD, 1270 Avenue of the Americas, New York, New York 10020.

NEW YORK TIMES, 229 W. 43rd St., New York, New York 10036.

PARENTS MAGAZINE, 52 Vanderbilt Ave., New York, New York 10017.

PHOTOPLAY, 205 E. 42nd St., New York, New York 10017.

(SMPE) SMPTE JOURNAL, 9. E. 41st St., New York, New York 10017.

SATURDAY REVIEW, 380 Madison Ave., New York, New York 10017.

SCIENCE DIGEST, 1775 Broadway, New York, New York 10019.

SCIENTIFIC AMERICAN, 415 Madison Ave., New York, New York 10017.

SIGHT AND SOUND, 255 Seventh Ave., New York, New York 10001.

TIME, Rockefeller Center, New York, New York 10020.

VARIETY, 154 W. 46th St., New York, New York 10036.

APPENDICES

KEY TO ABBREVIATIONS

AA — Allied Artists Corporation
AFR — Africa
ARC — American Releasing Corporation
ARG — Argentina
ART — Artclass
AST — Astor Pictures
AU — Australia
AUD — Audible Pictures
AUS — Austria
BEL — Belgium
BER — Bertad Pictures
BOL — Bolex Corporation
BRA — Brazil
BRI — British
BUL — Bulgaria
BV — Buena Vista (Disney)
CAN — Canada
CAP — Capitol Film Exchange
CHE — Chesterfield Pictures
CHI — China
CIN — Cinerama
COL — Columbia Pictures
COM — Commercial Biophone
CON — Consolidated Pictures
COS — Cosmopolitan Pictures
CUB — Cuba
CZE — Czechoslovakia
DCA — Distributor's Corporation of America
DEN — Denmark
ED — Edison Studios
EGY — Egypt
EL — Eagle-Lion Pictures
EMB — Embassy Pictures
FBO — Film Booking Organization
FC — Film Classics
FD — First Division
FIN — Finland
FN — First National Pictures
FOR — Formosa
FRA — France
GER — Germany
GN — Grand National
GOL — Goldwyn Pictures
GOT — Gotham Pictures
GRI — D. W. Griffith
HOL — Holland and the Netherlands
HUN — Hungary

INC — Thomas Ince
IND — Independent release
IRE — Ireland
ISR — Israel
ITA — Italy
JAP — Japan
KIN — Kinemacolor Corporation
KOR — Korea
LIP — Lippert Pictures
LOU — Louben Pictures
MAG — Magna Pictures
MAL — Malaya
MEX — Mexico
MGM — Metro-Goldwyn-Mayer
MON — Monogram Pictures
NOR — Norway
PAR — Paramount Pictures
PAT — Pathe and Pathe Freres
PHI — Philippine Islands

POL — Poland
POR — Portugal
PRE — Preferred Pictures
PRI — Principal Pictures
PRC — Producers Releasing Corporation
PWP — Public Welfare Pictures
PRZ — Prizma Pictures
RAY — Rayart Pictures
REA — Realart Pictures
REL — Reliance Pictures
REX — Rex Pictures
RKO — RKO-Pathe and RKO Radio Pictures
ROS — Rosemary Films
ROU — Roumania
RUS — Russia
SAR — Seven Arts
SEL — Selig Pictures
SG — Screen Guild Productions
SPA — Spain
SRO — Selznick Releasing Organization
SWE — Sweden
SWI — Switzerland
SYN — Syndicate Pictures
TCF — Twentieth Century-Fox
THA — Thailand
TOB — Tobis Florenfilms
TIF — Tiffany Pictures

TPE — Talking Picture Epics
TRI — Triangle Films
TUR — Turkey
UA — United Artists
UN — Universal Pictures
VIT — Vitagraph
WB — Warner Brothers Pictures
WW — World-Wide Pictures

APPENDIX ONE
NATURAL COLOR
AND TINTED FILMS

1895-1908		
AN ASTRONOMER'S DREAM	FRA	Pathecolor
CINDERELLA (sequences)	FRA	Pathecolor
THE DANCE OF ANNABELLE	ED	tinted
THE ENCHANTED GLASSES	FRA	Pathecolor
THE FLOWER FAIRY	FRA	Pathecolor
THE RED SPECTRE	FRA	Pathecolor
SALOME	FRA	Pathecolor
TRANSFORMATION	FRA	Pathecolor
WEIRD FANCIES	FRA	Pathecolor
THE WONDERFUL ALBUM	FRA	Pathecolor
1909		
THE BIRTH OF JESUS	FRA	Pathecolor
VISIT OF KING GEORGE AND QUEEN MARY TO INDIA	BRI	Kinemacolor
1910		
BIRTH OF A FLOWER	BRI	Kinemacolor
IN ANCIENT GREECE	FRA	Pathecolor
THE STORY OF NAPOLEON	BRI	Kinemacolor
1911		
CAIN AND ABEL	FRA	Pathecolor
THE CORONATION OF GEORGE V	BRI	Kinemacolor
THE DURBAR AT DELHI	BRI	Kinemacolor
THE INVESTITURE OF THE PRINCE OF WALES	BRI	Kinemacolor
ROUND THE WORLD IN TWO HOURS	BRI	Kinemacolor
THE MARGRAVE'S DAUGHTER	GER	
1912		
LA TOSCA	IND	Kinemacolor
1913		
THE CLANSMAN	IND	Kinemacolor
DAVID COPPERFIELD	BRI	tinted
DR. JEKYLL AND MR. HYDE	BRI	Kinemacolor
EAST LYNNE	BRI	tinted
THE RIVALS	BRI	Kinemacolor
1914		
THE EARL OF CAMELOT	BRI	Biocolor
THE LIFE OF OUR SAVIOR (LA PASSION)	FRA	Pathecolor
LITTLE LORD FAUNTLEROY	BRI	Kinemacolor
MAUD MULLER	BRI	Kinemacolor
MISSION BELLS	BRI	Kinemacolor
SPEAKING PICTURES	BRI	Biocolor
THE WORLD, THE FLESH AND THE DEVIL	BRI	Kinemacolor
1915		
THE BIRTH OF A NATION	GRI	tinted
GLADIOLI	BRI	Kinemacolor
LES MISERABLES	FRA	Pathecolor

THE PRIDE OF NATIONS	BRI	Biocolor
QUEEN MARGARET	BRI	Biocolor
A ROSE AMONG THE BRIARS	FRA	Pathecolor
THE WRATH OF THE GODS	INC	tinted
1916		
THE BELOVED VAGABOND	FRA	Pathecolor
INTOLERANCE	GRI	tinted
WITH THE FIGHTING FORCES OF EUROPE	BRI	Kinemacolor
1917		
JOAN THE WOMAN	PAR	tinted
OUR NAVY	PRZ	Prizma
A TALE OF TWO NATIONS	IND	unknown
1918		
THE GULF BETWEEN	IND	Technicolor
1919		
BROKEN BLOSSOMS	UA	tinted
EVERYWHERE IS PRIZMA	PRZ	Prizma
VICTORY PARADE	BRI	Gaumontcolor
1920		
THE ADVENTURER	TCF	tinted
BALI THE UNKNOWN	PRZ	Prizma
FIREBRAND TREVISON	TCF	tinted
FROM NOW ON	TCF	tinted
HEIDI OF THE ALPS	PRZ	Prizma
A MANHATTAN KNIGHT	TCF	tinted
ON THE FRINGE OF THE GLACIERS	IND	Artcolor
THE STRONGEST	TCF	tinted
THE TIGER'S CUB	TCF	tinted
WAY DOWN EAST (sequences)	UA	Technicolor
1921		
BUCKING THE LINE	TCF	tinted
THE JOLT	TCF	tinted
THE LAST TRAIL	TCF	tinted
LITTLE MISS HAWKSHAW	TCF	tinted
THE NIGHT HORSEMAN	TCF	tinted
QUEENIE	TCF	tinted
THE ROUGH DIAMOND	TCF	tinted
SHATTERED (SCHERBEN) (sequences)	GER	tinted
THE THREE MUSKETEERS	UA	tinted
WHILE THE DEVIL LAUGHS	TCF	tinted
1922		
THE BROADWAY PEACOCK	TCF	tinted
A CALIFORNIA ROMANCE	TCF	tinted
THE CUSTARD CUP	TCF	tinted
EVERYBODY STEP	IND	Musicolor
FLAMES OF PASSION (sequences)	BRI	Prizma
THE GLORIOUS ADVENTURE	BRI	Prizma
THE LIGHTS OF NEW YORK	TCF	tinted
MONTE CRISTO	TCF	tinted
THE RAGGED HEIRESS	TCF	tinted
TOLL OF THE SEA	IND	Technicolor
WEST OF CHICAGO	TCF	tinted
WHEN KNIGHTHOOD WAS IN FLOWER	PAR	tinted
1923		
ALIAS THE NIGHT WIND	TCF	tinted
BIG DAN	TCF	tinted
BRIGHT LIGHTS OF BROADWAY	PRI	tinted
CAMEO KIRBY	TCF	tinted
CUPID'S FIREMAN	TCF	tinted
THE ELEVENTH HOUR	TCF	tinted
THE EXILES	TCF	tinted

EYES OF THE FOREST	TCF	tinted
THE GUNFIGHTER	TCF	tinted
HELL'S HOLE	TCF	tinted
IF WINTER COMES	TCF	tinted
THE LONE STAR RANGER	TCF	tinted
MADNESS OF YOUTH	TCF	tinted
THE MAN WHO WON	TCF	tinted
MONNA VANNA	TCF	tinted
THE NET	TCF	tinted
NO MOTHER TO GUIDE HER	TCF	tinted
NORTH OF HUDSON BAY	TCF	tinted
RED LIGHT	GOL	tinted
ST. ELMO	TCF	tinted
SECOND-HAND LOVE	TCF	tinted
THE SILENT COMMAND	TCF	tinted
SKID PROOF	TCF	tinted
SOFT BOILED	TCF	tinted
STRANGERS OF THE NIGHT	MGM	tinted
THE TEN COMMANDMENTS (sequences)	PAR	Technicolor
THIS FREEDOM	TCF	tinted
TIMES HAVE CHANGED	TCF	tinted
TRUXTON KING	TCF	tinted
VANITY FAIR	PRZ	Prizma
THE VIRGIN QUEEN	PRZ	Prizma
WHEN ODDS ARE EVEN	TCF	tinted
THE WHITE ROSE	UA	tinted

1924

THE BANDOLERO	MGM	tinted
THE BRASS BOWL	TCF	tinted
CIRCUS COWBOY	TCF	tinted
CYTHEREA	FN	Technicolor
DANTE'S INFERNO	TCF	tinted
DAUGHTERS OF THE NIGHT	TCF	tinted
DEADWOOD COACH	TCF	tinted
FLAMES OF DESIRE	TCF	tinted
GREED (sequences)	MGM	tinted
HE WHO GETS SLAPPED	MGM	tinted
HONOR AMONG MEN	TCF	tinted
THE IRON HORSE	TCF	tinted
IT IS THE LAW	TCF	tinted
THE LAST MAN ON EARTH	TCF	tinted
LAWLESS MEN	IND	tinted
THE MAN WHO PLAYED SQUARE	TCF	tinted
MARRIED FLIRTS	MGM	tinted
MY HUSBAND'S WIVES	TCF	tinted
THE NAVIGATOR	MGM	tinted
ROMANCE RANCH	TCF	tinted
THE SILENT ACCUSER	MGM	tinted
SINNERS IN SILK	MGM	tinted
UNDER THE RED ROBE	COS	tinted
THE UNINVITED GUEST (sequences)	MGM	Technicolor
WANDERER OF THE WASTELAND	PAR	Technicolor
WESTERN LUCK	TCF	tinted
WINNER TAKE ALL	TCF	tinted

1925

THE ANCIENT MARINER	TCF	tinted
THE BEST BAD MAN	TCF	tinted
THE BIG PARADE (sequences)	MGM	Technicolor
BRIGHT LIGHTS	MGM	tinted
CYRANO DE BERGERAC	FRA	Pathecolor
THE DESERT'S PRICE	TCF	tinted
DURAND OF THE BADLANDS	TCF	tinted

EAST LYNNE	TCF	tinted
THE EVERLASTING WHISPER	TCF	tinted
THE FOOL	TCF	tinted
THE GOLDEN STRAIN	TCF	tinted
THE HUNTED WOMAN	TCF	tinted
THE KING ON MAIN STREET (sequences)	PAR	Technicolor
LAZYBONES	TCF	tinted
LIGHTS OF OLD BROADWAY	MGM	tinted
THE LOST WORLD	FN	tinted
LUCKY HORSESHOE	TCF	tinted
MARIONETTES	IND	Technicolor
THE MERRY WIDOW (sequences)	MGM	Technicolor
NEVER THE TWAIN SHALL MEET	COS	tinted
PEAK OF FATE	GER	tinted
THE PHANTOM OF THE OPERA (sequences)	UN	Technicolor
POTEMKIN	RUS	tinted
PRETTY LADIES (sequences)	MGM	Technicolor
SALLY	FN	tinted
SCANDAL PROOF	TCF	tinted
SEVEN KEYS TO BALDPATE	PAR	tinted
SPLENDID ROAD	FN	tinted
THE SPORTING VENUS	MGM	tinted
STAGE STRUCK (sequences)	PAR	Technicolor
SUN UP	MGM	tinted
THANK YOU	TCF	tinted
THE THREE MASKS	FRA	Pathecolor
TIMBER WOLF	TCF	tinted
THE TOWER OF LIES	MGM	tinted
THE UNHOLY THREE	MGM	tinted
THE WHEEL	TCF	tinted
WHEN THE DOOR OPENED	TCF	tinted
WINGS OF YOUTH	TCF	tinted

1926

AN AMERICAN VENUS (sequences)	PAR	Technicolor
BEAU GESTE (sequences)	PAR	Technicolor
BEN-HUR (sequences)	MGM	Technicolor
BERTHA, THE SEWING MACHINE GIRL	TCF	tinted
BLACK PARADISE	TCF	tinted
THE BLACK PIRATE	UA	Technicolor
BLUE BOY (short)	MGM	Technicolor
THE BLUE EAGLE	TCF	tinted
BUFFALO BILL'S LAST FIGHT (short)	MGM	Technicolor
THE CANYON OF LIGHT	TCF	tinted
CLEOPATRA (short)	MGM	Technicolor
THE COUNTRY BEYOND	TCF	tinted
THE COWBOY AND THE COUNTESS	TCF	tinted
EARLY TO WED	TCF	tinted
THE FIRST YEAR	TCF	tinted
FLAMING FOREST	MGM	tinted
THE FLYING HORSEMAN	TCF	tinted
THE GENTLE CYCLONE	TCF	tinted
THE GILDED BUTTERFLY	TCF	tinted
THE GREAT K & A TRAIN ROBBERY	TCF	tinted
HARD BOILED	TCF	tinted
IRENE (sequences)	TCF	Technicolor
THE LILY	TCF	tinted
THE MAN FOUR-SQUARE	TCF	tinted
MARRY MONTH OF MAY	TCF	tinted
MATRIMONY BLUES	TCF	tinted
MICHAEL STROGOFF (sequences)	UA	Technicolor
MIKE	MGM	tinted
MONA LISA (short)	MGM	Technicolor
MORE PAY —LESS WORK	TCF	tinted

NO MAN'S GOLD	TCF	tinted
THE PALACE OF PLEASURE	TCF	tinted
SANDY	TCF	tinted
THE SEA BEAST	WB	Technicolor
SIBERIA	TCF	tinted
THE SILVER TREASURE	TCF	tinted
SUMMER BACHELORS	TCF	tinted
30 BELOW ZERO	TCF	tinted
THREE BAD MEN	TCF	tinted
TONY RUNS WILD	TCF	tinted
THE VIRGIN QUEEN (short)	MGM	Technicolor
THE VISION (short)	MGM	Technicolor
THE VOLCANO	PAR	tinted
WINGS OF THE STORM	TCF	tinted
WOMANPOWER	TCF	tinted

1927

ANGKOR	WB	tinted
FAITH OF MILLIONS	IND	unknown
THE FIRE BRIGADE (sequences)	MGM	Technicolor
THE KING OF KINGS (sequences)	PAT	Technicolor
THE JOY GIRL	TCF	Technicolor
MOTHER MACHREE	TCF	tinted
PAID TO LOVE	TCF	tinted
THE ROAD TO ROMANCE	MGM	tinted
THE SECOND HUNDRED YEARS	TCF	tinted
SINGED	TCF	tinted

1928

ACROSS TO SINGAPORE	MGM	tinted
THE AIR CIRCUS	TCF	tinted
CASANOVA (sequences)	MGM	Technicolor
CIRCUS ROOKIES	MGM	tinted
COURT MARTIAL	COL	Technicolor
THE ENEMY	MGM	tinted
THE GIRL-SHY COWBOY	TCF	tinted
HONOR BOUND	TCF	tinted
A HORSEMAN OF THE PLAINS	TCF	tinted
ME GANGSTER	TCF	tinted
THE MYSTERY MANSION	TCF	tinted
NAPOLEON	MGM	tinted
NONE BUT THE BRAVE	TCF	Technicolor
THE PATSY	MGM	tinted
PLASTERED IN PARIS	TCF	tinted
THE PLAY GIRL	TCF	tinted
RED HAIR (sequence)	PAR	Technicolor
THE RIVER PIRATE	TCF	tinted
STREET ANGEL	TCF	tinted
A THIEF IN THE DARK	TCF	tinted
UNDER THE BLACK EAGLE	MGM	tinted
THE VIKING	MGM	Technicolor
THE WATER HOLE	PAR	Technicolor
THE WEDDING MARCH (sequences)	PAR	Technicolor
WHY SAILORS GO WRONG	TCF	tinted

1929

BROADWAY (sequences)	UN	Technicolor
BROADWAY MELODY (sequences)	MGM	Technicolor
DANCE OF LIFE (sequences)	PAR	Technicolor
THE DESERT SONG (sequences)	WB	Technicolor
FOOTLIGHTS AND FOOLS	FN	Technicolor
FOX MOVIETONE FOLLIES OF 1929 (sequences)	TCF	Multicolor
GLORIFYING THE AMERICAN GIRL (sequences)	WB	Technicolor
GOLD DIGGERS OF BROADWAY	WB	Technicolor
THE GREAT GABBO (sequences)	WW	Multicolor

HIS FIRST COMMAND (sequences)	PAT	Technicolor
THE HOLLYWOOD REVUE	MGM	Technicolor
LOVES OF CASANOVA	MGM	Technicolor
MAMBA	TIF	Technicolor
MARRIED IN HOLLYWOOD	TCF	Multicolor
THE MYSTERIOUS ISLAND	MGM	Technicolor
ON WITH THE SHOW	WB	Technicolor
PARIS	FN	Technicolor
RED HOT RHYTHM (sequence)	PAT	Technicolor
REDSKIN	PAR	Technicolor
RIO RITA	RKO	Technicolor
SHOW OF SHOWS	WB	Technicolor
SUNNY SIDE UP	TCF	Multicolor

1930

BRIDE OF THE REGIMENT	FN	Technicolor
CHASING RAINBOWS (sequences)	MGM	Technicolor
DIXIANA (sequences)	RKO	Technicolor
FOLLOW THRU	PAR	Technicolor
THE GENERAL LINE (OLD AND NEW)	RUS	tinted
GOLDEN DAWN	WB	Technicolor
HARMONY HEAVEN	BRI	unknown
HELL'S ANGELS (sequences)	UA	Technicolor
HIT THE DECK (sequences)	MGM	Technicolor
HOLD EVERYTHING	WB	Technicolor
KING OF JAZZ	UN	Technicolor
LEATHERNECKING	RKO	Technicolor
THE LIFE OF THE PARTY	WB	Technicolor
LORD BYRON OF BROADWAY (sequences)	MGM	Technicolor
THE LOTTERY BRIDE (sequences)	UA	Technicolor
MAMMY (sequences)	WB	Technicolor
NO, NO, NANETTE (sequences)	FN	Technicolor
PARAMOUNT ON PARADE (sequences)	PAR	Technicolor
PUTTIN' ON THE RITZ (sequences)	UA	Technicolor
THE ROGUE SONG	MGM	Technicolor
SALLY	FN	Technicolor
SHOWGIRL IN HOLLYWOOD (sequences)	FN	Technicolor
SON OF THE GODS (sequences)	FN	Technicolor
SONG OF THE FLAME	FN	Technicolor
SONG OF THE WEST	WB	Technicolor
SWEET KITTY BELLAIRE	WB	Technicolor
TOAST OF THE LEGION (sequences)	FN	Technicolor
UNDER A TEXAS MOON	WB	Technicolor
THE VAGABOND KING	PAR	Technicolor
VIENNESE NIGHTS	WB	Technicolor
WHOOPEE	UA	Technicolor

1931

BRIGHT LIGHTS	FN	Technicolor
FANNY FOLEY HERSELF	RKO	Technicolor
FIFTY MILLION FRENCHMEN	WB	Technicolor
GOOFY GOAT (short)	TCF	Multicolor
KISS ME AGAIN	FN	Technicolor
THE RUNAROUND (LOVABLE AND SWEET)	RKO	Technicolor
WOMAN HUNGRY	FN	Technicolor

1932

DOCTOR X	WB	Technicolor
FLOWERS AND TREES (short)	RKO	Technicolor
LES GAITES DE L'ESCADRON	FRA	unknown
MANHATTAN PARADE	WB	Technicolor

1933

BELOW THE SEA (sequences)	COL	Technicolor
THE MYSTERY OF THE WAX MUSEUM	WB	Technicolor

THE SKIPPER OF THE OSPREY	BRI	Raycol
ZOO IN BUDAPEST	TCF	tinted

1934

THE CAT AND THE FIDDLE (sequences)	MGM	Technicolor
HOLLYWOOD PARTY (sequences)	MGM	Technicolor
HOUSE OF ROTHCHILD (sequences)	UA	Technicolor
KID MILLIONS (sequences)	UA	Technicolor
LA CUCURACHA		

1935

BECKY SHARP	RKO	Technicolor
LEGONG	IND	unknown
THE LITTLE COLONEL (sequences)	TCF	Technicolor
RADIO FOLLIES (sequences)	BRI	Dufaycolor

1936

ALLEGRETTO (short)	IND	Gasparcolor
BLUE SEA	RUS	unknown
CAPTAIN CALAMITY	GN	Hirlicolor
CAVALCADE OF TEXAS (short)	UN	Telco-Color
COLOR CARNIVAL (short)	RUS	unknown
THE DANCING PIRATE	RKO	Technicolor
DE LA SARTEN AL FUEGO	MGM	Hirlicolor
THE DEVIL ON HORSEBACK	GN	Hirlicolor
EL CAPITAN TORMENTA	MGM	Hirlicolor
EL DIABLO SE DIVIERTE	MGM	Hirlicolor
THE GARDEN OF ALLAH	UA	Technicolor
GOD'S COUNTRY AND THE WOMAN	WB	Technicolor
NIGHTINGALE, LITTLE NIGHTINGALE	RUS	unknown
THE PHANTOM OF SANTA FE	IND	Hirlicolor
RAMONA	TCF	Technicolor
TALKING HANDS (short)	BRI	Harmonicolor
TRAIL OF THE LONESOME PINE	PAR	Technicolor
TRADE TATTOO (short)	BRI	Gasparcolor

1937

ACADEMY AWARD REVIEW OF WALT DISNEY CARTOONS	RKO	Technicolor
THE BAD MAN OF BRIMSTONE	MGM	sepia
THE BOLD CABALLERO	REP	Hirlicolor
CORONATION FILM	BRI	Technicolor
CORONATION FILM	FRA	Francita
EBB TIDE	PAR	Technicolor
MAYTIME	MGM	sepia
NOTHING SACRED	UA	Technicolor
OLD SOLDIERS NEVER DIE (short)	BRI	Dufaycolor
PAGLIACCI	FRA	Chemicolor
THE PRISONER OF ZENDA	UA	sepia
SAILS AND SAILORS (short)	BRI	Dufaycolor
THE SHEIK STEPS OUT	REP	tinted
SNOW WHITE AND THE SEVEN DWARFS	RKO	Technicolor
SOUVENIRS (short)	BRI	Dufaycolor
A STAR IS BORN	UA	Technicolor
VICTORIA THE GREAT (sequence)	RKO	Technicolor
VOGUES OF 1938	UA	Technicolor
WE'RE IN THE LEGION NOW	GN	Hirlicolor
WHEN'S YOUR BIRTHDAY? (sequence)	RKO	Technicolor
WINGS OF THE MORNING	TCF	Technicolor

· 1938

ADVENTURES OF ROBIN HOOD	WB	Technicolor
ADVENTURES OF TOM SAWYER	UA	Technicolor
DIVORCE OF LADY X	UA	Technicolor
DRUMS	UA	Technicolor
FLASH GORDON'S TRIP TO MARS (serial)	UN	tinted
THE GIRL OF THE GOLDEN WEST	MGM	sepia
GOLDWYN FOLLIES	UA	Technicolor
GOLD IS WHERE YOU FIND IT	WB	Technicolor
HEART OF THE NORTH	WB	Technicolor
HER JUNGLE LOVE	PAR	Technicolor

KENTUCKY	TCF	Technicolor
MAY NIGHT	RUS	unknown
MEN WITH WINGS	PAR	Technicolor
MY LUCKY STAR (sequence)	TCF	sepia
SIXTY GLORIOUS YEARS	RKO	Technicolor
STABLEMATES	MGM	sepia
SWEETHEARTS	MGM	Technicolor
TALBOT OF CANADA	CAN	Kodachrome
VALLEY OF THE GIANTS	WB	Technicolor
WYOMING	MGM	sepia

1939

BROADWAY SERENADE	MGM	sepia
DODGE CITY	WB	Technicolor
DRUMS ALONG THE MOHAWK	TCF	Technicolor
FOUR FEATHERS	UA	Technicolor
THE GENTLEMAN FROM ARIZONA	MON	Cinecolor
GONE WITH THE WIND	MGM	Technicolor
GULLIVER'S TRAVELS	PAR	Technicolor
HOLLYWOOD CAVALCADE	TCF	Technicolor
THE ICE FOLLIES OF 1939 (sequence)	MGM	Technicolor
JESSE JAMES	TCF	Technicolor
LAND OF LIBERTY (sequences)	MGM	Technicolor
LET FREEDOM RING	MGM	sepia
LITTLE HUMPBACK HORSE	RUS	unknown
THE LITTLE PRINCESS	TCF	Technicolor
LOVE ON THE RANGE (short)	BRI	Dufaycolor
LOVE ON THE WING (short)	CAN	Dufaycolor
LURE OF THE WASTELAND	MON	Telco-Color
THE MIKADO	UN	Technicolor
THE OKLAHOMA KID	WB	sepia
THE PRIVATE LIVES OF ELIZABETH AND ESSEX	WB	Technicolor
THE RAINS CAME	TCF	sepia
SOROCHINSK FAIR	RUS	unknown
STAND UP AND FIGHT	MGM	sepia
SWANEE RIVER	TCF	Technicolor
THE WIZARD OF OZ (sequences)	MGM	Technicolor
THE WOMEN (sequence)	MGM	Technicolor

1940

ARIZONA	COL	tinted
BITTER SWEET	MGM	Technicolor
THE BLUE BIRD	TCF	Technicolor
CHAD HANNA	TCF	Technicolor
DAS BAD AUF DER TENNE	GER	Agfacolor
DAS KLEINE JOFKONZERT	GER	Agfacolor
DOCTOR CYCLOPS	PAR	Technicolor
DOWN ARGENTINE WAY	TCF	Technicolor
FANTASIA	RKO	Technicolor
FIGARO, ODER EIN TOLLER TAG	GER	Agfacolor
IRENE (sequence)	RKO	Technicolor
ISLE OF DESTINY	RKO	Cosmocolor
MARYLAND	TCF	Technicolor
NORTHWEST MOUNTED POLICE	PAR	Technicolor
NORTHWEST PASSAGE	MGM	Technicolor
OF MICE AND MEN	UA	sepia
OVER THE MOON	UA	Technicolor
PINOCCHIO	RKO	Technicolor
QUEEN OF DESTINY	RKO	Technicolor
THE RETURN OF FRANK JAMES	TCF	Technicolor
THE THIEF OF BAGDAD	UA	Technicolor
TYPHOON	PAR	Technicolor
UNTAMED	PAR	Technicolor
WIR BEIDE LIEBTEN KATHERINA	GER	Agfacolor

1941

ALOMA OF THE SOUTH SEAS	PAR	Technicolor
BAHAMA PASSAGE	PAR	Technicolor
BELLE STARR	TCF	Technicolor
BILLY THE KID	MGM	Technicolor
BLOOD AND SAND	TCF	Technicolor
BLOSSOMS IN THE DUST	MGM	Technicolor
DIVE BOMBER	WB	Technicolor
DUMBO	RKO	Technicolor
FIESTA	UA	Technicolor
FRAUEN SIND DOCH BESSERE DIPLOMATEN	GER	Agfacolor
LOUISIANA PURCHASE	PAR	Technicolor
MR .BUG GOES TO TOWN	PAR	Technicolor
MOON OVER MIAMI	TCF	Technicolor
RELUCTANT DRAGON	RKO	Technicolor
SHEPHERD OF THE HILLS	PAR	Technicolor
SMILIN' THROUGH	MGM	Technicolor
THAT NIGHT IN RIO	TCF	Technicolor
VIRGINIA	PAR	Technicolor
WEEK-END IN HAVANA	TCF	Technicolor
WESTERN UNION	TCF	Technicolor
ZIEGFELD GIRL	MGM	sepia

1942

ARABIAN NIGHTS	UN	Technicolor
BAMBI	RKO	Technicolor
BEYOND THE BLUE HORIZON	PAR	Technicolor
THE BLACK SWAN	TCF	Technicolor
CAPTAINS OF THE CLOUDS	WB	Technicolor
DIE GOLDENE STADT	GER	Agfacolor
DIE GROSSE FREIHEIT	GER	Agfacolor
THE FOREST RANGERS	PAR	Technicolor
JUNGLE BOOK	UA	Technicolor
THE MOON AND SIXPENCE (sequence)	UA	Technicolor
MY GAL SAL	TCF	Technicolor
QUEEN VICTORIA	BRI	Technicolor
REAP THE WILD WIND	PAR	Technicolor
SALUDOS AMIGOS	RKO	Technicolor
SONG OF THE ISLANDS	TCF	Technicolor
SONS OF THE SEA	WB	Technicolor
SPRINGTIME IN THE ROCKIES	TCF	Technicolor
THUNDERBIRDS	TCF	Technicolor
TO THE SHORES OF TRIPOLI	TCF	Technicolor
TORTILLA FLAT	MGM	sepia

1943

BEST FOOT FORWARD	MGM	Technicolor
THE BOYAR'S PLOT	RUS	Agfacolor
COBRA WOMAN	UN	Technicolor
CONEY ISLAND	TCF	Technicolor
CRASH DIVE	TCF	Technicolor
DESERT SONG	WB	Technicolor
THE DESPERADOS	COL	Technicolor
DIXIE	PAR	Technicolor
DUBARRY WAS A LADY	MGM	Technicolor
FOR WHOM THE BELL TOLLS	PAR	Technicolor
THE GANG'S ALL HERE	TCF	Technicolor
THE GREAT MR. HANDEL	BRI	Technicolor
HAPPY GO LUCKY	PAR	Technicolor
HEAVEN CAN WAIT	TCF	Technicolor
HELLO, FRISCO, HELLO	TCF	Technicolor
IMMENSEE	GER	Agfacolor
JEEP HERDERS	PLA	Kodachrome
LASSIE COME HOME	MGM	Technicolor
MY FRIEND FLICKA	TCF	Technicolor

THE PHANTOM OF THE OPERA	UN	Technicolor
REPORT FROM THE ALEUTIANS	IND	Technicolor
RIDING HIGH	PAR	Technicolor
SALUTE TO THE MARINES	MGM	Technicolor
SWEET ROSIE O'GRADY	TCF	Technicolor
THIS IS THE ARMY	WB	Technicolor
THOUSANDS CHEER	MGM	Technicolor
VICTORY THROUGH AIR POWER	UA	Technicolor
WHITE SAVAGE	UN	Technicolor

1944

ALI BABA AND THE FORTY THIEVES	UN	Technicolor
AN AMERICAN ROMANCE	MGM	Technicolor
BATHING BEAUTY	MGM	Technicolor
BECKY SHARP (re-issue)	FC	Cinecolor
BELLE OF THE YUKON	RKO	Technicolor
BROADWAY RHYTHM	MGM	Technicolor
BUFFALO BILL	TCF	Technicolor
CAN'T HELP SINGING	UN	Technicolor
THE CLIMAX	UN	Technicolor
COVER GIRL	COL	Technicolor
DANCING PIRATE (re-issue)	FC	Cinecolor
DETOUR TO DANGER	PLA	Kodachrome
THE FIGHTING LADY	TCF	Kodachrome
DIE FLEDERMAUS	GER	Agfacolor
FRENCHMAN'S CREEK	PAR	Technicolor
GREENWICH VILLAGE	TCF	Technicolor
GYPSY WILDCAT	UN	Technicolor
HOME IN INDIANA	TCF	Technicolor
IRISH EYES ARE SMILING	TCF	Technicolor
KISENGA, MAN OF AFRICA	BRI	Technicolor
KISMET	MGM	Technicolor
LADY IN THE DARK	PAR	Technicolor
MEET ME IN ST. LOUIS	MGM	Technicolor
THE MEMPHIS BELLE	PAR	Kodachrome
NATIONAL VELVET	MGM	Technicolor
NOTHING SACRED (re-issue)	FC	Cinecolor
OPFERGANG	GER	Agfacolor
THE PEOPLE'S CHOICE	PLA	Kodachrome
PIN UP GIRL	TCF	Technicolor
THE PRINCESS AND THE PIRATE	RKO	Technicolor
RAINBOW ISLAND	PAR	Technicolor
SHINE ON, HARVEST MOON (sequence)	WB	Technicolor
SOMETHING FOR THE BOYS	TCF	Technicolor
A STAR IS BORN (re-issue)	FC	Cinecolor
THE STORY OF DR. WASSELL	PAR	Technicolor
THE THREE CABALLEROS	RKO	Technicolor
UP IN ARMS	RKO	Technicolor
WILSON	TCF	Technicolor
WITH THE MARINES AT TARAWA	IND	Kodachrome

1945

ANCHORS AWEIGH	MGM	Technicolor
BARON MUENCHHAUSEN	GER	Agfacolor
BLITHE SPIRIT	UA	Technicolor
BRING ON THE GIRLS	PAR	Technicolor
COLONEL BLIMP	UA	Technicolor
DIAMOND HORSESHOE	TCF	Technicolor
THE DOLLY SISTERS	TCF	Technicolor
THE ENCHANTED FOREST	PRC	Cinecolor
FRONTIER GAL	UN	Technicolor
INCENDIARY BLONDE	PAR	Technicolor
IT'S A PLEASURE	RKO	Technicolor
KOLBERG	GER	Agfacolor

LEAVE HER TO HEAVEN	TCF	Technicolor
NOB HILL	TCF	Technicolor
NORTHWEST TRAIL	SG	Cinecolor
THE PICTURE OF DORIAN GRAY (sequences)	MGM	Technicolor
ROUGH RIDERS OF CHEYENNE	REP	Magnacolor
SALOME —WHERE SHE DANCED	UN	Technicolor
SAN ANTONIO	WB	Technicolor
SON OF LASSIE	MGM	Technicolor
SONG OF OLD WYOMING	PRC	Cinecolor
A SONG TO REMEMBER	COL	Technicolor
THE SPANISH MAIN	RKO	Technicolor
SPORTS PARADE, MOSCOW	RUS	Agfacolor
STATE FAIR	TCF	Technicolor
SUDAN	UN	Technicolor
A THOUSAND AND ONE NIGHTS	COL	Technicolor
THRILL OF A ROMANCE	MGM	Technicolor
THUNDERHEAD, SON OF FLICKA	TCF	Technicolor
TONIGHT AND EVERY NIGHT	COL	Technicolor
WARRIORS OF FAITH	CZE	unknown
WHERE DO WE GO FROM HERE?	TCF	Technicolor
WONDER MAN	RKO	Technicolor
YOLANDA AND THE THIEF	MGM	Technicolor

1946

BANDIT OF SHERWOOD FOREST	COL	Technicolor
BLUE SKIES	PAR	Technicolor
CAESAR AND CLEOPATRA	UA	Technicolor
CALIFORNIA	PAR	Technicolor
CANYON PASSAGE	UN	Technicolor
CARAVAN TRAIL	PRC	Cinecolor
CENTENNIAL SUMMER	TCF	Technicolor
COLORADO SERENADE	PRC	Cinecolor
COURAGE OF LASSIE	MGM	Technicolor
DEATH VALLEY	SG	Cinecolor
DO YOU LOVE ME?	TCF	Technicolor
DUEL IN THE SUN	SRO	Technicolor
EASY TO WED	MGM	Technicolor
THE EXILE	UN	Sepiatone
FIGHTING GUARDSMAN	COL	Technicolor
GALLANT BESS	MGM	Cinecolor
GLINKA	RUS	Sovcolor
GOD'S COUNTRY	SG	Cinecolor
THE HARVEY GIRLS	MGM	Technicolor
HENRY V	UA	Technicolor
HOLIDAY IN MEXICO	MGM	Technicolor
HOME ON THE RANGE	REP	Magnacolor
I'VE ALWAYS LOVED YOU	REP	Technicolor
THE JOLSON STORY	COL	Technicolor
THE KID FROM BROOKLYN	RKO	Technicolor
LAUGHING LADY	BRI	Technicolor
MAKE MINE MUSIC	RKO	Technicolor
THE MAN FROM RAINBOW VALLEY	REP	Magnacolor
MARGIE	TCF	Technicolor
THE MICHIGAN KID	UN	Cinecolor
NIGHT AND DAY	WB	Technicolor
A NIGHT IN PARADISE	UN	Technicolor
OUT CALIFORNIA WAY	REP	Trucolor
THE RAIDER (WESTERN APPROACHES)	BRI	Technicolor
THE RENEGADES	COL	Technicolor
ROMANCE OF THE WEST	PRC	Cinecolor
SAN ANTONIO	WB	Technicolor
SANTA FE UPRISING	REP	Magnacolor
SMOKY	TCF	Technicolor
SONG OF THE SOUTH	RKO	Technicolor

STAIRWAY TO HEAVEN	UN	Technicolor
THE STONE FLOWER	RUS	Agfacolor
THREE COMRADES	RUS	Agfacolor
THREE LITTLE GIRLS IN BLUE	TCF	Technicolor
TILL THE CLOUDS ROLL BY	MGM	Technicolor
THE TIME, THE PLACE AND THE GIRL	WB	Technicolor
THE VIRGINIAN	PAR	Technicolor
WAKE UP AND DREAM	TCF	Technicolor
WILD WEST	PRC	Cinecolor
THE YEARLING	MGM	Technicolor
THE ZIEGFELD FOLLIES	MGM	Technicolor

1947

ADVENTURE ISLAND	PAR	Cinecolor
ADVENTURES OF DON COYOTE	IND	Cinecolor
ALONG THE OREGON TRAIL	REP	Trucolor
APACHE ROSE	REP	Trucolor
BANNISTER BABY LAND (short)	IND	Fullcolor
BASE BRAWL (short)	PAR	Polacolor
BELLS OF OLD TOWN	SWE	Cinecolor
BELLS OF SAN ANGELO	REP	Trucolor
BILL AND COO	REP	Trucolor
BLACK GOLD	AA	Cinecolor
BLACK NARCISSUS	UA	Technicolor
CAPTAIN FROM CASTILLE	TCF	Technicolor
CARNIVAL IN COSTA RICA	TCF	Technicolor
THE CIRCUS COMES TO CLOWN (short)	PAR	Polacolor
CURLEY	UA	Cinecolor
DESERT FURY	PAR	Technicolor
DOWN TO EARTH	COL	Technicolor
DREAMS THAT MONEY CAN BUY	IND	Kodachrome
FABULOUS JOE	UA	Cinecolor
FIESTA	MGM	Technicolor
FOREVER AMBER	TCF	Technicolor
FUN AND FANCY FREE	RKO	Technicolor
GOLDWYN FOLLIES (re-issue)	FC	Fullcolor
GOOD NEWS	MGM	Technicolor
GUNFIGHTERS	COL	Technicolor
THE HOMESTRETCH	TCF	Technicolor
I WONDER WHO'S KISSING HER NOW?	TCF	Technicolor
LAST FRONTIER UPRISING	REP	Magnacolor
LAST OF THE REDMEN	COL	Vitacolor
LIFE WITH FATHER	WB	Technicolor
LIGHT OVER RUSSIA	RUS	Agfacolor
MOTHER WORE TIGHTS	TCF	Technicolor
MY HEART GOES CRAZY (LONDON TOWN)	BRI	Technicolor
MY WILD IRISH ROSE	WB	Technicolor
ON THE OLD SPANISH TRAIL	REP	Trucolor
THE PERILS OF PAULINE	PAR	Technicolor
THE PRIVATE AFFAIRS OF BEL AMI (sequences)	UA	Technicolor
RED STALLION	EL	Cinecolor
RETURN OF RIN TIN TIN	EL	Vitacolor
ROBIN HOOD OF TEXAS	REP	Trucolor
ROBINSON CRUSOE	RUS	Sovcolor
SCARED TO DEATH	SG	Cinecolor
THE SECRET LIFE OF WALTER MITTY	RKO	Technicolor
THE SHOCKING MISS PILGRIM	TCF	Technicolor
SINBAD THE SAILOR	RKO	Technicolor
SLAVE GIRL	UN	Technicolor
SONG OF SCHEHERAZADE	UN	Technicolor
SPRING TIME IN THE SIERRAS	REP	Trucolor
THE SWORDSMAN	COL	Technicolor
TALE OF SIBERIA	RUS	Agfacolor
TAWNY PIPIT	UN	Technicolor

THAT'S MY GAL	REP	Trucolor
THIS HAPPY BREED	UN	Technicolor
THIS TIME FOR KEEPS	MGM	Technicolor
THUNDER IN THE VALLEY	TCF	Technicolor
TYCOON	RKO	Technicolor
UNCONQUERED	PAR	Technicolor
UNDER CALIFORNIA STARS	REP	Trucolor
UNDER COLORADO SKIES	REP	Trucolor
THE UNFINISHED DANCE	MGM	Technicolor
THE VIGILANTES RETURN	UN	Cinecolor
WILDFIRE	SG	Cinecolor

1948

ADVENTURES OF DON JUAN	WB	Technicolor
ADVENTURES OF GALLANT BESS	EL	Cinecolor
ALBUQUERQUE	PAR	Cinecolor
THE ANGRY GOD	UA	Fullcolor
APARTMENT FOR PEGGY	TCF	Technicolor
THE BIG SOMBRERO	COL	Cinecolor
BLACK BART	UN	Technicolor
BLANCHE FURY	EL	Technicolor
THE BOY WITH GREEN HAIR	RKO	Technicolor
CALIFORNIA FIREBRAND	REP	Trucolor
CLIMBING THE MATTERHORN	MON	Ansco Color
CORONER CREEK	COL	Cinecolor
A DATE WITH JUDY	MGM	Technicolor
DEAD MAN'S GOLD	SG	Cinecolor
DEEP WATERS	TCF	sepia
EASTER PARADE	MGM	Technicolor
EMPEROR WALTZ	PAR	Technicolor
ENCHANTED VALLEY	EL	Cinecolor
EYES OF TEXAS	REP	Trucolor
FIGHTER SQUADRON	WB	Technicolor
THE GALLANT BLADE	COL	Technicolor
THE GAY RANCHERO	REP	Trucolor
GIVE MY REGARDS TO BROADWAY	TCF	Technicolor
GRAND CANYON TRAIL	REP	Trucolor
GREEN GRASS OF WYOMING	TCF	Technicolor
HERE COMES TROUBLE	UA	Cinecolor
HILLS OF HOME	MGM	Technicolor
AN IDEAL HUSBAND	TCF	Technicolor
JASSY	UN	Technicolor
JOAN OF ARC	RKO	Technicolor
THE KISSING BANDIT	MGM	Technicolor
THE LAST OF THE WILD HORSES	SG	sepia
LOADED PISTOLS	COL	Cinecolor
LOVES OF CARMEN	COL	Technicolor
LUCK OF THE IRISH	TCF	tinted
LUXURY LINER	MGM	Technicolor
THE MAGIC HORSE	RUS	Magicolor
THE MAN FROM COLORADO	COL	Technicolor
MELODY TIME	RKO	Technicolor
MICHAEL O'HALLORAN	MON	Cinecolor
MICKEY	EL	Cinecolor
THE MILLER'S DAUGHTER	FRA	Rouxcolor
NIGHTTIME IN NEVADA	REP	Trucolor
NORTHWEST STAMPEDE	EL	Cinecolor
THE OLYMPIC GAMES OF 1948	EL	Technichrome
ON AN ISLAND WITH YOU	MGM	Technicolor
ONE SUNDAY AFTERNOON	WB	Technicolor
THE PALEFACE	PAR	Technicolor
PANHANDLE	AA	sepia
THE PIRATE	MGM	Technicolor
THE PLUNDERERS	REP	Trucolor

POPEYE MEETS HERCULES (short)	PAR	Polacolor
PRINCE OF THIEVES	COL	Cinecolor
THE RED SHOES	EL	Technicolor
RELENTLESS	COL	Technicolor
THE RETURN OF OCTOBER	COL	Technicolor
RETURN OF THE BADMEN	RKO	Technicolor
RETURN OF WILDFIRE	LIP	Cinecolor
RIVER LADY	UN	Technicolor
ROMANCE ON THE HIGH SEAS	WB	Technicolor
ROPE	WB	Technicolor
SCUDDA HOO, SCUDDA HAY	TCF	Technicolor
SECRET LAND	MGM	Technicolor
SHAGGY	PAR	Cinecolor
SIXTEEN FATHOMS DEEP	MON	Ansco Color
THE SMUGGLERS	EL	Technicolor
SO DEAR TO MY HEART	RKO	Technicolor
SOFIA	FC	Cinecolor
SON OF GOD'S COUNTRY	REP	Trucolor
A SONG IS BORN	RKO	Technicolor
STRAWBERRY ROAN	COL	Cinecolor
SUMMER HOLIDAY	MGM	Technicolor
SWORD OF THE AVENGER	EL	sepia
TALE OF THE NAVAJOS	MGM	Technicolor
TAP ROOTS	UN	Technicolor
TASK FORCE	WB	Technicolor
THAT LADY IN ERMINE	TCF	Technicolor
THREE DARING DAUGHTERS	MGM	Technicolor
THREE GODFATHERS	MGM	Technicolor
THREE MUSKETEERS	MGM	Technicolor
TIMBER TRAIL	REP	Trucolor
TWO GUYS FROM TEXAS	WB	Technicolor
UNKNOWN ISLAND	FC	Cinecolor
THE UNTAMED BREED	COL	Technicolor
WHEN MY BABY SMILES AT ME	TCF	Technicolor
WHISPERING SMITH	PAR	Technicolor
WHO KILLED "DOC" ROBIN?	UA	Cinecolor
WORDS AND MUSIC	MGM	Technicolor
YOU WERE MEANT FOR ME	TCF	Technicolor

1949

BAGDAD	UN	Technicolor
THE BARKLEYS OF BROADWAY	MGM	Technicolor
THE BEAUTIFUL BLONDE FROM BASHFUL BEND	TCF	Technicolor
THE BIG CAT	EL	Technicolor
THE BLUE LAGOON	UN	Technicolor
BONNIE PRINCE CHARLIE	TCF	Technicolor
BRIMSTONE	REP	Trucolor
CALAMITY JANE AND SAM BASS	UN	Technicolor
CANADIAN PACIFIC	TCF	Cinecolor
CHALLENGE TO LASSIE	MGM	Technicolor
CHRISTOPHER COLUMBUS	UN	Technicolor
CINDERELLA	RKO	Technicolor
A CONNECTICUT YANKEE IN KING ARTHUR'S COURT	PAR	Technicolor
COWBOY AND THE INDIANS	COL	sepia
DANCING IN THE DARK	TCF	Technicolor
DAUGHTER OF THE WEST	FC	Cinecolor
DOWN DAKOTA WAY	REP	Trucolor
EL PASO	PAR	Cinecolor
THE FAR FRONTIER	REP	Trucolor
THE FIGHTING REDHEAD	EL	Cinecolor
THE GAL WHO TOOK THE WEST	UN	Technicolor
GOLDEN STALLION	REP	Trucolor
GRAND CANYON	SG	sepia
HELLFIRE	REP	Trucolor

ICHABOD AND MR. TOAD	RKO	Technicolor
IN THE GOOD OLD SUMMERTIME	MGM	Technicolor
INSPECTOR GENERAL	WB	Technicolor
IT'S A GREAT FEELING	WB	Technicolor
JOLSON SINGS AGAIN	COL	Technicolor
THE LAST BANDIT	REP	Trucolor
THE LAWTON STORY (PRINCE OF PEACE)	IND	Cinecolor
LIFE IN BLOOM (MICHURIN)	RUS	Agfacolor
LITTLE WOMEN	MGM	Technicolor
LOOK FOR THE SILVER LINING	WB	Technicolor
LUST FOR GOLD	COL	sepia
THE MAN ON THE EIFFEL TOWER	RKO	Ansco Color
MIGHTY JOE YOUNG	RKO	tinted
MOTHER IS A FRESHMAN	TCF	Technicolor
THE MUTINEERS	COL	Technicolor
MY DREAM IS YOURS	WB	Technicolor
NEPTUNE'S DAUGHTER	MGM	Technicolor
OH , YOU BEAUTIFUL DOLL	TCF	Technicolor
ON THE TOWN	MGM	Technicolor
RED CANYON	UN	Technicolor
THE RED PONY	REP	Technicolor
RED STALLION OF THE ROCKIES	EL	Cinecolor
RIDE, RYDER, RIDE	EL	Cinecolor
RIDERS OF THE PONY EXPRESS	IND	unknown
RIDERS OF THE WHISTLING PINES	COL	Cinecolor
RIM OF THE CANYON	COL	Cinecolor
ROLL, THUNDER, ROLL	EL	Cinecolor
SAMSON AND DELILAH	PAR	Technicolor
SAND	TCF	Technicolor
SARABAND	EL	Technicolor
SAVAGE SPLENDOR	RKO	Kodachrome
SCOTT OF THE ANTARCTIC	EL	Technicolor
THE SECRET GARDEN (sequences)	MGM	Technicolor
SHE WORE A YELLOW RIBBON	RKO	Technicolor
SLIGHTLY FRENCH	COL	sepia
SOME OF THE BEST (sequences)	MGM	Technicolor
SONG OF INDIA	COL	sepia
SOUTH OF ST. LOUIS	WB	Technicolor
STAMPEDE	MON	sepia
STATE DEPARTMENT FILE 649	FC	Cinecolor
THE STORY OF SEABISCUIT	WB	Technicolor
STREETS OF LAREDO	PAR	Technicolor
THE SUN COMES UP	MGM	Technicolor
SUZANNA PASS	REP	Trucolor
TAKE ME OUT TO THE BALL GAME	MGM	Technicolor
THAT FORSYTE WOMAN	MGM	Technicolor
THAT MIDNIGHT KISS	MGM	Technicolor
TULSA	EL	Technicolor
UNDER CAPRICORN	WB	Technicolor
YES, SIR, THAT'S MY BABY	UN	Technicolor
THE YOUNGER BROTHERS	WB	Technicolor
YOU'RE MY EVERYTHING	TCF	Technicolor

1950

AN AMERICAN GUERRILLA IN THE PHILIPPINES	TCF	Technicolor
ANNIE GET YOUR GUN	MGM	Technicolor
BARRICADE	WB	Technicolor
BELLE OF OLD MEXICO	REP	Trucolor
BELLS OF CORONADO	REP	Trucolor
THE BLACK ROSE	TCF	Technicolor
THE BLAZING SUN	COL	sepia
BLUE GRASS OF KENTUCKY	MON	Cinecolor
THE BLUE LAMP	EL	Technicolor

BRANDED	PAR	Technicolor
BROKEN ARROW	TCF	Technicolor
BUCCANEER'S GIRL	UN	Technicolor
CARIBOO TRAIL	TCF	Cinecolor
CHEAPER BY THE DOZEN	TCF	Technicolor
COLT 45	WB	Technicolor
COMANCHE TERRITORY	UN	Technicolor
COPPER CANYON	PAR	Technicolor
COUNTY FAIR	MON	Cinecolor
COWBOY AND THE PRIZEFIGHTER	EL	Cinecolor
CURTAIN CALL AT CACTUS CREEK	UN	Technicolor
DAKOTA LIL	TCF	Cinecolor
DAUGHTER OF ROSIE O'GRADY	WB	Technicolor
DAVY CROCKET, INDIAN SCOUT	UA	Cinecolor
THE DESERT HAWK	UN	Technicolor
DESTINATION MOON	EL	Technicolor
DOUBLE CROSSBONES	UN	Technicolor
DUCHESS OF IDAHO	MGM	Technicolor
THE EAGLE AND THE HAWK	PAR	Technicolor
FANCY PANTS	PAR	Technicolor
FIGHTING PIMPERNELL	BRI	Technicolor
THE FLAME AND THE ARROW	WB	Technicolor
FRENCHIE	UN	Technicolor
THE GREAT MISSOURI RAID	PAR	Technicolor
THE HAPPY YEARS	MGM	Technicolor
HALLS OF MONTEZUMA	TCF	Technicolor
HIGH LONESOME	UA	Technicolor
I'LL GET BY	TCF	Technicolor
INDIAN UPRISING	COL	SuperCinecolor
IROQUOIS TRAIL	UA	Cinecolor
KANSAS RAIDERS	UN	Technicolor
THE KID FROM TEXAS	UN	Technicolor
KIM	MGM	Technicolor
KING SOLOMON'S MINES	MGM	Technicolor
LET'S DANCE	PAR	Technicolor
MARK OF THE GORILLA	COL	sepia
MY BLUE HEAVEN	MGM	Technicolor
NANCY GOES TO RIO	MGM	Technicolor
NORTH OF THE GREAT DIVIDE	REP	Trucolor
THE OLD FRONTIER	REP	Trucolor
PAGAN LOVE SONG	MGM	Technicolor
THE PALOMINO	COL	Technicolor
PEGGY	UN	Technicolor
THE PETTY GIRL	COL	Technicolor
PIONEER MARSHAL	REP	Trucolor
RETURN OF THE FRONTIERSMAN	WB	Technicolor
ROCK ISLAND TRAIL	REP	Truolor
ROCKETSHIP X-M	LIP	tinted
ROGUES OF SHERWOOD FOREST	COL	Technicolor
SADDLE TRAMP	UN	Technicolor
SIERRA	UN	Technicolor
SINGING GUNS	REP	Trucolor
SUMMER STOCK	MGM	Technicolor
THE SUNDOWNERS	EL	Technicolor
SUNSET IN THE WEST	REP	Trucolor
TEA FOR TWO	WB	Technicolor
THREE LITTLE WORDS	MGM	Technicolor
THE TINDERBOX	EL	unknown
THE TOAST OF NEW ORLEANS	MGM	Technicolor
TRAIL OF ROBIN HOOD	REP	Trucolor
TREASURE ISLAND	RKO	Technicolor
TRIGGER, JR.	REP	Trucolor

TRIPOLI	PAR	Technicolor
TWILIGHT IN THE SIERRAS	REP	Trucolor
TWO WEEKS WITH LOVE	MGM	Technicolor
THE VANISHING WESTERNER	REP	Trucolor
WABASH AVENUE	TCF	Technicolor
THE WHITE TOWER	RKO	Technicolor
WYOMING MAIL	UN	Technicolor
ZHUKOVSKY	RUS	Sovcolor

1951

ACROSS THE WIDE MISSOURI	MGM	Technicolor
THE AFRICAN QUEEN	UA	Technicolor
ALICE IN WONDERLAND	RKO	Technicolor
ALICE IN WONDERLAND	BRI	Ansco Color
AN AMERICAN IN PARIS	MGM	Technicolor
ANNE OF THE INDIES	TCF	Technicolor
APACHE DRUMS	UN	Technicolor
THE BAREFOOT MAILMAN	COL	SuperCinecolor
BEST OF THE BADMEN	RKO	Technicolor
BIRD OF PARADISE	RKO	Technicolor
BLUE BLOOD	MON	Cinecolor
CALL ME MISTER	TCF	Technicolor
CAPTAIN HORATIO HORNBLOWER	WB	Technicolor
CATTLE DRIVE	UN	Technicolor
CAVALIER OF THE GOLDEN STAR	RUS	Agfacolor
CAVALRY SCOUT	MON	Cinecolor
CAVE OF OUTLAWS	UN	Technicolor
CIMARRON KID	UN	Technicolor
COPENHAGEN	BRI	Technichrome
CROSSWINDS	PAR	Technicolor
CUBAN FIREBALL	REP	Trucolor
DAVID AND BATHSHEBA	TCF	Technicolor
DISTANT DRUMS	WB	Technicolor
DRUMS IN THE DEEP SOUTH	RKO	SuperCinecolor
THE EMPEROR'S NIGHTINGALE	CZE	Agfacolor
EXCUSE MY DUST	MGM	Technicolor
FLAME OF ARABY	UN	Technicolor
FLAME OF STAMBOUL	COL	sepia
FLAMING FEATHER	PAR	Technicolor
FLIGHT TO MARS	MON	Cinecolor
FLYING LEATHERNECKS	RKO	Technicolor
FORT DEFIANCE	UA	Cinecolor
GOLDEN GIRL	TCF	Technicolor
THE GOLDEN HORDE	UA	Technicolor
THE GRAND CONCERT	RUS	Magicolor
THE GREAT CARUSO	MGM	Technicolor
HALF ANGEL	TCF	Technicolor
HAPPY GO LOVELY	RKO	Technicolor
HAVANA ROSE	REP	Trucolor
HEART OF THE ROCKIES	REP	Trucolor
THE HIGHWAYMAN	AA	Cinecolor
HONG KONG	PAR	Technicolor
HURRICANE ISLAND	COL	SuperCinecolor
I'D CLIMB THE HIGHEST MOUNTAIN	TCF	Technicolor
I'LL NEVER FORGET YOU	TCF	Technicolor
I'LL SEE YOU IN MY DREAMS	WB	Technicolor
IN OLD AMARILLO	REP	Trucolor
JUNGLE HEADHUNTERS	RKO	Kodachrome
THE LADY FROM TEXAS	UN	Technicolor
THE LAST OUTPOST	PAR	Technicolor
LIBERATED CHINA	CHI	unknown
LITTLE EGYPT	UN	Technicolor
THE LONGHORN	MON	sepia

LORNA DOONE	COL	Technicolor
THE LOST CONTINENT	LIP	tinted
LULLABY OF BROADWAY	WB	Technicolor
THE MAGIC CARPET	COL	SuperCinecolor
MAN IN THE SADDLE	COL	Technicolor
MARK OF THE RENEGADE	UN	Technicolor
MARK OF THE AVENGER	COL	Technicolor
MEET ME AFTER THE SHOW	TCF	Technicolor
MR. IMPERIUM	MGM	Technicolor
MOUSSORGSKY	RUS	Agfacolor
NEW MEXICO	UA	Ansco Color
OH, SUZANNA	REP	Trucolor
ON MOONLIGHT BAY	WB	Technicolor
ON THE RIVIERA	TCF	Technicolor
ON THE SUNNY SIDE OF THE STREET	COL	SuperCinecolor
THE PAINTED HILLS	MGM	Technicolor
PAINTING THE CLOUDS WITH SUNSHINE	WB	Technicolor
PANDORA AND THE FLYING DUTCHMAN	MGM	Technicolor
PASSAGE WEST	PAR	Technicolor
PREHISTORIC WOMEN	EL	Cinecolor
THE PRINCE WHO WAS A THIEF	UN	Technicolor
QUEBEC	PAR	Technicolor
QUO VADIS	MGM	Technicolor
RANCHO GRANDE	MEX	Cinecolor
RED MOUNTAIN	PAR	Technicolor
THE RIVER	UA	Technicolor
ROYAL WEDDING	MGM	Technicolor
SHOWBOAT	MGM	Technicolor
SILVER CANYON	COL	sepia
SILVER CITY	PAR	Technicolor
SLAUGHTER TRAIL	RKO	Cinecolor
SMUGGLER'S ISLAND	UN	Technicolor
SON OF THE PALEFACE	PAR	Technicolor
SOUTH OF CALIENTE	REP	Trucolor
SPOILERS OF THE PLAINS	REP	Trucolor
A STRANGE MARRIAGE	HUN	unknown
SWORD OF MONTE CRISTO	TCF	SuperCinecolor
TAKE CARE OF MY LITTLE GIRL	TCF	Technicolor
TALES OF HOFFMAN	BRI	Technicolor
TEN TALL MEN	COL	Technicolor
TEXAS CARNIVAL	MGM	Technicolor
TEXAS RANGERS	COL	SuperCinecolor
THIS IS KOREA	REP	Trucolor
TOMAHAWK	UN	Technicolor
TWO TICKETS TO BROADWAY	RKO	Technicolor
VALENTINO	COL	Technicolor
VALLEY OF FIRE	COL	sepia
VENGEANCE VALLEY	MGM	Technicolor
WARPATH	PAR	Technicolor
WHEN THE REDSKINS RODE	COL	SuperCinecolor
WHEN WORLDS COLLIDE	PAR	Technicolor
WHIRLWIND	COL	sepia

1952

AARON SLICK FROM PUNKIN CRICK	PAR	Technicolor
ABBOTT AND COSTELLO MEET CAPTAIN KIDD	WB	SuperCinecolor
ABOUT FACE	WB	Technicolor
AGAINST ALL FLAGS	UN	Technicolor
ALADDIN AND HIS LAMP	MON	Cinecolor
ALL ASHORE	COL	Technicolor
AMBUSH AT TOMAHAWK GAP	COL	Technicolor
AT SWORD'S POINT	RKO	Technicolor
BABES IN BAGDAD	UA	Exotic Color

BATTLE OF APACHE PASS	UN	Technicolor
BECAUSE YOU'RE MINE	MGM	Technicolor
THE BELLE OF NEW YORK	MGM	Technicolor
BELLES ON THEIR TOES	TCF	Technicolor
BEND OF THE RIVER	UN	Technicolor
LA BERGERE ET LE RAMONEUR	FRA	Technicolor
THE BIG TREES	WB	Technicolor
BLACKBEARD THE PIRATE	RKO	Technicolor
BLAZING FOREST	PAR	Technicolor
BONGOLO	IND	Gevacolor
BRAVE WARRIOR	COL	Technicolor
THE BRIGAND	COL	Technicolor
BRONCO BUSTER	UN	Technicolor
BUGLES IN THE AFTERNOON	WB	Technicolor
BWANA DEVIL	UA	Ansco Color
CALIFORNIA CONQUEST	COL	Technicolor
CAPTAIN PIRATE	COL	Technicolor
CARIBBEAN	PAR	Technicolor
CARSON CITY	WB	WarnerColor
CRIMSON PIRATE	WB	Technicolor
CRIPPLE CREEK	COL	Technicolor
DENVER AND THE RIO GRANDE	PAR	Technicolor
DUEL AT SILVER CREEK	UN	Technicolor
THE DUPONT STORY	IND	Technicolor
ELDFAGELN	IND	Agfacolor
FARGO	MON	sepia
THE FIREBIRD	UA	Technicolor
FORT OSAGE	AA	Cinecolor
GOLDEN HAWK	COL	Technicolor
THE GREATEST SHOW ON EARTH	PAR	Technicolor
HALF BREED	RKO	Technicolor
HANGMAN'S KNOT	COL	Technicolor
HAS ANYBODY SEEN MY GAL?	UN	Technicolor
HIAWATHA	AA	Cinecolor
HONEYCHILE	REP	Trucolor
HORIZONS WEST	UI	Technicolor
HURRICANE SMITH	PAR	Technicolor
I DREAM OF JEANNIE	REP	Trucolor
IMPORTANCE OF BEING EARNEST	UN	Technicolor
INDIAN UPRISING	COL	SuperCinecolor
IRON MISTRESS	WB	Technicolor
ISLAND OF DESIRE	UA	Technicolor
IVANHOE	MGM	Technicolor
IVORY HUNTER (WHERE NO VULTURES FLY)	UN	Technicolor
JACK IN THE BEANSTALK	WB	SuperCinecolor
THE JUNGLE	LIP	sepia
JUST FOR YOU	PAR	Technicolor
KANGAROO	TCF	Technicolor
KANSAS PACIFIC	AA	Cinecolor
KANSAS TERRITORY	MON	sepia
THE LADY IN THE IRON MASK	TCF	Natural Color
LATUKO	IND	Technicolor
LEONARDO DA VINCI (sequences)	IND	Gevacolor
THE LION AND THE HORSE	WB	WarnerColor
THE LONGHORN	AA	sepia
LOVELY TO LOOK AT	MGM	Technicolor
LURE OF THE WILDERNESS	TCF	Technicolor
LYDIA BAILEY	TCF	Technicolor
THE MAGIC BOX	BRI	Technicolor
THE MAVERICK	AA	sepia
MAYTIME IN MAYFAIR	BRI	Technicolor
THE MERRY WIDOW	MGM	Technicolor

THE MIRACLE OF (OUR LADY OF) FATIMA	WB	WarnerColor
MONTANA BELLE	RKO	Trucolor
MONTANA TERRITORY	COL	Technicolor
MONTEMARTE	FRA	Technicolor
MUTINY	UA	Technicolor
MYSTERY LAKE	IND	Ansco Color
NAKED SPUR	MGM	Technicolor
NIAGARA	TCF	Technicolor
NIGHT STAGE TO GALVESTON	COL	sepia
OKLAHOMA ANNIE	REP	Trucolor
OUTLAW WOMEN	LIP	Cinecolor
PLEASURE ISLAND (GIRLS OF PLEASURE ISLAND)	PAR	Technicolor
PLYMOUTH ADVENTURE	MGM	Technicolor
PONY SOLDIER	TCF	Technicolor
POWDER RIVER	TCF	Technicolor
THE QUIET MAN	REP	Technicolor
THE RAIDERS	UN	Technicolor
RAINBOW ROUND MY SHOULDER	COL	Technicolor
RAMBLE IN ERIN	IRE	Technicolor
RANCHO NOTORIOUS	RKO	Technicolor
RED SKIES OF MONTANA	TCF	Technicolor
ROAD TO BALI	PAR	Technicolor
ROCK GRAYSON'S WOMEN	PAR	Technicolor
RODEO	MON	Cinecolor
THE ROSE BOWL STORY	AA	Cinecolor
ROSE OF CIMARRON	TCF	Natural Color
ROYAL JOURNEY	UA	Eastman Color
THE SAVAGE	PAR	Technicolor
SCARAMOUCHE	MGM	Technicolor
SCARLET ANGEL	UN	Technicolor
SHE'S WORKING HER WAY THROUGH COLLEGE	WB	Technicolor
SINGING IN THE RAIN	MGM	Technicolor
SKIRTS AHOY	MGM	Technicolor
SOMEBODY LOVES ME	PAR	Technicolor
SOUND OFF	COL	SuperCinecolor
SPRINGFIELD RIFLE	WB	Warnercolor
STARS AND STRIPES FOREVER	TCF	Technicolor
STEEL TOWN	UN	Technicolor
STOP, YOU'RE KILLING ME!	WB	Warnercolor
THE STORY OF ROBIN HOOD	RKO	Technicolor
THE STORY OF WILL ROGERS	WB	Technicolor
SWEETHEART TIME	REP	Trucolor
TEMBO	RKO	Ansco Color
THIEF OF DAMASCUS	COL	Technicolor
3 FOR BEDROOM C	WB	Natural Color
TOTO A COLORI	ITA	Ferraniacolor
TOUGHEST MAN IN ARIZONA	REP	Trucolor
TREASURE OF LOST CANYON	UN	Technicolor
TROPIC ZONE	PAR	Technicolor
THE UNFORGETTABLE YEAR — 1919	RUS	Sovcolor
UNTAMED FRONTIER	UN	Technicolor
WACO	MON	sepia
WAGON TEAM	COL	sepia
WAIT TILL THE SUN SHINES NELLIE	TCF	Technicolor
WAY OF A GAUCHO	TCF	Technicolor
WHAT PRICE GLORY?	TCF	Technicolor
WHERE'S CHARLEY?	WB	Technicolor
THE WILD HEART	RKO	Technicolor
THE WILD NORTH	MGM	Ansco Color
WILD STALLION	MON	Cinecolor
WITH A SONG IN MY HEART	TCF	Technicolor
WOMAN OF THE NORTH COUNTRY	REP	Trucolor

THE WORLD IN HIS ARMS	UN	Technicolor
YANKEE BUCCANEER	UN	Technicolor

1953

AAN	UA	Technicolor
ADVENTURES OF NATSUKO	JAP	Fujicolor
AFFAIR IN MONTE CARLO	AA	Technicolor
AFFAIRS OF DOBIE GILLIS	MGM	Technicolor
ALL ASHORE	COL	Technicolor
ALL THE BROTHERS WERE VALIANT	MGM	Technicolor
AMBUSH AT TOMAHAWK GAP	COL	Technicolor
APRIL IN PARIS	WB	Technicolor
APPOINTMENT IN HONDURAS	RKO	Technicolor
ARENA	MGM	Ansco Color
ARROWHEAD	PAR	Technicolor
BACK TO GOD'S COUNTRY	UN	Technicolor
THE BANDWAGON	MGM	Technicolor
BECAUSE YOU'RE MINE	MGM	Technicolor
THE BEGGAR'S OPERA	WB	Technicolor
BELOW THE SAHARA	RKO	Technicolor
BENEATH THE TWELVE MILE REEF	TCF	Technicolor
BONJOUR PARIS	FRA	Technicolor
BORN TO THE SADDLE	AST	Cinecolor
BOTANY BAY	PAR	Technicolor
BY THE LIGHT OF THE SILVERY MOON	WB	Technicolor
CALAMITY JANE	WB	Technicolor
CALL ME MADAM	TCF	Technicolor
CAPTAIN JOHN SMITH AND POCAHONTAS	UA	Pathecolor
CAPTAIN SCARLET	UA	Technicolor
CAROLINE CHERIE	FRA	Technicolor
CHALLENGE OF THE WILD	UA	Eastman Color
THE CHARGE AT FEATHER RIVER	WB	WarnerColor
CITY BENEATH THE SEA	UN	Technicolor
CITY OF BAD MEN	TCF	Technicolor
COLUMN SOUTH	UN	Technicolor
CONQUEST OF COCHISE	COL	Technicolor
CONQUEST OF EVEREST	UA	Technicolor
CORONATION DAY	HOL	Gevacolor
CRUISIN' DOWN THE RIVER	COL	Technicolor
DANGEROUS WHEN WET	MGM	Technicolor
DECAMERON NIGHTS	RKO	Technicolor
DESERT LEGION	UN	Technicolor
DESERT SONG	WB	Technicolor
DESTINATION GOBI	TCF	Technicolor
DESTINY IN TROUBLE	IND	Ansco Color
DEVIL'S CANYON	RKO	Technicolor
DIAMOND QUEEN	WB	SuperCinecolor
DOWN AMONG THE SHELTERING PALMS	TCF	Technicolor
EAST OF SUMATRA	UN	Technicolor
EASY TO LOVE	MGM	Technicolor
THE EDDIE CANTOR STORY	WB	Technicolor
ESCAPE FROM FORT BRAVO	MGM	Ansco Color
EVERYTHING I HAVE IS YOURS	MGM	Technicolor
FAIR WIND TO JAVA	REP	Trucolor
FARMER TAKES A WIFE	TCF	Technicolor
FATHER'S DOING FINE	BRI	Technicolor
FIGHTER ATTACK	AA	Cinecolor
THE 5,000 FINGERS OF DR. T	COL	Technicolor
FLAMENCO	SPA	CineFotoColor
FLAME OF CALCUTTA	COL	Technicolor
FLAT TOP	AA	Cinecolor
FLIGHT TO TANGIER	PAR	Technicolor
FORT TI	COL	Technicolor

FORT VENGEANCE	AA	Cinecolor
GENTLEMEN PREFER BLONDES	TCF	Technicolor
GILBERT AND SULLIVAN	UA	Technicolor
THE GIRL NEXT DOOR	TCF	Technicolor
GIVE THE GIRL A BREAK	MGM	Technicolor
THE GOLDEN BLADE	UN	Technicolor
THE GREAT SIOUX UPRISING	UN	Technicolor
GREAT JESSE JAMES RAID	LIP	Ansco Color
GREEN MAGIC	ITA	Ferraniacolor
GUN BELT	UA	Technicolor
GUN FURY	COL	Technicolor
GUNSMOKE	UN	Technicolor
HANNAH LEE	REA	Pathecolor
HANS CHRISTIAN ANDERSEN	RKO	Technicolor
HERE COME THE GIRLS	PAR	Technicolor
THE HINDU	IND	Eastman Color
HIS MAJESTY O'KEEFE	WB	Technicolor
HIS ROYAL HIGHNESS	GER	Gevacolor
THE HOMESTEADERS	AA	sepia
HONDO	WB	WarnerColor
HOUDINI	PAR	Technicolor
HOUSE OF WAX	WB	WarnerColor
HOW TO MARRY A MILLIONAIRE	TCF	Technicolor
THE "I DON'T CARE" GIRL	TCF	Technicolor
I LOVE MELVIN	MGM	Technicolor
INFERNO	TCF	Technicolor
INVADERS FROM MARS	TCF	Cinecolor
IT STARTED IN PARADISE	AST	Technicolor
JACK McCALL, DESPERADO	COL	Technicolor
JAMAICA RUN	PAR	Technicolor
THE JAZZ SINGER	WB	Technicolor
JIGOKUMEN	JAP	Eastman Color
JOHNNY, THE GIANT KILLER	LIP	Technicolor
KANSAS PACIFIC	AA	Cinecolor
KING OF THE KHYBER RIFLES	TCF	Technicolor
KISS ME KATE	MGM	Ansco Color
KNIGHTS OF THE ROUND TABLE	MGM	Technicolor
THE LADY WANTS MINK	REP	Trucolor
LAST OF THE COMANCHES	COL	Technicolor
LATIN LOVERS	MGM	Technicolor
LAW AND ORDER	UN	Technicolor
LET'S DO IT AGAIN	COL	Technicolor
LILI	MGM	Technicolor
A LION IS IN THE STREETS	WB	Technicolor
THE LIVING DESERT	BV	Technicolor
LONE HAND	UN	Technicolor
LOUISIANA TERRITORY	RKO	Pathecolor
LOVE ISLAND	AST	Cinecolor
THE LUCKY BRIDE	RUS	Art Chrome Color
LUCRETIA BORGIA	ITA	Technicolor
MAN BEHIND THE GUN	WB	Technicolor
MAN FROM THE ALAMO	UN	Technicolor
MAN IN THE DARK	COL	sepia
MAN OF MUSIC	RUS	Magicolor
MASTER OF BALLENTRAE	WB	Technicolor
MEET ME AT THE FAIR	UN	Technicolor
MELBA	UA	Technicolor
MILLION DOLLAR MERMAID	MGM	Technicolor
MISS ROBIN CRUSOE	TCF	Eastman Color
MISS SADIE THOMPSON	COL	Technicolor
MISSISSIPPI GAMBLER	UN	Technicolor
MOGAMBO	MGM	Technicolor
MONEY FROM HOME	PAR	Technicolor

MONSOON	UA	Technicolor
MOULIN ROUGE	UA	Technicolor
NAKED SPUR	MGM	Technicolor
THE NEBRASKAN	COL	Technicolor
THE NEOPOLITAN TURK	ITA	Ferraniacolor
NIAGARA	TCF	Technicolor
PAGEANT OF RUSSIA	RUS	Chrome Color
PARIS EXPRESS	BRI	Technicolor
THE PATHFINDER	COL	Technicolor
PETER PAN	RKO	Technicolor
PONY EXPRESS	PAR	Technicolor
POWDER RIVER	TCF	Technicolor
PRINCE OF PIRATES	COL	Technicolor
PRISONER OF ZENDA	MGM	Technicolor
PRISONERS OF THE CASBAH	COL	Technicolor
PUCCINI	ITA	Technicolor
A QUEEN IS CROWNED	UN	Technicolor
RAIDERS OF THE SEVEN SEAS	UA	Technicolor
REBEL CITY	AA	sepia
REDHEAD FROM WYOMING	UN	Technicolor
RETURN TO PARADISE	UA	Technicolor
THE RETURN OF VASILI BOSTNIKOV	RUS	unknown
RIDE THE MAN DOWN	REP	Trucolor
RIDE, VAQUERO	MGM	Ansco Color
ROAR OF THE CROWD	AA	Cinecolor
ROB ROY	RKO	Technicolor
THE ROBE	TCF	Technicolor
ROYAL AFRICAN RIFLES	AA	Cinecolor
SAADIA	MGM	Technicolor
SABRE JET	UA	Cinecolor
SALOME	COL	Technicolor
SANGAREE	PAR	Technicolor
SCANDAL AT SCOURIE	MGM	Technicolor
THE SEA AROUND US	RKO	Technicolor
SEA DEVILS	RKO	Technicolor
SECOND CHANCE	RKO	Technicolor
SEMINOLE	UN	Technicolor
SERPENT OF THE NILE	COL	Technicolor
SHANE	PAR	Technicolor
SHARK RIVER	UA	Color Corp.
SHE'S BACK ON BROADWAY	WB	WarnerColor
SHIP OF DAMNED WOMEN	GER	Gevacolor
SINS OF JEZABEL	LIP	Ansco Color
SIREN OF BAGDAD	COL	Technicolor
SLAVES OF BABYLON	COL	Technicolor
SMALL TOWN GIRL	MGM	Technicolor
SNOWS OF KILAMANJARO	TCF	Technicolor
SO THIS IS LOVE	WB	Technicolor
SOMBRERO	MGM	Technicolor
SON OF BELLE STARR	AA	Cinecolor
SONG OF THE LAND	UA	Color Corp.
STAND AT APACHE RIVER	UN	Technicolor
THE STARS ARE SINGING	PAR	Technicolor
THE STORY OF THREE LOVES	MGM	Technicolor
THE STRANGER WORE A GUN	COL	Technicolor
SWEETHEARTS ON PARADE	REP	Trucolor
THE SWORD AND THE ROSE	RKO	Technicolor
TAKE ME TO TOWN	UN	Technicolor
TAKE THE HIGH GROUND	MGM	Ansco Color
TANGA TIKA	IND	Eastman Color
THOSE REDHEADS FROM SEATTLE	PAR	Technicolor
THREE MUSKETEERS	FRA	Gevacolor

THREE SAILORS AND A GIRL	WB	Technicolor
THUNDER BAY	UN	Technicolor
THUNDER OVER THE PLAINS	WB	WarnerColor
TITFIELD THUNDERBOLT	UN	Technicolor
TONIGHT AT 8:30	BRI	Technicolor
TONIGHT WE SING	TCF	Technicolor
TOPEKA	AA	sepia
TORCH SONG	MGM	Technicolor
TREASURE OF THE GOLDEN CONDOR	TCF	Technicolor
TRIUMPH OF YOUTH	RUS	Chrome Color
TROPIC ZONE	PAR	Technicolor
TUMBLEWEED	UN	Technicolor
THE TYRANT	SPA	CineFotoColor
THE VANQUISHED	PAR	Technicolor
VEILS OF BAGDAD	UN	Technicolor
VIGILANTE TERROR	AA	sepia
WAGONS WEST	AA	Cinecolor
WALKING MY BABY BACK HOME	UN	Technicolor
WAR ARROW	UN	Technicolor
WAR OF THE WORLDS	PAR	Technicolor
WAR PAINT	UA	Pathecolor
WHITE WITCH DOCTOR	TCF	Technicolor
WINGS OF THE HAWK	UN	Technicolor
YOUNG BESS	MGM	Technicolor

1954

ADVENTURES OF HAJJI BABA	TCF	DeLuxe Color
ADVENTURES OF NATSUKO	JAP	Fujicolor
ADVENTURES OF ROBINSON CRUSOE	UA	Pathecolor
AFRICA ADVENTURE	RKO	Pathecolor
AIDA	ITA	Ferraniacolor
ALASKA SEAS	PAR	Technicolor
ALEKO	RUS	Sovcolor
ALERTE AU SUD	FRA	unknown
THE AMERICANO	RKO	Technicolor
THE ANNA CROSS	RUS	Sovcolor
ANNAPURNA	IND	Technicolor
APACHE	UA	Technicolor
ARROW IN THE DUST	AA	Technicolor
ATHENA	MGM	Technicolor
L'AVENTURIER DE SEVILLE	SPA	Gevacolor
BAD DAY AT BLACK ROCK	MGM	Eastman Color
THE BAREFOOT CONTESSA	UA	Technicolor
BATTLE OF ROGUE RIVER	COL	Technicolor
THE BEACHCOMBER	BRI	Technicolor
BEACHHEAD	UA	Technicolor
BEAU BRUMMEL	MGM	Technicolor
LA BELLE OTERO	FRA-ITA	Eastman Color
BENGAL BRIGADE	UN	Technicolor
BETRAYED	MGM	Eastman Color
THE BLACK DAKOTAS	COL	Technicolor
BLACK HORSE CANYON	UN	Technicolor
THE BLACK KNIGHT	COL	Technicolor
BLACK SHIELD OF FALWORTH	UN	Technicolor
BLACK WIDOW	TCF	DeLuxe Color
THE BLONDE GYPSY	FRA	unknown
BLOOD AND LIGHT	FRA-SPA	Eastman Color
BORDER RIVER	UN	Technicolor
THE BOUNTY HUNTER	WB	WarnerColor
THE BOY FROM OKLAHOMA	WB	WarnerColor
BRIDE WITH A DOWRY	RUS	Sovcolor
THE BRIDGES AT TOKO-RI	PAR	Technicolor
BRIGADOON	MGM	Ansco Color
BROKEN LANCE	TCF	DeLuxe Color
A BULLET IS WAITING	COL	Technicolor

THE CAINE MUTINY	COL	Technicolor
CAPTAIN KIDD AND THE SLAVE GIRL	UA	Color Corp.
CAPTAIN SCARLETT	UA	unknown
CARMEN JONES	TCF	DeLuxe Color
CARNIVAL STORY	RKO	Agfacolor
CASANOVA'S BIG NIGHT	PAR	Technicolor
CATTLE QUEEN OF MONTANA	RKO	Technicolor
CAVALLERIA RUSTICANNA	AST	unknown
CHALLENGE OF THE WILD	UA	Color Corp.
CHARGE OF THE LANCERS	COL	Technicolor
CHATEAUX EN ESPAGNE	FRA	Eastman Color
THE COMMAND	WB	WarnerColor
CONCERT OF STARS	RUS	Magicolor
CONFLICT OF WINGS	BRI	Eastman Color
CONQUEST OF EVEREST	BRI	Technicolor
THE COWBOY	LIP	Eastman Color
CROSSED SWORDS	UA	Pathecolor
DAGOHOY	PHI	Ansco Color
DANCE LITTLE LADY	BRI	Eastman Color
DANGEROUS MISSION	RKO	Technicolor
DAWN AT SOCORRO	UN	Technicolor
DAY OF TRIUMPH	IND	Pathecolor
DAYS OF LOVE	ITA	Ferraniacolor
DEMITRIUS AND THE GLADIATORS	TCF	Technicolor
DESIREE	TCF	DeLuxe Color
DESTRY	UN	Technicolor
DEVIL GODDESS	COL	sepia
DIAL M FOR MURDER	WB	WarnerColor
DIE —WE'LL DO THE REST	FRA	Eastman Color
DRAGNET	WB	WarnerColor
DRUM BEAT	WB	WarnerColor
DRUMS ACROSS THE RIVER	UN	Technicolor
DRUMS OF TAHITI	COL	Technicolor
DUEL IN THE JUNGLE	WB	Technicolor
THE EGYPTIAN	TCF	DeLuxe Color
ELEPHANT WALK	PAR	Technicolor
FIRE OVER AFRICA	COL	Technicolor
FIREWORKS	GER	Eastman Color
FLAME AND THE FLESH	MGM	Technicolor
FOR BETTER OR WORSE	BRI	Eastman Color
FOUR GUNS TO THE BORDER	UA	Technicolor
THE FRENCH LINE	RKO	Technicolor
THE FUNNIEST SHOW ON EARTH	ITA	Ferraniacolor
THE GAMBLER FROM NATCHEZ	TCF	Technicolor
GARDEN OF EDEN	IND	Tri-Art Color
GARDEN OF EVIL	TCF	Technicolor
GATE OF HELL	JAP	Eastman Color
GENEVIEVE	UN	Technicolor
THE GLENN MILLER STORY	UN	Technicolor
GOD IS MY LANDLORD	IND	Kodachrome
GOG	UA	Color Corp.
THE GOLDEN COACH	ITA	Technicolor
THE GOLDEN DEMON	JAP	Eastman Color
THE GOLDEN MASK	BRI	Technicolor
THE GOLDEN MISTRESS	UA	Technicolor
GORILLA AT LARGE	TCF	Technicolor
LE GRAND JEU	FRA	Eastman Color
LA GRANDE SPERANZA	ITA	Ferraniacolor
GREEN FIRE	MGM	Eastman Color
GYPSY COLT	MGM	Ansco Color
HALF A CENTURY OF SONGS	ITA	Ferraniacolor
HANSEL AND GRETEL	RKO	Technicolor
HELL AND HIGH WATER	TCF	Technicolor
HELL BELOW ZERO	COL	Technicolor

HER 12 MEN	MGM	Ansco Color
THE HIGH AND THE MIGHTY	WB	WarnerColor
HIS MAJESTY O'KEEFE	WB	Technicolor
HIS ROYAL HIGHNESS	GER	Gevacolor
HIT THE DECK	MGM	Eastman Color
HONDO	WB	WarnerColor
HUNTERS OF THE DEEP	DCA	SuperCineColor
IF VERSAILLES WERE TOLD TO ME	FRA	Eastman Color
INSPECTOR GENERAL	RUS	Sovcolor
THE IRON GLOVE	COL	Technicolor
ISTANBUL	TUR	Kodachrome
IT'S THE PARIS LIFE	FRA	Gevacolor
JESSE JAMES VS. THE DALTONS	COL	Technicolor
JESSE JAMES' WOMEN	UA	Technicolor
JIVARO	PAR	Technicolor
JOAN AT THE STAKE	ITA	Gevacolor
JOHN WESLEY	BRI	Eastman Color
JOHNNY DARK	UN	Technicolor
JOHNNY GUITAR	REP	Trucolor
JUBILEE TRAIL	REP	Trucolor
JUNGLE MANEATERS	COL	sepia
JUNGLE MOON MEN	COL	sepia
KARAMOJA	IND	Eastman Color
KHYBER PATROL	UA	Color Corp.
KING OF THE KHYBER RIFLES	TCF	Technicolor
KING RICHARD AND THE CRUSADERS	WB	WarnerColor
KNOCK ON WOOD	PAR	Technicolor
THE LAST TIME I SAW PARIS	MGM	Technicolor
LAUGHING ANNE	REP	Technicolor
THE LAW VS. BILLY THE KID	COL	Technicolor
LEASE OF LIFE	BRI	Eastman Color
LIFE IN THE ARCTIC	RUS	Magicolor
LILACS IN THE SPRING	REP	Trucolor
THE LIVING DESERT	BV	Technicolor
LIVING IT UP	PAR	Technicolor
THE LONE GUN	UA	Color Corp.
LONG JOHN SILVER	TCF	Eastman Color
LOUISIANA TERRITORY	RKO	Pathecolor
LUCKY ME	WB	WarnerColor
MAD ABOUT MEN	BRI	Technicolor
THE MAD MAGICIAN	COL	Technicolor
MADAME DU BARRY	FRA-ITA	Eastman Color
MAGNIFICENT OBSESSION	UN	Technicolor
MAKE ME AN OFFER	BRI	unknown
MALAGA	BRI	Technicolor
MAM'ZELLE NITOUCHE	FRA	Eastman Color
MAN OF MUSIC	RUS	Magicolor
MAN WITH A MILLION	UA	Technicolor
MASTERSON OF KANSAS	COL	Technicolor
MAYURPANKH	INDIA	Gevacolor
MEN OF THE FIGHTING LADY	MGM	Ansco Color
MAXIMA	RUS	Magicolor
MISS ROBIN CRUSOE	TCF	Pathecolor
MONEY FROM HOME	PAR	Technicolor
THE NAKED JUNGLE	PAR	Technicolor
NEOPOLITAN CAROUSEL (HURDY GURDY)	ITA	Pathecolor
NEW FACES	TCF	Color Corp.
NIGHT PEOPLE	TCF	Technicolor
O DESTINO EM APUROS	BRA	Ansco Color
OBSESSION	FRA-ITA	Eastman Color
OUT OF THIS WORLD	IND	Technicolor
THE OUTCAST	REP	Trucolor
OUTLAW STALLION	COL	Technicolor

THE OUTLAW'S DAUGHTER	TCF	Eastman Color
OVERLAND PACIFIC	UA	Color Corp.
PAMPOSH	INDIA	Gevacolor
PAR ORDRE DU TSAR	FRA	Gevacolor
PARATROOPER	COL	Technicolor
PASSION	RKO	Technicolor
LA PENSIONNAIRE	ITA	Ferraniacolor
PHANTOM OF THE RUE MORGUE	WB	WarnerColor
PRIDE OF THE BLUE GRASS	AA	Color Corp.
PRINCE OF PLAYERS	TCF	DeLuxe Color
PRINCE VALIANT	TCF	Technicolor
PRINCESS OF THE NILE	TCF	Technicolor
THE PRINCESS SEN	JAP	Eastman Color
PUCCINI	ITA	Technicolor
THE PURPLE PLAIN	UA	Technicolor
QUAI DES BLONDES	FRA	Gevacolor
THE QUEEN IN AUSTRALIA	BRI	Ferraniacolor
A QUEEN'S ROYAL TOUR	UA	Eastman Color
QUEST FOR THE LOST CITY	RKO	Eastman Color
RACING BLOOD	TCF	SuperCineColor
THE RAID	TCF	Technicolor
RAILS INTO LARAMIE	UA	Technicolor
THE RAINBOW JACKET	BRI	Technicolor
RASPOUTINE	FRA	Eastman Color
REAR WINDOW	PAR	Technicolor
THE RED AND THE BLACK	FRA-ITA	Technicolor
RED GARTERS	PAR	Technicolor
RETURN TO TREASURE ISLAND	UA	Pathecolor
RHAPSODY	MGM	Technicolor
RIDE CLEAR OF DIABLO	UN	Technicolor
RIDERS TO THE STARS	UA	Color Corp.
RIDING SHOTGUN	WB	WarnerColor
RIMSKY-KORSAKOV	RUS	Sovcolor
RING OF FEAR	WB	WarnerColor
RIVER OF NO RETURN	TCF	Technicolor
ROB ROY	RKO	Technicolor
ROMEO AND JULIET	UA	Technicolor
ROSE MARIE	MGM	Eastman Color
ROYAL AFRICAN RIFLES	AA	Cinecolor
THE ROYAL TOUR OF QUEEN ELIZABETH AND PHILIP	TCF	Eastman Color
SALGIN	TUR	Kodachrome
SANTI-VINA	THA	Eastman Color
THE SARACEN BLADE	COL	Technicolor
SASKATCHEWAN	UN	Technicolor
SCARLET SPEAR	UA	Technicolor
SECRET OF THE INCAS	PAR	Technicolor
THE SEEKERS	BRI	Eastman Color
SEVEN BRIDES FOR SEVEN BROTHERS	MGM	Ansco Color
SHAHENSHAH	INDIA	Gevacolor
SHARK RIVER	UA	Cinecolor
SHIP OF DAMNED WOMEN	ITA	Gevacolor
THE SIEGE AT RED RIVER	TCF	Technicolor
SIGN OF THE PAGAN	UN	Technicolor
THE SILVER CHALICE	WB	WarnerColor
SILVER LODE	RKO	Technicolor
SINS OF JEZEBEL	LIP	Ansco Color
SITTING BULL	UA	Eastman Color
SIXTH CONTINENT	ITA	Technicolor
SO THIS IS PARIS	UN	Technicolor
SON OF SINBAD	RKO	Technicolor
SONG OF THE LAND	UA	Color Corp.
SOUTHWEST PASSAGE	UA	Pathecolor
THE SPELL OF IRELAND	IRE	unknown
A STAR IS BORN	WB	WarnerColor

STARS OF THE RUSSIAN BALLET	RUS	Sovcolor
STARS OF THE UKRAINE	RUS	Magicolor
STORMY, THE THOROUGHBRED	BV	Technicolor
STRATFORD ADVENTURE	COL	Eastman Color
THE STUDENT PRINCE	MGM	Ansco Color
SUSAN SLEPT HERE	RKO	Technicolor
TANGANYIKA	UN	Technicolor
TARANTELLA NAPOLETANA	ITA	Gevacolor
TAZA, SON OF COCHISE	UN	Technicolor
TENNESSEE CHAMP	MGM	Ansco Color
THEODORA, SLAVE EMPRESS	ITA	Pathecolor
THERE'S NO BUSINESS LIKE SHOW BUSINESS	TCF	DeLuxe Color
THEY RODE WEST	COL	Technicolor
THIS IS MY LOVE.	RKO	Pathecolor
THIS IS YOUR ARMY	IND	Technicolor
THREE COINS IN THE FOUNTAIN	TCF	DeLuxe Color
THREE FOR THE SHOW	COL	Technicolor
THREE HOURS TO KILL	COL	Technicolor
THREE RING CIRCUS	PAR	Technicolor
THREE YOUNG TEXANS	TCF	Technicolor
TONIGHT'S THE NIGHT	AA	Technicolor
TOP BANANA	UA	Color Corp.
TOWER OF LUST	FRA	Gevacolor
TRACK OF THE CAT	WD	WarnerColor
LA TRAVIATA	AST	Eastman Color
TREASURE OF THE UNTAMED	IND	Pathecolor
TROUBLE IN THE GLEN	REP	Trucolor
TRUE FRIENDS	RUS	Sovcolor
20,000 LEAGUES UNDER THE SEA	BV	Technicolor
ULYSSES	PAR	Technicolor
USSR TODAY	RUS	Magicolor
VALLEY OF THE KINGS	MGM	Eastman Color
THE VANISHING PRAIRIE	BV	Technicolor
VASILI'S RETURN	RUS	Magicolor
VERA CRUZ	UA	Technicolor
VIAGO IN ORIENTE	ITA	Ferraniacolor
THE VIOLENT MEN	COL	Technicolor
THE WALK	ITA	unknown
WAR ARROW	UN	Technicolor
WELCOME THE QUEEN	BRI	Eastman Color
WHITE CHRISTMAS	PAR	Technicolor
THE WHITE ORCHID	UA	Eastman Color
WOMAN'S WORLD	TCF	Technicolor
THE WORLD DANCES	IND	Colorama
YANKEE PASHA	UN	Technicolor
THE YELLOW MOUNTAIN	UN	Technicolor
THE YELLOW TOMAHAWK	UA	Color Corp.
YOUNG AT HEART	WB	WarnerColor

1955

ADVENTURE IN WARSAW	RUS	Polcolor
THE ADVENTURES OF GIACOMO CASANOVA	FRA-ITA	Eastman Color
THE AFRICAN LION	BV	Technicolor
AIN'T MISBEHAVIN'	UN	Technicolor
ALI BABA	FRA	Eastman Color
ALL THAT HEAVEN ALLOWS	UN	Technicolor
AMAZONIA —UNKNOWN LAND	ITA	Ferraniacolor
APACHE WOMEN	ARC	Pathecolor
ARTISTS AND MODELS	PAR	Technicolor
AS LONG AS THEY'RE HAPPY	BRI	Eastman Color
AT GUNPOINT	AA	Technicolor
ATTILA	FRA-ITA	Technicolor
BALLET OF ROMEO AND JULIET	RUS	Sovcolor
BATTLE CRY	WB	WarnerColor
THE BEACH	ITA	Ferraniacolor

BEDEVILLED	MGM	Eastman Color
THE BENNY GOODMAN STORY	UN	Technicolor
A BIG FAMILY	RUS	Sovcolor
BLOOD ALLEY	WB	WarnerColor
BENGAZI	RKO	Technicolor
BRING YOUR SMILE ALONG	COL	Technicolor
CASANOVA (see ADVENTURES OF		
CAPTAIN LIGHTFOOT	UN	Technicolor
LA CASTIGLIONE	FRA-ITA	Eastman Color
CAVALCADE OF SONG	ITA	Ferraniacolor
CHERI-BIBI	FRA-ITA	Ferraniacolor
CHIEF CRAZY HORSE	UN	Technicolor
THE COBWEB	MGM	Eastman Color
COCKLESHELL HEROES	COL	Technicolor
CONQUEST OF SPACE	PAR	Technicolor
THE CONSTANT HUSBAND	BRI	Eastman Color
CONTRABAND SPAIN	BRI	Technicolor
COUNT OF MONTE CRISTO	FRA	Gevacolor
COUNT THREE AND PRAY	COL	Technicolor
THE COURT MARTIAL OF BILLY MITCHELL	WB	WarnerColor
DADDY LONG LEGS	TCF	DeLuxe Color
DAVY CROCKETT	BV	Technicolor
THE DEEP BLUE SEA	TCF	DeLuxe Color
DESERT SANDS	UA	Technicolor
DESIREE	TCF	DeLuxe Color
DEVOTION	RUS	Sovcolor
DIANE	MGM	Eastman Color
DOCK	BEL	Gevacolor
DOCTOR AT SEA	BRI	Technicolor
DON GIOVANNI	BRI	Eastman Color
THE DRAGONFLY	RUS	Sovcolor
DRUM BEAT	WB	WarnerColor
DUEL ON THE MISSISSIPPI	COL	Technicolor
EAST OF EDEN	WB	WarnerColor
THE EMPEROR AND THE GOLEM	CZE	Sovcolor
ESCAPE TO BURMA	RKO	Technicolor
FABULOUS INDIA	INDIA	Technicolor
THE FAR HORIZONS	PAR	Technicolor
FIVE FROM BARSKA STREET	POL	Agfacolor
FIVE GUNS WEST	ARC	Pathecolor
FLAME OF THE ISLANDS	REP	Trucolor
FOOTSTEPS IN THE FOG	COL	Technicolor
FOXFIRE	UN	Technicolor
FUSS OVER FEATHERS	BRI	Eastman Color
GARDEN OF EDEN	IND	Eastman Color
GENTLEMEN MARRY BRUNETTES	UA	Technicolor
GEORDIE (see WEE GEORDIE)		
GIRL DAYS OF A QUEEN	AUS	Agfacolor
THE GIRL IN THE RED VELVET SWING	TCF	DeLuxe Color
THE GIRL RUSH	PAR	Technicolor
THE GLASS SLIPPER	MGM	Eastman Color
GOOD MORNING, MISS DOVE	TCF	DeLuxe Color
GRAND VARIETY	ITA	Ferraniacolor
LA GRANDE SAVÀNA	ITA	Ferraniacolor
LES GRANDES MANOEUVRES	FRA	Eastman Color
THE GRASSHOPPER	RUS	Sovcolor
THE GUN THAT WON THE WEST	COL	Technicolor
GUYS AND DOLLS	MGM	Eastman Color
HEARTBREAK RIDGE	FRA	Gevacolor
HEIDI AND PETER	UA	Eastman Color
HELL'S ISLAND	PAR	Technicolor
HOME AND DEFENCE	NOR	Gevacolor
HOUSE OF BAMBOO	TCF	DeLuxe Color

HOUSE OF RICORDI	FRA-ITA	Technicolor
HOW TO BE VERY, VERY POPULAR	TCF	DeLuxe Color
I DIED A THOUSAND TIMES	WB	WarnerColor
I HAD SEVEN DAUGHTERS	FRA-ITA	Ferraniacolor
IN THE SOVIET UNION	RUS	Sovcolor
THE INDIAN FIGHTER	UA	Technicolor
INDONESIA TODAY	RUS	Sovcolor
ISLAND OF ALLAH	IND	Ansco Color
IT'S A DOG'S LIFE	MGM	Eastman Color
IT'S ALWAYS FAIR WEATHER	MGM	Eastman Color
JAN HUS	CZE	Agfacolor
JEDDA	AUS	Gevacolor
JOHN AND JULIE	BRI	Eastman Color
JOSEPHINE AND MEN	BRI	Eastman Color
JUPITER'S DARLING	MGM	Eastman Color
KAMI-SHIBAI	JAP	Eastman Color
THE KENTUCKIAN	UA	Technicolor
KING'S RHAPSODY	UA	Eastman Color
THE KING'S THIEF	MGM	Eastman Color
KISMET	MGM	Eastman Color
KISS OF FIRE	UN	Technicolor
LADY AND THE TRAMP	BV	Technicolor
LADY GODIVA	UN	Technicolor
THE LAND	RUS	Ukraine Color
LAND OF THE PHARAOHS	WB	WarnerColor
THE LARK	ROU	Agfacolor
THE LAST COMMAND	REP	Trucolor
THE LAST FRONTIER	COL	Technicolor
LAUGHING IN THE SUNSHINE	BRI-SWE	Eastman Color
A LAWLESS STREET	COL	Technicolor
THE LEFT HAND OF GOD	TCF	DeLuxe Color
LETTER TO A VANDAL ANYWHERE	AU	Gevacolor
THE LITTLEST OUTLAW	BV	Technicolor
THE LONG GRAY LINE	COL	Technicolor
THE LOST CONTINENT	ITA	Ferraniacolor
LOVE IS A MANY SPLENDORED THING	TCF	DeLuxe Color
LOVE ME OR LEAVE ME	MGM	Eastman Color
LUCY GALLANT	PAR	Technicolor
LUDWIG II	GER	Technicolor
THE McCONNELL STORY	WB	WarnerColor
MADAME BUTTERFLY	JAP	Technicolor
MADDALENA	ITA	Technicolor
THE MAGNIFICENT MATADOR	TCF	Pathecolor
A MAN ALONE	REP	Trucolor
A MAN CALLED PETER	TCF	DeLuxe Color
THE MAN FROM BITTER RIDGE	UN	Eastman Color
THE MAN FROM LARAMIE	COL	Technicolor
THE MAN WHO LOVED REDHEADS	BRI	Eastman Color
MAN WITHOUT A STAR	UN	Technicolor
MAN'S WINGED HELPERS	RUS	Sovcolor
MANY RIVERS TO CROSS	MGM	Eastman Color
THE MARAUDERS	MGM	Eastman Color
MASK AND DESTINY	JAP	Eastman Color
MAU MAU!	IND	unknown
THE MILLER'S BEAUTIFUL WIFE	ITA	Eastman Color
MR. MENASH BUILDS A HOUSE	BRI	Eastman Color
MISTER ROBERTS	WB	WarnerColor
MOONFLEET	MGM	Eastman Color
MY SISTER EILEEN	COL	Technicolor
NAGANA	ITA	Eastman Color
THE NAKED DAWN	UN	Technicolor
NAKED SEA	RKO	Pathecolor
NANA	FRA-ITA	Eastman Color
NAPOLEON	FRA	Eastman Color
NEW EXPLORERS	BRI	Eastman Color

OASIS	GER	Eastman Color
ONE DESIRE	UN	Technicolor
ONE SUNDAY MORNING	POL	Agfacolor
ONLY THE FRENCH CAN (FRENCH CAN-CAN)	FRA	Technicolor
OUT OF THE CLOUDS	BRI	Eastman Color
PEARL OF THE SOUTH PACIFIC	RKO	Technicolor
PETE KELLY'S BLUES	WB	WarnerColor
PICNIC	COL	Technicolor
PREHISTORIC ADVENTURE	CZE	Agfacolor
PIRATES OF TRIPOLI	COL	Technicolor
A PRIZE OF GOLD	COL	Technicolor
THE PRODIGAL	MGM	Eastman Color
THE PURPLE MASK	UN	Technicolor
QUEEN MARGOT	FRA-ITA	Eastman Color
QUENTIN DURWARD	MGM	Eastman Color
THE RACERS	TCF	DeLuxe Color
THE RAINS OF RANCHIPUR	TCF	DeLuxe Color
RAISING A RIOT	BRI	Technicolor
RICHARD III	BRI	Technicolor
REBEL WITHOUT A CAUSE	WB	WarnerColor
THE RIVER GIRL	FRA-ITA	Eastman Color
ROAD TO DENVER	REP	Trucolor
ROBBER'S ROOST	UA	Eastman Color
RUN FOR COVER	PAR	Technicolor
RUSSIAN HOLIDAY	RUS	Sovcolor
SABAKA	UA	Technicolor
THE SAFETY MATCH	RUS	Sovcolor
SAMURAI	JAP	Eastman Color
SANTA FE PASSAGE	REP	Trucolor
THE SCARLET COAT	MGM	Eastman Color
THE SEA CHASE	WB	WarnerColor
THE SECOND GREATEST SEX	UN	Eastman Color
SEMINOLE UPRISING	COL	Technicolor
SEVEN CITIES OF GOLD	TCF	DeLuxe Color
SEVEN LITTLE FOYS	PAR	Technicolor
THE SEVEN YEAR ITCH	TCF	DeLuxe Color
SHAITAN	FRA-ITA	Eastman Color
SHAN-PO AND YING-TAI	CHI	unknown
SHOTGUN	AA	Technicolor
SIGN OF THE PAGAN	UN	Technicolor
SIMBA	BRI	Eastman Color
SIMON AND LAURA	BRI	Technicolor
SINCERELY YOURS	WB	WarnerColor
SIR ARNE'S TREASURE	SWE	Gevacolor
SMOKE SIGNAL	UN	Technicolor
SO THIS IS PARIS	UN	Technicolor
SOLDIER OF FORTUNE	TCF	DeLuxe Color
THE SON OF CAROLINE CHERIE	FRA	Technicolor
SON OF SINBAD	RKO	Technicolor
THE SPOILERS	UN	Technicolor
SQUARE FORTUNE	ITA	Eastman Color
STORM OVER THE NILE	BRI	Technicolor
THE STORY ABOUT A DOGGY AND A PUSSY	CZE	Agfacolor
STRANGE LADY IN TOWN	WB	WarnerColor
STRANGER ON HORSEBACK	UA	Ansco Color
SVENGALI	BRI	Eastman Color
SUMMERTIME	UA	Eastman Color
TALL MAN RIDING	WB	WarnerColor
TALL MEN	TCF	DeLuxe Color
TAM TAM MAYUMBE	AFR	Technicolor
TEN WANTED MEN	COL	Technicolor
THE TENDER TRAP	MGM	Eastman Color
TENNESSEE'S PARTNER	RKO	Eastman Color
TEXAS LADY	RKO	Technicolor

THAT LADY	TCF	Eastman Color
THIS ISLAND EARTH	UN	Technicolor
THE TIGER AND THE FLAME	INDIA	Technicolor
TIGER GIRL	RUS	Sovcolor
TIMBERJACK	REP	Trucolor
TO HELL AND BACK	UN	Technicolor
TO PARIS WITH LOVE	BRI	Technicolor
TOUCH AND GO	BRI	Technicolor
THE TOWER OF NESLE	FRA-ITA	Eastman Color
THE TREASURE OF PANCHO VILLA	RKO	Technicolor
THE TROUBLE WITH HARRY	PAR	Technicolor
ULYSSES	PAR	Technicolor
UNDERWATER!	RKO	Technicolor
UNTAMED	TCF	DeLuxe Color
VALUE FOR MONEY	BRI	Technicolor
THE VIEW FROM POMPEY'S HEAD	TCF	DeLuxe Color
VIOLENT SATURDAY	TCF	DeLuxe Color
VIOLETTES IMPERIALES	FRA	Gevacolor
THE VIRGIN QUEEN	TCF	DeLuxe Color
THE VISCOUNT OF BRAGELONNE	FRA-ITA	Eastman Color
WAKUMBA!	RKO	Technicolor
THE WARRIORS (THE DARK AVENGER)	AA	Eastman Color
WE FOUND A VALLEY	BRI	Ferraniacolor
WEE GEORDIE	BRI	Technicolor
WE'RE NO ANGELS	PAR	Technicolor
WHERE MOUNTAINS FLOAT	DEN	Eastman Color
WHITE FEATHER	TCF	Technicolor
WICHITA	AA	Technicolor
THE WOMAN FOR JOE	BRI	Technicolor
WORLD'S MOST BEAUTIFUL WOMAN	ITA	Eastman Color
WYOMING RENEGADES	COL	Technicolor
YELLOWNECK	REP	Trucolor
YOKIHI	JAP	Eastman Color
YOU KNOW WHAT SAILORS ARE	BRI	Technicolor
YOU'RE NEVER TOO YOUNG	PAR	Technicolor

1956

ABDULLA THE GREAT	TCF	Technicolor
ALEXANDER THE GREAT	UA	Technicolor
ALL FOR MARY	BRI	Technicolor
AN ALLIGATOR NAMED DAISY	BRI	Technicolor
THE AMAZON TRADER	WB	WarnerColor
THE AMBASSADOR'S DAUGHTER	UA	Technicolor
ANASTASIA	TCF	DeLuxe Color
THE ANIMAL WORLD	WB	Technicolor
ANYTHING GOES	PAR	Technicolor
AROUND THE WORLD IN 80 DAYS	UA	Eastman Color
AWAY ALL BOATS	UN	Technicolor
THE BABY AND THE BATTLESHIP	BRI	Eastman Color
BACKLASH	UN	Technicolor
BANDIDO	UA	DeLuxe Color
BATTLE OF RIVER PLATE	BRI	Technicolor
BEAST OF HOLLOW MOUNTAIN	UA	DeLuxe Color
BEL-AMI	FRA	Agfacolor
THE BEST THINGS IN LIFE ARE FREE	TCF	DeLuxe Color
BETWEEN HEAVEN AND HELL	TCF	DeLuxe Color
BEYOND MOMBASA	BRI	Technicolor
BHOWANI JUNCTION	MGM	Eastman Color
BIGGER THAN LIFE	TCF	DeLuxe Color
THE BIRDS AND THE BEES	PAR	Technicolor
THE BLACK TENT	BRI	Technicolor
BORIS GODUNOV	RUS	Sovcolor
THE BOTTOM OF THE BOTTLE	TCF	DeLuxe Color
THE BRAVE ONE	RKO-UN	Technicolor

THE BURNING HILLS	WB	WarnerColor
BUS STOP	TCF	DeLuxe Color
CANYON RIVER	AA	DeLuxe Color
CAROUSEL	TCF	DeLuxe Color
CE SOIR LES JUPONS VOLENT	FRA	Agfacolor
C'EST ARRIVE A ODEN	FRA	Eastman Color
CHARLEY MOON	BRI	Eastman Color
CHARLEY'S TANTE	GER	Eastman Color
LA CHATELAINE DU LIBAN	FRA-ITA	Eastman Color
COMANCHE	UA	DeLuxe Color
COME NEXT SPRING	REP	Trucolor
CONGO CROSSING	UN	Technicolor
THE CONQUEROR	RKO	Technicolor
THE COURT JESTER	PAR	Technicolor
LE COUTEAU SOUS LA GORGE	FRA	Eastman Color
D-DAY, THE SIXTH OF JUNE	TCF	DeLuxe Color
DAKOTA INCIDENT	REP	Trucolor
DAVY CROCKET AND THE RIVER PIRATES	BV	Technicolor
A DAY OF FURY	UN	Technicolor
LE DICIOTTENNI	ITA	Eastman Color
DON JUAN	FRA	Technicolor
DON JUAN'S FAREWELL	AUS	Agfacolor
DONATELLA	ITA	Eastman Color
DONNE SOLE	ITA	Ferraniacolor
THE EDDY DUCHIN STORY	COL	Technicolor
ESCONDIDA	MEX	unknown
ESCUELA DE MUSICA	MEX	unknown
ETERNAL LOVE	GER	Eastman Color
EVERYTHING BUT THE TRUTH	UN	Eastman Color
THE EXTRA DAY	BRI	unknown
THE FEMININE TOUCH	BRI	Technicolor
THE FIRST TEXAN	AA	Technicolor
THE FIRST TRAVELING SALESLADY	RKO	Technicolor
FORBIDDEN PLANET	MGM	Eastman Color
FOREIGN INTRIGUE	UA	Eastman Color
FOREVER DARLING	MGM	Eastman Color
FOUR GIRLS IN TOWN	UN	Technicolor
FRIENDLY PERSUASION	AA	DeLuxe Color
FROU-FROU	FRA	Eastman Color
FUN AT ST. FANNY'S	BRI	unknown
GABY	MGM	Eastman Color
THE GADFLY	RUS	Magicolor
LA GATA	SPA	Eastman Color
GIANT	WB	WarnerColor
GLORY	RKO	Technicolor
GREAT DAY IN THE MORNING	RKO	Technicolor
THE GREAT LOCOMOTIVE CHASE	BV	Technicolor
GUITARS OF LOVE	GER	Eastman Color
GUNSLINGER	ARC	Pathecolor
DER HAUPTMUN VON KOEPENICK	GER	Eastman Color
HE LAUGHED LAST	COL	Technicolor
HEMSOBORNA	SWE	Eastman Color
HEROES OF SHIPKA	RUS	Magicolor
HIGH SOCIETY	MGM	Technicolor
HILDA CRANE	TCF	DeLuxe Color
HOLLYWOOD OR BUST	PAR	Technicolor
HOT BLOOD	COL	Technicolor
HOUSE OF SECRETS	BRI	Technicolor
HUK!	UA	Eastman Color
I KILLED WILD BILL HICKOCK	UA	unknown
INVITATION TO THE DANCE	MGM	Technicolor
THE IRON PETTICOAT	MGM	Technicolor
ISLAND OF ALLAH	IND	Ansco Color
IT'S A WONDERFUL WORLD	BRI	Technicolor

IT'S A GREAT LIFE	BRI	Technicolor
IT'S NEVER TOO LATE	BRI	Eastman Color
JUBAL	COL	Technicolor
A KISS BEFORE DYING	UA	DeLuxe Color
THE LADYKILLERS	BRI	Technicolor
THE LAST HUNT	MGM	Eastman Color
THE LAST WAGON	TCF	DeLuxe Color
THE LIEUTENANT WORE SKIRTS	TCF	DeLuxe Color
LISBON	REP	Trucolor
THE LITTLEST OUTLAW	BV	Technicolor
THE LONE RANGER	WB	WarnerColor
LORSQUE L'ENFANT PARAIT	FRA	Eastman Color
LOSER TAKE ALL	BRI	Eastman Color
LOST	BRI	Eastman Color
LUST FOR LIFE	MGM	Metrocolor
MADAME BUTTERFLY	ITA	Technicolor
MAGIC FIRE	REP	Trucolor
MAM'ZELLE PIGALLE (CETTE SACREE GAMINE)	FRA	Eastman Color
THE MAN IN THE GRAY FLANNEL SUIT	TCF	DeLuxe Color
MAN OF AFRICA	BRI	Ferraniacolor
THE MAN WHO KNEW TOO MUCH	PAR	Technicolor
THE MAN WHO NEVER WAS	TCF	DeLuxe Color
MANFISH	UA	DeLuxe Color
MANNEQUINS DE PARIS	FRA	Eastman Color
THE MARCH HARE	BRI	unknown
MARIE ANTOINETTE	FRA-ITA	Technicolor
MASSACRE	TCF	Ansco Color
MEET ME IN LAS VEGAS	MGM	Eastman Color
MEILLEURE PART	FRA-ITA	Eastman Color
MILORD L'ARSOUILLE	FRA	Eastman Color
MIO FIGLIO NERONE	ITA	Eastman Color
THE MISSIONARY	FRA	unknown
MOBY DICK	WB	Technicolor
MOHAWK	TCF	Pathecolor
LA MORT EN CE JARDIN	FRA-MEX	Eastman Color
MOTHER	RUS	Sovcolor
THE MOUNTAIN	PAR	Technicolor
MOZART	AUS	Agfacolor
THE NAKED HILLS	AA	Pathecolor
NEVER SAY GOODBYE	UN	Technicolor
NIGHT AND FOG	FRA	Eastman Color
1905	RUS	Magicolor
NO PLACE TO HIDE	AA	DeLuxe Color
NOW AND FOREVER	BRI	Technicolor
ODONGO	COL	Technicolor
OH, ROSALINDA!	BRI	Technicolor
ON THE THRESHOLD OF SPACE	TCF	DeLuxe Color
THE OPPOSITE SEX	MGM	Metrocolor
OTHELLO	RUS	Sovcolor
PACIFIC DESTINY	BRI	Eastman Color
PAN, AMORE. E . . . (BREAD, LOVE AND . . .)	ITA	Eastman Color
PARIS PALACE HOTEL	FRA-ITA	Eastman Color
THE PHANTOM HORSE	JAP	Eastman Color
PICASSO	ITA	Ferraniacolor
PILLARS OF THE SKY	UA	Technicolor
PORT AFRIQUE	BRI	unknown
THE PROUD ONES	TCF	DeLuxe Color
THE QUEEN OF BABYLON	ITA-TCF	Ferraniacolor
QUINCANNON, FRONTIER SCOUT	UA	DeLuxe Color
RACCONTI ROMANI	ITA	Eastman Color
RAW EDGE	UN	Technicolor
THE RAWHIDE YEARS	UN	Technicolor
THE RED BALLOON (LE BALLON ROUGE)	FRA	Technicolor
RED SUNDOWN	UN	Technicolor

REPRISAL	COL	Technicolor
THE REVOLT OF MAMIE STOVER	TCF	DeLuxe Color
LA RISAIA	ITA	Eastman Color
RUN FOR THE SUN	UA	Technicolor
RUNNING TARGET	UA	DeLuxe Color
SAFARI	COL	Technicolor
SANTIAGO	WB	WarnerColor
SATELLITE IN THE SKY	WB	WarnerColor
SCANDAL IN SORRENTO	ITA	Eastman Color
THE SEARCHERS	WB	Technicolor
SECRETS OF LIFE	BV	Technicolor
SECRETS OF THE REEF	IND	Tri-Art Color
SERENADE	WB	WarnerColor
SEVEN MEN FROM NOW	WB	WarnerColor
7TH CAVALRY	COL	Technicolor
THE SHARKFIGHTERS	UA	Technicolor
SHOWDOWN AT ABILENE	UN	Technicolor
THE SILENT WORLD	COL	Eastman Color
SLIGHTLY SCARLET	RKO	Technicolor
SMILEY	TCF	Technicolor
SOLID GOLD CADILLAC (sequence)	COL	Technicolor
STAR IN THE DUST	UN	Technicolor
STAR OF INDIA	UA	Technicolor
SWAMP WOMEN	IND	Eastman Color
THE SWAN	MGM	Eastman Color
THE TAHITIAN	IND	Eastman Color
TARDES DE TOROS	SPA	Eastman Color
TEA AND SYMPATHY	MGM	Metrocolor
TEAHOUSE OF THE AUGUST MOON	MGM	Metrocolor
THE TEN COMMANDMENTS	PAR	Technicolor
TENSION AT TABLE ROCK	RKO	Technicolor
THAT CERTAIN FEELING	PAR	Technicolor
THRILLARAMA ADVENTURE	IND	Technicolor
THUNDER OVER ARIZONA	REP	Trucolor
TOWARD THE UNKNOWN	WB	WarnerColor
TOY TIGER	UN	Technicolor
TRAPEZE	UA	DeLuxe Color
TRIBUTE TO A BADMAN	MGM	Eastman Color
TWELFTH NIGHT	RUS	Magicolor
23 PACES TO BAKER STREET	TCF	DeLuxe Color
THE UNGUARDED MOMENT	UN	Technicolor
THE VAGABOND KING	PAR	Technicolor
WALK THE PROUD LAND	UN	Technicolor
WAR AND PEACE	PAR	Technicolor
WETBACKS	IND	Eastman Color
WHAT PRICE FREEDOM	GER	Agfacolor
WHITE VERTIGO	ITA	Ferraniacolor
A WOMAN'S DEVOTION	REP	Trucolor
WORLD WITHOUT END	AA	Technicolor
WRITTEN ON THE WIND	UN	Technicolor
YANG KWEI FEI	BV	Eastman Color
YOU CAN'T RUN AWAY FROM IT	COL	Technicolor
ZANZABUKU	REP	Trucolor

1957

ACCUSED OF MURDER	REP	Trucolor
ACTION OF THE TIGER	MGM	Technicolor
ADAM AND EVE	MEX	Eastman Color
THE ADMIRABLE CRICHTON	COL	Technicolor
THE ADVENTURES OF ARSENE LUPIN	FRA-ITA	Technicolor
LES AVENTURES DE TILL L'ESPIEGLE	FRA-GER	Technicolor
AN AFFAIR TO REMEMBER	TCF	DeLuxe Color
AFTER THE BALL	BRI	Eastman Color
ALBERT SCHWEITZER	IND	Eastman Color

ALL MINE TO GIVE	UN	Technicolor
AMANECER EN PUERTA ASCURA	SPA	Eastman Color
AND GOD CREATED WOMAN	FRA	Eastman Color
APRIL LOVE	TCF	DeLuxe Color
AS LONG AS THEY ARE BEAUTIFUL GIRLS	GER	Agfacolor
AUTUMN ROSES	GER	Agfacolor
BALLET TALES	RUS	Sovcolor
BAND OF ANGELS	WB	WarnerColor
THE BARRETTS OF WIMPOLE STREET	MGM	Metrocolor
BATTLE HYMN	UN	Technicolor
BEHIND THE SHOW WINDOW	RUS	Magicolor
BERNARDINE	TCF	DeLuxe Color
THE BIG LAND	WB	WarnerColor
BITTER SPEARS	SA	unknown
THE BOLSHOI BALLET	BRI	Eastman Color
BOMBERS B-52	WB	WarnerColor
BONSOIR PARIS, BONJOUR L'AMOUR	FRA	Eastman Color
BORIS GODUNOV	RUS	Sovcolor
BOY ON A DOLPHIN	TCF	DeLuxe Color
THE BRIDGE ON THE RIVER KWAI	COL	Technicolor
BUNDLE OF JOY	RKO	Technicolor
CANASTA DE CUENTOS MEXICANOS	MEX	Pathecolor
CAPTAIN FANTOM	ITA	unknown
CARNIVAL NIGHT	RUS	Sovcolor
CASINO DE PARIS	FRA-GER	Technicolor
LA CHATELAINE DU LIBAN	FRA	Eastman Color
CHECKPOINT	BRI	Eastman Color
LA CIUDAD DE LOS NINOS	MEX	unknown
COURAGE OF BLACK BEAUTY	TCF	DeLuxe Color
CURSE OF FRANKENSTEIN	BRI	WarnerColor
DANGEROUS EXILE	BRI	Technicolor
DANIEL BOONE, TRAIL BLAZER	REP	Trucolor
DAUGHTER OF MATA HARI	ITA	Ferraniacolor
A DAY IN MOSCOW	RUS	Sovcolor
DAY OF FEAR	SPA	unknown
DECISION AT SUNDOWN	COL	Technicolor
THE DEERSLAYER	TCF	DeLuxe Color
DESK SET	TCF	DeLuxe Color
DESIGNING WOMEN	MGM	Metrocolor
THE DEVIL'S HAIRPIN	PAR	Technicolor
DOCTOR AT LARGE	BRI	Technicolor
DON QUIXOTE	RUS	Sovcolor
DON'T GO NEAR THE WATER	MGM	Metrocolor
DRAGOON WELLS MASSACRE	AA	DeLuxe Color
ECHO OF THE MOUNTAINS	GER	Agfacolor
8 X 8	IND	Eastman Color
EINEWACHT IN VENEDIG	GER	Agfacolor
ELISA	FRA	Eastman Color
THE ENEMY BELOW	TCF	DeLuxe Color
ESCAPADE IN JAPAN	UN	Technicolor
EYE FOR AN EYE	FRA-ITA	Eastman Color
FAMOUS PAINTERS	ITA	unknown
A FAREWELL TO ARMS	TCF	DeLuxe Color
FAUSTINA	SPA	Eastman Color
FELICIDAD	MEX	unknown
FIRE DOWN BELOW	COL	Technicolor
FLESH AND THE SPUR	AI	Eastman Color
FLICKEN I FRACK	SWE	Eastman Color
FOLIES-BERGERE	FRA	Technicolor
FORBIDDEN DESERT	WB	WarnerColor
THE FORTY-FIRST	RUS	Sovcolor
FRANZ SCHUBERT	GER	Agfacolor
FREEDOM	AFR	Eastman Color

FUNNY FACE	PAR	Technicolor
LE GARCONNE	FRA	Agfacolor
THE GIRL CAN'T HELP IT	TCF	DeLuxe Color
THE GIRL FROM KORFU	GRE	Eastman Color
THE GIRL MOST LIKELY	RKO	Technicolor
THE GIRLS FROM IMMENHOF	GER	Agfacolor
THE GOOD COMPANIONS	BRI	Technicolor
GUN FOR A COWARD	UN	Eastman Color
GUN GLORY	MGM	Metrocolor
GUNFIGHT AT THE OK CORRAL	PAR	Technicolor
THE GUNS OF FORT PETTICOAT	COL	Technicolor
HANG TUAH	MAL	unknown
THE HARD MAN	COL	Technicolor
HEARTBREAK RIDGE	FRA	unknown
HEAVEN KNOWS, MR. ALLISON	TCF	DeLuxe Color
HEIDELBERG ROMANCE	GER	Agfacolor
HEROES DEL AIRE	SPA	Eastman Color
HEROES OF SHIPKA	RUS	Sovcolor
HERR PUNTILA UND SEIN KNECHTMATTI	AUS	Agfacolor
HIRTENLEID VOM KAISERTAL	GER	Agfacolor
HOLINDAY AM WOERTHERSEE	GER	Agfacolor
HIS TWO LOVES	ITA	Ferraniacolor
L'HOMME ET L'ENFANT	FRA	Eastman Color
THE HUNCHBACK OF NOTRE DAME	AA	Eastman Color
IMMORTAL GARRISON	UN	Technicolor
IMMORTAL MOZART	GER	Agfacolor
INTERLUDE	UN	Technicolor
ISLAND IN THE SUN	TCF	DeLuxe Color
ISTANBUL	UN	Technicolor
IT HAPPENED IN ROME (SOUVENIER D'ITALIE)	ITA	Technicolor
JE REVIENDRAI A KANDARA	FRA	Eastman Color
JET PILOT	RKO-UN	Technicolor
JOE BUTTERFLY	UN	Technicolor
JOHNNY TREMAIN	BV	Technicolor
JUHA	FIN	Eastman Color
KELLY AND ME	UN	Technicolor
THE KING AND FOUR QUEENS	UA	DeLuxe Color
KISS THEM FOR ME	TCF	DeLuxe Color
KOENIGIN LUISE	GER	Eastman Color
KOME	JAP	Eastman Color
DER KOMOEDIANT VON WIEN	GER	Agfacolor
LAST OF THE BADMEN	AA	DeLuxe Color
THE LAST PARADISE	ITA	Ferraniacolor
LEGEND OF THE LOST	UA	Technicolor
LES GIRLS	MGM	Metrocolor
LET'S BE HAPPY	AA	Technicolor
THE LITTLE HUT	MGM	Eastman Color
THE LIVING IDOL	MGM	Eastman Color
THE LOVE LOTTERY	BRI	unknown
LOVE SLAVES OF THE AMAZON	UN	Eastman Color
LOVING YOU	PAR	Technicolor
MALWA	RUS	Sovcolor
MANOEVERBALL	GER	Agfacolor
MELBOURNE RENDEZVOUS	IND	Agfacolor
MEN OF SHERWOOD FOREST	AST	Eastman Color
THE MEXICAN	RUS	Magicolor
MICHEL STROGOFF	FRA	Eastman Color
MIRACLE IN SOHO	BRI	Eastman Color
MISTER CORY	UN	Eastman Color
MITSOU	FRA	Eastman Color
MONPTI	GER	Agfacolor
MONTE CARLO STORY	UA	Technicolor
MY MAN GODFREY	UN	Eastman Color
NAKED PARADISE	AI	Pathecolor

THE NAKED EYE (sequence)	IND	Eastman Color
NEW YEAR'S SACRIFICE	CHI	Agfacolor
NO TIME FOR TEARS	BRI	unknown
NOVEL OF FEAR	BRI	unknown
OEDIPUS REX	CAN	Eastman Color
OH, MEN! OH, WOMEN!	TCF	DeLuxe Color
THE OKLAHOMAN	AA	Technicolor
OLD YELLER	BV	Technicolor
OMAR KHAYYAM	PAR	Technicolor
THE PAJAMA GAME	WB	WarnerColor
PAL JOEY	COL	Technicolor
PARADISE ON EARTH	FRA-ITA	Eastman Color
PARIS DOES STRANGE THINGS	WB	Technicolor
PARSON AND THE OUTLAW	COL	Technicolor
PASSIONATE STRANGER (sequences)	BRI	Eastman Color
PAWNEE	REP	Trucolor
LE PAYS D'OU JE VIENS	FRA	Technicolor
PERRI	BV	Technicolor
PEYTON PLACE	TCF	DeLuxe Color
THE PRIDE AND THE PASSION	UA	Technicolor
THE PRINCE AND THE SHOWGIRL	WB	Technicolor
PROLOG	RUS	Sovcolor
PUBLIC PIGEON NO. 1	RKO	Technicolor
QUIVITOQ	DEN	Agfacolor
QUANTEZ	UN	Eastman Color
LA RAGAZZA DELLE SALINE	GER-ITA	unknown
THE RAINMAKER	PAR	Technicolor
RAINTREE COUNTY	MGM	Technicolor
THE RESTLESS BREED	TCF	Eastman Color
REVOLT AT FORT LARAMIE	UA	DeLuxe Color
THE RIVER'S EDGE	TCF	DeLuxe Color
ROAD OF LIFE	RUS	Sovcolor
ROBBERY UNDER ARMS	BRI	Eastman Color
ROSE BERND (SINS OF ROSE BERND)	GER	Agfacolor
ROYAL COMMAND	GER	Agfacolor
RUN OF THE ARROW	RKO	Technicolor
SAME JAKKI	NOR	Eastman Color
SAYONARA	WB	Technicolor
THE SCEPTRE AND THE MACE	CAN	Eastman Color
DIE SCHOENE MUELLERIN	GER	Agfacolor
SEA WIFE	TCF	DeLuxe Color
SHIROS SAMMYAHU	JAP	Eastman Color
SILK STOCKINGS	MGM	Metrocolor
SISSI	AUS	Agfacolor
SLIM CARTER	UN	Eastman Color
SOROK PERVYL	RUS	Sovcolor
THE SPANISH GARDNER	BRI	Technicolor
THE SPIRIT OF ST. LOUIS	WB	WarnerColor
SPOILERS OF THE FOREST	REP	Trucolor
STARS IN YOUR EYES	BRI	unknown
THE STORY OF MANKIND	WB	Technicolor
DAS SUENDIGE DORF	GER	Agfacolor
THE SUN ALSO RISES	TCF	DeLuxe Color
TAHITI	FRA	Eastman Color
THE TALL STRANGER	AA	DeLuxe Color
THE TALL "T"	COL	Technicolor
TALPA	MEX	unknown
TAMMY AND THE BACHELOR	UN	Technicolor
TARZAN AND THE LOST SAFARI	MGM	Technicolor
TEN THOUSAND BEDROOMS	MGM	Metrocolor
THIS IS RUSSIA (sequences)	UN	Eastman Color
THREE GIRLS FROM THE RHINE	GER	Agfacolor
THREE MEN IN A BOAT	BRI	Eastman Color
THREE VIOLENT PEOPLE	PAR	Technicolor

TRAITORS	JAP	Eastman Color
DIE TRAPP FAMILE	GER	Eastman Color
TRUE AS A TURTLE	BRI	Eastman Color
THE TRUE STORY OF JESSE JAMES	TCF	DeLuxe Color
TYPHON A NAGAZAKI	FRA-JAP	Technicolor
L'ULTIMA NOTTE D'AMORE	ITA-SPA	Ferraniacolor
UND DIR LIEBE LACHT DAZU	GER	Eastman Color
UNDERCURRENT	JAP	Daiei Color
THE UNHOLY WIFE	RKO	Technicolor
UNKNOWN SATELLITE OVER TOKYO	JAP	Daiei Color
UOMINI E LUPI	ITA	Eastman Color
UROK ISTORIJL	BUL-RUS	Sovcolor
VICTORIA AND HER HUSSAR	GER	Agfacolor
THE VINTAGE	MGM	Metrocolor
THE VIRTUOUS BIGAMIST	FRA-ITA	Eastman Color
WALK INTO HELL	BRI	Eastman Color
WAR DRUMS	UA	DeLuxe Color
WENN AM SONNTAG ABEND DIE DORFMUSIK SPIELT	GER	Agfacolor
WESTWARD HO, THE WAGONS	BV	Technicolor
WHITE HORSE INN	GER	Agfacolor
WILL SUCCESS SPOIL ROCK HUNTER?	TCF	DeLuxe Color
THE WINGS OF EAGLES	MGM	Metrocolor
WOMAN OF THE RIVER	COL	Technicolor
YELLOW SQUADRON	SWE	Ferraniacolor
ZARAK	COL	Technicolor

1958

ALESKA DUNDIE	RUS-YUG	Agfacolor
LOS AMANTES DEL DESIERTO	SPA	Agfacolor
APACHE TERRITORY	COL	Eastman Color
AUNTIE MAME	WB	Technicolor
BACHELOR OF HEARTS	BRI	unknown
THE BADLANDERS	MGM	Metrocolor
THE BARBARIAN AND THE GEISHA	TCF	DeLuxe Color
BEAUTIFUL BUT DANGEROUS	TCF	DeLuxe Color
THE BEGGAR STUDENT	GER	Eastman Color
BEHIND THE MASK	BRI	unknown
BELL, BOOK AND CANDLE	COL	Technicolor
THE BIG COUNTRY	UA	Technicolor
THE BIG BEAT	UN	Eastman Color
THE BIG MONEY	BRI	Technicolor
LA BIGORNE CAPORAL DE FRANCE	FRA	Eastman Color
LES BIJOUTIERS DU CLAIR DE LUNE	FRA	Eastman Color
THE BLOB	PAR	DeLuxe Color
BLOOD OF THE VAMPIRE	BRI	Eastman Color
BONJOUR TRISTESSE (sequences)	COL	Technicolor
LE BOURGEOIS GENTILHOMME	FRA	Eastman Color
THE BRAVADOS	TCF	DeLuxe Color
THE BROTHERS KARAMAZOV	MGM	Metrocolor
THE BUCCANEER	PAR	Technicolor
BUCHANAN RIDES ALONE	COL	Columbia Color
BULLWHIP	AA	DeLuxe Color
CAT ON A HOT TIN ROOF	MGM	Metrocolor
CATTLE EMPIRE	TCF	DeLuxe Color
LE CERF-VOLANT DU BOUT DU MONDE	FRA	Eastman Color
A CERTAIN SMILE	TCF	DeLuxe Color
C'EST LA FAUTE D'ADAM	FRA	Eastman Color
CHAMANTS GARCONS	FRA	Eastman Color
CIRCUS FESTIVAL	RUS	Sovcolor
CIRCUS OF LOVE	GER	Agfacolor
LOS CLARINES DEL MIEDO	SPA	Eastman Color
THE COLD HEART	GER	Agfacolor
COLE YOUNGER, GUNFIGHTER	AA	DeLuxe Color

COWBOY	COL	Technicolor
DAMN YANKEES	WB	Technicolor
THE DANCING HEART	GER	Agfacolor
DANGEROUS EXILE	BRI	Eastman Color
DAVY	BRI	Technicolor
DAY OF THE BADMAN	UN	Eastman Color
THE DEEP SIX	WB	WarnerColor
THE DOCTOR'S DILEMMA	MGM	Metrocolor
DOSANGO	JAP	Eastman Color
L'EAU VIVE	FRA	Eastman Color
ELEPHANT GUN (NOR THE MOON BY NIGHT)	BRI	Eastman Color
EMBEZZLED HEAVEN	GER	Agfacolor
ENCHANTED ISLAND	WB	Technicolor
LA FATICHE DI ERCOLE	ITA	Eastman Color
FESTIVAL IN MOSCOW	RUS	Magicolor
LES FILS DE L'EAU	FRA	Eastman Color
FLAMES ON THE VOLGA	RUS	Sovcolor
THE FLUTE AND THE ARROW	SWE	Technicolor
THE FLY	TCF	DeLuxe Color
FORT MASSACRE	UA	DeLuxe Color
FRAULEIN	TCF	DeLuxe Color
FROM HELL TO TEXAS	TCF	DeLuxe Color
FROM THE EARTH TO THE MOON	WB	Technicolor
LA GARCONNE	FRA	Agfacolor
THE GEISHA BOY	PAR	Technicolor
GIDEON'S DAY (GIDEON OF SCOTLAND YARD)	BRI	Technicolor
THE GIFT OF LOVE	TCF	DeLuxe Color
GIGI	MGM	Metrocolor
GIRLS AT SEA	BRI	Eastman Color
GOHA	TUR	Agfacolor
GOLDEN MOUNTAINS	DEN	unknown
GOOD DAY FOR A HANGING	COL	Columbia Color
LA GRANDE STRADA ASSURRA	FRA-ITA	Ferraniacolor
LA GUERRA EMPIEZA EN CUBA	SPA	Eastman Color
GUITARS OF LOVE	GER	Eastman Color
GUNMAN'S WALK	COL	Technicolor
GUNSMOKE IN TUCSON	AA	DeLuxe Color
THE GYPSY AND THE GENTLEMAN	BRI	Eastman Color
HARRY BLACK AND THE TIGER	TCF	Technicolor
HERCULES	FRA	Eastman Color
HORROR OF DRACULA	UN	Technicolor
THE HORSE'S MOUTH	BRI	Technicolor
HOUSEBOAT	PAR	Technicolor
THE HUNTERS	TCF	DeLuxe Color
I WAS A TEENAGE FRANKENSTEIN (sequences)	AI	Pathecolor
IKARI NO KOTO	JAP	Eastman Color
ILL MET BY MOONLIGHT (see NIGHT AMBUSH)		
IM PRATER BLUCH'N WIEDER DIE BAEUME	AUS	Agfacolor
IN LOVE AND WAR	TCF	DeLuxe Color
IN THE PACIFIC	RUS	Eastman Color
INDISCREET	WB	Technicolor
INN OF THE SIXTH HAPPINESS	TCF	DeLuxe Color
ITALIEN REISE-LIEBE INBEGRIFFEN	GER	Eastman Color
JAZZGOSSEN	SWE	Eastman Color
JENNY	HOL-GER	Agfacolor
KATHY-O	UN	Eastman Color
THE LADY TAKES A FLYER	UN	Eastman Color
THE LAST OF THE FAST GUNS	UN	Eastman Color
LAST OF THE NOMADS	LAP	Eastman Color
THE LAW AND JAKE WADE	MGM	Metrocolor
LETTRE DE SIBERIE	FRA	Eastman Color
LIBERTE SURVEILLE	FRA-CZE	Agfacolor
THE LIGHT IN THE FOREST	BV	Technicolor
LONE RANGER AND THE LOST CITY OF GOLD	UA	Eastman Color

THE LONG HOT SUMMER	TCF	DeLuxe Color
THE LORD TAKES A BRIDE	JAP	Toei Color
MAD LITTLE ISLAND (ROCKETS GALORE)	BRI	Eastman Color
MADCHEN IN UNIFORM	GER	Agfacolor
MAN FROM GOD'S COUNTRY	AA	DeLuxe Color
MAN OF THE WEST	UA	DeLuxe Color
MARDI GRAS	TCF	DeLuxe Color
MARJORIE MORNINGSTAR	WB	WarnerColor
MARK OF THE HAWK	UN	Technicolor
MERRY ANDREW	MGM	Metrocolor
LA MINA	SPA-ITA	Ferraniacolor
LES MISERABLES	FRA	Technicolor
THE MISSOURI TRAVELER	BV	Technicolor
MITZOU	FRA	Eastman Color
MON ONCLE (MY UNCLE, MR. HULOT)	FRA	Eastman Color
MONEY, WOMEN AND GUNS	UN	Eastman Color
THE MOONRAKER	BRI	Technicolor
MOTHER INDIA	INDIA	Technicolor
MUCHACHITA DE VALLADOLID	SPA	Eastman Color
MUHOMATSU NO ISSHO	JAP	Agfacolor
NACHTS IM GRUENEN KAKADU	GER	Eastman Color
THE NAKED AND THE DEAD	WB	Technicolor
THE NAKED EARTH	TCF	DeLuxe Color
NARAYAMA BUSI-KO	JAP	Fujicolor
THE NARCOTICS STORY	IND	Eastman Color
NEXT TO NO TIME	BRI	Eastman Color
NIGHT AMBUSH (ILL MET BY MOONLIGHT)	BRI	Technicolor
THE NIGHT HEAVEN FELL	FRA	Eastman Color
NO ORDINARY SUMMER	RUS	Sovcolor
NO SUN IN VENICE	FRA-ITA	Eastman Color
NO TIME TO DIE	COL	Technicolor
THE OLD MAN AND THE SEA	WB	WarnerColor
OREGON PASSAGE	AA	DeLuxe Color
OTAR'S WIDOW	RUS	Sovcolor
PARDESI	RUS	Sovcolor
PARIS HOLIDAY	UA	Technicolor
UNE PARISIENNE	FRA	Technicolor
PARTY GIRL	MGM	Metrocolor
LE PASSAGER CLANDESTIN	AUS-FRA	Eastman Color
THE PERFECT FURLOUGH	UN	Eastman Color
PEZZO, CAPOPEZZO E CAPITANO	ITA-GER	Ferraniacolor
THE PRECIPICE	JAP	Agfacolor
THE PROUD REBEL	BV	Technicolor
QUANTRILL'S RAIDERS	AA	DeLuxe Color
QUEEN OF OUTER SPACE	AA	DeLuxe Color
QUIET FLOWS THE DON	RUS	Sovcolor
LA RAGAZZA DEL PALIO	ITA	Technicolor
RALLY 'ROUND THE FLAG, BOYS	TCF	DeLuxe Color
RAW WIND IN EDEN	UN	Eastman Color
THE RELUCTANT DEBUTANTE	MGM	Metrocolor
THE RETURN OF DRACULA (sequences)	UA	unknown
RETURN TO WARBOW	COL	Technicolor
REVENGE OF FRANKENSTEIN	COL	Technicolor
RICE	JAP	Eastman Color
THE RICKSHAW MAN	JAP	Agfacolor
RIDE A CROOKED TRAIL	UN	Eastman Color
ROAD TO THE STARS	RUS	Sovcolor
ROCK-A-BYE BABY	PAR	Technicolor
ROOTS OF HEAVEN	TCF	DeLuxe Color
SADDLE THE WIND	MGM	Metrocolor
SAGA OF HEMP BROWN	UN	Eastman Color
SANS FAMILLE	FRA	Eastman Color
SCANDAL IN BAD ISCHL	AUS	Agfacolor

7TH VOYAGE OF SINBAD	COL	Technicolor
SHE DIDN'T SAY NO	BRI	Technicolor
SHE-GODS OF SHARK REEF	AI	Pathecolor
THE SHEEPMAN	MGM	Metrocolor
SIERRA BARON	TCF	DeLuxe Color
SMILEY GETS A GUN	BRI	Technicolor
SNOWFIRE	AA	Eastman Color
SOLEDAD	ITA-SPA	Ferraniacolor
SOME CAME RUNNING	MGM	Metrocolor
SORCERER'S VILLAGE	FRA	Pathecolor
SOUTH PACIFIC	TCF	Technicolor
SOUTH SEAS ADVENTURE	IND	Technicolor
A SPANISH AFFAIR	PAR	Technicolor
STAGE STRUCK	BV	Technicolor
STORIES ABOUT LENIN (sequences)	RUS	Sovcolor
STORIES OF MY MOTHER	RUS	Sovcolor
STORY OF A PURE LOVE	JAP	unknown
THE STORY OF VICKIE	BV	Technicolor
THE STRANGE GODS	ARG	unknown
SYNNOVE SOLBAKKEN	SWE	Eastman Color
TABARIN	FRA	Eastman Color
TAMANGO	FRA	Eastman Color
TARZAN'S FIGHT FOR LIFE	MGM	Metrocolor
TEMPEST	PAR	Technicolor
THE TEMPTRESS	JAP	Eastman Color
THIS ANGRY AGE	COL	Technicolor
THIS HAPPY FEELING	UN	Pathecolor
TICHY DON	RUS	Sovcolor
A TIME TO LOVE AND A TIME TO DIE	UN	Eastman Color
TOM THUMB	MGM	Metrocolor
TONKA	BV	Technicolor
TOSCA	ITA	Eastman Color
TORPEDO RUN	MGM	Metrocolor
LA TOUR, PRENDS GARDE	FRA-ITA-YUG	Eastman Color
LE TRIPORTEUR	FRA	Technicolor
TRUTH ABOUT WOMEN	BRI	Eastman Color
TWILIGHT FOR THE GODS	UN	Eastman Color
UNE VIE (A LIFE)	FRA	Eastman Color
LA VENGANZA	SPA	Eastman Color
VERTIGO	PAR	Technicolor
THE VIKINGS	UA	Technicolor
VIRGIN ISLAND	BRI	unknown
WAR OF THE COLOSSAL BEAST	AI	Pathecolor
WHITE WILDERNESS	BV	Technicolor
WIEN, DU STADT MEINER TRAEUME	AUS	Agfacolor
WILD HERITAGE	UN	Eastman Color
WIND ACROSS THE EVERGLADES	WB	WarnerColor
THE WIND CANNOT READ	BRI	Eastman Color
WINDOM'S WAY	BRI	Eastman Color

1959

ALIAS JESSE JAMES	UA	Technicolor
THE AMBITIOUS ONE	FRA	Eastman Color
AMONG THE HEADHUNTERS	BRI	Eastman Color
THE ANGRY RED PLANET	IND	Eastman Color
ANTARCTIC CROSSING	BRI	Eastman Color
APRIL IN PORTUGAL (LA GRAN SENORA)	SPA	Eastman Color
ASK ANY GIRL	MGM	Metrocolor
AT RISK OF LIFE	RUS	Sovcolor
BABETTE GOES TO WAR	COL	Eastman Color
THE BANDIT OF ZHOBE	COL	Eastman Color
THE BEAUTIFUL ADVENTURE	GER	Agfacolor
BEHIND THE GREAT WALL	IND	DeLuxe Color
BELL, BOOK AND CANDLE	COL	Technicolor

BELOVED INFIDEL	TCF	DeLuxe Color
BEN-HUR	MGM	Technicolor
THE BEST OF EVERYTHING	TCF	DeLuxe Color
THE BIG CIRCUS	AA	Technicolor
THE BIG FISHERMAN	BV	Technicolor
BLACK ORPHEUS (ORFEO NEGRO)	FRA	Eastman Color
THE BLUE ANGEL	TCF	DeLuxe Color
BORN TO LOVE	MEX	unknown
THE BRIDAL PATH	BRI	Technicolor
THE BROKEN TALISMAN	IRAN	Agfacolor
BUEHNE FREI FUER MARIKA	GER	Eastman Color
CALYPSO	ITA-FRA	Eastman Color
CAMPBELL'S KINGDOM	BRI	Eastman Color
THE CAPTAIN'S TABLE	BRI	Eastman Color
CARAVAN TO RUSSIA	RUS	Sovcolor
CARMEN OF GRANADA	SPA	Eastman Color
CASH McCALL	WB	Technicolor
CHRISTINE	FRA	Eastman Color
COLLEGE BOARDING HOUSE	SPA	Eastman Color
COSTA AZZURRA	ITA	Eastman Color
COUNT YOUR BLESSINGS	MGM	Metrocolor
LA CUCURACHA	SPA	Eastman Color
DEATH IN THE SADDLE	CZE	Agfacolor
THE DEVIL'S PASS	FRA	Eastman Color
A DOG OF FLANDERS	TCF	DeLuxe Color
A DOUBLE TOUR	FRA	Eastman Color
DUBROVSKY	YUG-ITA	Eastman Color
800 LEAGUES ON THE AMAZON	MEX	unknown
THE EIGHTH DAY OF THE WEEK (sequence)	GER	Agfacolor
THE ENCHANTED MIRROR	RUS	Sovcolor
EUROPE BY NIGHT	FRA-ITA	Eastman Color
EVA	AUS	Agfacolor
THE FBI STORY	WB	Technicolor
FACE OF A FUGITIVE	COL	Eastman Color
FELICIDAD (HAPPINESS)	MEX	unknown
FERRY TO HONG KONG	BRI	Eastman Color
THE FIVE PENNIES	PAR	Technicolor
FLAME OVER INDIA	BRI	Eastman Color
THE FLYING FONTAINES	COL	Eastman Color
FOR THE FIRST TIME	MGM	Technicolor
FORBIDDEN ISLAND	COL	Columbia Color
4-D MAN	UN	DeLuxe Color
FOUR OF THE MOANA	FRA	Ansco Color
GIDGET	COL	Pathecolor
THE GOLDEN AGE OF FLEMISH PAINTING	HOL	Gevacolor
GOLIATH AND THE BARBARIANS	AI	Eastman Color
GREAT IS MY COUNTRY	RUS	Sovcolor
GREEN MANSIONS	MGM	Metrocolor
THE GREEN MARE	FRA	Eastman Color
GUNFIGHT AT DODGE CITY	UA	DeLuxe Color
THE GUNMAN FROM LAREDO	COL	Columbia Color
GUNSMOKE IN TUCSON	AA	DeLuxe Color
THE GYPSY CARON	GER	Eastman Color
THE H-MAN	COL	Eastman Color
A HANDFUL OF GRAIN	INDIA	Technicolor
THE HANGING TREE	WB	Technicolor
HELDEN (HEROES)	GER	Agfacolor
HELL BENT FOR LEATHER	UN	Eastman Color
HERCULES	WB	Pathecolor
HERCULES AND THE QUEEN OF LYDIA	FRA	Eastman Color
HOLE IN THE HEAD	UA	Eastman Color
HOLIDAY FOR LOVERS	TCF	DeLuxe Color
HORRORS OF THE BLACK MUSEUM	AI	Eastman Color
THE HORSE SOLDIERS	UA	DeLuxe Color

THE HOUND DOG MAN	TCF	DeLuxe Color
THE HOUND OF THE BASKERVILLES	UA	Technicolor
THE HOUSE OF INTRIGUE	AA	Ferraniacolor
THE HOUSE OF THE SEVEN HAWKS	MGM	tinted
THE HOUSE OF THE THREE GIRLS	AUS	Agfacolor
THE IDEAL WOMAN	GER	Agfacolor
THE IDIOT	RUS	Sovcolor
I'LL CARRY YOU ON MY HANDS	GER	Agfacolor
ILYA MOUROMETZ (see THE SWORD AND THE DRAGON)		
IMITATION OF LIFE	UN	Eastman Color
INDIA	INDIA	Gevacolor
THE INDIAN TOMB (DAS INDISCHE GRABMAL)	GER	Eastman Color
INVITATION TO MONTE CARLO	BRI	Technicolor
ISLAND FISHERMEN	FRA	Eastman Color
IT HAPPENED TO JANE	COL	Pathecolor
IT STARTED WITH A KISS	MGM	Metrocolor
JAZZ ON A SUMMER'S DAY	IND	Eastman Color
THE JAYHAWKERS	PAR	Technicolor
JOHN PAUL JONES	WB	Technicolor
LE JOUEUR (THE GAMBLER)	FRA	Eastman Color
THE JOURNEY	MGM	Metrocolor
JOURNEY TO THE CENTER OF THE EARTH	TCF	DeLuxe Color
KING OF THE WILD STALLIONS	AA	DeLuxe Color
LAST TRAIN FROM GUN HILL	PAR	Technicolor
LI'L ABNER	PAR	Technicolor
THE MAN WHO COULD CHEAT DEATH	PAR	Technicolor
THE MAN WHO UNDERSTOOD WOMEN	TCF	DeLuxe Color
MASTERS OF THE CONGO JUNGLE	BEL	Eastman Color
THE MATING GAME	MGM	Metrocolor
MEETINGS WITH THE DEVIL	FRA	Agfacolor
MEUS AMORES NO RIO	BRA	Agfacolor
A MIDSUMMER NIGHT'S DREAM	CZE	Eastman Color
THE MIRACLE	WB	Technicolor
MISS APRIL	SWE	Eastman Color
MISS CUPLE	SPA	Agfacolor
MISS STONE	YUG	Eastman Color
THE MOUSE THAT ROARED	COL	Pathecolor
THE MUMMY	UN	Technicolor
THE MYSTERIANS	JAP	Eastman Color
THE NAKED MAJA	UA	Technicolor
NEVER SO FEW	MGM	Metrocolor
NEVER STEAL ANYTHING SMALL	UN	Eastman Color
NORTH BY NORTHWEST	MGM	Technicolor
NORTHWEST FRONTIER (see FLAME OVER INDIA)		
THE NUDE GENERAL	JAP	Eastman Color
NUDIST PARADISE	BRI	Eastman Color
THE NUN'S STORY	WB	Technicolor
1001 ARABIAN NIGHTS	COL	Technicolor
OPERATION BULLSHINE	BRI	unknown
OPERATION PETTICOAT	UN	Eastman Color
THE OREGON TRAIL	TCF	DeLuxe Color
ORFEO NEGRO (see BLACK ORPHEUS)		
PARADISE AND MELTING POT	GER	Agfacolor
PASSPORT FOR THE WORLD	FRA	Eastman Color
LA PETITE	BUL	unknown
PILLOW TALK	UN	Eastman Color
POISON AT 2:30	SPA	Eastman Color
POLICARPO	ITA-FRA-SPA	Eastman Color
PORGY AND BESS	COL	Technicolor
POWER AMONG MEN	IND	Eastman Color
A PRIVATE'S AFFAIR	TCF	DeLuxe Color
THE RAGPICKER'S ANGEL	JAP	Agfacolor
THE REMARKABLE MR. PENNYPACKER	TCF	DeLuxe Color

RETIRO PARK	SPA-ITA	Agfacolor
RHAPSODIA PORTUGUESA	SPA	Eastman Color
RIDE LONESOME	COL	Pathecolor
RIO BRAVO	WB	Technicolor
THE SAD HORSE	TCF	DeLuxe Color
ST. VALENTINE'S DAY	SPA	Eastman Color
SAPPHIRE	BRI	Eastman Color
SAY ONE FOR ME	TCF	DeLuxe Color
SCENT OF MYSTERY	IND	Technicolor
DER SCHINDERHANNES	GER	Eastman Color
SERENADE OF A GREAT LOVE	GER	Technicolor
SHE GODS OF SHARK REEF	AI	Pathecolor
SIGN OF THE GLADIATOR	AI	Pathecolor
SLEEPING BEAUTY	BV	Technicolor
SMALL DRAMAS	POL	Agfacolor
THE SNOW QUEEN	UN	Eastman Color
SOLOMON AND SHEBA	UA	Technicolor
SON OF ROBIN HOOD	BRI	Eastman Color
SONATAS	SPA	Eastman Color
THE SOUND AND THE FURY	TCF	DeLuxe Color
THE STAR GOES TO THE SOUTH	YUG-CZE	Agfacolor
A SUMMER PLACE	WB	Technicolor
THE SWORD AND THE DRAGON	RUS	Technicolor
TANK FORCE (NO TIME TO DIE)	BRI	Technicolor
TARZAN'S GREATEST ADVENTURE	PAR	Eastman Color
THEY CAME TO CORDURA	COL	Eastman Color
THESE THOUSAND HILLS	TCF	DeLuxe Color
THIRD MAN ON THE MOUNTAIN	BV	Technicolor
THIS EARTH IS MINE	UN	Technicolor
THIS WAS PANCHO VILLA	MEX	unknown
THUNDER IN THE SUN	PAR	Technicolor
THE TINGLER (sequences)	COL	Eastman Color
TOBY TYLER	BV	Technicolor
TOMMY THE TOREADOR	BRI	Technicolor
THE TRAP	PAR	Technicolor
TREICHVILLE	FRA	Agfacolor
12 GIRLS AND ONE MAN	AUS	Agfacolor
THE UNFORGETTABLE ROAD	JAP	Eastman Color
UP AND DOWN	MEX	Eastman Color
UP PERISCOPE	WB	Technicolor
UPSTAIRS AND DOWNSTAIRS	BRI	Eastman Color
VARGAS INN	SPA	Eastman Color
VENETIAN HONEYMOON	SPA	Eastman Color
VIRGIN SACRIFICE	IND	Tropi-Color
WARLOCK	TCF	DeLuxe Color
THE WARRIOR AND THE SLAVE GIRL	COL	Eastman Color
WATUSI	MGM	Technicolor
WEAK WOMEN	FRA	Eastman Color
WESTBOUND	WB	WarnerColor
WHIRLPOOL	BRI	unknown
THE WHITE HERON	JAP	Agfacolor
THE WILD AND THE INNOCENT	UN	Eastman Color
WILD RAPTURE	UN	Eastman Color
THE WOMAN AND THE PUPPET	FRA	Eastman Color
A WOMAN OBSESSED	TCF	DeLuxe Color
THE WONDERFUL COUNTRY	UA	Technicolor
THE WRECK OF THE MARY DEARE	MGM	Metrocolor
YELLOWSTONE KELLY	WB	WarnerColor
THE YOUNG LAND	COL	Technicolor
ZAFRA	ARG	Agfacolor

1960

ADVENTURES OF HUCKLEBERRY FINN	MGM	Metrocolor
ADVENTURES OF JOSELITO AND TOM THUMB	MEX	Eastman Color

THE ALAMO	UA	Technicolor
ALL THE FINE YOUNG CANNIBALS	MGM	Metrocolor
AMERICA AS SEEN BY A FRENCHMAN	FRA	Eastman Color
AND QUIET FLOWS THE DON	RUS	Sovcolor
ANGRY ISLAND	JAP	Eastman Color
ASHES OF MEMORY	ITA	Ferraniacolor
AUSTERLITZ	FRA-ITA-YUG	Eastman Color
THE BATTLE FOR OUTER SPACE	JAP	Eastman Color
BELLES AND BALLETS	FRA	Eastman Color
BELLS ARE RINGING	MGM	Metrocolor
BLAZING SAND	ISR	Eastman Color
BLOOD AND ROSES	FRA-ITA	Technicolor
THE BOY AND THE PIRATES	UA	Eastman Color
THE BRAMBLE BUSH	WB	Technicolor
A BREATH OF SCANDAL	PAR	Eastman Color
THE BRIDES OF DRACULA	UI	Technicolor
BUTTERFIELD 8	MGM	Metrocolor
CAN-CAN	TCF	Technicolor
LE CAPITAN	FRA	Eastman Color
THE CAPTAIN FROM COLOGNE	GER	Agfacolor
CAPTAIN LESKI	YUG	Agfacolor
CHARLESTON	MEX	Eastman Color
CIMARRON	MGM	Metrocolor
CINDERFELLA	PAR	Technicolor
CIRCUS OF HORRORS	AI	Eastman Color
CIRCUS STARS	RUS	Sovcolor
COMANCHE STATION	COL	Eastman Color
THE COSSACKS	ITA	Technicolor
THE CROSS OF ST. ANNE	RUS	Sovcolor
THE CROWDED SKY	WB	Technicolor
THE CROWNING EXPERIENCE	IND	Technicolor
CRY FOR HAPPY	COL	Eastman Color
THE DARK AT THE TOP OF THE STAIRS	WB	Technicolor
THE DEAD ONE	IND	unknown
THE DEAR AUGUSTIN	GER	Agfacolor
DINOSAURUS!	UN	DeLuxe Color
DOCTOR IN LOVE	BRI	Technicolor
DREAMS CAME BY COACH	YUG	Eastman Color
ELMER GANTRY	UA	Technicolor
THE EMPTY CHAIR	MEX	Eastman Color
THE ENCHANTING SHADOW	FOR	Eastman Color
ESTHER AND THE KING	TCF	Technicolor
EXODUS	UA	Technicolor
THE FABULOUS SOUTH SEAS	GER	Agfacolor
FAITH, HOPE AND WITCHCRAFT	DEN	Eastman Color
FAST AND SEXY (ANNA FROM BROOKLYN)	COL	Technirama
FAUST	GER	Agfacolor
FLAMING STAR	TCF	DeLuxe Color
FOR THE LOVE OF MIKE	TCF	DeLuxe Color
FORBIDDEN SANDS	JAP	Shokitu Color
FRECKLES	TCF	DeLuxe Color
FROM THE TERRACE	TCF	DeLuxe Color
G. I. BLUES	PAR	Technicolor
GIANT OF THE VALLEY OF THE KINGS	IND	Eastman Color
A GIRL FOR THE SUMMER	FRA	Eastman Color
A GLASS OF WATER	GER	unknown
THE GRASS IS GREENER	UN	Technicolor
GUNS OF THE TIMBERLAND	WB	Technicolor
HANNIBAL	WB	WarnerColor
THE HAUNTED CASTLE	BER	Agfacolor
HEAD OF A TYRANT	ITA	Ferraniacolor
HEAVEN ON EARTH	ITA	Eastman Color
HELLER IN PINK TIGHTS	PAR	Technicolor
HERITAGE OF BJOERNDAL	AUS	unknown

HIGH TIME	TCF	DeLuxe Color
HEROD THE GREAT	AA	Eastman Color
HOME FROM THE HILL	MGM	Metrocolor
THE HOUND THAT THOUGHT HE WAS A RACCOON	BV	Technicolor
THE HOUSE OF USHER	AI	Pathecolor
THE HUNCHBACK	FRA	Eastman Color
I, SINNER	MEX	Eastman Color
ICE PALACE	WB	Technicolor
THE IMMORAL MR. TEAS	IND	Eastman Color
IT STARTED IN NAPLES	PAR	Technicolor
JACK THE RIPPER (sequence)	BRI	Eastman Color
JOHYO	JAP	Eastman Color
JOURNEY TO THE LOST CITY	AI	Eastman Color
JUNGLE CAT	BV	Technicolor
KATIA	FRA	Eastman Color
THE KEY (KAGI)	JAP	Agfacolor
KIDNAPPED	BV	Technicolor
KNIGHTS OF THE TEUTONIC ORDER	POL	Eastman Color
THE LAST DAYS OF POMPEII	UA	Eastman Color
THE LAST VOYAGE	MGM	Metrocolor
THE LAST WOMAN ON EARTH	IND	Eastman Color
LEDA (WEB OF PASSION)	FRA	Technicolor
LEGIONS OF THE NILE	TCF	DeLuxe Color
LITTLE RED RIDING HOOD	MEX	Eastman Color
THE LOST WORLD	TCF	DeLuxe Color
MACUMBA LOVE	UA	Eastman Color
THE MAGNIFICENT SEVEN	UA	DeLuxe Color
MARIE OF THE ISLES	FRA	Eastman Color
THE MARRIAGE-GO-ROUND	TCF	DeLuxe Color
MIDNIGHT LACE	UN	Eastman Color
THE MILLIONAIRESS	TCF	DeLuxe Color
MY SLAVE	THA	Kodachrome
THE NIGHTS OF LUCRETIA BORGIA	ITA	Eastman Color
NORTH TO ALASKA	TCF	DeLuxe Color
OCEAN'S 11	WB	Technicolor
ONCE MORE WITH FEELING	COL	Technicolor
ONE FOOT IN HELL	TCF	DeLuxe Color
ONE, TWO, THREE, FOUR	FRA	Technicolor
PANCHO VILLA Y LA VALENTINA	MEX	Eastman Color
PAW	DEN	Eastman Color
PEEPING TOM	BRI	Eastman Color
PEPE	COL	Technicolor
THE PIONEERS	FRA-BRA	Eastman Color
PLEASE DON'T EAT THE DAISIES	MGM	Metrocolor
POEM OF THE SEA	RUS	Sovcolor
PORTRAIT IN BLACK	UN	Eastman Color
PRISONER OF THE VOLGA	FRA-ITA	Eastman Color
PURPLE NOON	FRA	Eastman Color
THE RAT RACE	PAR	Technicolor
THE REGATTAS OF SAN FRANCISCO	FRA	Eastman Color
THE RIGHT OF MAN	FRA	Eastman Color
THE ROYAL BALLET	BRI	Eastman Color
THE SAND CASTLE (sequences)	IND	Eastman Color
SANDS OF THE DESERT	BRI	unknown
THE SAVAGE INNOCENTS	PAR	Technicolor
SANTA CLAUS	MEX	Eastman Color
LE SECRET DE CHEVALIER D'EON	FRA	Eastman Color
THE SECRET OF THE PURPLE REEF	TCF	DeLuxe Color
SEPTEMBER STORM	TCF	DeLuxe Color
SINS OF RACHEL CADE	WB	WarnerColor
A SONG TO REMEMBER	MEX	Eastman Color
SONG WITHOUT END	COL	Pathecolor
SORCERER'S VILLAGE	IND	Pathecolor
SPARTACUS	UN	Technicolor

SPRING AFFAIR	IND	tinted
STARS AT NOON	FRA	Eastman Color
THE STORY OF RUTH	TCF	DeLuxe Color
STRANGERS WHEN WE MEET	COL	Eastman Color
THE SUBTERRANEANS	MGM	Metrocolor
SUNRISE AT CAMPOBELLO	WB	Technicolor
THE SUPER HE-MAN	MEX	Eastman Color
SWAN LAKE	RUS	Eastman Color
SWISS FAMILY ROBINSON	WB	Technicolor
THE SWORD AND THE CROSS	ITA	Ferraniacolor
SWORD OF SHERWOOD FOREST	COL	Eastman Color
TARZAN THE MAGNIFICENT	PAR	Eastman Color
TELEGRAMS	ROU	Ansco Color
TEN WHO DARED	BV	Technicolor
THE THIEF IN THE BEDROOM	SWE	Eastman Color
THIRTEEN GHOSTS (sequences)	COL	Eastman Color
THE THREE TREASURES	JAP	Agfacolor
THIS LOVE AT THE END OF THE WORLD	ARG-ITA	Ferraniacolor
THUNDER IN CAROLINA	IND	Eastman Color
THE 3 WORLDS OF GULLIVER	COL	Eastman Color
THE TIME MACHINE	MGM	Metrocolor
TOO HOT TO HANDLE	BRI	unknown
TOSCA	ITA	unknown
THE TRIALS OF OSCAR WILDE (THE GREEN CARNATION)	BRI	Technicolor
TUNES OF GLORY	BRI	Technicolor
TWO FACES OF DR. JEKYLL	BRI	Technicolor
THE UNFORGIVEN	UA	Technicolor
UTAMARO, PAINTER OF WOMEN	JAP	Daiei Color
VOYAGE IN A BALLOON	FRA	Eastman Color
THE WACKIEST SHIP IN THE ARMY	COL	Eastman Color
WAKE ME WHEN IT'S OVER	TCF	DeLuxe Color
WALK TALL	TCF	DeLuxe Color
WHEN THE BELLS SOUND CLEARLY	AUS	Eastman Color
WHEN THE WOMAN BUTTS IN	CZE	Ansco Color
WHERE THE BOYS ARE	MGM	Metrocolor
WILD RIVER	TCF	DeLuxe Color
WILLIAM TELL	SWI	unknown
WITHOUT TRUMPET OR DRUM	FRA-GER	Eastman Color
THE WIZARD OF BAGHDAD	TCF	DeLuxe Color
THE WORLD AT NIGHT	WB	Technicolor
THE WORLD OF SUZIE WONG	PAR	Technicolor
YEARS OF YOUTH	RUS	Sovcolor
ZAZIE	FRA	Eastman Color

1961

ADA	MGM	Metrocolor
ALAKAZAM THE GREAT	JAP	Eastman Color
ALL HANDS ON DECK	TCF	DeLuxe Color
ALL IN A NIGHT'S WORK	PAR	Technicolor
ATLANTIS, THE LOST CONTINENT	MGM	Metrocolor
BABES IN TOYLAND	BV	Technicolor
BACHELOR FLAT	TCF	DeLuxe Color
BACHELOR IN PARADISE	MGM	Metrocolor
BACK STREET	UN	Eastman Color
THE BATTLE AT BLOODY BEACH	TCF	DeLuxe Color
THE BEST OF ENEMIES	COL	unknown
THE BIG GAMBLE	TCF	Eastman Color
THE BIG SHOW	TCF	DeLuxe Color
BIMBO THE GREAT	GER	Eastman Color
BLACK SILK	UA	DeLuxe Color
BLUE HAWAII	PAR	Technicolor
BREAKFAST AT TIFFANY'S	PAR	Technicolor
BY LOVE POSSESSED	UA	DeLuxe Color
CALL ME GENIUS	BRI	Technicolor

THE CANADIANS	TCF	DeLuxe Color
THE CANANEA PRISON	MEX	Eastman Color
CAPTAIN FRICASSE	FRA	Eastman Color
CARTHAGE IN FLAMES	FRA-ITA	Technicolor
EL CID	AA	Technicolor
CINDERELLA	RUS	Sovcolor
CLEAR SKIES	RUS	Sovcolor
THE COLOSSUS OF RHODES	ITA	Eastman Color
THE COMANCHEROS	TCF	DeLuxe Color
COME SEPTEMBER	UN	Technicolor
THE COSSACKS	RUS	Sovcolor
CURSE OF THE WEREWOLF	UN	Eastman Color
DARCLEE	ROU	Agfacolor
DAVID AND GOLIATH	AA	Eastman Color
THE DEADLY COMPANIONS	IND	Pathecolor
DESCRIPTION D'UN COMBAT	ISR	Eastman Color
DESERT WARRIOR	ITA-SPA	Eastman Color
THE DEVIL AT 4 O'CLOCK	COL	Eastman Color
DR. BLOOD'S COFFIN	BRI	Eastman Color
DON'T BOTHER TO KNOCK	BRI	Eastman Color
DREAMLAND OF DESIRE	GER	Agfacolor
DYNAMITE JACK	FRA	Eastman Color
THE END OF THE CANGACIEROS	BRA	Eastman Color
EVE AND THE HANDYMAN	IND	Eastman Color
THE FALSE STUDENT	JAP	Eastman Color
FAMOUS LOVE AFFAIRS	FRA	Eastman Color
FANNY	WB	Technicolor
THE FIERCEST HEART	TCF	DeLuxe Color
FIVE DAYS — FIVE NIGHTS	RUS-GER	Sovcolor
THE FLOWER DRUM SONG	UN	Technicolor
FRANCIS OF ASSISI	TCF	DeLuxe Color
GHOSTS IN ROME	ITA	Technicolor
GIDGET GOES HAWAIIAN	COL	Pathecolor
GOLIATH AND THE DRAGON	AI	Pathecolor
GORGO	MGM	Technicolor
THE GREAT OLYMPIAD	ITA	Eastman Color
GREYFRIAR'S BOBBY	BV	Technicolor
THE GUNS OF NAVARONE	COL	Eastman Color
GUNS OF THE BLACK WITCH	ITA	Pathecolor
THE HELLIONS	BRI	Technicolor
HIPPODROME	GER	Eastman Color
THE HONEYMOON MACHINE	MGM	Metrocolor
THE HUMAN PYRAMID	FRA	Eastman Color
I BOMBED PEARL HARBOR	JAP	Technicolor
THE ILLITERATE ONE	MEX	Eastman Color
I LOVE, YOU LOVE	FRA	Technicolor
JUANA GALLO	MEX	Eastman Color
KING IN SHADOW	GER	Agfacolor
KING OF KINGS	MGM	Technicolor
THE KING'S NEW CLOTHES	YUG	Eastman Color
KONGA	AI	Eastman Color
THE LADIES' MAN	PAR	Technicolor
THE LAST JUDGMENT (sequences)	FRA-ITA	Eastman Color
THE LAST REBEL	MEX	Eastman Color
THE LAST SUNSET	UN	Eastman Color
LITTLE RED RIDING HOOD AND HER THREE FRIENDS	MEX	Eastman Color
THE LITTLE SHEPHERD OF KINGDOM COME	TCF	DeLuxe Color
LOSS OF INNOCENCE	BRI	Eastman Color
LOVE AND THE FRENCHWOMAN (sequence)	FRA	Eastman Color
LOVE IN A GOLDFISH BOWL	PAR	Technicolor
LOVER COME BACK	UN	Eastman Color
MAEVA	IND	Ansco Color
MAGIC BOY	JAP	Magicolor
A MAJORITY OF ONE	WB	Technicolor

THE MAGIC FOUNTAIN	IND	Eastman Color
MARINES, LET'S GO	TCF	DeLuxe Color
THE MASK (sequences)	WB	Eastman Color
MASTER OF THE WORLD	AI	Pathecolor
MEXICO, LINDO Y QUERIDO	MEX	Eastman Color
THE MIGHTY CRUSADERS	ITA	Ferraniacolor
THE MINOTAUR	ITA	Technicolor
THE MIRACLE OF THE WOLVES	ITA	Eastman Color
MR. TOPAZE (I LIKE MONEY)	BRI	Technicolor
MISTY	TCF	DeLuxe Color
MORGAN THE PIRATE	MGM	Eastman Color
MYSTERIOUS ISLAND	COL	Eastman Color
NAKED TERROR	IND	Eastman Color
NATURE GIRL AND THE SLAVER	GER	Eastman Color
NIKKI, WILD DOG OF THE NORTH	BV	Technicolor
NOT TONIGHT, HENRY	IND	Eastman Color
NUDE ODYSSEY	FRA-ITA	Eastman Color
OF STARS AND MEN	IND	Eastman Color
OJOS TAPATIOS	MEX	Eastman Color
OLE REX	UN	Eastman Color
ON THE DOUBLE	PAR	Technicolor
ONE-EYED JACKS	PAR	Technicolor
ONE HUNDRED AND ONE DALMATIANS	BV	Technicolor
OTOTO (HER BROTHER)	JAP	Agfacolor
L'OURS (BEARS)	FRA	Eastman Color
THE PARENT TRAP	BV	Technicolor
PARRISH	WB	Technicolor
PETTICOAT PIRATES	BRI	unknown
THE PHARAOH'S WOMAN	UN	Eastman Color
THE PIRATE AND THE SLAVE GIRL	ITA	Ferraniacolor
THE PIT AND THE PENDULUM	AI	Pathecolor
THE PLEASURE OF HIS COMPANY	PAR	Technicolor
THE PIRATE OF BLACK HAWK	ITA	Ferraniacolor
PIRATES OF TORTUGA	TCF	DeLuxe Color
POCKETFUL OF MIRACLES	UA	Eastman Color
POSSE FROM HELL	UN	Eastman Color
POVESTJ PLAMENNYKH LET	RUS	Sovcolor
THE PRINCESS OF CLEVES	FRA	Eastman Color
THE PRIVATE LIFE OF ADAM AND EVE	UN	Spectacolor
THE PURPLE HILLS	TCF	DeLuxe Color
PUSS IN BOOTS	MEX	Eastman Color
THE QUEEN OF SPADES	RUS	Sovcolor
QUEEN OF THE PIRATES	ITA	Eastman Color
THE QUEEN'S GUARDS	BRI	Technicolor
RAISING THE WIND	BRI	Technicolor
THE RAPE OF THE SABINES	FRA-ITA	Eastman Color
THE RED CLOAK	ITA	Ferraniacolor
RETURN TO PEYTON PLACE	TCF	DeLuxe Color
A REVOLUTIONARY FAMILY	CHI	unknown
RING OF FIRE	MGM	Metrocolor
RITUAL OF LOVE	ITA-FRA	Eastman Color
THE ROMAN SPRING OF MRS. STONE	WB	Technicolor
ROMANOFF AND JULIET	UN	Technicolor
ROMMELL'S TREASURE	ITA	Technicolor
SCARLET SAILS	RUS	Sovcolor
SACRED WATERS	SWI-GER	unknown
THE SACRELIGIOUS HERO	JAP	Eastman Color
SAINT TROPEZ BLUES	FRA	Eastman Color
SAKYA (BUDDHA)	JAP	Eastman Color
THE SECOND TIME AROUND	TCF	DeLuxe Color
THE SECRET OF MONTE CRISTO	BRI	Eastman Color
SERENGETI SHALL NOT DIE	AA	Eastman Color
THE SIN OF MONA KENT	IND	DeLuxe Color

THE SINGER NOT THE SONG	BRI	Eastman Color
THE SKY ABOVE AND THE MUD BELOW	FRA	Agfacolor
SNOW WHITE AND THE 3 STOOGES	TCF	DeLuxe Color
SONG OF THE WOODS	RUS	Sovcolor
SPLENDOR IN THE GRASS	WB	Technicolor
THE STEEL CLAW	WB	Technicolor
THE STORY OF CHOONHYANG	KOR	Agfacolor
SUMMER AND SMOKE	PAR	Technicolor
SUN LOVER'S HOLIDAY	BRI	DeLuxe Color
SUSAN SLADE	WB	Technicolor
THE TAI WOMAN DOCTOR	CHI	Sovcolor
TAMMY TELL ME TRUE	UN	Eastman Color
TESS OF THE STORM COUNTRY	TCF	DeLuxe Color
THE THREE MUSKETEERS	FRA	Eastman Color
THE THIEF OF BAGDAD	ITA	DeLuxe Color
THREE TALES OF CHEKHOV (sequences)	RUS	Sovcolor
A THUNDER OF DRUMS	MGM	Metrocolor
THE TOUCHABLES	IND	Eastman Color
TWO LOVES	MGM	Metrocolor
TWO RODE TOGETHER	COL	Eastman Color
20,000 LEAGUES ACROSS THE EARTH	FRA-RUS	Sovcolor
UPSTAIRS AND DOWNSTAIRS	BRI	DeLuxe Color
VACATIONS IN ACAPULCO	MEX	Eastman Color
VANINA VANINI	FRA-ITA	Technicolor
VIVA JALISCO, QUE ES MI TERRA	MEX	Eastman Color
VIVE HENRI IV, VIVE L'AMOUR	FRA	Eastman Color
VOYAGE TO THE BOTTOM OF THE SEA	TCF	DeLuxe Color
WAKE UP, DEAR	FRA	Eastman Color
THE WARRIOR EMPRESS	COL	Eastman Color
WEST SIDE STORY	UA	Technicolor
WHITE NIGHTS	RUS	Sovcolor
THE WHITE WARRIOR	WB	Technicolor
WILD IN THE COUNTRY	TCF	DeLuxe Color
WINGS OF CHANCE	UN	Eastman Color
A WOMAN IS ALWAYS A WOMAN	FRA	Eastman Color
THE WONDERS OF ALADDIN	MGM	Eastman Color
THE WORLD BY NIGHT	WB	Technicolor
X-15	UA	Technicolor
THE YOUNG ONES	BRI	Eastman Color

1962

ADVENTURES OF A YOUNG MAN	TCF	DeLuxe Color
ALMOST ANGELS	BV	Technicolor
AXEL MUNTHE, DOCTOR OF SAN MICHELE	GER-ITA	unknown
LA BANDIDA	MEX	Eastman Color
BARABBAS	COL	Technicolor
BARON MUENCHAUSEN	CZE	Agfacolor
BIG RED	BV	Technicolor
BIRD OF PARADISE	FRA	Eastman Color
BOCCACCIO '70	ITA	Technicolor
BON VOYAGE	BV	Technicolor
BOY'S NIGHT OUT	MGM	Metrocolor
CARRY ON CRUISING	BRI	Eastman Color
CARTOUCHE	FRA	Eastman Color
CHALLENGE TO LIVE	JAP	Eastman Color
THE CHAPMAN REPORT	WB	Technicolor
CLEO FROM 5 TO 7 (sequence)	FRA	Eastman Color
CLEOPATRA'S DAUGHTER	FRA-ITA	Eastman Color
CONGEHOVDINGEN (THE MUSKETEERS)	DEN	Agfacolor
CONSTANTINE AND THE CROSS	ITA	Eastman Color
THE COUNT OF MONTE CRISTO	FRA	Eastman Color
THE COUNTERFEIT TRAITOR	PAR	Technicolor
DAMN THE DEFIANT!	BRI	Technicolor
DAMON AND PYTHIAS	MGM	Eastman Color

DANCE WITH ME INTO THE MORNING	AUS	Agfacolor
DANGEROUS CHARTER	IND	Technicolor
THE DAY THE EARTH STOOD STILL	UN	tinted
DIAMOND HEAD	COL	Eastman Color
DR. NO	BRI	Technicolor
THE DOLL	FRA	Eastman Color
EMBRACE OF FATE	THA	Kodachrome
END OF DESIRE	FRA	Eastman Color
ESCAPE FROM ZAHRAIN	PAR	Technicolor
EVERYMAN	AUS	Agfacolor
THE EXTRA	MEX	Eastman Color
A FAMILY DIARY	ITA	Technicolor
THE FIRST SPACESHIP ON VENUS	IND	Technicolor
FIVE WEEKS IN A BALLOON	TCF	DeLuxe Color
FLAMING SUN	MEX	Eastman Color
FOLLOW THAT DREAM	UA	DeLuxe Color
FOREVER MY LOVE	GER	Technicolor
40 POUNDS OF TROUBLE	UN	Eastman Color
FOUR HORSEMEN OF THE APOCALYPSE	MGM	Metrocolor
GALAPAGOS	GER	Agfacolor
GAY PURR-EE	WB	Technicolor
GERONIMO	UA	Technicolor
GIGOT	TCF	DeLuxe Color
A GIRL NAMED TAMIKO	PAR	Technicolor
GIRLS, GIRLS, GIRLS	PAR	Technicolor
GO TO BLAZES	BRI	Eastman Color
THE GRASS CUTTERS	JAP	Eastman Color
GYPSY	WB	Technicolor
THE GYPSY BARON	GER	Agfacolor
HATARI!	PAR	Technicolor
HERO'S ISLAND	UA	Technicolor
THE HORIZONTAL LIEUTENANT	MGM	Metrocolor
A HOUSE OF SAND	IND	Eastman Color
HOW THE WEST WAS WON	MGM	Technicolor
I, TOO, AM ONLY A WOMAN	GER	Agfacolor
I THANK A FOOL	MGM	Metrocolor
IF A MAN ANSWERS	UN	Eastman Color
IN SEARCH OF THE CASTAWAYS	BV	Technicolor
IT HAPPENED IN ATHENS	TCF	DeLuxe Color
THE IRON MASK	FRA	Eastman Color
JESSICA	UA	Technicolor
JOSEPH THE DREAMER	ISR	Eastman Color
JOURNEY TO THE SEVENTH PLANET	AI	Pathecolor
JUMBO	MGM	Metrocolor
KID GALAHAD	UA	DeLuxe Color
THE KNIGHT FROM PARDAILLAN	FRA	Eastman Color
KONGA YO	FRA	Eastman Color
LAD: A DOG	WB	Technicolor
LAFAYETTE	FRA	Technicolor
LATE SUMMER	JAP	Agfacolor
LAWRENCE OF ARABIA	COL	Technicolor
THE LEGEND OF LOBO	BV	Technicolor
A LIGHT IN THE PIAZZA	MGM	Metrocolor
THE LION	TCF	DeLuxe Color
LISA	TCF	DeLuxe Color
THE LITTLE HUMPBACK HORSE	RUS	Magicolor
LITTLE RED RIDING HOOD AND TOM THUMB AGAINST THE MONSTERS	MEX	Eastman Color
THE LOVERS OF TERUEL	FRA	Technicolor
THE LOVES OF SALAMMBO	ITA	DeLuxe Color
THE MAD FOX	JAP	Eastman Color
MADAME (MADAME SANS-GENE)	ITA-FRA-SPA	Technicolor
THE MAGIC SWORD	UA	Eastman Color
MAKE WAY FOR LILA	GER-SWE	Eastman Color

THE MAIN ATTRACTION	MGM	Metrocolor
MERMAIDS OF TIBURON	IND	Eastman Color
MERRILL'S MARAUDERS	WB	Technicolor
MR. HOBBS TAKES A VACATION	TCF	DeLuxe Color
MONDO CANE	ITA	Technicolor
MOON PILOT	BV	Technicolor
MORNING STAR	RUS	Sovcolor
MOSHI-MOSHI, HALLO, JAPAN	JAP-GER	Ansco Color
MOTHRA	JAP	Pathecolor
THE MUSIC MAN	WB	Technicolor
MUTINY ON THE BOUNTY	MGM	Technicolor
MY GEISHA	PAR	Technicolor
THE MYSTERIES OF PARIS	FRA	Eastman Color
NIGHT CREATURES	BRI	Eastman Color
NO MAN IS AN ISLAND	UN	Eastman Color
OPERATION KALIMANTAN	CZE	Agfacolor
PARIS, MY LOVE	ITA	Eastman Color
THE PHANTOM OF THE OPERA	UN	Technicolor
THE PIRATES OF BLOOD RIVER	COL	Eastman Color
PREMATURE BURIAL	AI	Pathecolor
RED SKY	MEX	Eastman Color
RIDE THE HIGH COUNTRY	MGM	Metrocolor
ROME ADVENTURE	WB	Technicolor
DER ROSENKAVALIER	BRI	Technicolor
SAMAR	WB	Technicolor
SATAN NEVER SLEEPS	TCF	DeLuxe Color
THE SAVAGE GUNS	BRI-SPA	Metrocolor
THE SECRET OF OUTER SPACE ISLAND	FRA	Eastman Color
SERGEANTS 3	UA	Technicolor
THE SIEGE OF SYRACUSE	ITA	Eastman Color
SIX BLACK HORSES	UN	Eastman Color
SODOM AND GOMORRAH	TCF	DeLuxe Color
SOME PEOPLE	BRI	Eastman Color
THE SOUND OF LIFE	RUS	Sovcolor
THE SPIRAL ROAD	UN	Eastman Color
SPRINGTIME FOR THE GIRLS	RUS	Sovcolor
STATE FAIR	TCF	DeLuxe Color
THE STEPS	ITA	Eastman Color
SWEET BIRD OF YOUTH	MGM	Metrocolor
THE SWEET NIGHTS	ITA	Eastman Color
SWINGING ALONG	TCF	DeLuxe Color
THE SWORDSMAN OF SIENA	MGM	Eastman Color
A SUMMER SUNDAY	ITA	Eastman Color
SWORD OF THE CONQUEROR	ITA	Eastman Color
TAIYO NO HAKABA (THE SUN'S BURIAL)	JAP	Eastman Color
TALES OF TERROR	AI	Pathecolor
TARAS BULBA	UA	Eastman Color
THE TARTARS	ITA	Technicolor
TARZAN GOES TO INDIA	MGM	Metrocolor
TENDER IS THE NIGHT	TCF	DeLuxe Color
THAT TOUCH OF MINK	UN	Eastman Color
THREE HENCHMEN OF LAMPAIO	BRA	Eastman Color
THE 300 SPARTANS	TCF	DeLuxe Color
TIARA TAHITI	BRI	Eastman Color
TI-KOYO AND HIS SHARK	ITA-FRA	Eastman Color
TINTIN AND THE MYSTERY OF THE GOLDEN FLEECE	FRA	Eastman Color
THE TRIUMPH OF MICHAEL STROGOFF	FRA	Eastman Color
TWO WEEKS IN ANOTHER TOWN	MGM	Metrocolor
A VERY PRIVATE AFFAIR	FRA	Eastman Color
VOLGA, VOLGA	RUS	Sovcolor
WALTZ OF THE TOREADORS	BRI	Eastman Color
WARRIOR'S REST	FRA	Eastman Color
WE JOINED THE NAVY	BRI	Eastman Color

THE WHITE HORSE	PAR	Eastman Color
WHO'S GOT THE ACTION?	PAR	Technicolor
THE WILD WESTERNERS	COL	Eastman Color
WITHOUT EACH OTHER	IND	Pathecolor
THE WONDERFUL WORLD OF THE BROTHERS GRIMM	MGM	Technicolor
THE WORLD BY NIGHT NO. 2	WB	Technicolor
THE WORLD'S GREATEST SUMMER (sequence)	IND	Eastman Color
YANG KWEI FEI	FOR	Eastman Color
THE YOUNG AND BEAUTIFUL ONES	MEX	Eastman Color
YOUNG GUNS OF TEXAS	TCF	DeLuxe Color

1963

ALVORADA	GER	Eastman Color
THE AMPHIBIOUS MAN	RUS	Sovcolor
AN AUTUMN AFTERNOON	JAP	Agfacolor
BALLAD OF A HUSSAR	RUS	Sovcolor
BEACH PARTY	AI	Pathecolor
BEING TWO ISN'T EASY	JAP	Agfacolor
THE BEST OF CINERAMA	CIN	Technicolor
THE BIG ROADS	FRA	Eastman Color
THE BIRDS	UN	Technicolor
BITTER HARVEST	BRI	Eastman Color
BLACK ZOO	AA	Eastman Color
A BLONDE LIKE THAT	FRA	Eastman Color
A BOY TEN FEET TALL	BRI	Eastman Color
BYE BYE BIRDIE	COL	Technicolor
CALL ME BWANA	UA	Eastman Color
CAPTAIN NEWMAN, M.D.	UN	Eastman Color
CAPTAIN SINBAD	MGM	Technicolor
THE CARDINAL	COL	Technicolor
CASTLE IN SWEDEN	FRA	Eastman Color
CATTLE KING	MGM	Eastman Color
THE CELESTIAN BROTHERS	RUS	Sovcolor
CHARADE	UN	Technicolor
THE CHECKERED FLAG	IND	Eastman Color
CLEOPATRA	TCF	DeLuxe Color
CODINE	ROU-FRA	Eastman Color
COME BLOW YOUR HORN	PAR	Technicolor
COME FLY WITH ME	MGM	Metrocolor
THE COURTSHIP OF EDDIE'S FATHER	MGM	Metrocolor
THE CRACKSMAN	BRI	Eastman Color
THE CREATION OF THE WORLD	FRA-CZE	unknown
CRITIC'S CHOICE	WB	Technicolor
THE DAY OF THE TRIFFIDS	AA	Eastman Color
THE DIABOLIC EMPRESS	FOR	Eastman Color
DIARY OF A MADMAN	UA	Technicolor
DOCTOR IN DISTRESS	BRI	Technicolor
DONOVAN'S REEF	PAR	Technicolor
DRUMS OF AFRICA	MGM	Metrocolor
THE FAST LADY	BRI	Technicolor
55 DAYS AT PEKING	AA	Technicolor
FLIPPER	MGM	Metrocolor
THE FLYING CLIPPER	GER	Technicolor
FOLLOW THE BOYS	MGM	Metrocolor
FOR LOVE OR MONEY	UN	Eastman Color
FOUR FOR TEXAS	WB	Technicolor
FROM RUSSIA WITH LOVE	UA	Technicolor
FROM SATURDAY TO MONDAY	ITA	Technicolor
FUN IN ACAPULCO	PAR	Technicolor
A GATHERING OF EAGLES	UN	Eastman Color
GHOST AT NOON	FRA-ITA	Technicolor
GIDGET GOES TO ROME	COL	Eastman Color
GLADIATORS 7	ITA	Technicolor
THE GREAT ESCAPE	UA	DeLuxe Color

DER GROSSE ATLANTIK	GER	Eastman Color
GUDRUN	DEN	Technicolor
THE GUN HAWK	AA	DeLuxe Color
HONOLULU-TOKYO-HONG KONG	JAP	Eastman Color
I COULD GO ON SINGING	UA	Eastman Color
IMPERIAL VENUS	ITA-FRA	Technicolor
IN THE COOL OF THE DAY	MGM	Metrocolor
THE INCREDIBLE JOURNEY	BV	Technicolor
IRMA LA DOUCE	UA	Technicolor
THE IRON MAIDEN (see THE SWINGIN' MAIDEN)		
ISLAND OF LOVE	WB	Technicolor
IT HAPPENED AT THE WORLD'S FAIR	MGM	Metrocolor
IT'S ALL HAPPENING	BRI	Eastman Color
JASON AND THE ARGONAUTS	COL	Eastman Color
THE JOHN GLENN STORY	WB	Eastman Color
KING KONG VS. GODZILLA	UN	Eastman Color
A KING WITHOUT DISTRACTIONS	FRA	Eastman Color
KINGS OF THE SUN	UA	DeLuxe Color
KISS OF THE VAMPIRE	UN	Eastman Color
KOHLHEISEL'S DAUGHTERS	GER	Agfacolor
LANDRU (BLUEBEARD)	FRA	Eastman Color
THE LEOPARD	ITA	Technicolor
LOVE IS A BALL	UA	Technicolor
McCLINTOCK	UA	Technicolor
MACBETH	IND	Technicolor
MADAME AKI	JAP	Eastman Color
MAGNET OF DOOM	FRA	Eastman Color
MANDARIN	FRA	Eastman Color
MANLOHUA	CHI	Sovcolor
MAN'S PARADISE	ITA	Technicolor
MARILYN (sequences)	TCF	DeLuxe Color
THE MARRIAGE OF FIGARO	FRA	Eastman Color
MARY MARY	WB	Technicolor
MATHIAS SANDORF	FRA	Eastman Color
MIRACLE OF THE WHITE STALLIONS	BV	Technicolor
THE MOUSE ON THE MOON	UA	Eastman Color
MOVE OVER, DARLING	TCF	DeLuxe Color
MURIEL	FRA	Eastman Color
MY HOBO	JAP	Eastman Color
MY SIX LOVES	PAR	Technicolor
MY SON, THE HERO	UA	Eastman Color
A NEW KIND OF LOVE	PAR	Technicolor
NINE HOURS TO RAMA	TCF	DeLuxe Color
THE NUTTY PROFESSOR	PAR	Technicolor
OF LOVE AND DESIRE	TCF	DeLuxe Color
ONE DAY A CAT ...	CZE	Agfacolor
OPERATION BIKINI	AI	tinted
PAPA'S DELICATE CONDITION	PAR	Technicolor
THE PRIZE	MGM	Metrocolor
RAMPAGE	WB	Technicolor
LE RAT L'AMERIQUE	FRA	Eastman Color
THE RAVEN	AI	Pathecolor
ROGOPAG	ITA	tinted
THE RUNNING MAN	BRI	Technicolor
RUSSIAN ROUNDABOUT	RUS	Sovcolor
SALADIN	EGY	Eastman Color
SAVAGE SAM	BV	Technicolor
SEVEN SEAS TO CALAIS	MGM	Eastman Color
SCHEHERAZADE	FRA	Eastman Color
SHOCK CORRIDOR (sequences)	AA	Eastman Color
SIEGE OF THE SAXONS	COL	Technicolor
THE SLAVE	ITA	Eastman Color
SNOW WHITE AND THE SEVEN JUGGLERS	SWI-GER	unknown

SPENCER'S MOUNTAIN	WB	Technicolor
STOLEN HOURS	UA	DeLuxe Color
STORIES ON THE SAND	ITA	Eastman Color
SUMMER HOLIDAY	BRI	Technicolor
SUMMER MAGIC	BV	Technicolor
SUNDAY IN NEW YORK	MGM	Metrocolor
THE SWINGIN' MAIDEN (THE IRON MAIDEN)	BRI	Eastman Color
THE SWORD IN THE STONE	BV	Technicolor
SWORD OF LANCELOT	UN	Eastman Color
TAKE HER, SHE'S MINE	TCF	DeLuxe Color
TAMAHINE	BRI	Eastman Color
TAMMY AND THE DOCTOR	UN	Eastman Color
TARZAN'S THREE CHALLENGES	MGM	Metrocolor
13 FRIGHTENED GIRLS	COL	Eastman Color
THREE LIVES OF THOMASINA	BV	Technicolor
THE THREEPENNY OPERA	GER	Technicolor
THE THRILL OF IT ALL	UN	Eastman Color
A TICKLISH AFFAIR	MGM	Metrocolor
TOM JONES	UA	Eastman Color
THE TREASURE OF SILVER LAKE	GER-YUG	Eastman Color
TWICE TOLD TALES	UA	Technicolor
TWIN SISTERS OF KYOTO	JAP	Eastman Color
UNDER THE YUM YUM TREE	COL	Eastman Color
VACATION BY THE SEA	ROU	Sovcolor
THE VIP'S	MGM	Metrocolor
THE WHEELER DEALERS	MGM	Metrocolor
WHO'S BEEN SLEEPING IN MY BED?	PAR	Technicolor
WHO'S MINDING THE STORE?	PAR	Technicolor
WINNETOU (PART 1)	GER-YUG	Eastman Color
WOMEN OF THE WORLD	ITA	Technicolor
THE WORLD AT NIGHT NO. 3	ITA	Technicolor
"X"—THE MAN WITH THE X-RAY EYES	AI	Eastman Color
THE YOUNG RACERS	AI	Pathecolor
ZORRO	SPA	Eastman Color

1964

ADVANCE TO THE REAR	MGM	Metrocolor
ALL MIXED UP	JAP	Eastman Color
ALL THESE WOMEN	SWE	Eastman Color
APACHE RIFLES	TCF	DeLuxe Color
BANEO A BANGKOK	FRA	Eastman Color
THE BARGEE	BRI	Technicolor
BATMANOVA, SINGING SLAVE	RUS	Sovcolor
THE BEAUTY JUNGLE	BRI	Eastman Color
BECKET	PAR	Technicolor
BEDTIME STORY	UN	Eastman Color
BIKINI BEACH	AI	Pathecolor
THE BLACK TULIP	FRA	Eastman Color
BLACK TORMENT	BRI	Eastman Color
BLOOD FEAST	IND	Eastman Color
THE BRASS BOTTLE	UN	Eastman Color
BREAD AND GAMES	GER	Agfacolor
BULLET FOR A BADMAN	UN	Eastman Color
THE CARPETBAGGERS	PAR	Technicolor
CARRY ON, CLEO	BRI	Eastman Color
THE CASTLE	DEN	Technicolor
THE CHALK GARDEN	UN	Technicolor
CHEYENNE AUTUMN	WB	Technicolor
CIRCUS WORLD	PAR	Technicolor
CODE 7, VICTIM 5	BRI	Technicolor
THE COMEDY OF TERRORS	AI	Pathecolor
THE CRIMSON BLADE	COL	Eastman Color
CROOKS IN CLOISTERS	BRI	Technicolor
THE CURSE OF THE MUMMY'S TOMB	BRI	Technicolor

CYRANO AND D'ARTAGNAN	SPA-FRA-ITA	Eastman Color
DARK PURPOSE	UN	Technicolor
THE DEAD ONE OF BEVERLY HILLS	GER	Eastman Color
THE DEVIL-SHIP PIRATES	BRI	Eastman Color
A DISTANT TRUMPET	WB	Technicolor
THE DISORDERLY ORDERLY	PAR	Technicolor
EAST OF SUDAN	BRI	Technicolor
EMIL AND THE DETECTIVES	BV	Technicolor
ENSIGN PULVER	WB	Technicolor
AN EVENING WITH THE ROYAL BALLET	BRI	Technicolor
EVERY DAY'S A HOLIDAY	BRI	Technicolor
THE EVIL OF FRANKENSTEIN	BRI	Eastman Color
THE FALL OF THE ROMAN EMPIRE	PAR	Technicolor
FANTOMAS	FRA	Eastman Color
FATHER CAME TOO	BRI	Eastman Color
FATHER GOOSE	UN	Technicolor
THE FINEST HOURS	BRI	Technicolor
THE FIRST MEN IN THE MOON	COL	Technicolor
FLIGHT FROM ASHIYA	UA	Eastman Color
FLIPPER'S NEW ADVENTURE	MGM	Metrocolor
FOR A FISTFUL OF DOLLARS	ITA-GER-SPA	Technicolor
FOR THOSE WHO THINK YOUNG	UA	Technicolor
GET YOURSELF A COLLEGE GIRL	MGM	Metrocolor
GERMANY GREETS KENNEDY	GER	Technicolor
THE GIRL AND THE PRESS PHOTOGRAPHER	DEN	Eastman Color
THE GIRL IN MOURNING	SPA	Eastman Color
GO FRANCE	FRA	Eastman Color
GO GO GO WORLD	ITA	Eastman Color
GODZILLA VS. THE THING	JAP	Eastman Color
GOLD FOR THE CAESARS	MGM	Technicolor
THE GOLDEN ARROW	ITA	Technicolor
GOLDFINGER	UA	Technicolor
GOLIATH AND THE VAMPIRES	ITA	Eastman Color
GOOD NEIGHBOR SAM	COL	Eastman Color
GOODBYE CHARLIE	TCF	DeLuxe Color
GORATH	JAP	Eastman Color
THE GORGON	BRI	Technicolor
THE GRIPSHOLM CASTLE	GER	Eastman Color
GUNFIGHT AT COMANCHE CREEK	AA	DeLuxe Color
A HALE-FELLOW WELL-MET	FRA	Eastman Color
THE HAPPY SIXTIES	SPA	Eastman Color
HEY THERE, IT'S YOGI BEAR	COL	Eastman Color
HONEYMOON HOTEL	MGM	Metrocolor
THE HOP PICKERS	CZE	Agfacolor
HOT ENOUGH FOR JUNE	BRI	unknown
HOUSE WITH AN ATTIC	RUS	Sovcolor
THE HUMAN VAPOR	JAP	Eastman Color
I'D RATHER BE RICH	UN	Eastman Color
THE INCREDIBLE MR. LIMPET	WB	Technicolor
INVITATION TO A GUNFIGHTER	UA	DeLuxe Color
THE ISLAND OF THE BLUE DOLPHINS	UN	Eastman Color
JACK AND JENNY	GER	Agfacolor
JOHN GOLDFARB, PLEASE COME HOME	TCF	DeLuxe Color
KATU	BRA	Eastman Color
THE KILLERS	UN	Pathecolor
KISSIN' COUSINS	MGM	Metrocolor
THE LAST WOMAN OF SHANG	CHI	Eastman Color
LAW OF THE LAWLESS	PAR	Technicolor
LEMONADE JOE	CZE	Agfacolor
THE LIVELY SET	UN	Eastman Color
LONDON IN THE RAW	BRI	Eastman Color
THE LONG SHIPS	COL	Technicolor
LOOKING FOR LOVE	MGM	Metrocolor

LOTNA	POL	Sovcolor
THE LOVERS OF THE FRANCE	FRA	Eastman Color
LYDIA	CAN	Technicolor
McHALE'S NAVY	UN	Pathecolor
MAIL ORDER BRIDE	MGM	Technicolor
THE MAN FROM RIO	FRA	Technicolor
MAN'S FAVORITE SPORT	UN	Technicolor
MARNIE	UN	Technicolor
MARRIAGE —ITALIAN STYLE	ITA	Eastman Color
MARY POPPINS	BV	Technicolor
THE MASQUE OF THE RED DEATH	AI	Pathecolor
MEDITERRANEAN HOLIDAY	CON	Technicolor
THE MISADVENTURES OF MERLIN JONES	BV	Technicolor
MONDO CANE NO. 2	ITA	Technicolor
MONEY AND SPIRIT	SWI	Eastman Color
MONTEVIDEO	GER	Eastman Color
THE MOON SPINNERS	BV	Technicolor
MUSCLE BEACH PARTY	AI	Pathecolor
MY FAIR LADY	WB	Technicolor
THE NASY RABBIT	IND	Technicolor
NOTHING BUT THE BEST	BRI	Eastman Color
OF STARS AND MEN	IND	Eastman Color
OLD SHATTERHAND	GER-YUG	Eastman Color
OLYMPIC WINTER GAMES AT INNSBRUCK	AUS	Agfacolor
PAJAMA PARTY	AI	Pathecolor
PARALLEL STREETS (sequences)	GER	Eastman Color
PARIS WHEN IT SIZZLES	PAR	Technicolor
THE PATSY	PAR	Technicolor
THE PINK PANTHER	UA	Technicolor
THE PLEASURE SEEKERS	TCF	DeLuxe Color
PYRO	AI	Panacolor
QUICK, BEFORE IT MELTS	MGM	Metrocolor
THE QUICK GUN	COL	Technicolor
RATAI (THE BODY)	JAP	Eastman Color
RED DESERT	ITA-FRA	Technicolor
RHINO!	MGM	Metrocolor
RIDE THE WILD SURF	COL	Pathecolor
RIO CONCHOS	TCF	DeLuxe Color
ROBIN AND THE SEVEN HOODS	WB	Technicolor
ROBINSON CRUSOE ON MARS	PAR	Technicolor
LA RONDE	FRA	Eastman Color
ROUSTABOUT	PAR	Technicolor
SAMSON AND THE SLAVE QUEEN	AI	Eastman Color
SCHOOL FOR SUICIDE	DEN	Eastman Color
THE SECRET INVASION	UA	DeLuxe Color
SEND ME NO FLOWERS	UN	Technicolor
7 FACES OF DR. LAO	MGM	Metrocolor
THE 7TH DAWN	UA	Technicolor
SEX AND THE SINGLE GIRL	WB	Technicolor
A SHOT IN THE DARK	UA	DeLuxe Color
633 SQUADRON	UA	DeLuxe Color
SLAVE TRADE IN THE WORLD TODAY	ITA	Eastman Color
SOFT HANDS	EGY	Eastman Color
THE SOLDIER'S TALE	BRI	Technicolor
THE SON OF CAPTAIN BLOOD	PAR	Technicolor
SOUTH OF TANA RIVER	DEN	unknown
STRANGE BEDFELLOWS	UN	Technicolor
TAGGERT	UN	Technicolor
TAMAHINE	MGM	Eastman Color
LOS TARANTOS	SPA	unknown
THOSE CALLOWAYS	BV	Technicolor
THREE NIGHTS OF LIFE	ITA	Technicolor
THREE NUTS IN SEARCH OF A BOLT (sequences)	IND	Eastman Color

A TIGER WALKS	BV	Technicolor
THE TIME TRAVELERS	AI	Pathecolor
TOPKAPI	UA	Eastman Color
THE UMBRELLAS OF CHERBOURG	FRA	Eastman Color
THE UNSINKABLE MOLLY BROWN	MGM	Metrocolor
VILLAGE SWEETNESS	FRA	Eastman Color
VIVA LAS VEGAS	MGM	Metrocolor
VOICE OF THE HURRICANE	IND	Technicolor
WEEKEND A ZUYDCOOTE	FRA	Eastman Color
WEEPING FOR A BANDIT	SPA	unknown
WHAT A WAY TO GO!	TCF	DeLuxe Color
WHERE LOVE HAS GONE	PAR	Technicolor
WHERE YOU FROM, JOHNNY?	FRA	Eastman Color
WHITE VOICES	FRA-ITA	Technicolor
WHY HUNGARIAN FILMS ARE BAD (sequence)	HUN	unknown
WILD AND WONDERFUL	UN	Eastman Color
WINNETOU, PART II	GER-YUG	unknown
WOMAN IS A WONDERFUL THING (sequences)	ITA-FRA	Eastman Color
WOMAN OF STRAW	BRI	Eastman Color
WONDERFUL LIFE	BRI	Technicolor
THE WORLD OF HENRY ORIENT	UA	DeLuxe Color
WORLD WITHOUT SUN	FRA	Eastman Color
THE YELLOW DEVIL	GER-YUG	Eastman Color
YESTERDAY, TODAY AND TOMORROW	ITA	Technicolor
YOLANDA	RUS	Sovcolor
ZULU	PAR	Technicolor

1965

THE AGONY AND THE ECSTASY	TCF	DeLuxe Color
AMANITA PESTILENS	CAN	Eastman Color
AN AMERICAN WIFE	ITA	Technicolor
AMONG VULTURES	GER-FRA-YUG	Eastman Color
THE AMOROUS ADVENTURES OF MOLL FLANDERS	PAR	Technicolor
AND A MAN CAME ...	ITA	Eastman Color
ANGELIQUE, MARQUISE DES ANGES	FRA-ITA-GER	Eastman Color
ARIZONA RAIDERS	COL	Technicolor
THE ART OF LOVE	UN	Technicolor
ATRAGON	JAP	Pathecolor
THE BATTLE OF THE BULGE	WB	Technicolor
THE BATTLE OF THE VILLA FIORITA	WB	Technicolor
BEACH BALL	PAR	Technicolor
BEACH BLANKET BINGO	AI	Pathecolor
BEFORE THE REVOLUTION (sequences)	ITA	Eastman Color
BEYOND THE ODER AND NEISSE	GER	Agfacolor
THE BIG SHOTS	FRA	Eastman Color
BILLIE	UA	Technicolor
BLACK SPURS	PAR	Technicolor
THE BLIND BIRD	RUS	Sovcolor
THE BLIZZARD	RUS	Sovcolor
BLOOD AND BLACK LACE	AA	Technicolor
BOEING BOEING	PAR	Technicolor
THE BOUNTY KILLER	EMB	Technicolor
THE BRIGAND OF KANDAHAR	BRI	Technicolor
BUS RILEY'S BACK IN TOWN	UN	Eastman Color
BWANA TOSHI NO UTA	JAP	Eastman Color
CASANOVA '70	ITA	Technicolor
CAT BALLOU	COL	Pathecolor
THE CINCINNATI KID	MGM	Metrocolor
CLARENCE, THE CROSS-EYED LION	MGM	Metrocolor
COAST OF SKELETONS	BRI	Technicolor
THE COLLECTOR	COL	Technicolor
CORRIDA FOR A SPY	FRA-SPA-GER	Eastman Color
CRACK IN THE WORLD	PAR	Technicolor
CRAZY PARADISE	DEN	Eastman Color

CRAZY PETE (PIERROT LE FOU)	FRA	Eastman Color
A DAN IN A SOLAR	CUB	Eastman Color
DEAD BIRDS	IND	Eastman Color
DEAR BRIGITTE	TCF	DeLuxe Color
DIE, DIE, MY DARLING	COL	Eastman Color
DIE, MONSTER, DIE	BRI	Pathecolor
DINGAKA	EMB	Technicolor
DO NOT DISTURB	TCF	DeLuxe Color
DO YOU KEEP A LION AT HOME?	CZE	Agfacolor
DR. GOLDFOOT AND THE BIKINI MACHINE	AI	Pathecolor
DR. PRAETORIUS	GER	Eastman Color
DR. TERROR'S HOUSE OF HORRORS	BRI	Technicolor
DR. WHO AND THE DALEKS	BRI	Technicolor
DOCTOR ZHIVAGO	MGM	Metrocolor
DOGORA	JAP	Eastman Color
DON'T TELL ME ANY STORIES	GER	Eastman Color
THE EARLY BIRD	BRI	Eastman Color
ECCO!	ITA	Technicolor
THE ENCHANTED DESNA	RUS	Sovcolor
THE ENCHANTED ISLES	POR-FRA	Agfacolor
THE ENCHANTING SHADOW	CHI	Sovcolor
THE FABULOUS ADVENTURE OF MARCO POLO	FRA-YUG	Eastman Color
THE FACE OF FU MANCHU	BRI	Technicolor
THE FAMILY JEWELS	PAR	Technicolor
FIVE GENTS' TRICK BOOK	JAP	Eastman Color
THE FLAMING YEARS	RUS	Agfacolor
THE FLIGHT OF THE PHOENIX	TCF	DeLuxe Color
THE FLOWER MARKET	ARG	unknown
FLUFFY	UN	Eastman Color
FOG	BRI	Eastman Color
FUNNY THINGS HAPPEN DOWN UNDER	AUT	Eastman Color
LE GENDARME A NEW YORK	FRA	Eastman Color
LE GENDARME DE SAINT-TROPEZ	FRA	Eastman Color
GENGHIS KHAN	COL	Technicolor
GHIDRAH, THE THREE-HEADED MONSTER	JAP	Eastman Color
THE GIRL AND THE MILLIONAIRE	DEN	Eastman Color
THE GIRL WHO DANCED INTO LIFE	HUN	Eastman Color
GIRL HAPPY	MGM	Metrocolor
THE GLORY GUYS	UA	DeLuxe Color
GO GO BIGBEAT	BRI	Eastman Color
GO GO MANIA	BRI	Technicolor
THE GOLDEN HEAD (MILLIE GOES TO BUDAPEST)	HUN-USA	Technicolor
THE GRAND SUBSTITUTION	CHI	Eastman Color
THE GREAT RACE	WB	Technicolor
THE GREAT SIOUX MASSACRE	COL	Technicolor
THE GREATEST STORY EVER TOLD	UA	Technicolor
THE GUIDE	INDIA	Pathecolor
GUNFIGHTERS OF CASA GRANDE	MGM	Metrocolor
THE HALLELUJAH TRAIL	UA	Technicolor
HAPPINESS	FRA	Eastman Color
HARLOW	PAR	Technicolor
HARUM SCARUM	MGM	Metrocolor
HARVEY MIDDLEMAN, FIREMAN	COL	Pathecolor
HEAVEN ON ONE'S HEAD	FRA	Eastman Color
THE HELL OF MANITOBA	GER-SPA	Eastman Color
HELLO, AMERICA	GER-SWI	unknown
HELP!	BRI	Eastman Color
THE HEROES OF TELEMARK	BRI	Technicolor
THE HIGH, BRIGHT SUN	BRI	Eastman Color
A HIGH WIND IN JAMAICA	TCF	DeLuxe Color
HORROR CASTLE	ITA	Eastman Color
HOW TO STUFF A WILD BIKINI	AI	Pathecolor
THE HUMAN DUPLICATORS	IND	Eastman Color
HUNTING THE LION WITH BOW AND ARROW	FRA	Kodachrome
I'LL TAKE SWEDEN	UA	Technicolor

IN THE SHADOW OF THE PAST	RUS	Sovcolor
INSIDE DAISY CLOVER	WB	Technicolor
THE INTELLIGENCE MEN	BRI	Eastman Color
THE IPCRESS FILE	BRI	Technicolor
IT'S NIFTY IN THE NAVY	DEN	Eastman Color
I'VE GOTTA HORSE	BRI	Technicolor
THE JERK	FRA-ITA	Eastman Color
JOHN F. KENNEDY: YEARS OF LIGHTNING, DAY OF DRUMS	PAR	Eastman Color
JOY IN THE MORNING	MGM	Metrocolor
JULIET OF THE SPIRITS	ITA	Technicolor
KIMBERLEY JIM	EMB	Agfacolor
A KING'S STORY	BRI	Eastman Color
THE KITE FROM THE OTHER SIDE OF THE WORLD	FRA-CHI	Eastman Color
THE KOUMIKO MYSTERY	FRA	Eastman Color
KWAIDAN	JAP	Eastman Color
LA BOHEME	WB	Technicolor
LADY L	MGM	Eastman Color
THE LITTLE GIRL, THE DOG AND THE SEAL	SWE	unknown
LORD JIM	COL	Technicolor
THE LOST WORLD OF SINBAD	JAP	Pathecolor
LOVE AND KISSES	UN	Technicolor
LOVE AT SEA	FRA	Eastman Color
THE LOVE GODDESSES (sequence)	CON	Technicolor
LOVE HAS MANY FACES	COL	Pathecolor
McHALE'S NAVY JOINS THE AIR FORCE	UN	Eastman Color
MADAM WHITE SNAKE	CHI	Eastman Color
MAJOR DUNDEE	COL	Pathecolor
THE MAN FROM BUTTON WILLOW	IND	Eastman Color
THE MAN FROM ISTANBUL	FRA	Eastman Color
MARIE CHANTAL VS. DR. KHA	FRA-SPA-ITA	Eastman Color
MARRIAGE ON THE ROCKS	WB	Technicolor
MARVELOUS ANGELIQUE	FRA	Eastman Color
MASQUERADE	BRI	Eastman Color
MEMETH (THE FLURRY)	RUS	Sovcolor
THE MERRY WIVES OF WINDSOR	AUS	Technicolor
MINNESOTA CLAY	ITA-FRA-SPA	Eastman Color
MISTER MOSES	UA	Technicolor
THE MOMENT OF TRUTH	SPA-ITA	Technicolor
THE MONKEY'S UNCLE	BV	Technicolor
MURIETA	WB	Eastman Color
NEVER TOO LATE	WB	Technicolor
NIGHTMARE IN THE SUN	IND	DeLuxe Color
NONE BUT THE BRAVE	WB	Technicolor
THE OIL PRINCE	GER-YUG	Eastman Color
ONE MILLION DOLLARS	ITA	Technicolor
ONE-WAY WAHINI	UA	Technicolor
OPERATION CROSSBOW	MGM	Metrocolor
OTHELLO	BRI	Technicolor
OUR MAN FLINT	TCF	DeLuxe Color
PARIS SECRET	BRI	Eastman Color
PARIS SEEN BY ...	FRA	Ektachrome
PINOCCHIO IN OUTER SPACE	UN	Eastman Color
A PISTOL FOR RINGO	ITA-SPA	Technicolor
PLANET OF THE VAMPIRES	ITA	Pathecolor
THE PLAYER PIANOS	SPA-FRA	Eastman Color
PRIMITIVE LONDON	BRI	Eastman Color
THE PYRAMID OF THE SUN GOD	GER-YUG	Eastman Color
RED LINE 7000	PAR	Technicolor
REVENGE OF THE GLADIATORS	PAR	Technicolor
THE REWARD	TCF	DeLuxe Color
RITE OF SPRING	POR	Eastman Color
THE ROYAL ROAD	SWE	Eastman Color
THE SANDPIPER	MGM	Metrocolor

SANDS OF THE KALAHARI	PAR	Technicolor
THE SATAN BUG	UA	DeLuxe Color
SAUL AND DAVID	ITA-SPA	Eastman Color
THE SECOND BEST SECRET AGENT IN THE WHOLE WIDE WORLD	BRI	Pathecolor
THE SECRET OF MY SUCCESS	MGM	Technicolor
THE SECRET OF THE THREE JUNKS	GER	Eastman Color
SERGEANT DEADHEAD	AI	Pathecolor
SEVEN GOLDEN MEN	ITA-FRA-SPA	Eastman Color
SEVEN WOMEN	MGM	Metrocolor
SEVENTEEN	DEN	Eastman Color
SHE	MGM	Metrocolor
SHENANDOAH	UN	Technicolor
THE SHEPHERD GIRL	CHI	Eastman Color
SHOTS IN THREE-QUARTER TIME	GER-AUS	Agfacolor
SKI PARTY	AI	Pathecolor
THE SKULL	PAR	Technicolor
SLALOM	ITA-FRA-EGY	Technicolor
SONG OF THE WORLD	FRA	Eastman Color
THE SONS OF KATIE ELDER	PAR	Technicolor
THE SOUND OF MUSIC	TCF	DeLuxe Color
SUMMER IN TYROL	DEN	Eastman Color
A SWINGIN' SUMMER	IND	Technicolor
THE SWORD OF ALI BABA	UN	Eastman Color
TABOOS OF THE WORLD	ITA	Technicolor
TABU NO. 2	ITA	Eastman Color
TALES OF A YOUNG SCAMP	GER	Eastman Color
TELL ME WHO TO KILL	FRA	Eastman Color
THE TENTH VICTIM	FRA-ITA	Technicolor
THAT DARN CAT	BV	Technicolor
THAT FUNNY FEELING	UN	Technicolor
THE THIRD DAY	WB	Technicolor
THOSE MAGNIFICENT MEN IN THEIR FLYING MACHINES	TCF	DeLuxe Color
THREE FACES OF A WOMAN	ITA	Technicolor
THREE HATS FOR LISA	BRI	Eastman Color
THREE WEEKS OF LOVE	JAP	Eastman Color
THUNDERBALL	UA	Technicolor
TICKLE ME	AA	DeLuxe Color
THE TIGER SPRAYS HIMSELF WITH DYNAMITE	JAP	Eastman Color
TOKYO OLYMPIAD	JAP	Eastman Color
THE TOMB OF LIGEIA	AI	Pathecolor
THE TOWN TAMER	PAR	Technicolor
TROUBLE IN BAHIA FOR OSS 117	FRA	Eastman Color
THE TRUTH ABOUT SPRING	UN	Technicolor
THE UGLY DACHSHUND	BV	Technicolor
UNCLE TOM'S CABIN	GER	Eastman Color
UP JUMPED A SWAGMAN	BRI	Technicolor
UP TO HIS EARS	FRA	Eastman Color
UPROAR IN HEAVEN	CHI	Sovcolor
THE VERMILION DOOR	CHI	Eastman Color
A VERY SPECIAL FAVOR	UN	Technicolor
VILLAGE OF THE GIANTS	EMB	Pathecolor
VIVA MARIA	FRA	Eastman Color
VON RYAN'S EXPRESS	TCF	DeLuxe Color
WAELSUNGENBLUT	GER	Eastman Color
WAR AND PEACE	RUS	Sovcolor
WAR GODS OF THE DEEP	AI	Pathecolor
THE WAR LORD	UN	Technicolor
THE WAR OF THE ZOMBIES	AI	Pathecolor
WE WILL REMEMBER	JAP	Eastman Color
WEEP FOR A BANDIT	SPA	Eastman Color
WHAT	ITA-BRI	Technicolor
WHAT'S NEW PUSSYCAT?	UA	DeLuxe Color

WHEN THE BOYS MEET THE GIRLS	MGM	Metrocolor
WHERE THE SPIES ARE	MGM	Metrocolor
WHERE WAS YOUR MAJESTY BETWEEN 3 AND 5?	HUN	Eastman Color
THE WHITE MOOR	ROU	Eastman Color
WHITE ROSE OF HONG KONG	JAP	Eastman Color
WILD WILD WINTER	UN	Technicolor
WILD WILD WORLD	ITA	Eastman Color
WILLY McBEAN AND HIS MAGIC MACHINE	MAG	Eastman Color
WINTER-A-GO-GO	COL	Pathecolor
THE WOMAN FROM BEIRUT	SPA-FRA-ITA	Eastman Color
THE YELLOW ROLLS-ROYCE	MGM	Metrocolor
THE YELLOW SLIPPERS	POL	unknown
YOUNG CASSIDY	MGM	Metrocolor
YOUNG FURY	PAR	Technicolor
ZEBRA IN THE KITCHEN	MGM	Metrocolor

1966

AFRICA ADDIO	ITA	Technicolor
AFTER THE FOX	UA	Technicolor
ALFIE	PAR	Technicolor
ALVAREZ KELLY	COL	Eastman Color
AMBUSH BAY	UA	DeLuxe Color
AN AMERICAN DREAM	WB	Technicolor
AND NOW MIGUEL	UN	Technicolor
ANY WEDNESDAY	WB	Technicolor
THE APPALOOSA	UN	Technicolor
ARABESQUE	UN	Technicolor
AROUND THE WORLD UNDER THE SEA	MGM	Metrocolor
ARRIVEDERCI, BABY	PAR	Technicolor
ARSHIN MAL ALAN	RUS	Sovcolor
ASSAULT ON A QUEEN	PAR	Technicolor
BANG, BANG, YOU'RE DEAD	AI	Technicolor
BATMAN	TCF	DeLuxe Color
THE BEACH UMBRELLA	ITA-FRA	Eastman Color
BEAU GESTE	UN	Technicolor
BEL AMI 2000	GER-AUS	Eastman Color
A BELLES DENTS (LIVING IT UP)	FRA-GER	Eastman Color
THE BIBLE	TCF	Technicolor
A BIG HAND FOR THE LITTLE LADY	WB	Technicolor
THE BIG RUNAROUND	FRA	Eastman Color
THE BIG T-N-T SHOW	AI	Technicolor
BIRDS DO IT	COL	Pathecolor
BLACK SUN	FRA	Eastman Color
BLINDFOLD	UN	Technicolor
BLOW-UP	BRI	Metrocolor
THE BLUE MAX	TCF	DeLuxe Color
BOLSHOI BALLET '67	PAR	Technicolor
BORN FREE	COL	Technicolor
BOY, DID I GET A WRONG NUMBER	UA	DeLuxe Color
BRIDE OF THE ANDES	JAP	Eastman Color
THE BRIDES OF FU-MANCHU	BRI	Technicolor
BRIDGE ANTI-GANGS	FRA	Eastman Color
BRIGITTE AND BRIGITTE (sequence)	FRA	Eastman Color
THE BUBBLE	IND	Eastman Color
A BULLET IN THE HEART	FRA	Eastman Color
CARRY ON COWBOY	BRI	Eastman Color
CARRY ON SCREAMING	BRI	Eastman Color
CAST A GIANT SHADOW	UA	DeLuxe Color
THE CAT	EMB	Pathecolor
CHAMBER OF HORRORS	WB	Technicolor

CHAPPAQUA	IND	Eastman Color
THE CHASE	COL	Technicolor
CHILDREN'S SICKNESSES	HUN	Sovcolor
THE CHRISTMAS THAT ALMOST WASN'T	ITA	Eastman Color
CINERAMA'S RUSSIAN ADVENTURE	IND	Sovcolor
A COMPLICATED MAN	JAP	Daieiscope
CONGRESS OF LOVE	GER-AUS	Eastman Color
THE COUNTESS FROM HONG KONG	UN	Technicolor
A COVENANT WITH DEATH	WB	Technicolor
CROOK'S HONOR	GER	Eastman Color
THE DAISIES	CZE	Corwo Color
DALEKS INVADE EARTH 2150 A.D.	BRI	Technicolor
DAPHNE	JAP	Eastman Color
THE DAYDREAMER	EMP	Eastman Color
DEAD HEAT ON A MERRY-GO-ROUND	COL	Eastman Color
THE DEFECTOR	SAR	Eastman Color
DESTINATION INNER SPACE	IND	Eastman Color
DIAMOND SAFARI	FRA	Eastman Color
DR. GOLDFOOT AND THE GIRL BOMBS	AI	Technicolor
DOCTOR IN CLOVER	BRI	Eastman Color
DRACULA — PRINCE OF DARKNESS	BRI	Technicolor
DUEL AT DIABLO	UA	DeLuxe Color
DYMKY (THE PIPES)	CZE-AUS	Eastman Color
EL GRECO	ITA-FRA	DeLuxe Color
THE ENDLESS SUMMER	IND	Kodachrome
EVERY DAY IS A HOLIDAY	SPA	Technicolor
AN EYE FOR AN EYE	EMB	Pathecolor
FAHRENHEIT 451	UN	Technicolor
THE FAMILY WAY	BRI	Eastman Color
THE FANTASTIC VOYAGE	TCF	DeLuxe Color
FANTOMAS TEARS LOOSE	FRA	Eastman Color
FAT SPY	IND	Eastman Color
FATA MORGANA	SPA	Eastman Color
FATHER'S TRIP	FRA	Eastman Color
THE FIGHTING PRINCE OF DONEGAL	DIS	Technicolor
FINDERS KEEPERS	UA	Eastman Color
A FINE MADNESS	WB	Technicolor
THE FLAME AND THE FIRE	CON	Eastman Color
FOLLOW ME, BOYS	DIS	Technicolor
FOR A FEW DOLLARS MORE	ITA-GER-SPA	Technicolor
FOR LOVE AND GOLD (L'ARMATA BRANCALEONE)	FRA-ITA	Technicolor
FRANKENSTEIN CONQUERS THE WORLD	JAP	Eastman Color
FRANKIE AND JOHNNY	UA	Technicolor
FUNERAL IN BERLIN	PAR	Technicolor
FUNNY MONEY	FRA	Eastman Color
A FUNNY THING HAPPENED ON THE WAY TO THE FORUM	UA	DeLuxe Color
GAMBARA TAI GARUGON	JAP	Eastman Color
GAMBIT	UN	Technicolor
THE GAME IS OVER	FRA	Eastman Color
THE GARDENER OF ARGENTEUIL	FRA	Eastman Color
THE GENTLE RAIN	BRA	Eastman Color
THE GHOST IN THE INVISIBLE BIKINI	AI	Pathecolor
THE GLASS-BOTTOMED BOAT	MGM	Metrocolor
GOAL! WORLD CUP 1966	BRI	Technicolor
GRAND PRIX	MGM	Metrocolor
THE GREAT ST. TRINIAN'S TRAIN ROBBERY	BRI	Eastman Color
THE GREAT WALL	JAP	Technicolor
THE GROUP	UA	DeLuxe Color
GUNPOINT	UN	Technicolor
GYPSY GIRL	BRI	Eastman Color
HARPER	WB	Technicolor
HAWAII	UA	DeLuxe Color

HEART TRUMP FOR OSS 117 IN TOKYO	FRA	Eastman Color
HOCUS POCUS	GER	Eastman Color
HOLD ON	MGM	Metrocolor
THE HOSTAGE	IND	Technicolor
THE HOT DAYS	ARG	Eastman Color
HOTEL PARADISO	MGM	Metrocolor
HOW TO STEAL A MILLION	TCF	DeLuxe Color
THE HUNCHBACK OF SOHO	GER	Eastman Color
I AM LOOKING FOR A MAN	GER	Eastman Color
IDEAL IN DANGER	TCF	DeLuxe Color
I HEAR ZATO-ICHI SINGING	JAP	Eastman Color
ILLUSION OF BLOOD	JAP	Eastman Color
IN THE TORRID WIND	SPA	Eastman Color
INCIDENT AT PHANTOM HILL	UN	Technicolor
JACK FROST	RUS	Sovcolor
JOHNNY RENO	PAR	Technicolor
JOHNNY TIGER	UN	Technicolor
KALEIDOSCOPE	BRI	Technicolor
KANCHENGUNGHA	INDIA	Eastman Color
THE KILL (see THE GAME IS OVER)		
KING OF HEARTS	FRA	Eastman Color
KISS THE GIRLS AND MAKE THEM DIE	COL	Technicolor
THE LACE WARS (FETES GALANTES)	RUM-FRA	Eastman Color
LADY OF THE RAILS	CZE	Corwo Color
THE LAST OF THE SECRET AGENTS?	PAR	Technicolor
LET'S KILL UNCLE	UN	Technicolor
LET'S NOT GET ANGRY	FRA	Eastman Color
THE LETTER	GER	Eastman Color
LT. ROBIN CRUSOE, U.S.N.	BV	Technicolor
THE LIQUIDATOR	MGM	Metrocolor
LISOLETTE VON DER PFALZ	GER	Eastman Color
LONG LEGS — LONG FINGERS	GER	Eastman Color
THE LOST COMMAND	COL	Pathecolor
MADAME X	UN	Technicolor
MADE IN ITALY	ITA	Technicolor
MADE IN PARIS	MGM	Metrocolor
MADE IN U.S.A.	FRA	Eastman Color
MADEMOISELLE DE MAUPIN	ITA-FRA SPA-YUG	Technicolor
MAKE LIKE A THIEF	FIN	Eastman Color
A MAN AND A WOMAN	FRA	Eastman Color
THE MAN CALLED FLINTSTONE	COL	Eastman Color
A MAN COULD GET KILLED	UN	Technicolor
A MAN FOR ALL SEASONS	COL	Technicolor
THE MAN FROM MARRAKECH	FRA	Eastman Color
THE MAN WHO LAUGHS	ITA	Eastman Color
MARA OF THE WILDERNESS	AA	DeLuxe Color
MARTIN SOLDAT	FRA	Eastman Color
A MATTER OF HONOR	ITA-FRA	Technicolor
MAYA	MGM	Technicolor
THE MERMAID	CHI	unknown
A MIDSUMMER NIGHT'S DREAM	COL	Pathecolor
MODESTY BLAISE	TCF	DeLuxe Color
MOMENT TO MOMENT	UN	Technicolor
THE MONA LISA HAS BEEN STOLEN	FRA-ITA	Eastman Color
MONDAY OR TUESDAY (sequences)	YUG	Corwo Color
MOONLIGHTING WIVES	IND	DeLuxe Color
MUNSTER GO HOME	UN	Technicolor
MURDERER'S ROW	COL	Technicolor
MY FIRST GIRL FRIEND	ARG	Eastman Color
NAKED PREY	PAR	Technicolor
NAMU — THE KILLER WHALE	UA	DeLuxe Color

NASHVILLE REBEL	AI	Technicolor
THE NAVY VS. THE NIGHT MONSTERS	IND	DeLuxe Color
NEVADA SMITH	PAR	Eastman Color
NIGHT IN BANGKOK	JAP	Eastman Color
THE NIGHT OF THE GRIZZLY	PAR	Technicolor
NIGHTS OF FAREWELL	RUS	Sovcolor-Eastman Color
NOT WITH MY WIFE, YOU DON'T	WB	Technicolor
THE NUN	FRA	Eastman Color
ONCE A GREEK	GER	Eastman Color
ONE MILLION YEARS, B.C.	BRI	Technicolor
ONE SPY TOO MANY	MGM	Metrocolor
OPERATION AIR RAID: BED MUFFLER	KOR	Eastman Color
OPERATION SAN GENNARO	ITA-GER-FRA	Eastman Color
THE OSCAR	EMB	Pathecolor
OUR INCREDIBLE WORLD	BRI	Eastman Color
OUT OF SIGHT	UN	Technicolor
THE PAD (AND HOW TO USE IT)	UN	Technicolor
PALACES OF A QUEEN	BRI	Eastman Color
PARADISE, HAWAIIAN STYLE	PAR	Technicolor
PARANOIA (sequences)	ITA-FRA	unknown
PENELOPE	MGM	Metrocolor
PEOPLE ON WHEELS	CZE	Corwo Color
PEPPER	ARG	Eastman Color
PHARAOH	POL	Eastman Color
PICTURE MOMMY DEAD	EMB	Pathecolor
A PISTOL FOR RINGO	ITA	Eastman Color
A PLACE CALLED GLORY	SPA-GER	Pathecolor
THE PLAGUE OF THE ZOMBIES	BRI	DeLuxe Color
THE POPPY IS ALSO A FLOWER	IND	Eastman Color
THE POSTMAN GOES TO WAR	FRA	Eastman Color
PRESS FOR TIME	BRI	Eastman Color
THE PROFESSIONALS	COL	Technicolor
PROMISE HER ANYTHING	PAR	Technicolor
THE PSYCHOPATH	BRI	Technicolor
THE QUILLER MEMORANDUM	BRI	Eastman Color
RAGE	COL	Pathecolor
THE RARE BREED	UN	Technicolor
RASPUTIN — THE MAD MONK	TCF	DeLuxe Color
RED TOMAHAWK	PAR	Pathecolor
RELAX, FREDDIE	DEN	Eastman Color
REPREHENSIBLE JAPAN	JAP	Eastman Color
THE RETURN OF RINGO	ITA	Eastman Color
RETURN OF THE SEVEN	UA	DeLuxe Color
RIDE BEYOND VENGEANCE	COL	Pathecolor
RIDE IN THE WHIRLWIND	IND	Eastman Color
RIFIFI IN PANAMA	FRA	Eastman Color
RINGS AROUND THE WORLD	COL	Technicolor
ROMEO AND JULIET	BRI	Pathecolor
THE RUSSIANS ARE COMING, THE RUSSIANS ARE COMING	UA	DeLuxe Color
THE SAINT LIES IN WAIT	FRA	Eastman Color
THE SAND PEBBLES	TCF	DeLuxe Color
THE SANDWICH MAN	BRI	Eastman Color
SANTA'S CHRISTMAS CIRCUS	IND	Eastman Color
SAVAGE PAMPAS	ARG-SPA	Eastman Color
THE SECOND TRUTH	FRA	Eastman Color
SECRET AGENT FIREBALL	ITA	Eastman Color
SECRET AGENT SUPER DRAGON	ITA-FRA	Technicolor
THE SECRET SEVEN	ITA-MGM	Eastman Color
THE SENSATION OF THE CENTURY	JAP	Eastman Color
SEVEN GOLDEN MEN STRIKE AGAIN	ITA	Technicolor
SHOOT LOUD, LOUDER . . . I DON'T UNDERSTAND	ITA	Technicolor

THE SILENCERS	COL	Pathecolor
THE SINGING NUN	MGM	Metrocolor
SKI FASCINATION	GER	Eastman Color
SLEEPING BEAUTY	RUS	Sovcolor
THE SLEEPING SENTINEL	FRA	Eastman Color
SMOKY	TCF	DeLuxe Color
SON OF A GUNFIGHTER	SPA	Metrocolor
SPINOUT	MGM	Metrocolor
SPY IN YOUR EYE	AI	Pathecolor
THE SPY WITH A COLD NOSE	BRI	Pathecolor
THE SPY WITH MY FACE	MGM	Metrocolor
STAGECOACH	TCF	DeLuxe Color
STOP THE WORLD — I WANT TO GET OFF	WB	Technicolor
THE SULTANS	FRA	Eastman Color
THE SWINGER	PAR	Technicolor
THE TAKING OF POWER BY LOUIS XIV	FRA	Eastman Color
10:30 P.M. SUMMER	IND	Technicolor
TENDER HOODLUM	FRA	Eastman Color
TEXAS ACROSS THE RIVER	UN	Technicolor
THANK YOU VERY MUCH	ITA	Technicolor
THAT RIVIERA TOUCH	BRA	Eastman Color
THEY'RE A WEIRD MOB	AUT	Eastman Color
THE THIRD YOUTH	RUS	Sovcolor
THREE ON A COUCH	COL	Pathecolor
THUNDERBIRDS ARE GO	BRI	Technicolor
TO TRAP A SPY	MGM	Metrocolor
TOBRUK	UN	Technicolor
TOO SOON TO DIE	ITA-FRA	Eastman Color
THE TORN CURTAIN	UN	Technicolor
THE TRAMPLERS	ITA	Eastman Color
THE TRAP	BRI	Eastman Color
TRIPLE CROSS	FRA	Eastman Color
THE TROUBLE WITH ANGELS	COL	Pathecolor
TRUNK TO CAIRO	AI	Pathecolor
TWO KOVNEY LEMELS	ISR	Technicolor
THE VENETIAN AFFAIR	MGM	Metrocolor
A VIRGIN FOR THE PRINCE	ITA-FRA	Technicolor
WACO	PAR	Technicolor
WALK, DON'T RUN	COL	Technicolor
WARNING SHOT	PAR	Technicolor
WAY OUT	IND	Eastman Color
WAY . . . WAY OUT	TCF	DeLuxe Color
WEEKEND AT DUNKIRK	FRA	Eastman Color
WHAT DID YOU DO IN THE WAR, DADDY?	UA	DeLuxe Color
WHAT'S UP, TIGER LILY?	AI	Eastman Color
WHERE THE BULLETS FLY	BRI	Eastman Color
WHITE, RED, YELLOW, PINK (sequence)	ITA	Technicolor
THE WILD ANGELS	AI	Pathecolor
WINNETOU III	GER	Eastman Color
THE WITCHES	BRI	Technicolor
WITH THE LIVES OF OTHERS	FRA-ITA	Eastman Color
WOMEN OF THE PREHISTORIC PLANET	IND	DeLuxe Color
THE WRONG BOX	BRI	Technicolor
THE YEAR OF THE HORSE	IND	Eastman Color
YOU ARE LIKE A WILD CHRYSANTHEMUM	JAP	Eastman Color
YOU'RE A BIG BOY NOW	SAR	Pathecolor

ADDENDA FOR 1967

1967

ACCIDENT	BRI	Eastman Color
THE ADVENTURERS	FRA	Eastman Color
THE ADVENTURES OF BULLWHIP GRIFFIN	DIS	Technicolor
AFRICA — TEXAS STYLE	PAR	Eastman Color
AFTER YOU, COMRADE	AFR	Technicolor
ALL MAD ABOUT HIM	FRA	Eastman Color
THE AMBUSHERS .	COL	Technicolor
EL AMOR BRUJO	SPA	Eastman Color
ANOTHER MAN'S WIFE	SPA	Eastman Color
THE ARNAUDS	FRA	Eastman Color
BAD TIME FOR SQUEALERS	FRA	Eastman Color
THE BALLAD OF JOSIE	UN	Technicolor
BANNING	UN	Technicolor
BAREFOOT IN THE PARK	PAR	Technicolor
BATOUK	FRA	Eastman Color
BEACH RED	UA	DeLuxe Color
BEAUTY OF THE DAY (BELLE DE JOUR)	FRA	Eastman Color
BEDAZZLED	TCF	DeLuxe Color
THE BENEFIT OF THE DOUBT	BRA	unknown
BERSERK	COL	Technicolor
BIG DUEL IN THE NORTH SEA	JAP	Eastman Color
THE BIG GRASSHOPPER	FRA	Eastman Color
THE BIG MOUTH	COL	Pathecolor
THE BIG SOFTIE (LE GRAND DADAIS)	FRA	Eastman Color
THE BIG VACATION	FRA	unknown
BIKE BOY	IND	Eastman Color
BILLION DOLLAR BRAIN	UA	Technicolor
BITTER FRUIT	FRA-YUG-ITA	Eastman Color
THE BOBO	WB	Technicolor
BONDITIS	SWI	Technicolor
BONNIE AND CLYDE	WB	Technicolor
BORN LOSERS	AI	Pathecolor
BOYS AND GIRLS	FRA-BEL	Eastman Color
THE BUSY BODY	PAR	Technicolor
CAMELOT	WB	Technicolor
THE CAPER OF THE GOLDEN BULLS	EMB	Pathecolor
CAPRICE	TCF	DeLuxe Color
CARMEN BABY	YUG-GER	Eastman Color
CASINO ROYALE	COL	Technicolor
CASTLE OF EVIL	IND	Eastman Color
THE CATALINA CAPER	IND	unknown
CHAPPAQUA	UN	unknown
CHARLIE, THE LONESOME COUGAR	DIS	Technicolor
THE CHINESE GIRL	FRA	Eastman Color
A CHOICE OF KILLERS	FRA-ITA	Eastman Color
THE CHRISTMAS KID	USA-SPA	Movielab
CHUKA	PAR	Pathecolor
CLAMBAKE	UA	Technicolor
C'MON, LET'S LIVE A LITTLE	PAR	Technicolor
THE COLLECTOR	FRA	Eastman Color
COME SPY WITH ME	TCF	DeLuxe Color
THE COMEDIANS	MGM	Metrocolor
COOL HAND LUKE	WB	Technicolor
THE COOL ONES	WB	Technicolor
THE CORRUPT ONES	GER	Technicolor
COUNTERPOINT	UN	Technicolor
CUSTER OF THE WEST	CIN	Technicolor
DAISIES	CZE	unknown
THE DAWNING NATION (YOWAKE NO KUNI)	JAP	Eastman Color
THE DAY THE FISH CAME OUT	GRE	DeLuxe Color

DEADLIER THAN THE MALE	FRA	Technicolor
THE DEADLY AFFAIR	BRI	Technicolor
THE DEADLY BEES	BRI	Technicolor
DEATH AND HOMICIDE	GER	Eastman Color
A DEGREE OF MURDER	GER	Eastman Color
DEVIL'S ANGELS	AI	Pathecolor
THE DEVIL'S OWN	BRI	DeLuxe Color
THE DIRTY DOZEN	MGM	Metrocolor
DIVORCE ITALIAN STYLE	COL	Technicolor
DOCTOR DOOLITTLE	TCF	DeLuxe Color
DOCTOR FAUSTUS	COL	Technicolor
DOCTOR, YOU'VE GOT TO BE KIDDING	MGM	Metrocolor
DON'T LOSE YOUR HEAD	BRI	Technicolor
DON'T MAKE WAVES	MGM	Metrocolor
THE DOUBLE MAN	BRI	Technicolor
DOUBLE TROUBLE	MGM	Metrocolor
THE DRUMS OF TABU	USA-SPA	Movielab
EASY COME, EASY GO	PAR	Technicolor
EIGHT ON THE LAM	UA	DeLuxe Color
EL DORADO	PAR	Technicolor
ELVIRA MADIGAN	SWE	Eastman Color
THE ENCHANTED FOREST	CAMBODIA	unknown
ENTER LAUGHING	COL	Pathecolor
A FAITHFUL SOLDIER OF PANCHO VILLA	MEX	Eastman Color
FANTOMAS AGAINST SCOTLAND YARD	FRA	Eastman Color
FAR FROM THE MADDING CROWD	MGM	Metrocolor
FAR FROM VIET-NAM	FRA	unknown
THE FASTEST GUITAR ALIVE	MGM	Metrocolor
FATHOM	TCF	DeLuxe Color
THE FEARLESS VAMPIRE KILLERS	MGM	Metrocolor
THE FICKLE FINGER OF FATE	SPA-USA	Movielab
FIRST TO FIGHT	WB	Metrocolor
FITZWILLY	UA	DeLuxe Color
FIVE ASHORE FOR SINGAPORE	FRA	Eastman Color
THE FLIM FLAM MAN	TCF	DeLuxe Color
THE FLYING MATCHMAKER	ISR	unknown
FOLLOW THAT CAMEL	BRI	Eastman Color
FORT UTAH	PAR	Technicolor
FOUR STARS	IND	Eastman Color
THE FOX	CAN	DeLuxe Color
FRANK'S GREATEST ADVENTURE	IND	Technicolor
FRANKENSTEIN CREATED WOMAN	BRI	DeLuxe Color
FUNNYMAN	IND	unknown
GAMERA VS. GYAOS	JAP	Eastman Color
GAMES	UN	Technicolor
GAPPA — TRIPHIBIAN MONSTER	JAP	Eastman Color
GENTLE GIANT	PAR	Eastman Color
THE GIRL AND THE GENERAL	ITA	unknown
GLORIOUS TIMES IN THE SPEEART	GER	Eastman Color
THE GNOME-MOBILE	DIS	Technicolor
GOHAKU MUIKA	JAP	Eastman Color
THE GOOD, THE BAD AND THE UGLY	ITA	Technicolor
GOOD MORNING . . . AND GOODBYE	IND	unknown
GOOD TIME	COL	DeLuxe
THE GRADUATE	EMB	Technicolor
LES GRAND MEULNES	FRA	Eastman Color
GRAND SLAM	ITA-GER-SPA	unknown
GUESS WHO'S COMING TO DINNER	COL	DeLuxe Color
A GUIDE FOR THE MARRIED MAN	TCF	DeLuxe Color
GUNFIRE IN ABILENE	UN	Technicolor
GUNN	PAR	Technicolor
HALF A SIXPENCE	PAR	Technicolor
THE HAPPENING	COL	Technicolor

THE HAPPIEST MILLIONAIRE	DIS	Technicolor
HEAD OF THE FAMILY	ITA-FRA	Eastman Color
HELL ON WHEELS	IND	Technicolor
HELL'S ANGELS ON WHEELS	IND	Eastman Color
THE HELLBENDERS	ITA	Pathecolor
THE HILLS RUN RED	ITA	Technicolor
THE HIPPIE REVOLT	IND	Technicolor
THE HIRED KILLER	ITA	Technicolor
HOMBRE	TCF	DeLuxe Color
THE HONEY POT	UA	Technicolor
HOODLUM'S SUN	FRA	Eastman Color
HORIZON	FRA	Eastman Color
HOSTILE GUNS	PAR	Technicolor
HOT RODS TO HELL	MGM	Metrocolor
HOTEL	WB	Technicolor
HOUR OF THE GUN	UA	DeLuxe Color
HOUSE OF 1,000 DOLLS	AI	Technicolor
HOW I WON THE WAR	BRI	DeLuxe Color
HOW TO SUCCEED IN BUSINESS WITHOUT REALLY TRYING	UA	DeLuxe Color
HUELGA	IND	unknown
HURRY SUNDOWN	PAR	Technicolor
I, A MAN	IND	Eastman Color
I AM MEXICO	FRA	Eastman Color
I BELONG TO ME	DEN	Eastman Color
I EVEN MET A HAPPY GYPSY	YUG	Eastman Color
I KILLED RASPUTIN	FRA	Eastman Color
I'LL NEVER FORGET WHAT'S 'IS NAME	BRI	Technicolor
AN IDIOT IN PARIS	FRA	Eastman Color
IN LIKE FLINT	TCF	DeLuxe Color
IN THE CLAWS OF THE GOLDEN DRAGON	GER-ITA-YUG	Eastman Color
IN THE HEAT OF THE NIGHT	UA	DeLuxe Color
INSIDE NORTH VIETNAM	IND	Eastman Color
ISLAND OF TERROR	BRI	Eastman Color
IT	BRI	Technicolor
JACK OF DIAMONDS	MGM	Metrocolor
JAGUAR	FRA	Eastman Color
JOHNNY YUMA	ITA	Eastman Color
THE JOKERS	UN	Technicolor
LA JUDOKA AGENT SECRET	FRA	Eastman Color
THE JUNGLE BOOK	DIS	Technicolor
JUST LIKE A WOMAN	BRI	Eastman Color
KAJA, I'LL KILL YOU	YUG	Eastman Color
KATERINA IZMAILOVA	RUS	Sovcolor
KILL A DRAGON	UA	DeLuxe Color
THE KILLING GAME	FRA	Eastman Color
KING'S PIRATE	UN	Technicolor
KNIVES OF THE AVENGER	ITA	Technicolor
LAMIEL	FRA	Eastman Color
THE LAST CHALLENGE	MGM	Metrocolor
THE LAST SAFARI	BRI	Technicolor
LAW OF SURVIVAL	FRA	Eastman Color
LET'S GO, YOUNG GUY!	JAP	Eastman Color
LIGHTNING BOLT	ITA-SPA	Technicolor
LIVE FOR LIFE	FRA	Eastman Color
THE LONG DUEL	BRI	Eastman Color
THE LOVE-INS	COL	Pathecolor
LOVE FOR AN IDIOT	JAP	Eastman Color
LUV	COL	Pathecolor
MADE IN ITALY	ITA	Technicolor
THE MAGNIFICIENT TWO	BRI	Eastman Color
MAMAIA	FRA	Eastman Color

A MAN CALLED DAGGER	MGM	Metrocolor
A MAN TO KILL	FRA-SPA	Eastman Color
THE MAN WHO BETRAYED THE MAFIA	FRA	Eastman Color
THE MAN WHO WAS WORTH MILLIONS	FRA	Eastman Color
MARAT/SADE	UA	unknown
MAROC 7	BRI	Eastman Color
MATCHLESS	ITA	DeLuxe Color
THE MIKADO	WB	Technicolor
MISUNDERSTOOD	FRA-ITA	Technicolor
MONDO HOLLYWOOD	IND	Pathecolor
MONKEYS GO HOME	DIS	Technicolor
THE MONSTERS OF LONDON CITY	GER	unknown
MORE THAN A MIRACLE	MGM	Metrocolor
THE MUMMY'S SHROUD	TCF	unknown
MY LOVE, MY LOVE	FRA	Eastman Color
THE NAKED RUNNER	WB	Technicolor
NAVAJO JOE	ITA-SPA	Technicolor
NIGHT OF THE GENERALS	COL	Technicolor
NO STARS IN THE JUNGLE	PERU	Eastman Color
THE NUDE RESTAURANT	IND	Eastman Color
OEDIPUS REX	ITA	Technicolor
OH, DAD, POOR DAD, MAMA'S HUNG YOU IN THE CLOSET AND I'M FEELIN' SO SAD	PAR	Technicolor
OLA AND JULIA	SWE	unknown
THE OLDEST PROFESSION IN THE WORLD	FRA-ITA-GER	Eastman Color
ONE TOO MANY	FRA	Eastman Color
THE 1,000,000 EYES OF SU-MURN	AI	Technicolor
OPERATION KID BROTHER	UA	Technicolor
OSCAR	FRA	Eastman Color
THE OTHER ONE	FRA	unknown
THE OTHER WORLD OF WINSTON CHURCHILL	BRI	Eastman Color
OUR MOTHER'S HOUSE	MGM	Metrocolor
THE OUTSIDERS	MEX	Eastman Color
PEKING REMEMBERED	IND	unknown
THE PENTHOUSE	PAR	Eastman Color
PEPPERMINT FRAPPE	SPA	Eastman Color
THE PERILS OF PAULINE	UN	Pathecolor
THE PHANTOM OF SOHO	GER	unknown
THE PICASSO LOOK	FRA	Eastman Color
PILLAGED	FRA	Eastman Color
A PISTOL SHOT	RUS	Sovcolor
PLAYTIME	FRA	Eastman Color
POINT BLANK	MGM	Metrocolor
POOR COW	BRI	Eastman Color
PREHISTORIC WOMEN	BRI	Technicolor
THE PRESIDENT'S ANALYST	PAR	Technicolor
PRETTY POLLY	UN	Technicolor
PRETTY-BOY AND ROSA	DEN	unknown
PRIVILEGE	BRI	Technicolor
THE PRODUCERS	EMB	Pathecolor
THE PROJECTED MAN	BRI	Technicolor
THE RAPE	FRA-SWE	Eastman Color
RED DRAGON	ITA-GER-USA	Technicolor
THE RED MANTLE	DEN-SWE-ICE	Eastman Color
REFLECTIONS IN A GOLDEN EYE	WB	Technicolor
THE RELUCTANT ASTRONAUT	UN	Technicolor
THE RETURN OF MAJIN	JAP	Eastman Color
RHEINSBERG	GER	Eastman Color
THE RIDE TO HANGMAN'S TREE	UN	Technicolor
RIOT ON SUNSET STRIP	AI	Pathecolor
THE ROAD TO CORINTH	FRA	Eastman Color
ROBBERY	BRI	Pathecolor

A ROSE FOR EVERYONE	ITA	Technicolor
ROSIE	UN	Technicolor
ROUGH NIGHT IN JERICHO	UN	Technicolor
ROUND TRIP	CON	unknown
SADISIMO	ITA	unknown
ST. VALENTINE'S DAY MASSACRE	TCF	DeLuxe Color
THE SAMURAI	FRA	Eastman Color
SAMURAI (PART 2)	JAP	Eastman Color
SAMURAI (PART 3)	JAP	Eastman Color
SASAKI KOJIRO	JAP	unknown
SAUTERELLE	FRA	unknown
THE SAVAGE EYE	ITA	Technicolor
SAVAGE PAMPAS	SPA	unknown
THE SCANDAL	FRA	Eastman Color
SCANDAL IN THE FAMILY	ARG-SPA	unknown
SCATTERED CLOUDS	JAP	Eastman Color
THE SEA PIRATE	FRA-SPA-ITA	Eastman Color
SEVEN GUYS AND A GAL	FRA-ITA-RUM	Eastman Color
SEVENTH CONTINENT	YUG	Eastman Color
THE SEVENTH FLOOR	ITA	Eastman Color
THE SHUTTERED ROOM	BRI	Technicolor
SIEGFRIED	GER-YUG	Eastman Color
SKI ON THE WILD SIDE	IND	Eastman Color
SMASHING TIME	BRI	unknown
SONG OF THE FIREMAN	CZE	Eastman Color
THE SORCERERS	BRI	Eastman Color
SORREL FLOWER	FRA	Eastman Color
THE SPIRIT IS WILLING	PAR	Technicolor
SPREE	IND	Pathecolor
A SPY'S SKIN	FRA-GER-ITA	unknown
STEW IN THE CARIBBEAN	FRA	Eastman Color
THE STRANGER	ITA-FRA	unknown
STRANGER IN THE HOUSE	BRI	Eastman Color
SULLIVAN'S EMPIRE	UN	unknown
SURFARI	IND	Eastman Color
THE SWAN LAKE	SA	Eastman Color
THE TAMING OF THE SHREW	COL	Technicolor
TAMMY AND THE MILLIONAIRE	UN	Pathecolor
TARZAN AND THE GREAT RIVER	PAR	Eastman Color
TATTOO	GER	unknown
THE TERRORNAUTS	EMB	Pathecolor
THEATRE DE MONSIEUR ET MADAME KABAL	FRA	Eastman Color
THEY CAME FROM BEYOND SPACE	EMB	Pathecolor
THE THIEF	FRA	Eastman Color
THIS IS JOY	ARG	Eastman Color
THOROUGHLY MODERN MILLIE	UN	Technicolor
THOSE FANTASTIC FLYING FOOLS	UN	Technicolor
THREE BITES OF THE APPLE	MGM	Metrocolor
THEY ARE NOT ORANGES, THEY ARE HORSES	DEN	Eastman Color
THREE MEN IN SEARCH OF A TROLL	DEN	Eastman Color
THREE NIGHTS OF LOVE	HUN	Eastman Color
THUNDER ALLEY	AI	unknown
THE TIGER AND THE PUSSYCAT	ITA	Pathecolor
THE TIGER MAKES OUT	COL	Eastman Color
TO EACH HIS OWN	ITA	Technicolor
TO HELL WITH THE PRIEST	ARG	Eastman Color
TO SIR WITH LOVE	COL	Technicolor
TOM THUMB	MEX	Eastman Color
TOMORROW'S ANOTHER DAY	SPA	Eastman Color
TONITE LET'S ALL MAKE LOVE IN LONSON	BRI	unknown
TONY ROME	TCF	DeLuxe Color
TOPO GIGIO AND THE MISSILE WAR	JAP-ITA	Eastman Color
THE TRAITORS OF SAN ANGEL	ARG-USA	Eastman Color

THE TRIP	AI	unknown
TWO FOR THE ROAD	TCF	DeLuxe Color
TWO OF THREE THINGS I KNOW ABOUT HER	FRA	Eastman Color
UNTAMABLE ANGELIQUE	FRA-GER-ITA	Eastman Color
UP THE DOWN STAIRCASE	WB	Technicolor
THE UPPER HAND (RIFIFI DU PANAMA)	FRA	unknown
VALI	FRA	unknown
VALLEY OF MYSTERY	UN	Technicolor
VALLEY OF THE DOLLS	TCF	DeLuxe Color
THE VIKING QUEEN	TCF	DeLuxe Color
THE VIOLENT ONES	IND	unknown
THE VISCOUNT SETTLES ACCOUNTS	FRA-ITA-SPA	Eastman Color
WAIT UNTIL DARK	WB	Technicolor
WAR — ITALIAN STYLE	ITA	Technicolor
WAR AND PEACE III	RUS	Sovcolor
WAR KILL	PHI	DeLuxe Color
THE WAR WAGON	UN	Technicolor
WATERHOLE NO. 3	PAR	Technicolor
THE WAY WEST	UA	DeLuxe Color
WELCOME TO HARD TIMES	MGM	Metrocolor
WHAT AM I BID?	IND	Technicolor
WHEN THE COOKIE CRUMBLES	JAP	Eastman Color
WHERE TO LIVE AFTER RAIN?	YUG	unknown
WHO KNOWS?	ITA	Eastman Color
WHO'S MINDING THE MINT?	COL	Pathecolor
THE WILD REBELS	IND	Technicolor
WILD, WILD PLANET	ITA	Eastman Color
WINNETOU AND HIS FRIEND OLD FIREHAND	GER	Eastman Color
A WITCH WITHOUT A BROOM	SPA	Movielab
WITH JOYOUS HEART	FRA	Eastman Color
WOMAN TIMES SEVEN	EMB	Pathecolor
WOULD YOU MARRY ME?	ARG-SPA	Eastman Color
YOU ONLY LIVE TWICE	UA	Technicolor
YOUNG AMERICANS	COL	Technicolor
YOUNG GIRLS OF ROCHEFORT	FRA	Eastman Color
THE YOUNG WARRIORS	UN	Technicolor
ZATO — ICHI'S RAMBLING TRAVELS	JAP	Eastman Color

APPENDIX TWO
WIDESCREEN FILMS

	1900		
LUMIERE FILMS		FRA	Widescreen
CINEORAMA		FRA	Cineorama
	1921		
J'ACCUSE		FRA	Polyvision
WIDESCOPE PRESENTATION		IND	Widescope
	1922		
MAGIRAMA PROGRAM		FRA	Polyvision
	1924		
TRI-ERGON		GER	Tri-Ergon
	1925		
NAPOLEON		FRA	Polyvision
NORTH OF '36		PAR	Magnascope
THE THUNDERING HERD		PAR	Magnascope
	1926		
OLD IRONSIDES		PAR	Magnascope
	1927		
THE AMERICAN		IND	Natural Vision
CHANG		PAR	Magnascope
THE LAST WALTZ		PAR	Magnascope
TWINKLETOES		FN	Magnascope
WINGS		PAR	Magnascope
	1929		
FOX MOVIETONE FOLLIES OF 1929		TCF	Grandeur
HAPPY DAYS		TCF	Grandeur
POUR CONSTRUIRE UN FEU		FRA	Hypergonar
WE'RE IN THE NAVY NOW		PAR	Magnifilm
WATERLOO		FRA	Polyvision
WE'RE IN THE NAVY NOW		PAR	Magnifilm
	1930		
THE BAT WHISPERS		UA	65mm film
THE BIG TRAIL		TCF	Grandeur
BILLY THE KID		MGM	Realife
DANGER LIGHTS		RKO	Natural Vision
KISMET		WB	65mm film
	1931		
GREAT MEADOW		MGM	Realife
THE LASH		WB	65mm film
	1939		
STAGECOACH		UA	Magnascope
VITARAMA (NEW YORK WORLD'S FAIR)		IND	Vitarama
	1948		
PORTRAIT OF JENNY		SRO	Magnascope

	1952		
MILLION DOLLAR MERMAID		MGM	Magnascope
THIS IS CINERAMA		CIN	Cinerama
THE WILD HEART		RKO	Magnascope
	1953		
BENEATH THE 12-MILE REEF		TCF	CinemaScope
THE COMMAND		WB	CinemaScope
HOW TO MARRY A MILLIONAIRE		TCF	CinemaScope
KNIGHTS OF THE ROUND TABLE		MGM	CinemaScope
NIAGARA		TCF	Magnascope
THE ROBE		TCF	CinemaScope
	1954		
ADVENTURES OF HAJJI BABA		TCF	CinemaScope
ATHENA		MGM	CinemaScope
BAD DAY AT BLACK ROCK		MGM	CinemaScope
BLACK SHIELD OF FALWORTH		UN	CinemaScope
BLACK WIDOW		TCF	CinemaScope
BRIGADOON		MGM	CinemaScope
BROKEN LANCE		TCF	CinemaScope
CARMEN JONES		TCF	CinemaScope
CATTLE QUEEN OF MONTANA		RKO	SuperScope
DEMITRIUS AND THE GLADIATORS		TCF	CinemaScope
DESIREE		TCF	CinemaScope
THE EGYPTIAN		TCF	CinemaScope
GARDEN OF EVIL		TCF	CinemaScope
GREEN FIRE		MGM	CinemaScope
HELL AND HIGH WATER		TCF	CinemaScope
THE HIGH AND THE MIGHTY		WB	CinemaScope
KING RICHARD AND THE CRUSADERS		WB	CinemaScope
KING OF THE KHYBER RIFLES		TCF	CinemaScope
LUCKY ME		WB	CinemaScope
NEW FACES		TCF	CinemaScope
NIGHT PEOPLE		TCF	CinemaScope
PRINCE VALIANT		TCF	CinemaScope
RING OF FEAR		WB	CinemaScope
RIVER OF NO RETURN		TCF	CinemaScope
ROSE-MARIE		MGM	CinemaScope
SEVEN BRIDES FOR SEVEN BROTHERS		MGM	CinemaScope
SIGN OF THE PAGAN		UN	CinemaScope
THE SILVER CHALICE		WB	CinemaScope
SITTING BULL		UA	CinemaScope
A STAR IS BORN		WB	CinemaScope
THE STUDENT PRINCE		MGM	CinemaScope
THERE'S NO BUSINESS LIKE SHOW BUSINESS		TCF	CinemaScope
THREE COINS IN THE FOUNTAIN		TCF	CinemaScope
THREE RING CIRCUS		PAR	VistaVision
TRACK OF THE CAT		WB	CinemaScope
20,000 LEAGUES UNDER THE SEA		BV	CinemaScope
VERA CRUZ		UA	SuperScope
WHITE CHRISTMAS		PAR	VistaVision
A WOMAN'S WORLD		TCF	CinemaScope
	1955		
ARTISTS AND MODELS		PAR	VistaVision
AT GUNPOINT		AA	CinemaScope
BATTLE CRY		WB	CinemaScope
BEDEVILLED		MGM	CinemaScope
BENGAZI		RKO	SuperScope
BLOOD ALLEY		WB	CinemaScope
THE BOLD AND THE BRAVE		RKO	SuperScope
CAPTAIN LIGHTFOOT		UN	CinemaScope
THE CHARGE OF THE RURALES		MEX	SuperScope
CHIEF CRAZY HORSE		UN	CinemaScope

CINERAMA HOLIDAY	CIN	Cinerama
THE COBWEB	MGM	CinemaScope
COUNT THREE AND PRAY	COL	CinemaScope
THE COURT MARTIAL OF BILLY MITCHELL	WB	CinemaScope
DADDY LONG LEGS	TCF	CinemaScope
DEEP BLUE SEA	TCF	CinemaScope
DESERT SANDS	UA	SuperScope
THE DESPERATE HOURS	PAR	VistaVision
DIANE	MGM	CinemaScope
EAST OF EDEN	WB	CinemaScope
ESCAPE TO BURMA	RKO	SuperScope
THE FAR HORIZONS	PAR	VistaVision
GENTLEMEN MARRY BRUNETTES	UA	CinemaScope
THE GIRL IN THE RED VELVET SWING	TCF	CinemaScope
THE GIRL RUSH	PAR	VistaVision
GOOD MORNING, MISS DOVE	TCF	CinemaScope
GUYS AND DOLLS	MGM	CinemaScope
HELEN OF TROY	WB	CinemaScope
HELL ON FRISCO BAY	WB	CinemaScope
HELL'S ISLAND	PAR	VistaVision
HIT THE DECK	MGM	CinemaScope
HOUSE OF BAMBOO	TCF	CinemaScope
HOW TO BE VERY, VERY POPULAR	TCF	CinemaScope
I DIED A THOUSAND TIMES	WB	CinemaScope
THE INDIAN FIGHTER	UA	CinemaScope
INTERRUPTED MELODY	MGM	CinemaScope
IT'S A DOG'S LIFE	MGM	CinemaScope
IT'S ALWAYS FAIR WEATHER	MGM	CinemaScope
JUPITER'S DARLING	MGM	CinemaScope
THE KENTUCKIAN	UA	CinemaScope
THE KING'S THIEF	MGM	CinemaScope
KISMET	MGM	CinemaScope
LADY AND THE TRAMP	BV	CinemaScope
LAND OF THE PHARAOHS	UN	CinemaScope
THE LAST FRONTIER	COL	CinemaScope
THE LEFT HAND OF GOD	TCF	CinemaScope
THE LONG GRAY LINE	COL	CinemaScope
LONG JOHN SILVER	DCA	CinemaScope
LOVE IS A MANY-SPLENDORED THING	TCF	CinemaScope
LOVE ME OR LEAVE ME	MGM	CinemaScope
LUCY GALLANT	PAR	VistaVision
THE McCONNELL STORY	WB	CinemaScope
THE MAGNIFICENT MATADOR	TCF	CinemaScope
A MAN CALLED PETER	TCF	CinemaScope
THE MAN FROM LARAMIE	COL	CinemaScope
MANY RIVERS TO CROSS	MGM	CinemaScope
MISTER ROBERTS	WB	CinemaScope
MOONFLEET	MGM	CinemaScope
MY SISTER EILEEN	COL	CinemaScope
OKLAHOMA	IND	Todd-AO
PEARL OF THE SOUTH PACIFIC	RKO	SuperScope
PETE KELLY'S BLUES	WB	CinemaScope
PICNIC	COL	CinemaScope
PRINCE OF PLAYERS	TCF	CinemaScope
THE PRODIGAL	MGM	CinemaScope
THE PURPLE MASK	UN	CinemaScope
QUENTIN DURWARD	MGM	CinemaScope
THE RACERS	TCF	CinemaScope
THE RAINS OF RANCHIPUR	TCF	CinemaScope
REBEL WITHOUT A CAUSE	WB	CinemaScope
THE RETURN OF JACK SLADE	AA	SuperScope
THE ROSE TATTOO	PAR	VistaVision
RUN FOR COVER	PAR	VistaVision

THE SCARLET COAT	MGM	CinemaScope
THE SEA CHASE	WB	CinemaScope
THE SECOND GREATEST SEX	UN	CinemaScope
SEVEN CITIES OF GOLD	TCF	CinemaScope
SEVEN LEAGUES	MEX	SuperScope
THE SEVEN LITTLE FOYS	PAR	VistaVision
THE SEVEN YEAR ITCH	TCF	CinemaScope
SOLDIER OF FORTUNE	TCF	CinemaScope
SON OF SINBAD	RKO	SuperScope
STRANGE LADY IN TOWN	WB	CinemaScope
STRATEGIC AIR COMMAND	PAR	VistaVision
THE TALL MEN	TCF	CinemaScope
THE TENDER TRAP	MGM	CinemaScope
TENNESSEE'S PARTNER	RKO	SuperScope
TEXAS LADY	RKO	SuperScope
THAT LADY	TCF	CinemaScope
THREE FOR THE SHOW	COL	CinemaScope
TO CATCH A THIEF	PAR	VistaVision
TO HELL AND BACK	UN	CinemaScope
THE TREASURE OF PANCHO VILLA	RKO	SuperScope
THE TROUBLE WITH HARRY	PAR	VistaVision
UNDERWATER!	RKO	SuperScope
UNTAMED	TCF	CinemaScope
THE VIEW FROM POMPEY'S HEAD	TCF	CinemaScope
THE VIOLENT MAN	COL	CinemaScope
VIOLENT SATURDAY	TCF	CinemaScope
THE VIRGIN QUEEN	TCF	CinemaScope
THE WARRIORS	AA	CinemaScope
WE'RE NO ANGELS	PAR	VistaVision
WHITE FEATHER	TCF	CinemaScope
WICHITA	AA	CinemaScope
YOU LUCKY PEOPLE	BRI	CameraScope
YOU'RE NEVER TOO YOUNG	PAR	VistaVision

1956

ACCUSED OF MURDER	REP	Naturama
AN AFFAIR TO REMEMBER	TCF	CinemaScope
ALEXANDER THE GREAT	UA	CinemaScope
THE AMBASSADOR'S DAUGHTER	UA	CinemaScope
ANASTASIA	TCF	CinemaScope
ANYTHING GOES	PAR	VistaVision
AROUND THE WORLD IN 80 DAYS	UA	Todd-AO
AWAY ALL BOATS	UN	VistaVision
BANDIDO	UA	CinemaScope
BATTLE HYMN	UN	CinemaScope
THE BATTLE OF RIVER PLATE	BRI	VistaVision
THE BEAST OF HOLLOW MOUNTAIN	UA	CinemaScope
THE BEST THINGS IN LIFE ARE FREE	TCF	CinemaScope
BETWEEN HEAVEN AND HELL	TCF	CinemaScope
BHOWANI JUNCTION	MGM	CinemaScope
BIGGER THAN LIFE	TCF	CinemaScope
THE BIRDS AND THE BEES	PAR	VistaVision
THE BOTTOM OF THE BOTTLE	TCF	CinemaScope
THE BRAVE ONE	RKO	CinemaScope
THE BURNING FUSE	FRA-ITA	Dyaliscope
THE BURNING HILLS	WB	CinemaScope
BUS STOP	TCF	CinemaScope
CANYON RIVER	AA	CinemaScope
CAROUSEL	TCF	CinemaScope 55
LA CHATELAINE DU LIBAN	FRA-ITA	CinemaScope
THE COCKLESHELL HEROES	COL	CinemaScope
COMANCHE	UA	CinemaScope
THE CONQUEROR	RKO	CinemaScope
THE COURT JESTER	PAR	VistaVision

LE COUTEAU SOUS LA GORGE	FRA	Cinepanoramic
D-DAY, THE SIXTH OF JUNE	TCF	CinemaScope
THE DESPERADOES ARE IN TOWN	TCF	Regalscope
DIMANCHE	FRA	Franscope
DOCTOR AT SEA	BRI	VistaVision
DONATELLA	ITA	CinemaScope
THE EDDIE DUCHIN STORY	COL	CinemaScope
THE FIRST TEXAN	AA	CinemaScope
FIVE GUINEAS A WEEK	BRI	CosmoScope
THE FORBIDDEN PLANET	MGM	CinemaScope
FOUR GIRLS IN TOWN	UN	CinemaScope
FREEDOM	IND	VistaVision
GABY	MGM	CinemaScope
THE GIRL CAN'T HELP IT	TCF	CinemaScope
GLORY	RKO	SuperScope
GREAT DAY IN THE MORNING	RKO	SuperScope
THE GREAT LOCOMOTIVE CHASE	BV	CinemaScope
HIGH SOCIETY	MGM	VistaVision
HILDA CRANE	TCF	CinemaScope
HOLLYWOOD OR BUST	PAR	VistaVision
L'HOMME ET L'ENFANT	FRA	CinemaScope
HOT BLOOD	COL	CinemaScope
INTERNATIONAL POLICE	BRI	CinemaScope
INVASION OF THE BODY SNATCHERS	AA	SuperScope
IT HAPPENED IN ADEN	FRA	Dyaliscope
JE REVIENDRAI A KANDARA	FRA	CinemaScope
JUBAL	COL	CinemaScope
JUKA	FIN	AgaScope
THE KING AND I	TCF	CinemaScope 55
A KISS BEFORE DYING	UA	CinemaScope
THE LAST HUNT	MGM	CinemaScope
THE LAST WAGON	TCF	CinemaScope
THE LEATHER SAINT	PAR	VistaVision
THE LIEUTENANT WORE SKIRTS	TCF	CinemaScope
LISBON	REP	Naturama
LOVE ME TENDER	TCF	CinemaScope
LUST FOR LIFE	MGM	CinemaScope
THE MAN IN THE GRAY FLANNEL SUIT	TCF	CinemaScope
THE MAN WHO KNEW TOO MUCH	PAR	VistaVision
THE MAN WHO NEVER WAS	TCF	CinemaScope
MANNEQUINS DE PARIS	FRA	Franscope
THE MAVERICK QUEEN	REP	Naturama
MEET ME IN LAS VEGAS	MGM	CinemaScope
LA MEILLEURE PART	FRA-ITA	CinemaScope
MILORD L'ARSOULLIE	FRA	CinemaScope
MOHAWK	TCF	WideVision
THE MOUNTAIN	PAR	VistaVision
ODONGO	BRI	CinemaScope
ON THE THRESHOLD OF SPACE	TCF	CinemaScope
THE OPPOSITE SEX	MGM	CinemaScope
PARDNERS	PAR	VistaVision
PICASSO (sequences)	FRA	CinemaScope
PILLARS OF THE SKY	UN	CinemaScope
PITY FOR THE VAMPS	FRA	Dyaliscope
THE POWER AND THE PRIZE	MGM	CinemaScope
THE PROUD AND THE PROFANE	PAR	VistaVision
THE PROUD ONES	TCF	CinemaScope
THE RAINMAKER	PAR	VistaVision
THE REVOLT OF MAMIE STOVER	TCF	CinemaScope
RICHARD III	UA	VistaVision
RUN FOR THE SUN	UA	SuperScope
SAFARI	COL	CinemaScope
SATELLITE IN THE SKY	WB	CinemaScope
THE SCARLET HOUR	PAR	VistaVision

THE SEARCH FOR BRIDEY MURPHY	PAR	VistaVision
THE SEARCHERS	WB	VistaVision
SECRETS OF LIFE (sequences)	BV	CinemaScope
SEVEN WONDERS OF THE WORLD	CIN	Cinerama
THE SHARKFIGHTERS	UA	CinemaScope
SIMON AND LAURA	UN	VistaVision
SLIGHTLY SCARLET	RKO	SuperScope
STAGECOACH TO FURY	TCF	Regalscope
STARS IN YOUR EYES	BRI	SpectaScope
STORM OVER THE NILE	COL	CinemaScope
THE SWAN	MGM	CinemaScope
TEA AND SYMPATHY	MGM	CinemaScope
THE TEAHOUSE OF THE AUGUST MOON	MGM	CinemaScope
TEENAGE REBEL	TCF	CinemaScope
THE TEN COMMANDMENTS	PAR	VistaVision
THAT CERTAIN FEELING	PAR	VistaVision
THREE VIOLENT PEOPLE	PAR	VistaVision
THUNDER OVER ARIZONA	REP	Naturama
TRAPEZE	UA	CinemaScope
TRIBUTE TO A BAD MAN	MGM	CinemaScope
23 PACES TO BAKER STREET	TCF	CinemaScope
THE VAGABOND KING	PAR	VistaVision
WALK THE PROUD LAND	UN	CinemaScope
WAR AND PEACE	PAR	VistaVision
WEDDING IN MONACO	MGM	CinemaScope
WESTWARD HO, THE WAGONS	BV	CinemaScope
THE WOMEN OF PITCAIRN ISLAND	TCF	Regalscope
WORLD WITHOUT END	AA	CinemaScope
YOU CAN'T RUN AWAY FROM IT	COL	CinemaScope

1957

THE ABOMINABLE SNOWMAN	TCF	Regalscope
ACTION OF THE TIGER	MGM	CinemaScope
AFFAIR IN RENO	REP	Naturama
APACHE WARRIOR	TCF	Regalscope
APRIL LOVE	TCF	CinemaScope
BACK FROM THE DEAD	TCF	Regalscope
THE BARRETTS OF WIMPOLE STREET	MGM	CinemaScope
BEAU JAMES	PAR	VistaVision
BERNARDINE	TCF	CinemaScope
THE BLACK TENT	BRI	VistaVision
THE BLACK WHIP	TCF	Regalscope
BOMBERS B-52	WB	CinemaScope
BOY ON A DOLPHIN	TCF	CinemaScope
THE BRIDGE ON THE RIVER KWAI	COL	CinemaScope
THE BUSTER KEATON STORY	PAR	VistaVision
CANASTA DE CUENTOS MEXICANOS	MEX	CinemaScope
CE SOIR LES JUPONS VOLENT	FRA	Dyaliscope
CHINA GATE	TCF	CinemaScope
COPPER SKY	TCF	Regalscope
DANGEROUS EXILE	BRI	VistaVision
THE DEERSLAYER	TCF	CinemaScope
DESIGNING WOMEN	MGM	CinemaScope
DESK SET	TCF	CinemaScope
THE DEVIL'S HAIRPIN	PAR	VistaVision
LE DICIOTTENNI	ITA	SuperFilmScope
DOCTOR AT LARGE	BRI	VistaVision
DON QUIXOTE	RUS	Sovscope
DON'T GO NEAR THE WATER	MGM	CinemaScope
THE DOOR IN THE WALL	IND	VistaVision
DRAGOON WELLS MASSACRE	AA	CinemaScope
DUEL AT APACHE WELLS	REP	Naturama
THE ENEMY BELOW	TCF	CinemaScope
ESCAPADE IN JAPAN	UN	Technirama

FANTASIA (re-issue)	BV	SuperScope
FIRE DOWN BELOW	COL	CinemaScope
FORTY GUNS	TCF	CinemaScope
FUN AT ST. FANNY'S	BRI	CinemaScope
FUNNY FACE	PAR	VistaVision
LA GATA	SPA	CinemaScope
GHOST RIVER	TCF	Regalscope
GOD IS MY PARTNER	TCF	Regalscope
THE GOOD COMPANIONS	BRI	CinemaScope
GUN FOR A COWARD	UN	CinemaScope
GUN GLORY	MGM	CinemaScope
A HATFUL OF RAIN	TCF	CinemaScope
HE WHO MUST DIE	FRA	CinemaScope
HEAR ME GOOD	PAR	VistaVision
HEAVEN KNOWS, MR. ALLISON	TCF	CinemaScope
THE HELEN MORGAN STORY	WB	CinemaScope
HELL'S CROSSROADS	REP	Naturama
THE HIRED GUN	MGM	CinemaScope
HOUSE OF NUMBERS	MGM	CinemaScope
HOUSE OF SECRETS	BRI	VistaVision
THE HUNCHBACK OF NOTRE DAME	AA	CinemaScope
INTERLUDE	UN	CinemaScope
THE IRON PETTICOAT	MGM	VistaVision
ISABELLE IS AFRAID OF MEN	FRA	Dyaliscope
ISLAND IN THE SUN	TCF	CinemaScope
ISTANBUL	UN	CinemaScope
IT HAPPENED IN ROME	ITA	Technirama
IT'S A WONDERFUL WORLD	BRI	Spectascope
JAILHOUSE ROCK	MGM	CinemaScope
JET PILOT	UN	SuperScope
JOE BUTTERFLY	UN	CinemaScope
KELLY AND ME	UN	CinemaScope
THE KING AND FOUR QUEENS	UA	CinemaScope
KISS THEM FOR ME	TCF	CinemaScope
KRONOS	TCF	Regalscope
THE LAND UNKNOWN	UN	CinemaScope
THE LAST OF THE BADMEN	AA	CinemaScope
LES GIRLS	MGM	CinemaScope
LET'S BE HAPPY	AA	CinemaScope
THE LIVING IDOL	MGM	CinemaScope
THE LONELY MAN	PAR	VistaVision
LOSER TAKE ALL	BRI	CinemaScope
LOVING YOU	PAR	VistaVision
LURE OF THE SWAMP	TCF	Regalscope
MAN AFRAID	UN	CinemaScope
MAN IN THE SHADOW	UN	CinemaScope
MAN OF A THOUSAND FACES	UN	CinemaScope
THE MARCH HARE	BRI	CinemaScope
THE MIDNIGHT STORY	UN	CinemaScope
MIO FIGLIO NERONE	FRA-ITA	CinemaScope
MISTER CORY	UN	CinemaScope
THE MONTE CARLO STORY	UA	Technirama
MY MAN GODFREY	UN	CinemaScope
NIGHT PASSAGE	UN	Technirama
NO DOWN PAYMENT	TCF	CinemaScope
NO SUN IN VENICE	FRA-ITA	CinemaScope
OASIS	FRA	CinemaScope
OH, MEN! OH, WOMEN!	TCF	CinemaScope
THE OKLAHOMAN	AA	CinemaScope
OMAR KHAYYAM	PAR	VistaVision
PANAMA SAL	REP	Naturama
PLUNDER ROAD	TCF	Regalscope
THE PRIDE AND THE PASSION	UA	VistaVision
QUANTEZ	UN	CinemaScope

THE QUIET GUN	TCF	Regalscope
RACCONTI ROMANI	ITA	CinemaScope
RAINTREE COUNTY	MGM	Panavision
RIDE A VIOLENT MILE	TCF	Regalscope
LA RISAIA	ITA	CinemaScope
THE RIVER'S EDGE	TCF	CinemaScope
ROCKABILLY BABY	TCF	Regalscope
THE SAD SACK	PAR	VistaVision
SAYONARA	WB	Technirama
SEA WIFE	TCF	CinemaScope
SEARCH FOR PARADISE	IND	Cinerama
THE SEVENTH SIN	MGM	CinemaScope
SHORT CUT TO HELL	PAR	VistaVision
SILK STOCKINGS	MGM	CinemaScope
SMILEY	TCF	CinemaScope
THE SPANISH GARDNER	BRI	VistaVision
THE SPIRIT OF ST. LOUIS	WB	CinemaScope
SPOILERS OF THE FOREST	REP	Naturama
THE STORM RIDER	TCF	Regalscope
THE SUN ALSO RISES	TCF	CinemaScope
THE TALL STRANGER	TCF	CinemaScope
TALPA	MEX	CinemaScope
TAMMY AND THE BACHELOR	UN	CinemaScope
TARNISHED ANGELS	UN	CinemaScope
THE TATTERED DRESS	UN	CinemaScope
TEN THOUSAND BEDROOMS	MGM	CinemaScope
THIS COULD BE THE NIGHT	MGM	CinemaScope
THREE MEN IN A BOAT	BRI	CinemaScope
THRILLARAMA ADVENTURE	IND	Thrillarama
THE TIN STAR	PAR	VistaVision
TIP ON A DEAD JOCKEY	MGM	CinemaScope
THE TRUE STORY OF JESSE JAMES	TCF	CinemaScope
UNDER FIRE	TCF	Regalscope
UNKNOWN TERROR	TCF	Regalscope
UOMINI E LUPI	ITA	CinemaScope
I VAMPIRI	ITA	CinemaScope
THE VINTAGE	MGM	CinemaScope
THE WAY TO THE GOLD	TCF	CinemaScope
THE WAYWARD BUS	TCF	CinemaScope
THE WAYWARD GIRL	REP	Naturama
WILD AS THE WIND	PAR	VistaVision
WILL SUCCESS SPOIL ROCK HUNTER?	TCF	CinemaScope
YOUNG AND DANGEROUS	TCF	Regalscope
ZARAK	COL	CinemaScope

1958

LOS AMANTES DEL DESIERTO	SPA	CinemaScope
AMBUSH AT CIMARRON PASS	TCF	Regalscope
AVIORAMA	ITA	Aviorama
ANOTHER TIME, ANOTHER PLACE	PAR	VistaVision
THE BADLANDERS	MGM	CinemaScope
THE BEGGAR STUDENT	GER	SuperScope
THE BIG COUNTRY	UA	Technirama
LES BIJOUTIERS DU CLAIR DE LUNE	FRA	CinemaScope
BITTER VICTORY	COL	CinemaScope
BLOOD ARROW	TCF	Regalscope
BONJOUR TRISTESSE	COL	CinemaScope
THE BONNIE PARKER STORY	AI	Superama
THE BRAVADOS	TCF	CinemaScope
BULLWHIP	AA	CinemaScope
THE CAMP ON BLOOD ISLAND	BRI	Megascope
CATTLE EMPIRE	TCF	CinemaScope
A CERTAIN SMILE	TCF	CinemaScope
CES DAMES PREFERENT LE MAMBO	FRA	Franscope

CINETARIUM	GER	Cinetarium
CIRCARAMA	IND	Circarama
COLE YOUNGER, GUNFIGHTER	AA	CinemaScope
COUNT FIVE AND DIE	AA	CinemaScope
DAVY	BRI	Technirama
DAY OF THE BADMEN	UN	CinemaScope
DESIRE UNDER THE ELMS	PAR	VistaVision
DESERT HELL	TCF	Regalscope
DOSANGO	JAP	CinemaScope
DUNKIRK	BRI	Metroscope
L'EAU VIVE	FRA	Franscope
ESCAPE FROM RED ROCK	TCF	Regalscope
FAMILY DOCTOR	FRA	Franscope
FATICHE DI ERCOLE	ITA	Dyaliscope
THE FEMALE ANIMAL	UN	CinemaScope
THE FIEND WHO WALKED THE WEST	TCF	CinemaScope
FLOOD TIDE	UN	CinemaScope
THE FLUTE AND THE ARROW (EN DJUNGELSAGA)	SWE	AgaScope
THE FLY	TCF	CinemaScope
FORT MASSACRE	UA	CinemaScope
FRANKENSTEIN —1970	AA	CinemaScope
FRAULEIN	TCF	CinemaScope
FROM HELL TO TEXAS	TCF	CinemaScope
GANG WAR	TCF	Regalscope
THE GIFT OF LOVE	TCF	CinemaScope
GIGI	MGM	CinemaScope
LA GRANDE STRADA ASSURRA	FRA-ITA	SuperScope
GUNMAN'S WALK	COL	CinemaScope
GUNSMOKE IN TUCSON	AA	CinemaScope
HARRY BLACK AND THE TIGER	TCF	CinemaScope
HENRY (re-issue)	UA	SuperScope
THE HIGH COST OF LOVING	MGM	CinemaScope
HIGH FLIGHT	COL	CinemaScope
HOT SPELL	PAR	VistaVision
THE HUNTERS	TCF	CinemaScope
I ACCUSE!	MGM	CinemaScope
I KARI NO KOTO	JAP	CinemaScope
IMITATION GENERAL	MGM	CinemaScope
INCOGNITO	FRA	Dyaliscope
INTENT TO KILL	TCF	CinemaScope
JUVENILE JUNGLE	REP	Naturama
THE KEY	COL	CinemaScope
KING CREOLE	PAR	VistaVision
THE LADY TAKES A FLYER	UN	CinemaScope
THE LAST PARADISE (L'ULTIMO PARADISO)	ITA	Ultrascope
THE LAW AND JAKE WADE	MGM	CinemaScope
LIBERTE SEREVEILLE	FRA-CZE	Franscope
THE LONG HOT SUMMER	TCF	CinemaScope
THE LORD TAKES A BRIDE	JAP	CinemaScope
LOVE ALONG A RIVER	FIN	AgaScope
A LOVE STORY	GER	Plastorama
MACHINE GUN KELLY	AI	Superama
MAMZELLE PIGALE (CETTE SACREE GAMINE)	FRA	CinemaScope
THE MAN FROM GOD'S COUNTRY	AA	CinemaScope
MAN IN THE SHADOW	UN	CinemaScope
MARACAIBO	PAR	VistaVision
MARK OF THE HAWK	UN	SuperScope
THE MATCHMAKER	PAR	VistaVision
MERRY ANDREW	MGM	CinemaScope
THE NAKED AND THE DEAD	WB	WarnerScope
NAKED EARTH	TCF	CinemaScope
THE NIGHT HEAVEN FELL	FRA	CinemaScope

THE NOTORIOUS MR. MONKS	REP	Naturama
ONCE UPON A HORSE	UN	CinemaScope
OREGON PASSAGE	AA	CinemaScope
PANAMA SAL	REP	Naturama
PARDISI	RUS	Sovscope
PARIS HOLIDAY	UA	Technirama
QUANTRILL'S RAIDERS	AA	CinemaScope
RAGAZZA DEL PALIO	ITA	Technirama
RAW WIND IN EDEN	UN	CinemaScope
THE RELUCTANT DEBUTANTE	MGM	CinemaScope
RIDE A CROOKED TRAIL	UN	CinemaScope
ROCK-A-BYE BABY	PAR	VistaVision
ROSURA A LAS DIEZ	ARG	Alexscope
SADDLE THE WIND	MGM	CinemaScope
ST. LOUIS BLUES	PAR	VistaVision
SEVEN HILLS OF ROME	MGM	Technirama
THE SHEEPMAN	MGM	CinemaScope
SHOWDOWN AT BOOT HILL	TCF	Regalscope
SIERRA BARON	TCF	CinemaScope
SING BOY SING	TCF	CinemaScope
SMILEY GETS A GUN	TCF	CinemaScope
SOUTH PACIFIC	TCF	Todd-AO
SOUTH SEAS ADVENTURE	CIN	Cinerama
SPACE MASTER X-7	TCF	Regalscope
SPANISH AFFAIR	PAR	VistaVision
THE STORY OF A PURE LOVE	JAP	CinemaScope
STRANGE GODS	ARG	CinemaScope
TAMANGO	FRA	CinemaScope
TARZAN AND THE LOST SAFARI	UN	RKO-Scope
TEACHER'S PET	PAR	VistaVision
THE TEMPTRESS	JAP	CinemaScope
TEN NORTH FREDERICK	TCF	CinemaScope
THIS ANGRY AGE (THE SEA WALL)	COL	Technirama
THIS HAPPY FEELING	UN	CinemaScope
THUNDERING JETS	TCF	Regalscope
A TIME TO LOVE	UN	CinemaScope
TOUR, PRENDS BARDE	FRA-ITA	Dyaliscope
UNDERWATER WARRIOR	MGM	CinemaScope
VERTIGO	PAR	VistaVision
THE VIKINGS	UA	Technirama
LES VIOLENTS	FRA	Dyaliscope
THE VOICE IN THE MIRROR	UN	CinemaScope
WHITE WILDERNESS	BV	SuperScope
WILD HERITAGE	UN	CinemaScope
WINDJAMMER	IND	CineMiracle
YOUNG AND WILD	REP	Naturama
THE YOUNG LIONS	TCF	CinemaScope

1959

ALASKA PASSAGE	TCF	Regalscope
ALIAS JESSE JAMES	UA	VistaVision
THE ALLIGATOR PEOPLE	TCF	CinemaScope
THE ANGRY HILLS	MGM	CinemaScope
APPOINTMENT WITH A SHADOW	UN	CinemaScope
ASK ANY GIRL	MGM	CinemaScope
THE ATOM ON THE FARM	IND	Cinedome
BABETTE GOES TO WAR	COL	CinemaScope
BEHIND THE GREAT WALL	IND	Totalscope
THE BELOVED INFIDEL	TCF	CinemaScope
THE BEAT GENERATION	MGM	CinemaScope
BEN-HUR	MGM	Panavision 70
THE BEST OF EVERYTHING	TCF	CinemaScope
THE BIG FISHERMAN	BV	Panavision 70

THE BIG OPERATOR	MGM	CinemaScope
THE BLACK ORCHID	PAR	VistaVision
THE BLUE ANGEL	TCF	CinemaScope
BLUE DENIM	TCF	CinemaScope
BOBBIKINS	TCF	CinemaScope
BUT NOT FOR ME	PAR	VistaVision
CALYPSO	ITA-FRA	Totalscope
THE CAPTAIN'S DAUGHTER	RUS	Sovscope
CINESPHERE	IND	Vista-Dome
COMPULSION	TCF	CinemaScope
COSTA ASSURA (COTE D'AZUR)	ITA	Dyaliscope
COUNT YOUR BLESSINGS	MGM	CinemaScope
DESIGN FOR SUBURBAN LIVING	IND	Quadravision
THE DEVIL'S PASS	FRA	CinemaScope
THE DIARY OF ANNE FRANK	TCF	CinemaScope
A DOG OF FLANDERS	TCF	CinemaScope
DON'T GIVE UP THE SHIP	PAR	VistaVision
DUBROVSKY	YUG-ITA	Totalscope
800 LEAGUES ON THE AMAZON	MEX	Mexiscope
THE ENCHANTED MIRROR	RUS	Kinopanorama
FERRY TO HONG KONG	BRI	CinemaScope
THE FIVE PENNIES	PAR	VistaVision
FLAME OVER INDIA	BRI	CinemaScope
FLAMING FRONTIER	TCF	Regalscope
FOR THE FIRST TIME	MGM	Technirama
FOUR FAST GUNS	UN	CinemaScope
THE FOUR HUNDRED BLOWS	FRA	Dyaliscope
GIDGET	COL	CinemaScope
GLIMPSES OF THE USA	IND	Septorama
GOLIATH AND THE BARBARIANS	AI	Totalscope
GREAT IS MY COUNTRY	RUS	Kinopanorama
THE GREAT WAR (LA GRANDE GUERRA)	ITA-FRA	CinemaScope
GREEN MANSIONS	MGM	CinemaScope
THE GREEN MARE	FRA	Franscope
GUNFIGHT AT DODGE CITY	UA	CinemaScope
THE H-MAN	COL	Tohoscope
HADAKA NO YAIKO (THE NUDE GENERAL)	JAP	Tohoscope
THE HEADLESS GHOST	AI	Dyaliscope
HELL BENT FOR LEATHER	UN	CinemaScope
HERCULES	COL	Dyaliscope
HERCULES AND THE QUEEN OF LYDIA	FRA-ITA	Dyaliscope
HERE COME THE JETS	TCF	Regalscope
HOLIDAY FOR LOVERS	TCF	CinemaScope
HORRORS OF THE BLACK MUSEUM	AI	CinemaScope
HOUND DOG MAN	TCF	CinemaScope
HOUSE OF INTRIGUE	AA	CinemaScope
I, MOBSTER	TCF	CinemaScope
IDLE ON PARADE	BRI	CinemaScope
IN BURNING DARKNESS	ARG	Alexscope
ISLAND FISHERMAN	FRA	Dyaliscope
IT STARTED WITH A KISS	MGM	CinemaScope
THE JAYHAWKERS	PAR	VistaVision
JOHN PAUL JONES	WB	Technirama
JOURNEY TO THE CENTER OF THE EARTH	TCF	CinemaScope
KIKU AND ISAMU	JAP	CinemaScope
KING OF THE WILD STALLIONS	AA	CinemaScope
KORKARLEN (THE SOUL SHALL BEAR WITNESS)	SWE	AgaScope
LAST TRAIN FROM GUN HILL	PAR	VistaVision
LIBEL	MGM	Metroscope
LONE TEXAN	TCF	Regalscope
LI'L ABNER	PAR	VistaVision
MAN OR GUN	REP	Naturama
THE MAN WHO DIED TWICE	REP	Naturama

THE MAN WHO UNDERSTOOD WOMEN	TCF	CinemaScope
MASTERS OF THE CONGO JUNGLE	BEL	CinemaScope
THE MATING GAME	MGM	CinemaScope
A MIDSUMMER NIGHT'S DREAM	CZE	CinemaScope
THE MIRACLE	WB	Technirama
MIRACLE OF THE HILLS	TCF	CinemaScope
MISS STONE	YUG	Totalscope
THE NAKED MAJA	UA	Technirama
NATURE GIRL AND THE SLAVER	IND	Dynavision
THE NAVY LARK	BRI	CinemaScope
NEVER SO FEW	MGM	CinemaScope
NEVER STEAL ANYTHING SMALL	UN	CinemaScope
NIGHT OF THE QUARTER MOON	MGM	CinemaScope
NO PLACE TO LAND	REP	Naturama
NORTH BY NORTHWEST	MGM	VistaVision
NUDE IN A WHITE CAR	FRA	CinemaScope
THE OREGON TRAIL	TCF	CinemaScope
PILLOW TALK	UN	CinemaScope
PORGY AND BESS	COL	Todd-AO
A PRIVATE'S AFFAIR	TCF	CinemaScope
QUEEN OF OUTER SPACE	AA	CinemaScope
THE REMARKABLE MR. PENNYPACKER	TCF	CinemaScope
RETURN OF THE FLY	TCF	CinemaScope
RHAPSODIA PORTUGUESA	SPA	Totalvision
THE RICKSHAW MAN	JAP	Tohoscope
RIDE LONESOME	COL	CinemaScope
THE ROAD A YEAR LONG	YUG	CinemaScope
THE ROOKIE	TCF	CinemaScope
THE SAD HORSE	TCF	CinemaScope
SAY ONE FOR ME	TCF	CinemaScope
SCENT OF MYSTERY	IND	Todd-AO
SERENADE TO A BIG LOVE	GER	Technirama
SIGN OF THE GLADIATOR	AI	Colorscope
SLEEPING BEAUTY	BV	Technirama 70
SOLOMON AND SHEBA	UA	Technirama 70
SON OF ROBIN HOOD	TCF	CinemaScope
THE SOUND AND THE FURY	TCF	CinemaScope
SOVIET AGRICULTURAL ACHIEVEMENT EXHIBITION	RUS	Circarama
STRANGER IN MY ARMS	TCF	CinemaScope
THE SWORD AND THE DRAGON (ILYA MOUROMETZ)	RUS	Sovscope
TANK FORCE (NO TIME TO DIE)	BRI	CinemaScope
THESE THOUSAND HILLS	TCF	CinemaScope
THEY CAME TO CORDURA	COL	CinemaScope
THIRST FOR LOVE	MEX	Camerascope
THIS EARTH IS MINE	UN	CinemaScope
UP PERISCOPE	WB	WarnerScope
VENETIAN HONEYMOON	FRA	Totalvision
VLAK BEZ VOSNOG REDA	YUG	Totalvision
WARLOCK	TCF	CinemaScope
WARRIOR AND THE SLAVE GIRL	COL	SuperCinescope
THE WHITE HERON (SHIRASAGUI)	JAP	CinemaScope
THE WILD AND THE INNOCENT	UN	CinemaScope

1960

ADVENTURES OF HUCKLEBERRY FINN	MGM	CinemaScope
THE ALAMO	UA	Todd-AO
ALL THE FINE YOUNG CANNIBALS	MGM	Panavision
AMERICA AS SEEN BY A FRENCHMAN	FRA	Dyaliscope
THE APARTMENT	UA	Panavision
AUSTERLITZ	FRA-ITA-YUG	Dyaliscope
BATTLE FOR OUTER SPACE	JAP	Tohoscope
BELLS ARE RINGING	MGM	CinemaScope
BLOOD AND ROSES (ET MOURIR DE PLASIR)	FRA-ITA	Technirama
BUTTERFIELD 8	MGM	CinemaScope

CAN-CAN	TCF	Todd-AO
LE CAPITAN (THE YOKEL)	FRA	Dyaliscope
CIMARRON	MGM	CinemaScope
COMANCHE STATION	COL	CinemaScope
THE COSSACKS	ITA	Totalscope
CRACK IN THE MIRROR	TCF	CinemaScope
CRESUS	FRA	Franscope
CRY FOR HAPPY	COL	CinemaScope
THE DAY THEY ROBBED THE BANK OF ENGLAND	MGM	Metroscope
THE DEAD ONE	IND	Ultrascope
DESIRE IN THE DUST	TCF	CinemaScope
DIALOGS OF THE CARMELITES	FRA	Dyaliscope
DINOSAURUS!	UN	CinemaScope
ESTHER AND THE KING	TCF	CinemaScope
EXODUS	UA	Panavision 70
FAST AND SEXY (ANNA FROM BOOKLYN)	COL	Technirama
FLAMING STAR	TCF	CinemaScope
FOR THE LOVE OF MIKE	TCF	CinemaScope
FRECKLES	TCF	CinemaScope
FROM THE TERRACE	TCF	CinemaScope
A GIRL FOR THE SUMMER	FRA	Dyaliscope
THE GRASS IS GREENER	UN	Technirama
HANNIBAL	WB	SuperCinescope
HEAD OF A TYRANT (JUDITH AND HOLOPHERNES)	ITA	Totalscope
HIGH TIME	TCF	CinemaScope
HOME FROM THE HILL	MGM	CinemaScope
HOUSE OF USHER	AI	CinemaScope
THE HUNCHBACK	FRA	Dyaliscope
IT STARTED IN NAPLES	PAR	VistaVision
JAZZ BOAT	COL	CinemaScope
JOKYO (WOMAN'S TESTAMENT)	JAP	CinemaScope
JOURNEY TO THE LOST CITY	AI	Colorscope
THE KEY (KAGI)	JAP	CinemaScope
KEY WITNESS	MGM	CinemaScope
KNIGHTS OF THE TEUTONIC ORDER	POL	Dyaliscope
THE LAST DAYS OF POMPEII	UA	SuperTotalscope
THE LAST WOMAN ON EARTH	IND	Vitascope
LEGIONS OF THE NILE	TCF	CinemaScope
LET'S MAKE LOVE	TCF	CinemaScope
THE LOST WORLD	TCF	CinemaScope
THE MAGNIFICENT SEVEN	UA	Panavision
THE MARRIAGE-GO-ROUND	TCF	CinemaScope
MANIA (FLESH AND THE FIENDS)	BRI	Vitascope
A MATTER OF MORALS	BRI-SWE	AgaScope
MODERATO CANTABILE	FRA	CinemaScope
MORANBONG	FRA	Dyaliscope
MURDER, INC.	TCF	CinemaScope
MY SECOND BROTHER (NIANCHAN)	JAP	CinemaScope
THE NIGHTS OF LUCRETIA BORGIA	ITA	Totalscope
NORTH TO ALASKA	TCF	CinemaScope
OCEAN'S 11	WB	Panavision
OF MEN AND MONEY (I-RO-HA-NI-HO-HE-YO)	JAP	CinemaScope
ONE FOOT IN HELL	TCF	CinemaScope
ONE, TWO, THREE, FOUR	FRA	Technirama 70
PEPE	COL	Panavision
PLEASE DON'T EAT THE DAISIES	MGM	CinemaScope
POEM OF THE SEA	RUS	Sovscope
PRISONER OF THE VOLGA	FRA-ITA	Totalscope
THE REGATTAS OF SAN FRANCISCO	FRA	CinemaScope
LE SECRET DE CHEVALIER D'EON	FRA	Dyaliscope
SECRET MEETING (MIKKAI)	JAP	CinemaScope
THE SECRET OF THE PURPLE REEF	TCF	CinemaScope

SEPTEMBER STORM	TCF	CinemaScope
SHOOT THE PIANIST! (TIREZ SUR LE PIANISTE)	FRA	Dyaliscope
SINK THE BISMARK!	TCF	CinemaScope
SONG WITHOUT END	COL	CinemaScope
SONS AND LOVERS	TCF	CinemaScope
SPARTACUS	UN	Technirama 70
THE STORY OF RUTH	TCF	CinemaScope
STRANGERS WHEN WE MEET	COL	CinemaScope
THE SUBTERRANEANS	MGM	CinemaScope
THE SUPER HE-MAN (EL SUPERMACHO)	MEX	Mexiscope
SWISS FAMILY ROBINSON	BV	Panavision
THE SWORD AND THE CROSS (SLAVES OF CARTHAGE)	ITA	CineTotalscope
SWORD OF SHERWOOD FOREST	COL	Megascope
THE THIRD VOICE	TCF	CinemaScope
THIRTEEN FIGHTING MEN	TCF	CinemaScope
THE THREE TREASURES	JAP	Tohoscope
THIS LOVE AT THE END OF THE WORLD	ARG-ITA	CinemaScope
THREE GIRLS NAMED ANNA (TRI ANE)	YUG	Totalvision
TRAPPED IN TANGIERS	TCF	SuperCinescope
TOSCA	ITA	CinemaScope
TRIALS OF OSCAR WILDE (THE GREEN CARNATION)	BRI	Technirama
THE UNFORGIVEN	UA	Technirama
UTAMARO, PAINTER OF WOMEN	JAP	DaieiScope
VOYAGE IN A BALLOON	FRA	Dyaliscope
THE WACKIEST SHIP IN THE ARMY	COL	CinemaScope
WAKE ME WHEN IT'S OVER	TCF	CinemaScope
WALK TALL	TCF	CinemaScope
WAR (RAT)	YUG	Totalscope
WHEN A WOMAN GOES UPSTAIRS	JAP	CinemaScope
WHERE THE BOYS ARE	MGM	Panavision
WILD RIVER	TCF	CinemaScope
WIZARD OF BAGDAD	TCF	CinemaScope
THE WORLD AT NIGHT	WB	Technirama
YOUNG JESSE JAMES	TCF	CinemaScope

1961

ADA	MGM	CinemaScope
ALL HANDS ON DECK	TCF	CinemaScope
ANIMAS TRUJANO	MEX	CinemaScope
BACHELOR FLAT	TCF	CinemaScope
BACHELOR IN PARADISE	MGM	Panavision
THE BATTLE AT BLOODY BEACH	TCF	CinemaScope
THE BIG GAMBLE	TCF	CinemaScope
THE BIG SHOW	TCF	CinemaScope
THE CANADIANS	TCF	CinemaScope
THE CANANEA PRISON	MEX	Mexiscope
CAPTAIN FRACASSE	FRA	Dyaliscope
CARTHAGE IN FLAMES	FRA-ITA	Technirama
EL CID	AA	Technirama 70
THE COMANCHEROS	TCF	CinemaScope
THE COLOSSUS OF RHODES	ITA	SuperTotalscope
COME SEPTEMBER	UN	CinemaScope
DAVID AND GOLIATH	AA	Totalscope
THE DEADLY COMPANIONS	PA	Panavision
THE DEVIL PLAYED THE BALALAIKA	GER	CinemaScope
FAMOUS LOVE AFFAIRS	FRA	Dyaliscope
THE FIERCEST HEART	TCF	CinemaScope
FLIGHT OF THE LOST BALLOON	BRI	SpectraScope
FOUL PLAY (LES MAUVAIS COUPS)	FRA	Cinegraphiscope
FLOWER DRUM SONG	UN	Panavision
FRANCIS OF ASSISI	TCF	CinemaScope
THE GAME OF TRUTH	FRA	Dyaliscope
GOLIATH AND THE DRAGON	AI	Colorscope
THE GUNS OF NAVARONE	COL	CinemaScope

HAPPINESS IS WITHIN US (NAMONAKU MAZUSHIKU UTSUKUSHIKU)	JAP	Tohoscope
L'HISTOIRE DES ANNES DE FEU (see POVESTJ PLAMENNYKH LET)		
THE HONEYMOON MACHINE	MGM	CinemaScope
HOUSE OF FRIGHT (JEKYLL'S INFERNO)	AI	Megascope
I LOVE, YOU LOVE	FRA	Ultrascope
THE INNOCENTS	TCF	CinemaScope
KING OF KINGS	MGM	Technirama 70
LAST YEAR IN MERIENBAD	FRA	Dyaliscope
THE LIONS ARE LOOSE	FRA	Dyaliscope
LOLA	FRA	Franscope
LOVE IN A GOLDFISH BOWL	PAR	Panavision
THE LOVE OF ALIOCHA	RUS	Sovscope
THE MAGIC FOUNTAIN	IND	Ultrascope
MAN TRAP	PAR	Panavision
MARINES, LET'S GO	TCF	CinemaScope
THE MIGHTY CRUSADERS	ITA	SuperCinescope
THE MINOTAUR	ITA	Totalscope
THE MIRACLE OF THE WOLVES	FRA	Dyaliscope
MISTY	TCF	CinemaScope
MORGAN THE PIRATE	MGM	CinemaScope
MOTHER COURAGE AND HER CHILDREN	GER	CinemaScope
NIGHT GUEST	CZE	CinemaScope
NUDE ODESSEY	FRA-ITA	Totalscope
ON THE DOUBLE	PAR	Panavision
ONE-EYED JACKS	PAR	VistaVision
OTOTO (HER BROTHER)	JAP	CinemaScope
THE PHARAOH'S WOMAN	UN	CinemaScope
THE PIT AND THE PENDULUM	AI	Panavision
PIRATES OF TORTUGA	TCF	CinemaScope
POCKETFUL OF MIRACLES	UA	Panavision
POVESTJ PLAMENNYKH LET	RUS	70mm
THE PURPLE HILLS	TCF	CinemaScope
PUSS IN BOOTS (EL GATO CON BOTAS)	MEX	CinemaScope
QUEEN OF THE PIRATES	ITA	SuperCinescope
THE QUEEN'S GUARDS	BRI	CinemaScope
QUI ETES-VOUS, MR. SORGE	FRA-JAP	CinemaScope
RETURN TO PEYTON PLACE	TCF	CinemaScope
SCARLET SAILS	RUS	Sovscope
SANCTUARY	TCF	CinemaScope
THE SECOND TIME AROUND	TCF	CinemaScope
THE SECRET OF MONTE CRISTO	BRI	Dyaliscope
SEVEN WOMEN FROM HELL	TCF	CinemaScope
THE SLACK REINS (LE BRIDE SUR LE COUR)	FRA	CinemaScope
SNOW WHITE AND THE 3 STOOGES	TCF	CinemaScope
THE STORY OF CHOONHYANG	KOR	CinemaScope
SUMMER AND SMOKE	PAR	Panavision
A TAXI FOR TOBRUK	FRA	Dyaliscope
TESS OF THE STORM COUNTRY	TCF	CinemaScope
THE THREE MUSKETEERS	FRA	Dyaliscope
THE THIEF OF BAGDAD	ITA	CinemaScope
A THUNDER OF DRUMS	MGM	CinemaScope
TIRE-AU-FLANC (THE SAD SACK)	FRA	Franscope
TWO LOVES	MGM	CinemaScope
20,000 EYES	TCF	CinemaScope
VIVE HENRI IV, VIVE L'AMOUR	FRA	Dyaliscope
VOYAGE TO THE BOTTOM OF THE SEA	TCF	CinemaScope
THE WARRIOR EMPRESS	COL	CinemaScope
THE WAYSIDE PEBBLE	JAP	Tohoscope
WEST SIDE STORY	UA	Panavision 70
THE WHITE WARRIOR	WB	Dyaliscope
WILD IN THE COUNTRY	TCF	CinemaScope

A WOMAN IS ALWAYS A WOMAN	FRA	Franscope
THE WONDERS OF ALADDIN	MGM	CinemaScope
THE WORLD BY NIGHT	WB	Technirama
X-15	UA	Panavision

1962

ADVENTURES OF A YOUNG MAN	TCF	CinemaScope
ADVISE AND CONSENT	COL	Panavision
ARSENE LUPIN AGAINST ARSENE LUPIN	FRA	Dyaliscope
BARABBAS	COL	Technirama 70
BELLS WITHOUT JOY	FRA	Dyaliscope
BILLY BUDD	AA	CinemaScope
THE CABINET OF CALIGARI	TCF	CinemaScope
CARTOUCHE	FRA	Dyaliscope
CHALLENGE TO LIVE	JAP	Tohoscope
CLEOPATRA'S DAUGHTER	ITA	UltraScope
CONSTANTINE AND THE CROSS	ITA	Totalscope
THE COUNT OF MONTE CRISTO	FRA	Dyaliscope
CRIME DOES NOT PAY	FRA	CinemaScope
CUPOLA (DOME)	JAP	CinemaScope
THE DANCE (LA GAMBERGE)	FRA	Dyaliscope
DANGEROUS CHARTER	IND	Panavision
THE DENUNCIATION	FRA	Franscope
THE DEVIL AND THE 10 COMMANDMENTS	FRA	Franscope
THE DOLL (LA POUPEE)	FRA	Franscope
EDUCATION SENTIMENTALE	FRA	Dyaliscope
EMILE'S BOAT	FRA	Dyaliscope
ESCAPE FROM ZAHRIN	PAR	Panavision
THE FIRST SPACESHIP ON VENUS	JAP	Totalvision
FIVE WEEKS IN A BALLOON	TCF	CinemaScope
FOLLOW THAT DREAM	UA	Panavision
40 POUNDS OF TROUBLE	UN	Panavision
THE FOUR HORSEMEN OF THE APOCALYPSE	MGM	CinemaScope
THE GENTLEMAN D'EPSOM	FRA	Totalscope
GERONIMO	UA	Panavision
GIGOT	TCF	CinemaScope
A GIRL NAMED TAMIKO	PAR	Panavision
THE GOLD OF THE SEVEN SAINTS	WB	WarnerScope
GOOD LUCK, CHARLIE	FRA	Franscope
THE GRASS CUTTERS (KUSA-O KARU MUSUME)	JAP	CinemaScope
GYPSY	WB	Technirama
HERO'S ISLAND	UA	Panavision
HORACE '62	FRA	Dyaliscope
THE HORIZONTAL LIEUTENANT	MGM	CinemaScope
HOW THE WEST WAS WON	MGM	Cinerama
THE HUSTLER	TCF	CinemaScope
IT HAPPENED IN ATHENS	TCF	CinemaScope
THE IRON MASK	FRA	Dyaliscope
JESSICA	UA	Panavision
JULES AND JIM	FRA	Franscope
JUMBO	MGM	Panavision
THE KNIGHT FROM PARDAILLAN	FRA	Franscope
LAFAYETTE	FRA	Technirama 70
LAWRENCE OF ARABIA	COL	Panavision 70
LEMMY FOR THE GIRLS	FRA	Dyaliscope
A LIGHT IN THE PIAZZA	MGM	CinemaScope
LISA	TCF	CinemaScope
THE LONGEST DAY	TCF	CinemaScope
LOVE AT 20	FRA	Totalscope
THE LOVERS OF TERUEL	FRA	Totalscope
THE LOVES OF SALAMMBO	ITA	CinemaScope
THE MAD FOX (KOIYA KOI NAS UNA KOI)	JAP	Colorscope
MAN OF THE FIRST CENTURY	CZE	CinemaScope

MERMAIDS OF TIBURON	IND	Aquascope
MR. HOBBS TAKES A VACATION	TCF	CinemaScope
A MONKEY IN WINTER	FRA	Totalscope
MOTHRA	JAP	Tohoscope
THE MUSIC MAN	WB	Technirama 70
MUTINY ON THE BOUNTY	MGM	Panavision 70
MY GEISHA	PAR	Technirama
THE MYSTERIES OF PARIS	FRA	Dyaliscope
PERIOD OF ADJUSTMENT	MGM	Panavision
THE PIRATES OF BLOOD RIVER	COL	Megascope
PREMATURE BURIAL	AI	Panavision
THE PRINCESS OF CLEAVES	FRA	Dyaliscope
RIDE THE HIGH COUNTRY	MGM	CinemaScope
THE RIGHT APPROACH	TCF	CinemaScope
SANJURO	JAP	Tohoscope
SARANG (BANG SONNIM OMONI)	KOR	CinemaScope
SATAN NEVER SLEEPS	TCF	CinemaScope
SERGEANTS 3	UA	Panavision
THE SEVEN CAPITAL SINS	FRA	Dyaliscope
THE SIEGE OF SYRACUSE	ITA	Dyaliscope
SODOM AND GOMORRAH	TCF	CinemaScope
SORCERY (MALEFICES)	FRA	Dyaliscope
SPRINGTIME FOR THE GIRLS	RUS	Sovscope
STATE FAIR	TCF	CinemaScope
STRANGERS IN THE CITY	IND	Scanoscope
SWEET BIRD OF YOUTH	MGM	CinemaScope
SWEET VIOLENCE	FRA	CinemaScope
SWINGING ALONG	TCF	CinemaScope
THE SWORDSMAN OF SIENA	MGM	CinemaScope
SUNDAYS AND CYBELE	FRA	Franscope
THE SUN'S BURIAL (TAIYO NOHAKABA)	JAP	Grandscope
TALES OF TERROR	AI	Panavision
TARAS BULBA	UA	Panavision
TARZAN GOES TO INDIA	MGM	CinemaScope
TENDER IS THE NIGHT	TCF	CinemaScope
THE 300 SPARTANS	TCF	CinemaScope
TINTIN AND THE MYSTERY OF THE GOLDEN FLEECE	FRA	Dyaliscope
THE TRIUMPH OF MICHAEL STROGOFF	FRA	Dyaliscope
TWO FOR THE SEESAW	UA	Panavision
TWO WEEKS IN ANOTHER TOWN	MGM	CinemaScope
VOLGA, VOLGA	RUS	Kinopanorama
WARRIOR'S REST	FRA	Franscope
WHO'S GOT THE ACTION?	PAR	Panavision
THE WONDERFUL WORLD OF THE BROTHERS GRIMM	MGM	Cinerama
THE WORLD BY NIGHT NO. 2	WB	Technirama
YOUNG GUNS OF TEXAS	TCF	CinemaScope

1963

BANANA PEEL	FRA	Franscope
BAY OF ANGELS	FRA	CinemaScope
BE CAREFUL, LADIES	FRA	Franscope
BEACH PARTY	AI	Panavision
THE BIG GRAB (MELODIE EN SOUS-SOL)	FRA	Dyaliscope
THE BIG ROADS	FRA	Franscope
BLACK ZOO	AA	Panavision
BUDDHA	JAP	Technirama 70
BYE BYE BIRDIE	COL	Panavision
THE CARDINAL	COL	Panavision
CASTLE IN SWEDEN	FRA	Franscope
CLEOPATRA	TCF	Todd-AO
COME FLY WITH ME	MGM	Panavision
THE CONDEMNED OF ALTONA	TCF	CinemaScope
THE COURTSHIP OF EDDIE'S FATHER	MGM	Panavision

THE DARK ROOM OF DAMOCLES	HOL	Franscope
THE DAY AND THE HOUR	FRA	Franscope
THE DAY OF THE TRIFFIDS	AA	CinemaScope
THE DIABOLIC EMPRESS	FOR	CinemaScope
THE EMPIRE OF THE NIGHT	FRA	Totalscope
55 DAYS AT PEKING	AA	Totalscope
THE FLYING CLIPPER	GER	70mm
FOLLOW THE BOYS	MGM	Panavision
FORT OF THE MAD	FRA	Dyaliscope
GERMINAL	FRA	Dyaliscope
GLADIATORS 7	ITA	Techniscope
THE GOOD CAUSES	FRA	Franscope
THE GREAT ESCAPE	UA	Panavision
HARAKIRI (STEPPUKU)	JAP	Grandscope
THE HAUNTING	MGM	Panavision
HONOLULU-TOKYO-HONG KONG	JAP	Tohoscope
THE HOOK	MGM	Panavision
I COULD GO ON SINGING	UA	Panavision
IN THE COOL OF THE DAY	MGM	Panavision
IRMA LA DOUCE	UA	Panavision
ISLAND OF LOVE	WB	Panavision
IT HAPPENED AT THE WORLD'S FAIR	MGM	Panavision
KINGS OF THE SUN	UA	Panavision
LONELY LANE (HOROKI)	JAP	Tohoscope
LOVE IS A BALL	UA	Panavision
McCLINTOCK!	UA	Panavision
MADAME AKI	JAP	Tohoscope
MAGNET OF DOOM (L'AINE DES FERCHAUX)	FRA	Franscope
LE MAGOT DE JOSEFA (JOSEFA'S LOOT)	FRA	Franscope
MANDARIN	FRA	Dyaliscope
MANIAC (FLESH AND THE FIENDS)	COL	Megascope
MARILYN	TCF	CinemaScope
MATHIAS SANDORF	FRA	CinemaScope
MOVE OVER, DARLING	TCF	CinemaScope
THE MURDERER	FRA	Franscope
MY SIX LOVES	PAR	VistaVision
NINE HOURS TO RAMA	TCF	CinemaScope
ONE DAY A CAT ...	CZE	CinemaScope
AN OPTOMISTIC TRAGEDY	RUS	70mm
THE PRIZE	MGM	Panavision
LA PROSTITUTION	FRA	CinemaScope
LE RAT L'AMERIQUE	FRA	Totalvision
THE RAVEN	AI	Panavision
ROMAN RHYTHM	FRA	Franscope
ROOTS OF STONE	SA	Dyaliscope
RUSSIAN ROUNDABOUT	RUS	Circlorama
SEVEN SEAS TO CALAIS	MGM	CinemaScope
SCHEHERAZADE	FRA	Superpanorama 70
THE SLAVE	ITA	CinemaScope
SPENCER'S MOUNTAIN	WB	Panavision
THE SWORD AND THE BALANCE	FRA	Franscope
SWORD OF LANCELOT (LANCELOT AND GUINEVERE)	UN	Panavision
TAKE HER, SHE'S MINE	TCF	CinemaScope
TARZAN'S THREE CHALLENGES	MGM	Dyaliscope
THE THREEPENNY OPERA	GER	CinemaScope
THUNDER ISLAND	TCF	CinemaScope
A TICKLISH AFFAIR	MGM	Panavision
TILL THE END OF THE WORLD	FRA	Franscope
TOYS IN THE ATTIC	UA	Panavision
THE TREASURE OF SILVER LAKE	GER-YUG	CinemaScope
TWILIGHT OF HONOR	MGM	Panavision
TWIN SISTERS OF KYOTO	JAP	Grandscope
THE UNKNOWN OF HONG KONG	FRA	Dyaliscope
THE VIP'S	MGM	Panavision

VICE AND VIRTUE	FRA	Franscope
THE WHEELER DEALERS	MGM	Panavision
WHO'S BEEN SLEEPING IN MY BED?	PAR	Panavision
WINNETOU (PART I)	GER-YUG	CinemaScope
THE YELLOW CANARY	TCF	CinemaScope
THE ZANY INNOCENTS	FRA	Franscope
ZLOTO	POL	CinemaScope
ZORRO	SPA	SuperScope

1964

ADVANCE TO THE REAR	MGM	Panavision
BANEO A BANGKOK	FRA	Franscope
BATMANOVA, SINGING SLAVE	RUS	Kinopanorama
BECKET	PAR	Panavision
THE CALM	RUS	Sovscope
THE CARPETBAGGERS	PAR	Panavision
THE CHAIN	BUL	CinemaScope
CHEYENNE AUTUMN	WB	Panavision 70
CHILDREN OF THE DAMNED	MGM	Panavision
CIRCUS WORLD	PAR	Technirama 70
CODE 7, VICTIM 5	BRI	Techniscope
THE COMEDY OF TERRORS	AI	Panavision
THE CONJUGAL LIFE	FRA	Franscope
COOKING WITH BUTTER	FRA	Franscope
THE CRIMSON BLADE	COL	Megascope
DAY DREAM	JAP	Shokitu Vision
A DAY OF HAPPINESS	RUS	Sovscope
DEATH, WHERE IS YOUR VICTORY?	FRA	Totalscope
THE DEVIL-SHIP PIRATES	BRI	Megascope
THE DIARY OF A CHAMBERMAID	FRA	Franscope
DINNER FOR SAVAGES	FRA	Dyaliscope
A DISTANT TRUMPET	WB	Panavision
ENSIGN PULVER	WB	Panavision
THE FALL OF THE ROMAN EMPIRE	PAR	Panavision 70
FANTOMAS	FRA	Franscope
THE FELINES	FRA	Franscope
FIND THE IDOL	FRA	Franscope
FLIGHT FROM ASHIYA	UA	Panavision
FOR A FISTFULL OF DOLLARS	ITA-GER-SPA	Techniscope
FOR THOSE WHO THINK YOUNG	UA	Techniscope
FREE ESCAPE	FRA	Franscope
GODZILLA VS. THE THING	JAP	CinemaScope
GOLD FOR THE CAESARS	MGM	CinemaScope
THE GOLDEN ARROW	ITA	Technirama
GOLIATH AND THE VAMPIRES	ITA	Colorscope
THE GOOD SOUP	FRA	Franscope
GOODBYE CHARLIE	TCF	CinemaScope
GORATH	JAP	TohoScope
THE GRIPSHOLM CASTLE	GER	CinemaScope
GUNFIGHT AT COMANCHE CREEK	AA	Panavision
GUNS AT BATASI	BRI	CinemaScope
HONEYMOON HOTEL	MGM	Panavision
JOHN GOLDFARB, PLEASE COME HOME	TCF	CinemaScope
KISSIN' COUSINS	MGM	Panavision
THE LAST STEP	FRA	Totalvision
THE LAST WOMAN OF SHANG	CHI	Shawscope
LAW OF THE LAWLESS	PAR	Techniscope
THE LIVING AND THE DEAD	RUS	Sovscope
THE LOVERS OF THE FRANCE	FRA	Franscope
MAIL ORDER BRIDE	MGM	Panavision
MAN IN THE MIDDLE	TCF	CinemaScope
MANHUNTERS	POL	Dyaliscope
THE MASQUE OF THE RED DEATH	AI	Panavision
MEDITERRANEAN HOLIDAY	CON	Cinerama

MONSIEUR	FRA	Franscope
MONTEVIDEO	GER	Panavision
MUSCLE BEACH PARTY	AI	Panavision
MY FAIR LADY	WB	Panavision 70
THE NASTY RABBIT	IND	Techniscope
OLD SHATTERHAND	GER-ITA	Techniscope
100,000 DOLLARS IN THE SUN	FRA-JUG	Franscope
THE OUTRAGE	MGM	Panavision
PAJAMA PARTY	AI	Panavision
PARIAHS OF GLORY	FRA	Dyaliscope
PATATE	FRA	Dyaliscope
THE PINK PANTHER	UA	Technirama
THE PLEASURE SEEKERS	TCF	CinemaScope
PRESSURE OF GUILT	JAP	TohoScope
QUICK, BEFORE IT MELTS	MGM	Panavision
THE QUICK GUN	COL	Techniscope
RATAI	JAP	Grandscope
RIO CONCHOS	TCF	CinemaScope
ROBIN AND THE SEVEN HOODS	WB	Panavision
ROBINSON CRUSOE ON MARS	PAR	Techniscope
LA RONDE	FRA	Franscope
ROUSTABOUT	PAR	Techniscope
SAMSON AND THE SLAVE QUEEN	AI	Colorscope
SAMURAI FROM NOWHERE	JAP	Grandscope
THE SECRET INVASION	UA	Panavision
SEE VENICE AND DIE	FRA	Dyaliscope
SHOCK TREATMENT	TCF	CinemaScope
A SHOT IN THE DARK	UA	Panavision
SIGNPOST TO MURDER	MGM	Panavision
633 SQUADRON	UA	Panavision
TAMAHINE	MGM	CinemaScope
THE THIN RED LINE	AA	CinemaScope
36 HOURS	MGM	Panavision
TIME STOOD STILL	ITA	CinemaScope
THE UNSINKABLE MOLLY BROWN	MGM	Panavision
VILLAGE SWEETNESS	FRA	CinemaScope
THE VISIT	TCF	CinemaScope
VIVA LAS VEGAS	MGM	Panavision
WEEPING FOR A BANDIT	SPA	CinemaScope
WHAT A WAY TO GO!	TCF	CinemaScope
WHERE LOVE HAS GONE	PAR	Techniscope
WHITE VOICES	FRA-ITA	Techniscope
WINNETOU (PART II)	GER-YUG	CinemaScope
A WOMAN'S LIFE	JAP	CinemaScope
ZULU	PAR	Technirama

1965

ADVENTURE STARTS HERE	SWE	Franscope
THE AGONY AND THE ECSTASY	TCF	Todd-AO
THE AMOROUS ADVENTURES OF MOLL FLANDERS	PAR	Panavision
ATRAGON	JAP	TohoScope
THE BATTLE OF THE BULGE	WB	Panavision 70
THE BATTLE OF THE VILLA FIORITA	WB	Panavision
BEACH BLANKET BINGO	AI	Panavision
BILLIE	UA	Techniscope
BLACK SPURS	PAR	Techniscope
THE BLIZZART	RUS	Sovscope 70
THE BOUNTY KILLER	EMB	Techniscope
BRAINSTORM	WB	Panavision
BUNNY LAKE IS MISSING	COL	Panavision
COAST OF SKELETONS	BRI	Techniscope
CORRIDA FOR A SPY	FRA-SPA-GER	CinemaScope
CRAZY PETE	FRA	CinemaScope
A DAY IN A SOLAR	CUB	CinemaScope

DEAR BRIGITTE	TCF	CinemaScope
DIE, MONSTER, DIE	BRI	CinemaScope
DINGAKA	EMB	CinemaScope
DO NOT DISTURB	TCF	CinemaScope
DR. GOLDFOOT AND THE BIKINI MACHINE	AI	Panavision
DR. PRAETORIUS	GER	Panavision
DR. WHO AND THE DALEKS	BRI	Techniscope
DOCTOR ZHIVAGO	MGM	Panavision
DOUBLE-BARRELED DETECTIVE STORY	IND	Scanoscope
THE ENCHANTED DESNA	RUS	Sovscope 70
THE FACE OF FU MANCHU	BRI	Techniscope
FIRST DAY OF LIBERTY	POL	CinemaScope
THE FLAMING YEARS	RUS	Sovscope 70
GENGHIS KHAN	COL	Panavision
THE GIRL DANCED INTO LIFE	HUN	CinemaScope
GIRL HAPPY	MGM	Panavision
THE GLORY GUYS	UA	Panavision
THE GRAND SUBSTITUTION	CHI	ShawScope
THE GREAT RACE	WB	Panavision
THE GREAT SIOUX MASSACRE	COL	CinemaScope
THE GREATEST STORY EVER TOLD	UA	Panavision 70
GUNFIGHTERS OF CASA GRANDE	MGM	CinemaScope
THE HALLELUJAH TRAIL	UA	Panavision 70
HARLOW	PAR	Panavision
THE HEROES OF TELEMARK	BRI	Panavision
A HIGH WIND IN JAMAICA	TCF	CinemaScope
HORROR CASTLE	ITA	CinemaScope
HOW TO STUFF A WILD BIKINI	AI	Panavision
IN HARM'S WAY	PAR	Panavision
INSIDE DAISY CLOSER	WB	Panavision
KIMBERLEY JIM	EMB	Scanoscope
THE LOST WORLD OF SINBAD	JAP	Tohoscope
MADAM WHITE SNAKE	CHI	ShawScope
MAJOR DUNDEE	COL	Panavision
MARRIAGE ON THE ROCKS	WB	Panavision
MARVELOUS ANGELIQUE	FRA	Dyaliscope
MISTER MOSES	UA	Panavision
THE MOMENT OF TRUTH	SPA-ITA	Techniscope
MY BLOOD RUNS COLD	WB	Panavision
NEVER TOO LATE	WB	Panavision
NONE BUT THE BRAVE	WB	Panavision
ON A NICE SUMMER DAY	FRA	Franscope
ONCE A THIEF	MGM	Panavision
ONE MILLION DOLLARS	ITA	Techniscope
ONE WAY WAHINI	UA	Techniscope
ONIBABA	JAP	TohoScope
OPERATION CROSSBOW	MGM	Panavision
THE ORGAN	CZE	CinemaScope
OTELLO	BRI	Panavision
A PATCH OF BLUE	MGM	Panavision
PLANET OF THE VAMPIRES	ITA	CinemaScope
A RAGE TO LIVE	UA	Panavision
RAPTURE	TCF	CinemaScope
THE REAL BARGAIN	FRA	Franscope
RETURN FROM THE ASHES	UA	Panavision
REVENGE OF THE GLADIATORS	PAR	Techniscope
THE REWARD	TCF	CinemaScope
THE ROUNDERS	MGM	Panavision
SAMYONG	KOR	CinemaScope
THE SANDPIPER	MGM	Panavision
SANDS OF THE KALAHARI	PAR	Panavision
THE SATAN BUG	UA	Panavision
THE SECRET OF MY SUCCESS	MGM	Panavision

THE SECRET OF THE THREE JUNKS	GER	Ultrascope
SERGEANT DEADHEAD	AI	Panavision
SEVEN GOLDEN MEN	ITA-FRA-SPA	CinemaScope
SEVEN WOMEN	MGM	Panavision
SHE	MGM	CinemaScope
THE SHEPHERD GIRL	CHI	ShawScope
SKI PARTY	AI	Panavision
THE SONS OF KATIE ELDER	PAR	Panavision
THE SOUND OF MUSIC	TCF	Todd-AO
THE SQUEAKER	GER	Ultrascope
A SWINGIN' SUMMER	IND	Techniscope
THAT TENDER AGE	FRA	Dyaliscope
THE THIRD DAY	WB	Panavision
THOSE MAGNIFICENT MEN IN THEIR FLYING MACHINES	TCF	Todd-AO
THREE FACES OF A WOMAN	ITA	Techniscope
THREE WEEKS OF LOVE	JAP	CinemaScope
THE THUNDER OF GOD	FRA	Franscope
THUNDERBALL	UA	Panavision
TICKLE ME	AA	Panavision
TOWN TAMER	PAR	Techniscope
A TRAP FOR CINERELLA	FRA	Franscope
TWO ON A GUILLOTINE	WB	Panavision
UNCLE TOM'S CABIN	GER	SuperPanorama 70
UP FROM THE BEACH	TCF	CinemaScope
THE VAMPIRE OF DUSELDORF	FRA	Franscope
THE VERMILION DOOR	CHI	CinemaScope
VON RYAN'S EXPRESS	TCF	CinemaScope
WAR AND PEACE	RUS	Sovscope 70
WAR GODS OF THE DEEP	AI	Panavision
THE WAR LORD	UN	Panavision
THE WAR OF THE ZOMBIES	AI	CinemaScope
WE WILL REMEMBER	JAP	CinemaScope
WHEN THE BOYS MEET THE GIRLS	MGM	Panavision
WHERE THE SPIES ARE	MGM	Panavision
WILD WILD WINTER	UN	Techniscope
WILD WILD WORLD	ITA	CinemaScope
YOUNG FURY	PAR	Techniscope

1966

ALVAREZ KELLY	COL	Panavision
THE AMORIST	JAP	CinemaScope
THE APPALOOSA	UN	Techniscope
ARABESQUE	UN	Panavision
THE ARMY NAKANO SCHOOL	JAP	CinemaScope
AROUND THE WORLD UNDER THE SEA	MGM	Panavision
ARRIVEDERCI, BABY	PAR	Panavision
ARSHIN MAL ALAN	RUS	Sovscope
ASSAULT ON A QUEEN	PAR	Panavision
BEAU GESTE	UN	Techniscope
THE BIBLE	TCF	D-150
THE BIG RUNAROUND	FRA	Panavision
BLACK SUN	FRA	Franscope
BLINDFOLD	UN	Panavision
THE BLUE MAX	TCF	CinemaScope
BORN FREE	COL	Panavision
BRIDE OF THE ANDES	JAP	Tohoscope
BRIGADE ANTI-GANGS	FRA	Franscope
CAST A GIANT SHADOW	UA	Panavision
THE CHASE	COL	Panavision
CHEVSSURSKAJA BALLADA	RUS	Sovscope
CINERAMA'S RUSSIAN ADVENTURE	IND	Sovscope 70
COLD DAYS	HUN	CinemaScope
A COMPLICATED MAN	JAP	DaieiScope

APPENDIX THREE
THIRD-DIMENSIONAL FILMS

	1903		
LUMIERE SHORTS		FRA	anaglyph
	1921		
PLASTICON		IND	anaglyph
PLASTIGRAMS		IND	anaglyph
	1922		
LUNA-CY		PAT	Stereoscopiks
M.A.R.S.		IND	Teleview
THE POWER OF LOVE		IND	Fairall
OUCH		PAT	Stereoscopiks
A RUNAWAY TAXI		PAT	Stereoscopiks
ZOWIE		PAT	Stereoscopiks
	1930		
CAMPUS SWEETHEARTS		IND	Natural Vision
	1935		
LUMIERE SHORTS		FRA	anaglyph
	1936		
AUDIOSCOPIKS		MGM	anaglyph
THE BEGGAR'S WEDDING		ITA	anaglyph
	1937		
YOU CAN NEARLY TOUCH IT		GER	polaroid
	1938		
NEW AUDIOSCOPIKS		MGM	anaglyph
	1939		
SIX GIRLS RIDE INTO THE WEEKEND		GER	polaroid
CHRYSLER WORLD'S FAIR FILM		IND	polaroid
	1940		
FILM CONCERT		RUS	parallax stereogram
PENNSYLVANIA RAILROAD FILM		IND	polaroid
	1941		
THREE-DIMENSIONAL MURDER		MGM	anaglyph
	1946		
ROBINSON CRUSOE		RUS	parallax stereogram
	1948		
ALEKO		RUS	parallax stereogram
LALIM		RUS	parallax stereogram
NIGHT IN MAY		RUS	parallax stereogram
QUEEN JULIANA		HOL	Veri-Vision
STAR OF THE SCREEN		HOL	Veri-Vision
	1951		
AROUND IS AROUND		BRI	Stereo-Techniques
BLACK SWAN		BRI	Stereo-Techniques
LONDON TRIBUTE		BRI	Stereo-Techniques
NOW IS THE TIME		BRI	Stereo-Techniques

ROYAL RIVER	BRI	Stereo-Techniques
A SOLID EXPLANATION	BRI	Stereo-Techniques

1952

ARTIST'S EXAMINATION	HUN	polaroid
BWANA DEVIL	UA	Natural Vision
MAY DAY 1952	HUN	polaroid
WALK IN THE ZOO	BRI	Stereo-Techniques

1953

ARENA	MGM	polaroid
ASSIGNMENT A-BOMB	IND	polaroid
BANDIT ISLAND	LIP	Stereo-Techniques
CEASE FIRE	PAR	polaroid
THE CHARGE AT FEATHER RIVER	WB	Natural Vision
COLLEGE CAPERS	LIP	Stereo-Techniques
CORONATION OF QUEEN ELIZABETH	BRI	Stereo-Techniques
A DAY IN THE COUNTRY	LIP	Stereo-Techniques
DEVIL'S CANYON	RKO	polaroid
FLIGHT TO TANGIER	PAR	polaroid
FORT TI	COL	polaroid
THE FORTUNE HUNTERS	CHI	unknown
THE GLASS WEB	UN	polaroid
GUN FURY	COL	polaroid
HANNAH LEE	UA	Stereo-Techniques
HONDO	WB	Natural Vision
HOUSE OF WAX	WB	Natural Vision
THE HYPNOTIC HICK	UN	polaroid
I, THE JURY	UA	polaroid
INFERNO	TCF	polaroid
IT CAME FROM OUTER SPACE	UN	polaroid
JUMPING OUT SUNDAY	JAP	polaroid
KISS ME KATE	MGM	polaroid
LAS VEGAS ATOM BLAST	IND	polaroid
LOUISIANA TERRITORY	RKO	polaroid
MAN IN THE DARK	COL	polaroid
MARCIANO-WALCOTT FIGHT	UA	Stereo-Techniques
THE MAZE	AA	polaroid
MELODY	RKO	polaroid
MILWAUKEE-CHICAGO BASEBALL GAME	IND	polaroid
MISS SADIE THOMPSON	COL	polaroid
THE MOONLIGHTER	WB	Natural Vision
MOTOR RHYTHM	RKO	polaroid
NAT KING COLE	UN	polaroid
THE OWL AND THE PUSSYCAT	BRI	Stereo-Techniques
PARDON MY BACKFIRE	COL	polaroid
POPEYE, ACE OF SPACE	PAR	polaroid
SANGAREE	PAR	polaroid
SECOND CHANCE	RKO	polaroid
SPOOKS	COL	polaroid
THE STRANGER WORE A GUN	COL	polaroid
THE TELL-TALE HEART	COL	polaroid
THIS IS TRIORAMA	BOL	Triorama
THOSE REDHEADS FROM SEATTLE	PAR	polaroid
WINGS OF THE HAWK	UN	polaroid

1954

BOO MOON	PAR	polaroid
CAT WOMEN OF THE MOON	IND	polariod
CREATURE FROM THE BLACK LAGOON	UN	polaroid
DANGEROUS MISSION	RKO	polaroid
DIAL M FOR MURDER	WB	Natural Vision
DRUMS OF TAHITI	COL	polaroid
THE FRENCH LINE	RKO	polaroid
GOG	UA	polaroid
GORILLA AT LARGE	TCF	polaroid
JESSE JAMES VS. THE DALTONS	COL	polaroid

LUMBERJACK RABBIT	WB	Natural Vision
THE MAD MAGICIAN	COL	polaroid
MONEY FROM HOME	PAR	polaroid
THE NEBRASKAN	COL	polaroid
THE PHANTOM OF THE RUE MORGUE	WB	Natural Vision
SON OF SINBAD	RKO	polaroid
SOUTHWEST PASSAGE	UA	polaroid
TAZA, SON OF COCHISE	UN	polaroid
A WAY OF THINKING	IND	Ramsdell

1955

THE RETURN OF THE CREATURE	UN	polaroid

1960

SEPTEMBER STORM	TCF	polaroid
13 GHOSTS	COL	anaglyph

1961

THE MASK	WB	anaglyph

1962

PARADISIO	IND	anaglyph

1966

THE BUBBLE	IND	Space Vision

APPENDIX FOUR
PIONEER SOUND FILMS

AT-All Talking   PT-Part Talking   SS-Synchronized Sound

c1900

CYRANO DE BERGERAC (AT)	FRA	Chronophone
HAMLET (AT)	FRA	Chronophone
LITTLE TICH AND HIS BIG BOOTS (AT)	BRI	unknown
SARAH BERNHARDT (AT)	FRA	Chronophone

1902

YVETTE GUILBERT (AT)	FRA	Chronophone
THE DRESS (AT)	FRA	Chronophone

1905

ANNA HELD (AT)	IND	Cameraphone
BLANCHE RING (AT)	IND	Cameraphone
EVA TANGUAY (AT)	IND	Cameraphone

1908

COON SONG (AT)	IND	Cameraphone
THE CORSICAN BROTHERS (AT)	IND	Cameraphone
SCENE IN A TURKISH BATH (AT)	IND	Cameraphone

1909

THE OPERA MARTHA (AT)	FRA	Lumiere

1910

UNCLE TOM'S CABIN (AT)	VIT	Lyman Howe

1911

CORONATION OF KING GEORGE V (SS)	KIN	unknown
FATE (SS)	REX	Lyman Howe
THE GRAY OF THE DAWN (SS)	REL	Lyman Howe
THE MIKADO (AT)	BRI	Animatophone

1912

THE CHARGE OF THE LIGHT BRIGADE (SS)	ED	Kinetophone
THE INDIAN GIRL'S REVENGE (SS)	ED	Kinetophone

1913

PAGLIACCI (AT)	IND	Vi-T-Phone

1914

ALMOST TOO LATE (AT)	COM	Biophone
CHILDREN'S CAKE WALK (AT)	COM	Biophone
FAUST ARIA (AT)	COM	Biophone
HARRY LAUDER —HIMSELF (AT)	SEL	Selig system
HER SACRIFICE (AT)	COM	Biophone
MIGNON (AT)	COM	Biophone
MYSTERIOUS WIRELESS (AT)	COM	Biophone
MYSTERY OF CORBY CASTLE (AT)	COM	Biophone
POLISH JEW (AT)	COM	Biophone
SEVEN OF CLUBS (AT)	COM	Biophone
SHADOW DANCE (AT)	COM	Biophone
SPANISH SERENADE (AT)	COM	Biophone
SPEAKING PICTURES (AT)	COM	Biophone
TELEPHONE FROM THE GRAVE (AT)	COM	Biophone
ZEDA (AT)	COM	Biophone

	1915		
BARBER OF SEVILLE ARIA (AT)		COM	Biophone
THE BIRTH OF A NATION (SS)		GRI	Lyman Howe
CARMEN ARIA (AT)		COM	Biophone
FAMILY DIAMOND (AT)		COM	Biophone
PAGLIACCI ARIA (AT)		COM	Biophone
TALES OF HOFFMANN (AT)		COM	Biophone
TYROL IN ARMS (AT)		COM	Biophone
	1916		
L'AMICA		ITA	unknown
RAPSODIA SANTANICA		ITA	unknown
	1921		
DREAM STREET (PT)		UA	Phonokinema
	1923		
THE COVERED WAGON (SS)		PAR	Phonofilm
	1924		
LOVE'S OLD SWEET SONG (AT)		TCF	Phonofilm
PRESIDENT CALVIN COOLIDGE (AT)		TCF	Phonofilm
TRI-ERGON FILMS (AT)		GER	Tri-Ergon
	1925		
CYRANO DE BERGERAC (AT)		FRA	unknown
	1926		
ANTIDOTE (AT)		BRI	British Acoustic
THE BETTER 'OLE (SS)		WB	Vitaphone
CHANGING THE GUARD AT BUCKINGHAM PALACE (AT)		BRI	British Acoustic
DON JUAN (SS)		WB	Vitaphone
NEW YORK PHILHARMONIC (AT)		WB	Vitaphone
RETRIBUTION (SS)		TCF	Phonofilm
SAINT JOAN (AT)		BRI	British Acoustic
SENTENCE OF DEATH (AT)		BRI	British Acoustic
A WET NIGHT (AT)		BRI	British Acoustic
WHAT PRICE GLORY? (SS)		TCF	Movietone
	1927		
FOX MOVIETIME NEWSREEL (AT)		TCF	Movietone
GEORGE BERNARD SHAW (AT)		TCF	Movietone
THE JAZZ SINGER (PT)		WB	Vitaphone
KITTY (PT)		BRI	unknown
SEVENTH HEAVEN (SS)		TCF	Movietone
SHOW GIRL (SS)		RAY	unknown
SUNRISE (SS)		TCF	Movietone
WHEN A MAN LOVES (SS)		WB	Vitaphone
WINGS (SS)		PAR	Photophone
	1928		
ACROSS THE ATLANTIC (SS)		WB	Vitaphone
ADORATION (SS)		FN	Movietone
AIR CIRCUS (PT)		TCF	Movietone
ALIAS JIMMY VALENTINE (PT)		MGM	Movietone
ANNAPOLIS (SS)		RKO	Photophone
AS WE LIE (AT)		BRI	Movietone
THE AWAKENING (SS)		UA	Movietone
BABY CYCLONE (SS)		MGM	Movietone
THE BARKER (PT)		FN	Movietone
THE BATTLE OF THE SEXES (SS)		UA	Movietone
BEGGARS OF LIFE (PT)		PAR	Movietone
BEWARE OF MARRIED MEN (SS)		WB	Vitaphone
BLINDFOLD (SS)		TCF	Movietone
BLOCKADE (PT)		RKO	Photophone
CAPTAIN SWAGGER (SS)		RKO	Photophone
CAUGHT IN THE FOG (PT)		WB	Vitaphone
THE CAVALIER (SS)		TIF	Photophone

THE CIRCUS KID (PT)	FBO	Photophone
COLLEGE SWING (AT)	PAR	Movietone
CRIMSON CITY (SS)	WB	Vitaphone
DOMESTIC TROUBLES (SS)	WB	Vitaphone
DRY MARTINI (SS)	TCF	Movietone
THE FAMILY PICNIC (SS)	TCF	Movietone
FAZIL (SS)	TCF	Movietone
FISHERMAN OF POSILLIPO (SS)	ART	unknown
FIVE AND TEN CENT ANNIE (SS)	WB	Vitaphone
FORTUNE'S FOOL (SS)	LOU	unknown
FOUR SONS (SS)	TCF	Movietone
GANG WAR (PT)	FBO	Photophone
GERALDINE (PT)	RKO	Photophone
GIVE AND TAKE (SS)	UN	Movietone
GLORIOUS BETSY (PT)	WB	Vitaphone
GOODBYE KISS (SS)	FN	Movietone
GREASED LIGHTNING (AT)	UN	Movietone
HAUNTED HOUSE (SS)	FN	Movietone
THE HOMECOMING (SS)	PAR	Movietone
INTERFERENCE (AT)	PAR	Movietone
LADIES NIGHT IN A TURKISH BATH (AT)	FN	Movietone
LIGHTS OF NEW YORK (AT)	WB	Vitaphone
THE LION AND THE MOUSE (AT)	WB	Vitaphone
LILAC TIME (SS)	FN	Movietone
LITTLE SNOB (SS)	WB	Vitaphone
LONESOME (PT)	UN	Movietone
MAN, WOMAN AND WIFE (SS)	UN	Movietone
MARKED MONEY (SS)	RKO	Photophone
ME GANGSTER (SS)	TCF	Movietone
MELODY OF LOVE (AT)	UN	Movietone
MIDNIGHT TAXI (PT)	WB	Vitaphone
MOTHER KNOWS BEST (PT)	TCF	Movietone
MOTHER MACHREE (SS)	TCF	Movietone
MY MAN (PT)	WB	Vitaphone
NED McCOBB'S DAUGHTER (SS)	RKO	Photophone
NIGHT WATCH (SS)	FN	Movietone
ON TRIAL (AT)	WB	Vitaphone
THE PATRIOT (SS)	PAR	Movietone
PAY AS YOU ENTER (SS)	WB	Vitaphone
PLASTERED IN PARIS (SS)	TCF	Movietone
POWDER MY BACK (SS)	WB	Vitaphone
PREP AND PEP (SS)	TCF	Movietone
THE PERFECT CRIME (PT)	FBO	Photophone
RACE FOR LIFE (SS)	WB	Vitaphone
RED DANCE (SS)	TCF	Movietone
REVENGE (SS)	UA	Movietone
RILEY THE COP (SS)	TCF	Movietone
RINTY OF THE DESERT (SS)	WB	Vitaphone
THE RIVER (PT)	TCF	Movietone
RIVER PIRATE (SS)	TCF	Movietone
RIVER WOMAN (SS)	GOT	unknown
SAWDUST PARADISE (SS)	PAR	Movietone
SCARLET SEAS (SS)	FN	Movietone
SHADY LADY (PT)	RKO	Photophone
SHOW FOLKS (PT)	RKO	Photophone
SHOW PEOPLE (SS)	MGM	Movietone
THE SINGIN' FOOL (PT)	WB	Vitaphone
STATE STREET SADIE (PT)	WB	Vitaphone
STEPPING HIGH (PT)	FBO	Photophone
TENDERLOIN (AT)	WB	Vitaphone
THE TERROR (AT)	WB	Vitaphone
THE TOILERS (SS)	TIF	Photophone
VARSITY (PT)	PAR	Movietone
WARMING UP (SS)	PAR	Movietone
WOMEN THEY TALK ABOUT (PT)	WB	Vitaphone

1929

ACQUITTED (AT)	COL	Movietone
ALIBI (AT)	UA	Movietone
APPLAUSE (AT)	PAR	Movietone
AROUND THE WORLD VIA GRAF ZEPPELIN (SS)	TPE	unknown
THE AVIATOR (AT)	WB	Vitaphone
THE AWFUL TRUTH (AT)	RKO	Photophone
BACHELOR GIRL (PT)	COL	Movietone
BACHELOR'S CLUB (SS)	PAT	Photophone
BARNUM WAS RIGHT (AT)	UN	Movietone
BATTLE OF PARIS (AT)	PAR	Movietone
BEHIND THAT CURTAIN (AT)	TCF	Movietone
THE BELLAMY TRIAL (PT)	WB	Vitaphone
THE BETRAYAL (SS)	PAR	Movietone
BEWARE OF BACHELORS (PT)	WB	Vitaphone
BIG NEWS (AT)	RKO	Photophone
BIG TIME (AT)	TCF	Movietone
BLACK MAGIC (SS)	TCF	Movietone
BLACK WATERS (AT)	WW	unknown
BLACKMAIL (AT)	BRI	Movietone
BLUE SKIES (SS)	TCF	Movietone
BRIDE OF THE DESERT (AT)	RAY	unknown
THE BRIDGE OF SAN LUIS REY (PT)	MGM	Movietone
BROADWAY (AT)	UN	Movietone
BROADWAY BABIES (PT)	FN	Movietone
BROADWAY MELODY (AT)	MGM	Movietone
BROADWAY SCANDALS (AT)	COL	Movietone
BROKEN HEARTED (PT)	TRI	unknown
BULLDOG DRUMMOND (AT)	UA	Movietone
BYE BYE BUDDY (PT)	TRI	unknown
THE CANARY MURDER CASE (AT)	PAR	Movietone
CAPTAIN LASH (SS)	TCF	Movietone
CAREERS (PT)	FN	Movietone
CARELESS AGE (AT)	FN	Movietone
THE CARNATION KID (PT)	PAR	Movietone
CHASING THRU EUROPE (SS)	TCF	Movietone
CHILDREN OF THE RITZ (SS)	FN	Movietone
CHINATOWN NIGHTS (AT)	PAR	Movietone
CHRISTINA (PT)	TCF	Movietone
CLEAR THE DECKS (PT)	UN	Movietone
CLOSE HARMONY (AT)	PAR	Movietone
COCKEYED WORLD (AT)	TCF	Movietone
THE COCOANUTS (AT)	PAR	Movietone
THE COHENS AND KELLYS IN ATLANTIC CITY (PT)	UN	Movietone
COLLEGE COQUETTE (AT)	COL	Movietone
COLLEGE LIFE (AT)	UN	Movietone
COME ACROSS (PT)	UN	Movietone
CONDEMNED (AT)	UA	Movietone
CONQUEST (AT)	WB	Vitaphone
COQUETTE (AT)	UA	Movietone
DAMAGED SOULS (SS)	PWP	unknown
DANCE HALL (AT)	RKO	Photophone
DANCE OF LIFE (AT)	PAR	Movietone
DANGEROUS CURVES (AT)	PAR	Movietone
DANGEROUS WOMAN (AT)	PAR	Movietone
DARK SKIES (AT)	CAP	unknown
DARK STREETS (AT)	FN	Movietone
DARKENED ROOMS (AT)	PAR	Movietone
DELIGHTFUL ROGUE (AT)	RKO	Photophone
DESERT NIGHTS (SS)	MGM	Movietone
THE DESERT SONG (AT)	MGM	Movietone
DEVIL MAY CARE (AT)	MGM	Movietone
DIVINE LADY (SS)	FN	Movietone
DIVORCE MADE EASY (AT)	PAR	Movietone

THE DOCTOR'S SECRET (AT)	PAR	Movietone
THE DONOVON AFFAIR (AT)	COL	Movietone
DRAG (AT)	FN	Movietone
THE DRAKE CASE (AT)	UN	Movietone
THE DUKE STEPS OUT (PT)	MGM	Movietone
DUMMY (AT)	PAR	Movietone
DYNAMITE (AT)	RKO	Photophone
ETERNAL LOVE (SS)	UA	Movietone
EVANGELINE (PT)	UA	Movietone
EVIDENCE (AT)	WB	Vitaphone
EXALTED FLAPPER (SS)	TCF	Movietone
FALL OF EVE (AT)	COL	Movietone
FANCY BAGGAGE (PT)	WB	Vitaphone
FAR CALL (SS)	TCF	Movietone
FASHIONS IN LOVE (AT)	PAR	Movietone
FAST LIFE (AT)	FN	Movietone
FATHER AND SON (PT)	COL	Movietone
THE FEATHER (SS)	UA	Movietone
FIGHTING THE WHITE SLAVE TRAFFIC (PT)	BER	unknown
FLIGHT (AT)	COL	Movietone
FLYING FEET (SS)	MGM	Movietone
FLYING FOOL (AT)	RKO	Photophone
FLYING MARINE (PT)	COL	Movietone
FOOTLIGHTS AND FOOLS (AT)	FN	Movietone
FORWARD PASS (AT)	FN	Movietone
FOUR DEVILS (PT)	TCF	Movietone
FOUR FEATHERS (SS)	PAR	Movietone
FOX MOVIETONE FOLLIES OF 1929 (AT)	TCF	Movietone
FROM HEADQUARTERS (PT)	WB	Vitaphone
FROZEN JUSTICE (AT)	TCF	Movietone
FROZEN RIVER (PT)	WB	Vitaphone
FUGITIVES (SS)	TCF	Movietone
GAMBLERS (AT)	WB	Vitaphone
GENERAL CRACK (AT)	WB	Vitaphone
GENTLEMEN OF THE PRESS (AT)	PAR	Movietone
THE GHOST TALKS (AT)	TCF	Movietone
THE GIRL FROM HAVANA (AT)	TCF	Movietone
THE GIRL FROM WOOLWORTH'S (AT)	FN	Movietone
THE GIRL IN THE GLASS CAGE (PT)	FN	Movietone
GIRL O' THE PORT (AT)	RKO	Photophone
THE GIRL ON THE BARGE (PT)	UN	Movietone
GIRL OVERBOARD (PT)	UN	Movietone
GIRLS GONE WILD (SS)	TCF	Movietone
GLAD RAG DOLL (AT)	WB	Vitaphone
GLORIFYING THE AMERICAN GIRL (AT)	PAR	Movietone
THE GODLESS GIRL (PT)	RKO	Photophone
GOLD DIGGERS OF BROADWAY (AT)	WB	Vitaphone
THE GREAT GABBO (AT)	WW	unknown
THE GREAT POWER (PT)	WB	Vitaphone
THE GREENE MURDER CASE (AT)	PAR	Movietone
GREYHOUND LIMITED (PT)	WB	Vitaphone
HALF MARRIAGE (AT)	RKO	Photophone
HALFWAY TO HEAVEN (AT)	MGM	Movietone
HALLELUJAH! (AT)	MGM	Movietone
HANDCUFFED (AT)	RAY	unknown
HARD TO GET (AT)	FN	Movietone
HARDBOILED ROSE (PT)	WB	Vitaphone
HEARTS IN DIXIE (AT)	TCF	Movietone
HEARTS IN EXILE (AT)	WB	Vitaphone
HELL'S HEROES (AT)	UN	Movietone
HER PRIVATE AFFAIR (AT)	RKO	Photophone
HER PRIVATE LIFE (AT)	FN	Movietone
HIGH TREASON (AT)	BRI	Movietone

HIGH VOLTAGE (AT)	RKO	Photophone
HIS CAPTIVE WOMAN (PT)	FN	Movietone
HIS GLORIOUS NIGHT (AT)	MGM	Movietone
HIS LUCKY DAY (PT)	UN	Movietone
HOLD YOUR MAN (AT)	UN	Movietone
HOLLYWOOD REVUE OF 1929 (AT)	MGM	Movietone
HOMESICK (SS)	TCF	Movietone
HONKY TONK (AT)	WB	Vitaphone
HOT FOR PARIS (AT)	TCF	Movietone
THE HOTTENTOT (AT)	WB	Vitaphone
HOUSE OF HORROR (PT)	FN	Movietone
HOUSE OF SECRETS (AT)	CHE	unknown
HUNGARIAN RHAPSODY (SS)	PAR	Movietone
HUNTED (AT)	RKO	Photophone
HUNTING TIGERS IN INDIA (AT)	TPE	unknown
HURRICANE (AT)	COL	Movietone
IDAHO RED (SS)	RKO	Photophone
ILLUSION (AT)	PAR	Movietone
IN OLD ARIZONA (AT)	TCF	Movietone
IN OLD CALIFORNIA (AT)	AUD	unknown
IN THE HEADLINES (AT)	WB	Vitaphone
INNOCENTS OF PARIS (AT)	PAR	Movietone
THE INVADERS (SS)	SYN	unknown
THE IRON MASK (PT)	UA	Movietone
IS EVERYBODY HAPPY? (AT)	WB	Vitaphone
ISLE OF LOST SHIPS (AT)	FN	Movietone
IT CAN BE DONE (PT)	UN	Movietone
IT'S A GREAT LIFE (AT)	MGM	Movietone
JAZZ HEAVEN (AT)	RKO	Photophone
JEALOUSY (AT)	PAR	Movietone
JOY STREET (SS)	TCF	Movietone
THE KIBITZER (AT)	PAR	Movietone
KID GLOVES (PT)	WB	Vitaphone
THE KISS (SS)	MGM	Movietone
THE LADY LIES (AT)	PAR	Movietone
LADY OF CHANCE (PT)	MGM	Movietone
LADY OF THE PAVEMENTS (PT)	UA	Movietone
THE LAST OF MRS. CHENEY (PT)	MGM	Movietone
THE LAST PERFORMANCE (PT)	UN	Movietone
THE LAST WARNING (PT)	UN	Movietone
LEATHERNECKING (PT)	RKO	Photophone
THE LETTER (AT)	PAR	Movietone
LIGHT FINGERS (PT)	COL	Movietone
LINDA (SS)	FD	unknown
THE LITTLE WILDCAT (PT)	WB	Vitaphone
LOOPING THE LOOP (SS)	PAR	Movietone
THE LOVE DOCTOR (AT)	PAR	Movietone
LOVE IN THE DESERT (PT)	RKO	Photophone
LOVE, LIVE AND LAUGH (AT)	TCF	Movietone
THE LOVE PARADE (AT)	PAR	Movietone
THE LOVE TRAP (PT)	UN	Movietone
LUCKY BOY (PT)	TIF	Photophone
MADAME X (AT)	MGM	Movietone
MADONNA OF AVENUE A (PT)	WB	Vitaphone
MAKING THE GRADE (PT)	TCF	Movietone
MAN AND THE MOMENT (PT)	FN	Movietone
THE MAN I LOVE (AT)	PAR	Movietone
A MAN'S MAN (SS)	MGM	Movietone
MAN MUST FIGHT (AT)	PAR	Movietone
MARIANNE (AT)	MGM	Movietone
MASKED EMOTIONS (SS)	TCF	Movietone
MASQUERADE (AT)	TCF	Movietone
MELODY LANE (AT)	UN	Movietone

MEN ARE LIKE THAT (AT)	PAR	Movietone
MIDNIGHT DADDIES (AT)	WW	unknown
MIDSTREAM (PT)	TIF	Photophone
MILLION DOLLAR COLLAR (PT)	WB	Vitaphone
MISTER ANTONIO (AT)	TIF	Photophone
MODERN LOVE (PT)	UN	Movietone
MOLLY AND ME (PT)	TIF	Photophone
A MOST IMMORAL LADY (AT)	FN	Movietone
MOULIN ROUGE (SS)	WW	unknown
MYSTERIES OF LIFE (SS)	PWP	unknown
MYSTERIOUS ISLAND (PT)	MGM	Movietone
THE NAKED TRUTH (SS)	PWP	unknown
NAUGHTY BABY (SS)	FN	Movietone
NEW ORLEANS (PT)	TIF	Photophone
NIGHT PARADE (AT)	RKO	Photophone
NIX ON DAMES (AT)	TCF	Movietone
NO DEFENSE (PT)	WB	Vitaphone
NOAH'S ARK (SS)	WB	Vitaphone
NOT QUITE DECENT (PT)	TCF	Movietone
NOTHING BUT THE TRUTH (AT)	PAR	Movietone
OFFICE SCANDAL (PT)	RKO	Photophone
THE OKLAHOMA KID (AT)	SYN	unknown
ON WITH THE SHOW (PT)	WB	Vitaphone
ONE STOLEN NIGHT (PT)	WB	Vitaphone
ONE WOMAN IDEA (SS)	TCF	Movietone
OVERLAND BOUND (AT)	PRE	unknown
PAGAN (SS)	MGM	Movietone
PARIS BOUND (AT)	RKO	Photophone
PHANTOM IN THE HOUSE (AT)	CON	unknown
PICCADILLY (SS)	WW	unknown
PLEASURE CRAZED (AT)	TCF	Movietone
POINTED HEELS (AT)	PAR	Movietone
THE PRINCE AND THE BALLET DANCER (SS)	WW	unknown
PRISONERS (PT)	FN	Movietone
PROTECTION (SS)	TCF	Movietone
QUEEN OF THE NIGHT CLUBS (AT)	WB	Vitaphone
RAINBOW MAN (AT)	PAR	Movietone
RED HOT RHYTHM (AT)	RKO	Photophone
RED HOT SPEED (PT)	UN	Movietone
RED WINE (SS)	TCF	Movietone
REDSKIN (SS)	PAR	Movietone
THE RESCUE (SS)	UA	Movietone
RETURN OF SHERLOCK HOLMES (AT)	PAR	Movietone
RIO RITA (AT)	RKO	Photophone
RIVER OF ROMANCE (AT)	PAR	Movietone
ROAD SHOW (AT)	MGM	Movietone
ROMANCE OF THE RIO GRANDE (AT)	TCF	Movietone
ROMANCE OF THE UNDERWORLD (SS)	TCF	Movietone
ROYAL BOX (AT)	WB	Vitaphone
SAILOR'S HOLIDAY (AT)	RKO	Photophone
SAL OF SINGAPORE (PT)	RKO	Photophone
SALLY (AT)	FN	Movietone
SALUTE (AT)	TCF	Movietone
THE SAP (PT)	WB	Vitaphone
THE SATURDAY NIGHT KID (AT)	WB	Vitaphone
SATURDAY'S CHILDREN (PT)	FN	Movietone
SAY IT WITH SONGS (AT)	WB	Vitaphone
SEA FURY (PT)	ROS	unknown
SEVEN FACES (AT)	TCF	Movietone
SEVEN FOOTPRINTS TO SATAN (SS)	FN	Movietone
SEVEN KEYS TO BALDPATE (AT)	RKO	Photophone
SEX MADNESS (SS)	PWP	unknown
SHANGHAI LADY (AT)	UN	Movietone

THE SHANNONS OF BROADWAY (AT)	UN	Movietone
SHE GOES TO WAR (PT)	UA	Movietone
THE SHOPWORN ANGEL (PT)	PAR	Movietone
SHOULD A GIRL MARRY? (PT)	RAY	unknown
SHOW BOAT (PT)	UN	Movietone
SHOW OF SHOWS (AT)	WB	Vitaphone
SIDE STREET (AT)	TCF	Movietone
SIN SISTER (SS)	TCF	Movietone
SKIN DEEP (AT)	WB	Vitaphone
SKINNER STEPS OUT (AT)	UN	Movietone
SKY HAWK (AT)	TCF	Movietone
SMILING IRISH EYES (AT)	FN	Movietone
SO THIS IS COLLEGE? (AT)	MGM	Movietone
SONG OF KENTUCKY (AT)	TCF	Movietone
SONG OF LOVE (AT)	COL	Movietone
SONNY BOY (PT)	WB	Vitaphone
THE SOPHOMORE (AT)	RKO	Photophone
SOUTH SEA ROSE (AT)	TCF	Movietone
THE SPIELER (PT)	RKO	Photophone
THE SQUALL (AT)	FN	Movietone
SQUARE SHOULDERS (PT)	RKO	Photophone
STARK MAD (AT)	WB	Vitaphone
STOLEN KISSES (PT)	WB	Vitaphone
STRANGE CARGO (AT)	RKO	Photophone
STREET GIRL (AT)	RKO	Photophone
STRONG BOY (SS)	TCF	Movietone
THE STUDIO MURDER MYSTERY (AT)	PAR	Movietone
SUNNY SIDE UP (AT)	TCF	Movietone
SWEETIE (AT)	PAR	Movietone
SYNCOPATION (AT)	RKO	Photophone
THE TAMING OF THE SHREW (AT)	UA	Movietone
TANNED LEGS (AT)	RKO	Photophone
TAXI THIRTEEN (PT)	FBO	Photophone
THEY HAD TO SEE PARIS (AT)	TCF	Movietone
THE THIRTEENTH CHAIR (AT)	MGM	Movietone
THIS IS HEAVEN (PT)	UA	Movietone
THIS THING CALLED LOVE (AT)	PAR	Movietone
THREE LIVE GHOSTS (AT)	UA	Movietone
THRU DIFFERENT EYES (AT)	TCF	Movietone
THUNDERBOLT (AT)	PAR	Movietone
TIGER ROSE (AT)	WB	Vitaphone
THE TIME, THE PLACE AND THE GIRL (AT)	WB	Vitaphone
TIMOTHY'S QUEST (AT)	GOT	unknown
TOMMY ATKINS (AT)	WW	unknown
TONIGHT AT TWELVE (AT)	UN	Movietone
THE TRESPASSER (AT)	UA	Movietone
THE TRIAL OF MARY DUGAN (AT)	MGM	Movietone
TWIN BEDS (AT)	FN	Movietone
TWO WEEKS OFF (PT)	FN	Movietone
U-BOAT 9 (SS)	BER	unknown
UNHOLY NIGHT (AT)	MGM	Movietone
UNMASKED (AT)	ART	unknown
THE VAGABOND LOVER (AT)	RKO	Photophone
THE VALIANT (AT)	TCF	Movietone
THE VERY IDEA (AT)	RKO	Photophone
THE VIRGINIAN (AT)	PAR	Movietone
THE VOICE OF THE CITY (AT)	MGM	Movietone
THE VOICE WITHIN (PT)	TIF	Photophone
WAGON MASTER (PT)	UN	Movietone
WEARY RIVER (PT)	FN	Movietone
WELCOME DANGER (AT)	PAR	Movietone
WHEEL OF LIFE (AT)	PAR	Movietone
WHY BRING THAT UP? (AT)	TCF	Movietone

WHY GO HOME? (AT)		TCF	Movietone
WILD PARTY (AT)		PAR	Movietone
THE WOLF OF WALL STREET (AT)		PAR	Movietone
WOLF SONG (PT)		PAR	Movietone
WOMAN TO WOMAN (AT)		TIF	Photophone
WORDS AND MUSIC (AT)		TCF	Movietone
YOUNG NOWHERES (AT)		FN	Movietone
YOUNGER GENERATION (PT)		COL	Movietone
	1930		
BRIDE 68 (PT)		TOB	unknown
CITY GIRL (PT)		TCF	Movietone
FIGHTING LEGION (PT)		ALL	unknown
LOVE IN THE RING (PT)		ALL	unknown
PARADE OF THE WEST (PT)		UN	Movietone
WHITE DEVIL (PT)		GER	unknown
	1931		
BEN-HUR (re-issue) (SS)		MGM	Movietone
THE BIG PARADE (re-issue) (SS)		MGM	Movietone
CITY LIGHTS (SS)		UA	Movietone
THE PHANTOM OF THE OPERA (re-issue) (PT)		UN	Movietone
WAY DOWN EAST (re-issue) (SS)		IND	unknown
	1932		
MR. ROBINSON CRUSOE (SS)		UA	Movietone
	1940		
FOUR MOTHERS		WB	VitaSound
SANTA FE TRAIL		WB	VitaSound
	1941		
FANTASIA		RKO	FantaSound
	1952		
THIS IS CINERAMA		CIN	CineramaSound
	1953		
ALL THE BROTHERS WERE VALIANT		MGM	Stereophonic
BENEATH THE TWELVE-MILE REEF		TCF	Stereophonic
BLOWING WILD		WB	Stereophonic
THE CADDY		PAR	Stereophonic
CALAMITY JANE		WB	Stereophonic
CEASE FIRE		PAR	Stereophonic
THE CHARGE AT FEATHER RIVER		WB	Stereophonic
CRUISIN' DOWN THE RIVER		COL	Stereophonic
DEVIL'S CANYON		RKO	Stereophonic
THE 5,000 FINGERS OF DR. T		COL	Stereophonic
FORT TI		COL	Stereophonic
FROM HERE TO ETERNITY		COL	Stereophonic
GILBERT AND SULLIVAN		UA	Stereophonic
HOUSE OF WAX		WB	Stereophonic
HOW TO MARRY A MILLIONAIRE		TCF	Stereophonic
ISLAND IN THE SKY		WB	Stereophcnic
IT CAME FROM OUTER SPACE		UN	Stereophonic
JULIUS CAESAR		MGM	Stereophonic
LET'S DO IT AGAIN		COL	Stereophonic
THE MAZE		AA	Stereophonic
MELBA		UA	Stereophonic
MISS SADIE THOMPSON		COL	Stereophonic
MISSION OVER KOREA		COL	Stereophonic
MOGAMBO		MGM	Stereophonic
THE ROBE		TCF	Stereophonic
ROBOT MONSTER		UA	Stereophonic
SCARED STIFF		PAR	Stereophonic
SECOND CHANGE		RKO	Stereophonic
SHANE		PAR	Stereophonic
THE STRANGER WORE A GUN		COL	Stereophonic

TAKE THE HIGH GROUND		MGM	Stereophonic
WAR OF THE WORLDS		PAR	Stereophonic
WINGS OF THE HAWK		UN	Stereophonic
YOUNG BESS		MGM	Stereophonic
	1954		
BETRAYED		MGM	Perspecta
THE COMMAND		WB	Perspecta
THE EGYPTIAN		TCF	Stereophonic
DUEL IN THE SUN (re-issue)		SRO	Perspecta
GONE WITH THE WIND (re-issue)		MGM	Perspecta
HELL AND HIGH WATER		TCF	Stereophonic
THE HIGH AND THE MIGHTY		WB	Stereophonic
THE JOLSON STORY (re-issue)		COL	Stereophonic
KNIGHTS OF THE ROUND TABLE		MGM	Perspecta
LUCKY ME		WB	Perspecta
NEW FACES		TCF	Stereophonic
NIGHT PEOPLE		TCF	Stereophonic
LES REVOLTES DE LOMANACH		FRA	Stereophonic
ROSE-MARIE		MGM	Perspecta
THE ROSE TATTOO		PAR	Perspecta
RING OF FEAR		WB	Perspecta
RUN FOR COVER		PAR	Perspecta
STRATEGIC AIR COMMAND		PAR	Stereophonic
THREE COINS IN THE FOUNTAIN		TCF	Stereophonic
TO CATCH A THIEF		PAR	Perspecta
WE'RE NO ANGELS		PAR	Perspecta
WHITE CHRISTMAS		PAR	Perspecta
	1955		
CINERAMA HOLIDAY		CIN	CineramaSound

INDEX

INDEX

ASPECTS OF FILM

An Arno Press Collection

Adler, Mortimer J. **Art and Prudence.** 1937
Conant, Michael. **Anti-Trust in the Motion Picture Industry.** 1960
Croy, Homer. **How Motion Pictures Are Made.** 1918
Drinkwater, John. **The Life and Adventures of Carl Laemmle.** 1931
Hacker, Leonard. **Cinematic Design.** 1931
Hepworth, T[homas] C[raddock]. **The Book of the Lantern.** 1899
Johnston, Alva. **The Great Goldwyn.** 1937
Klingender, F.D. and Stuart Legg. **Money Behind the Screen.** 1937
Limbacher, James L. **Four Aspects of the Film.** 1969
Manvell, Roger, ed. **The Cinema 1950.** 1950
Manvell, Roger, ed. **The Cinema 1951.** 1951
Manvell, Roger, ed. **The Cinema 1952.** 1952
Marchant, James, ed. **The Cinema in Education.** 1925
Mayer, J.P. **British Cinemas and Their Audiences.** 1948
Sabaneev, Leonid. **Music for the Films.** 1935
Seabury, William Marston. **Motion Picture Problems.** 1929
Seldes, Gilbert. **The Movies Come from America.** 1937
U.S. House of Representatives, Committee on Education. **Motion Picture Commission: Hearings.** 1914
U.S. House of Representatives, Committee on Education. **Federal Motion Picture Commission: Hearings.** 1916
U.S. Senate, Temporary National Economic Committee. **Investigation of Concentration of Economic Power.** 1941
Weinberg, Herman G. **Josef von Sternberg.** 1967